Politician
in Uniform

Gen. Lew Wallace on horseback, n.d. *Indiana Historical Society, M0292.*

Politician in Uniform

General Lew Wallace and the Civil War

Christopher R. Mortenson

UNIVERSITY OF OKLAHOMA PRESS : NORMAN

Library of Congress Cataloging-in-Publication Data

Names: Mortenson, Christopher R., 1975– author.
Title: Politician in uniform : General Lew Wallace and the Civil War / Christopher R.
    Mortenson.
Description: Norman : University of Oklahoma Press, [2019] | Includes bibliographical
    references and index.
Identifiers: LCCN 2018027387 | ISBN 978-0-8061-6195-2 (hardcover : alk. paper)
Subjects: LCSH: Wallace, Lew, 1827–1905. | Generals—United States—Biography. |
    Statesmen—United States—Biography. | Generals—Selection and appointment—
    United States. | United States—History—Civil War, 1861–1865—Political aspects. |
    United States—History—Civil War, 1861–1865—Campaigns.
Classification: LCC E467.1.W2 M67 2019 | DDC 973.7/4772092 [B] —dc23
LC record available at https://lccn.loc.gov/2018027387

The paper in this book meets the guidelines for permanence and durability of the Committee
on Production Guidelines for Book Longevity of the Council on Library Resources, Inc. ∞

For my beautiful Autumn

Contents

List of Illustrations   *ix*

Preface   *xi*

Acknowledgments   *xiii*

Introduction   *3*

ONE   Militia, Mexico, and Politics   *9*

TWO   "The Fruits of Victory"   *20*

THREE   Forts Henry and Donelson   *35*

FOUR   Shiloh   *54*

FIVE   "On the Shelf" and Off to Cincinnati   *71*

SIX   Columbus, Buell, and Morgan   *96*

SEVEN   "A Command Worthy of His Rank"   *115*

EIGHT   "A Forlorn Hope"   *131*

NINE   Victory and Mexico   *150*

TEN   Assassination and Andersonville   *169*

Conclusion   *190*

Notes   *199*

Bibliography   *251*

Index   *259*

Illustrations

Figures

Gen. Lew Wallace on horseback   *frontispiece*
Lew Wallace   *89*
Gen. Lew Wallace, ca. 1861–65   *89*
Gen. Lew Wallace, ca. 1860–65   *90*
Governor Oliver P. Morton   *91*
Gen. Charles F. Smith   *91*
Gen. Ulysses S. Grant   *92*
Maj. Gen. Henry W. Halleck   *92*
Gen. Don Carlos Buell   *92*
Governor Augustus W. Bradford   *93*
Gen. Jubal A. Early   *94*
Judge Advocate Gen. Joseph Holt   *94*
Military commission, 1865   *94*
Trial of Capt. Henry Wirz   *95*

Maps

Forts Henry and Donelson, February 1862   *42*
Fort Donelson and Union Divisions, 15 February 1862   *45*
Crump's Landing to Pittsburg Landing, April 1862   *56*
Union Camps near Pittsburg Landing, 6 April 1862   *61*
The Battle of Monocacy, 9 July 1864   *139*

Preface

Arising politician from Indiana, Lew Wallace became a Civil War general through political connections. As the war developed, political generals contributed to the Union war effort in multiple ways. This book evaluates Wallace's service for the Union. While he had much success as a regimental commander, he experienced troubles at the brigade and division levels. Some natural rivalry and tension between West Pointers and political generals may have caused ill will between Wallace and professionally trained officers, but other factors also contributed to his difficulties. A temperamental officer who often embraced a more martial or "rough" conception of manhood, Wallace often sought out mentors but then quickly found reasons to fault them. Wallace's lack of respect for his superiors led him to occasionally criticize or be rude to them. Moreover, General Wallace vigorously sought chances to see glorious action in the field but then failed to perform well when given the opportunity.

Despite creating problems for himself, such as his recurrent unwillingness to give speeches and recruit soldiers for the Union, Wallace concluded his Civil War service having contributed both politically and militarily to the war effort. For example, the general came to the aid of the Union right flank at Fort Donelson, performed admirably on the second day of the Battle of Shiloh, and defended Cincinnati in 1862. He came to the defense of southern Indiana and continued to grudgingly assist in recruiting new troops in 1863. He administered Baltimore and the Middle Department and set up an adequate defense at the Monocacy River in 1864. Wallace also accepted politically risky assignments on high-profile military commissions in 1862 and 1865. His service as a volunteer general demonstrates how a politician in uniform should be evaluated differently than most professionally trained officers.

Acknowledgments

I would like to thank Professors Joseph G. Dawson III, Brian M. Linn, Walter D. Kamphoefner, R. J. Q. Adams, Peter J. Hugill, and Vernon L. Volpe for valuable guidance and criticism in beginning and completing this project. Texas A&M University and Ouachita Baptist University provided much of the necessary funding and time for research. Librarians and archivists from institutions in Arkansas, Texas, Indiana, and Washington, D.C., guided me to and through small and massive collections. My colleagues in the School of Social Sciences at Ouachita continue to be more supportive than this historian deserves.

Paul Springer encouraged me to submit a manuscript to Adam Kane at the University of Oklahoma Press, leading to an excellent experience with some of the most personable and professional editors I have met. My parents, Melvin and Carol Mortenson, have never failed me. Kobey Mortenson and Tracy Van Cleave have been sources of never-ending encouragement. And Autumn Mortenson's patience and understanding will always be indispensable.

Politician
in Uniform

Introduction

Lew Wallace is famous for the popular and enduring novel *Ben-Hur* (1880), as well as his negotiations with William H. Bonney ("Billy the Kid") during the Lincoln County Wars of 1878–81 in New Mexico Territory. The writing of his novel and Wallace's time in New Mexico have received much attention from scholars and popular writers. Wallace's Civil War military career has also been covered. But while some treatments of Wallace provide adequate narratives, most authors may be too easily convinced by Wallace's own memoir.[1] Probing analyses of all aspects of his generalship during the conflict are in short supply.

Political generals of the Civil War era received their commissions mainly by virtue of political connections. Although some had military experience—usually limited—they had not attended the United States Military Academy. All had experience in politics before the war. In offering such commissions to these men, President Abraham Lincoln hoped to gain the support of various constituencies—from citizens of the same state, ethnicity, or political party as the political appointees. The war needed nationwide support and turning to politicians helped.[2] Wallace was one such politician and officer.

It is important to remember that America had a long tradition of turning politicians, or civilians in general, into military officers, and many of them performed well. As historian David Work has pointed out, Nathaniel Greene, Henry Knox, Andrew Jackson, William Henry Harrison, John Quitman, and Alexander Doniphan had no military education prior to leading men in battle. This tradition led many Americans, leading into the Civil War, to believe that those who did not attend West Point could still be great generals.[3] In fact, nineteenth-century Americans regularly argued about the primacy of "genius" or "expertise" as they applied to a number of professions, including the army.[4] The war between North and South altered these assumptions to a degree.

No matter one's opinion, at the time, Lincoln needed these officers. The president did not have enough professionally trained military men to go around. Such a large volunteer army needed far more than the 754 West Pointers who agreed to serve in the greater Union army. Sixteen separate field armies, each including the smaller corps, divisions, and brigades, would need a number of senior and junior officers to take charge. And while the politicians who filled the gaps did not tend to fare as well on the battlefield, they often proved themselves as administrators. They also tended to be of greater and more positive influence when it came to dealing with contentious issues, such as slavery and the ruckus created by disloyal persons. Furthermore, as Work points out, these men were often great speakers who could, through speeches and recruiting drives, provide "evidence that key members of the political class stood by the president, despite" recurring defeats and setbacks. For that matter, "Lincoln did not expect all of the politicians to become field commanders. Thus, their lack of military experience was not necessarily a liability. The president intended to employ them in ways that would make the best use of their talents and do the most to help win the war."[5]

Nevertheless, some historians, including Brooks D. Simpson, question Lincoln's employment of such political generals during the Civil War. Simpson argues that the "political benefits of making such appointments" did not outweigh their military costs. Furthermore, according to Simpson, appointments that were justified as political necessities actually incurred political costs; the blunders of political generals "contributed to a military situation in the summer of 1864 where the northern public, anticipating decisive victory with [Gen. Ulysses S.] Grant in command, began to wonder whether it was worth it to continue the struggle."[6]

Thomas Goss, on the other hand, argues that such interpretations place too much attention on "the stereotype of political generals as inept tacticians, ambitious schemers, and military failures." Agreeing largely with Work, Goss suggests that one should not evaluate officers solely on "military criteria." Lincoln certainly did not; he wanted generals who could move "the Union war effort closer to eventual political and military victory." Political generals seemed to be better at the former. One downside, however, to the use of both West Pointers and politicians was that the regulars saw the war as a "military problem requiring a focus on the battlefield to destroy the enemy army and seize strategic points, while the politically adept amateurs [more often] viewed the rebellion as a partisan political struggle for power and political allegiance in both the South and in

Washington." Differing views led the two types of officers to disagree, quarrel, and scheme against each other. The "resulting friction between West Pointers and political generals eroded Northern morale and damaged the war effort."[7]

Even if Simpson offers a sound evaluation of a "typical" political general during the Civil War, Lew Wallace was not typical. For example, his appointment as a general was a result of his military accomplishments as well as his political connections. The courage he displayed at Romney, Virginia, and Fort Donelson helped to secure a promotion. Moreover, it can be argued that Wallace's service incurred few political costs for the Lincoln administration. His handling of challenges in Maryland during the election of 1864, his leadership at the Battle of Monocacy, Maryland, and his defense of Cincinnati, Ohio, were all politically beneficial.

Lew Wallace was one of many volunteer generals who received commissions during the Civil War. Biographers assert that Wallace was one of the better volunteer generals.[8] In evaluating such an assertion, one must pay special attention to the general's courage, leadership, political contributions, intelligence, and physical fitness, but also his ability to work with other commanders. All of these qualities benefited an effective senior volunteer commander. Wallace cannot be charged with exhibiting cowardliness or lacking physical ability. On the other hand, he occasionally demonstrated poor judgment and rash behavior, and some writers may overlook or downplay the fact that he consistently failed to get along with professionally trained generals.

A number of older works on Wallace have discussed his military career at length, but with only occasional or insufficient scrutiny of the flawed man and soldier. All provide adequate narratives of the general's Civil War years, but the authors demonstrate too much sympathy for their subject. For example, Irving McKee, in *"Ben-Hur" Wallace*, describes the general's role at Fort Donelson, Tennessee, and notes that Ulysses S. Grant gave him less credit for the victory than was given to Charles F. Smith. On the other hand, McKee neglects to explain why Wallace's actions at Donelson may have frustrated Grant, his immediate superior, and helped to contribute to misunderstandings later.[9]

McKee and other authors often provide adequate descriptions of those Civil War events involving Wallace, and they sometimes elaborate on the difficulties of the Indianan's military career. But, for example, Lee Scott Thiesen (in his dissertation) concludes his discussion of the Battle of Shiloh by stating that most "of Wallace's difficulties were not of his own making."[10] A team of authors, Robert and Katherine Morsberger, also provide noticeably sympathetic explanations of

Wallace's actions at Shiloh and afterward, relying too often on his autobiography to explain controversial actions and events.[11] This book provides a less sympathetic, more objective, analysis of Wallace's Civil War years, juxtaposing his autobiography with evidence in archival materials and other published primary sources.[12]

Wallace's relationships with other generals are a crucial part of understanding his service in the Civil War. America's dual military tradition, citizen soldier and regular soldier, has been an important part of United States military history. Wallace is an ideal subject for a study of the evolving relationships between regular and volunteer officers during the nineteenth century.[13] Such relationships are crucial to an understanding of this general's successes and failures. While Wallace's successes as a colonel quickly led to his rise to major general, his inability to get along with superiors resulted in a reversal of fortune. As a general, he had an aggravating and hostile relationship with Chief of Staff Henry Halleck as well as with Secretary of War Edwin Stanton, and his relations with General Grant suffered as the war progressed. Such problems led to a continual shuffling of Wallace's assignments, but he was politically valuable enough for the Lincoln administration to maintain him in uniform.[14]

The Indianan's troubles with trained officers, and what often materialized as an attitude problem, might best be explained with reference to nineteenth-century ideas on manhood. Amy S. Greenberg differentiates between two competing masculinities in antebellum America, restrained manhood and martial manhood. The former "was practiced by men . . . who grounded their identities in their families, in the evangelical practice of their Protestant faith, and in success in the business world." On the other side of the spectrum, "Martial men rejected the moral standards that guided restrained men; they often drank to excess with pride, and they reveled in their physical strength and ability to dominate both men and women." They "believed that the masculine qualities of strength, aggression, and even violence, better defined a true man than did the firm and upright manliness of restrained men. At times they embraced the 'chivalry' of knighthood or other masculine ideals from the past." Such martial men "were not necessarily ruffians, although restrained men might say they were. Both martial manhood, and the primitive manhood that emerged in the late-nineteenth century, celebrated martial virtues, strength, bravery, and idealized the adventurous outsider."[15]

Lorien Foote, on the other hand, refers to gentlemen and "roughs" in her monograph on manhood during the Civil War, with the two holding views very similar to those of the restrained and martial men mentioned in Greenberg's work. Foote, however, emphasizes the place of honor in the discussion, especially for the more martial ruffians. She also is correct to assert that "Northern men, to a greater extent than their southern counterparts, did not conform to a singular understanding of manhood or to a uniform ideal of what constituted manly behavior." It appears that "consciously or subconsciously, men chose from a spectrum of options when they pieced together the component parts of their manly identities. At the same time, men shared a common goal or expectation: others would recognize and respect their manhood."[16]

Other scholars concentrate on a dominant self-made manhood that emerged with the growing republic and its market economy; it seemed to triumph over an earlier communal manhood, the newly dominant form being a "chronically anxious, temperamentally restless manhood—a manhood that carries with it the constant burden of proof." This restlessness, or obsession, could be self-destructive for some.[17] At any rate, Wallace straddled the line between these dueling manhoods but more often veered toward the martial and rough notions of what it meant to be a man, maybe even in reaction to the era of the self-made man.[18]

West Pointers, however, often embraced a more restrained, gentlemanly, and communal manhood. They were professionals who dedicated themselves to serving their country, and who had acquired a code of ethics and behavior instilled in them while attending the United States Military Academy. West Point taught them to put duty and country before their own reputations, that following orders without complaint was the ideal, and civilian authority was to be respected; in such a manner, they would establish their honor. They professed to avoid rude and rash behavior, indiscipline, selfishness, and political fights. Political generals, including Wallace, appeared to embrace all of these negatives, leading to numerous differences between them and those who claimed a special expertise in waging war. Considering such differing views of Wallace and educated generals, his sour relationships with Halleck, Grant, and Smith make more sense. One might argue that the volunteer from the Old Northwest wanted to be one of those professionals, but also could not let go of a more martial notion of manhood embraced by many volunteer soldiers of that era.[19]

Despite such problems, Wallace did have some ability. Historian Thomas B. Buell, in *The Warrior Generals*, discusses the careers of two political generals. He asserts that "fighting spirit, courage, intelligence, stamina, and good fortune" allowed the most able men to deal with the obligations of being a Civil War general. A senior officer's duties included the competent use of a combat force while also ensuring its good condition, morale, and discipline. Matters of transportation, supply, communication, information gathering, and the acquisition of good maps could greatly aid the leader of a division or corps. A commander might also have to interact with irregular troops and disloyal locals. Senior officers would further need to get along with an area's general populace, its elected officials, and its newspapermen.[20]

Wallace often, but not always, excelled with regard to the last category, even though he regularly tried to avoid such duties. Thus, his true value to the Federal war effort can be understood since, according to historian Bruce Catton, to "win the war the Northern government had to get and keep the support of any number of separate groups, factions, and classes." Lincoln accomplished this partly by making generals of "civilian leaders in whom the members of those highly divergent groups strongly believed."[21] Demonstrating much spirit and courage, Wallace did not always use intelligence to his advantage, or realize the value of good maps. In addition, he often argued with regular officers. These faults nearly derailed his generalship near Shiloh Church.

In fact, the different viewpoints and troubles of officers like Wallace led Halleck, among others, to expect failure from political generals "so utterly destitute of military education and military capacity." He did not believe that such men might be born with a military genius that trumped learned intellect. Halleck even went as far as stating that it was "little better than murder to give important commands to such men as [Nathaniel] Banks, [Benjamin] Butler, [John] McClernand, [Franz] Sigel, and Lew. Wallace, and yet it seems impossible to prevent it."[22] While Wallace's accomplishments never managed to fully win over Stanton, Halleck, and Grant, they demonstrate how political generals should be evaluated differently than most professionally trained officers; their political contributions to the Union could be even more valuable than the military actions of mediocre West Pointers such as Don Carlos Buell or the more controversial George McClellan.

ONE

Militia, Mexico, and Politics

Lewis Wallace's grandfather, Andrew Wallace, settled in the growing town of Brookville, Indiana, during the first decade of the nineteenth century, and the family soon gained prominence. Andrew had been a storekeeper, surveyor, and publisher in Pennsylvania and Ohio before moving west to Indiana. His household eventually included seven sons and one daughter. Andrew secured, for his oldest son, David, an appointment to the U.S. Military Academy through William Henry Harrison, then a U.S. congressman, who befriended Andrew in Cincinnati, Ohio. Andrew had supplied Harrison's troops during the War of 1812.[1]

David Wallace's time at West Point was gratifying to his father, considering that, according to Andrew, John Paul Jones was the cadet's great uncle.[2] David Wallace did well at the academy, graduating in 1821. He was asked to teach mathematics there, and served in that capacity for two years. Wallace then resigned his commission, moving back to Brookville to study law.[3] While David did not remain in the army, his experience and the stories about John Paul Jones had a great effect on the personality and desires of his second son, Lewis. In fact, according to Lew, among "the earliest of my recollections is the gray uniform of Cadet [David] Wallace," and none "of the good man's after honors exalted him in my eyes like that scant garment."[4]

David soon opened a law office in Brookville and married Esther French Test, the daughter of a local politician, John Test. The connections to two Indiana politicians of note, Harrison and Test, probably led the young lawyer to pursue politics as a Whig. After serving in the lower house of the state legislature for three years, David was elected lieutenant governor of Indiana in 1831.

By that time, Esther Wallace had given birth to three boys, William, Lewis, and John.[5] The family, in 1832, moved west to Covington, where David could better serve Indiana and his own interests in law and merchandising. During the move from Brookville to Covington, Lew and his little brother John contracted scarlet fever. John died while the family rested in Indianapolis.[6]

In 1834, the Wallace family again experienced tragedy. Esther died from consumption. His mother's death, combined with his father's numerous travels, led Lew to disobey school masters and guardians in Crawfordsville, Indiana. He eventually developed a love for reading, but formal schooling never excited the future general and author. After three years of traveling and campaigning as lieutenant governor, Lew's father returned to Crawfordsville with a new wife, Zerelda Gray Sanders. William and Lew shunned and disobeyed their stepmother, but she worked hard to eventually earn their trust and love. Zerelda and David, however, failed to break Lew of his rebellious ways.[7]

David's frequent absences may have been a product of the times and the emergence of the self-made man, which produced fathers who spent less and less time with their children. Nineteenth-century Americans often stressed that mothers played the greatest part in helping male children bridge the gap between boyhood and manhood, something that would be understandably difficult for Zerelda to manage. According to some scholars of gender, academic institutions, mothers, and the boy culture of the era were supposed to help boys learn to contain their wildest behaviors as they reached adulthood. For Lew, this combination of influences worked to an extent, but he largely grew to embrace notions of manhood that seemed more martial or rough, rather than restrained or gentlemanly. In fact, a much older Lew fondly remembered a boy culture that encouraged aggression, including the "dare," in which young men would dare each other to complete dangerous feats in order to prove their courage. Such lessons seemed to have the greatest influence on the boy and man.[8]

A future political general would certainly need political connections, and Lew Wallace derived many from the acquaintances and reputation attained by his father, who died in 1859.[9] The peak of David's political career occurred in 1837 when the Whig easily won a bid to become Indiana's next governor. He sponsored spending on ambitious internal improvements, hoping to bring better roads, canals, and railroads to the state.[10] As a result of the election, the family moved once again, this time to Indianapolis.

In addition to the connections gained from the family name, his father's governorship indirectly brought young Lew around to more academic interests. The state library in Indianapolis, while not large, encouraged in him a love for reading and writing that never faded. But, at the same time, a few books from the state library and his father's collection moved the youngster to do something rather rash. Those volumes described Mexico and the Spanish settlement of Latin America. He further read about the Texas Revolution, Sam Houston, and the defeat of General Antonio Lopez de Santa Anna. Consequently, the teenager and a companion unsuccessfully tried to round up people to go to Texas and join the Texas Navy shortly after that republic's war for independence.[11] This failed attempt demonstrated the future army officer's tendency to pursue glorious adventures and embrace a more martial manhood, instead of the lucrative occupations and restraint that his father earnestly recommended.[12] Many historians have lamented the propensity of many Civil War generals, especially politically appointed officers, to shy away from risky and intense battles. Wallace, on the other hand, demonstrated early in life his wish to attain glory and honor through such endeavors.

Despite his growing love of books, Lew continued to be quite the truant, and it likely took some time and energy for David Wallace to convince his son to study law. Lew approached these studies with little enthusiasm; it was merely a means to make a living and support a family. In the meantime, the teenager found much more enjoyment in a militia company that he joined in 1841, as well as his related study of Winfield Scott's *Infantry Tactics*.[13] The Marion (County) Rifles, as the unit was called, soon elected Wallace to be their second sergeant, and he relished the chance to drill and train for a battle. The experience, and some natural ability, certainly helped to prepare him for later service in the Mexican War and the Civil War, where he excelled as a colonel, but it did not adequately prepare him for higher command.

According to Wallace, time with the Marion Rifles solidified that fighting, or martial, spirit that seemed to possess him in later years. One instance especially affected an impressionable young officer. Wallace's company of militia had a rival, a troop called the "City Greys." That organization assembled first, and it consisted of wealthier, older, and more established citizens of Indianapolis. Tension abounded since the "Rifles despised the aristocratic airs of the Greys" while "the Greys laughed at the Rifles," eventually referring to them derogatorily as "Arabs." They could have called them "roughs," given the competing masculinities of the day.[14]

The Marion Rifles got revenge for the name-calling and turned-up noses during a mock battle for a town celebration. The battle initially went as planned, the Greys attacking and the Rifles returning fire. However, in the heat of this pretend fight, the captain of the Rifles ignored the schedule. The company was supposed to retreat, but the captain forgot to order the men to fall back. As might be expected, the "mêlée that ensued was tremendous."[15] The Rifles won the fight and managed to take prisoners. In addition to cementing a passion for the military and encouraging his embrace of martial manhood, this incident foreshadowed future incidents during Wallace's career. The captain had succeeded by not following the script, or the rules, and this experience (or at least his evolving memory of it) may have encouraged an older Wallace to deviate from rules and orders during the Civil War, sometimes for the good, but often for the bad.

Such pursuits were good preparation for a future colonel of infantry, but not for a lawyer. Father Wallace took the son under his wing, helping him to study, but Lew could not keep his mind on such practical endeavors. And as the day approached for the nineteen-year-old Wallace to take the bar exam to become a lawyer, the Mexican War began. His earlier excitement over Texas, and his love of books on Mexico, could not be contained once the United States and Mexico had exchanged declarations of war.

Along with others, Wallace reported to the chambers of Supreme Court Justice Isaac Blackford for the bar exam, and a bailiff took the applicants to a quiet room in order to take the essay test. The young Indianan worked on the exam until approximately 2:00 A.M. but realized that he had not done well. Putting the exam in the provided envelope, he included a flippant, if not disrespectful, note to Justice Blackford: "I hope the foregoing answers will be to your satisfaction more than they are to mine; whether they are or not, I shall go to Mexico."[16] The answers did not satisfy the judge, who replied that the "Court interposes no objection to your going to Mexico."[17] A license to practice law did not accompany the letter, so Wallace happily formed a company of recruits and became a second lieutenant in the 1st Indiana Infantry.

Wallace later claimed that he needed only three days to fill the company.[18] The group soon elected officers: James P. Drake was the captain, and John McDougal became the first lieutenant.[19] The men elected Wallace to be the second lieutenant. The election of officers was important because it set the stage for Wallace's first confrontation with a superior officer. He had few problems with Captain Drake, but McDougal and Wallace seldom saw eye to eye. Early in life, Lew had rebelled against his father's authority, and this propensity to irritate superiors continued in Texas and Mexico. He never learned how to be a dutiful and patient follower, something taken for granted by his father and by other officers trained at the United States Military Academy.[20]

The city of Indianapolis held a farewell celebration, drawing thousands of citizens, to wish luck to the company.[21] Then the volunteer soldiers proceeded by train to the Ohio River, merely the first leg of a one-month voyage to Mexico. While at camp on the Ohio River, Wallace's company was assigned to the 1st Indiana Regiment, part of the Indiana Brigade under Brig. Gen. Joseph Lane.[22] The Indianans arrived at Brazos de Santiago, near the mouth of the Rio Grande, in late July of 1846.[23]

The 1st Indiana had already suffered six deaths due to illness by 25 July.[24] Nevertheless, Lieutenant Wallace wrote to his brother, raving about the climate in Brazos de Santiago while describing problems that would mirror his Civil War experience. On a positive note, the "sun and continual sea-breeze which sweeps around me seems to have made a favorable compact with my constitution." But diseases infected and killed others in his company, seven men having been buried the day before while another seven were "unfit for duty," leading Wallace to say that "we live in the midst of death."[25]

Wallace loved "the continual excitement—the increasing change of character and scene—with which I come in daily contact."[26] However, following such a comment, the Indianan described the beginnings of his first serious confrontation with a superior officer. According to the young second lieutenant, John "McDougal is beginning to show the tyrannical nature given him by public opinion in years gone by. Impositions and unjust exactions are beginning to be read to us every morning or so." Moreover, McDougal "can *lie* as sweetly as a . . . [bird] can sing." The elder lieutenant was promoted to captain when Drake became a colonel, and subsequently became domineering. Wallace, however, was not interested in making real, lasting peace.[27]

While Wallace learned that such treatment did not endear men to their leader, knowledge that would be an asset to him in the Civil War, he had not learned, and appeared uninterested in learning, how to subtly or openly get along with an immediate superior in such a situation.[28] In addition, the episode seemed to mirror the dueling conceptions of manhood that Lorien Foote associates with later Civil War soldiers and officers. McDougal represented the "gentleman" who insists on discipline and restraint, while Wallace was the "rough" who rebels from the rules and discipline that many Americans abhorred as violations of their rights as U.S. citizens.[29]

By October, many more soldiers had become sick, and they were frustrated with the medical care that the army provided. Wallace joked that the volunteers believed, and hoped, that one particular doctor had drowned. But "alas! for the hopes of all who had been sick, who most devoutly wished it might be true, and looked upon the occurrence as one in which the interposition of Providence was clearly visible, the gentleman made his appearance in camp and commenced his duties day before yesterday." The lieutenant believed him and his two assistants to be "beautiful specimen[s] of the genus 'Quack'" because wherever "they proceed, whenever they administer medicine, death is the consequent attendant."[30]

The young Indianan also hoped that his unit might "be called into more active service, and a chance offered us to redeem the tarnished honor of our state." He voiced such concerns even before an Indiana regiment embarrassed the state at the Battle of Buena Vista in February 1847. Wallace's regiment had received little action, as would be the case for the remainder of the war, and he desperately yearned for some sort of honorable fight. Thus, Wallace was "burning to see more active service, and pray but for one engagement before we return home." While the young officer never witnessed a major battle in Mexico, he acquired some understanding of logistics and supply, mentioning that he "went with the companies which escorted the 250 [wagon] train as far as Matamoras, and yet think it the most beautiful sight I ever saw. As each wagon was drawn by five mules, the whole of them together, from front to rear, covered a track two miles in length."[31]

While Wallace gained some experience in dealing with supply and sickness, both possibly being of value during the Civil War, his negative attitude was more important to his future. He hated the lack of a good fight, and he continued to anguish over his inability to prove his bravery and attain honor for the home state. He largely blamed Gen. Zachary Taylor, a haughty and unkempt officer, at least in Wallace's opinion, for the lack of action. Taylor commanded the Army of Occupation during the Mexican War. This negative view of a long-serving officer, a professional by early nineteenth-century standards, never left the mind of the future political general.

The quarrel with McDougal only intensified, Wallace finding ways to infuriate the captain. McDougal had been sending information back to Indiana, much of it critical of the lieutenant. According to the senior officer, Wallace argued that McDougal was sick, drunk, and unfit for duty because of a desire to become captain. Wallace denied that he was plotting to take his superior's rank. As for the captain's supposed drunkenness, "to the best of my recollection I never stated or wrote it; if I did, why *men have eyesight, and so have witnesses.*"[32] A dispute over Wallace owing the company some money, as well as accusations that he stole some supplies, eventually led to a court of inquiry. The young officer was acquitted, but the incident certainly made matters worse.[33]

The 1st Indiana's first major mission after landing at Brazos de Santiago was to occupy and secure the town of Matamoras. Wallace liked the "beautiful city which has sheltered us for so long a time and almost re accustomed [*sic*] us to the pleasures and conveniences of civilized life," but the labor at Matamoras was tedious, continuous, and not so honorable in his opinion. The impatient lieutenant gained some valuable insights at Matamoras about occupying a city: "[O]fficers and soldiers are perpetually busy. Day and night find us on an eternal trot." He came to understand the myriad of duties involved as this "man is to be seen here, that Mexican is to be taken there, while scouting parties are coming and going at all hours, and pickets and patrol guards traversing every street and . . . alley in the place."[34] This experience must have been useful when Wallace found himself occupying and guarding the state of Maryland for the Union in 1864–65.

Furthermore, by March of 1847, Wallace's dislike for Taylor turned into intense hatred. The Hoosier agonized because a poor performance by the 2nd Indiana Infantry in the Battle of Buena Vista, in February, had embarrassed the state. Taylor accused the regiment of cowardice in retreating during that battle, and despite the fact that many regrouped to join again in the battle, the charge greatly damaged Indiana's reputation.[35] The controversy over Buena Vista created even more animosity toward the seasoned general. The haughty and unkempt officer, in Wallace's opinion, blamed the Indiana regiment for problems during the battle in order to ensure his reputation, as well as those of his friends, including Jefferson Davis of Mississippi. The hatred exhibited for such long-serving, trained officers never left the mind of the future political general.

After the Battle of Buena Vista, Wallace heard rumors that Taylor was in trouble, and he relayed his mixture of joy and chagrin to his brother on 4 March.[36] He believed that the rumors would mean action for the 1st Indiana Regiment, as it eventually marched for Monterrey. However, while a major battle had been fought there in September of 1846, the war had now moved to other locales. As a result, Wallace never experienced the combat that he longed for.[37]

The 1st Indiana Regiment left Mexico for New Orleans on 24 May 1847, their term of service expiring, in order to be mustered out. Wallace returned to Indianapolis to study law with his father, eventually applying again to take the state bar exam. This time he passed.[38] In the meantime, the Mexican War veteran spent much of 1848 campaigning against Zachary Taylor, who was running for president.[39] The son of a former governor tried to use his political clout to prevent the Indiana delegation to the 1848 Whig convention from supporting Taylor. He failed, and likely irritated fellow Whigs in the process. Upon the setback, he did not rally around the party's nominee. In fact, the new lawyer became an investor in a Free-Soil publication based in Indianapolis. While he likely had little interest in the antislavery sentiments of the periodical's readers, he wrote a number of anti-Taylor articles on its behalf. In the end, Indiana's electoral votes went to Taylor, Wallace lost a lot of money in the venture, and he forced himself out of the Whig Party by angering influential politicians and being unwilling to make amends. As he later stated, Wallace had no choice but to become "a Democrat—one of the straitest [sic] of the sect."[40]

Wallace practiced law in Covington, Fountain County, from 1850 to 1853. He began his practice there because Covington was close to the town of Crawfordsville, Indiana, the home of Susan Elston. The young lawyer was in love with Susan and hoped to make a name for himself in Covington in order to impress the young lady's father. The couple married in 1852, and they soon had a son named Henry.[41] In marrying Susan, Wallace made a good choice; the two were madly in love until his death, and, more importantly for his political career, the Covington lawyer gained a powerful brother-in-law. Henry S. Lane had married Susan's sister, and he already knew Wallace since the two had served together in Mexico, Lane as a major. Lane would eventually be a U.S. senator from Indiana, as well as a Republican Party leader in the state from the organization's inception. His brother-in-law's support went a long way toward securing Wallace an appointment as a brigadier general of Union armies during the Civil War.

Many lawyers dabbled in politics, and Wallace was no exception. While residing in Covington, he attained his first elective office in 1850, that of prosecuting attorney for Fountain County. It was not a glamorous position, but it allowed the holder to earn some money, gain practical work experience, and to make political and business connections.[42] The aspiring politician attained this office in part due to a rash and unprofessional stunt, a success that clouded his judgment for some time to come. A state constitutional convention was held in 1850, and Wallace supported Judge Joseph Ristine to be a delegate to that convention. Ristine managed to get Wallace some work in the county clerk's office, and the young lawyer was obliged to write some editorials on the candidate's behalf in a Democratic paper. The opposing candidate, a Mr. Mallory, countered those editorials with some of his own, subtly calling in to question Ristine's and Wallace's integrity.

As a result, the rash twenty-three-year-old proceeded to the next stop of a debate tour, waited for Mallory to speak, and then approached the podium to counter the remarks. When Ristine's opponent tried to stop him from speaking because Wallace was not an actual candidate, the Covington lawyer recounted that he hit Mallory, buried his "fingers deep in his 'guzzle,' turned his head sideways, and hit him five good ones on the jaw. He never touched me once." Even though the fighter had warned the sheriff of his plan, the affair still "was bold and rash in the extreme." The sheriff quickly brought the instigator before a judge, who fined him three dollars, but then insisted that everyone help Wallace pay the fine. The assembled crowd, and the county in general, seemed to agree that Wallace had a right to confront the man who challenged his integrity, a sort of frontier justice in a region more likely to embrace notions of martial manhood. Most importantly, the incident helped the fledgling politician attain his first office. But in the future, the success of this event seemed to convince Wallace that rash, bold, aggressive behavior could bail him out of any bind.[43] It worked on the frontier, but as stakes became higher, he tended to make enemies with such behavior.[44]

After marrying Susan, Wallace moved to her hometown of Crawfordsville, in Montgomery County. He practiced law there, with several interruptions, from 1853 till his death in 1905. The Hoosier's highest political office, before the Civil War, materialized four years after moving to the town. In 1856, this strong supporter of Stephen Douglas and his policies received the Democratic Party's nomination for state senator from Montgomery County.[45] With the Wallace name, the support of Susan's father and Henry S. Lane, and his acquired boldness and confidence, the fledgling politician won the fall election and served into 1859.[46]

Wallace was not reelected in 1858, and the reason for his loss is unclear. It likely mirrored the losing campaigns of other Democrats during those years. The Kansas-Nebraska Act and the *Dred Scott* decision fueled the emergence of the Republican Party and cost many Democrats their positions. And for that matter, Wallace was seldom able to make good friends, professionally or personally. The one-term senator often irritated others, sometimes with his abundant pride over his own writings and presentations. Shortly after his victory in 1856, which was followed by the usual speeches and editorials, a local newspaper sarcastically claimed that Wallace "has commenced the task of revising Webster's Unabridged Dictionary and will have it transposed into verse, for the use of infant Schools," adding that "Mr. Wallace is a wonderful genius."[47] While his ability to write and speak made him an ideal recruiter during the next war, some listeners and readers saw much arrogance in his work, sometimes eroding his political support.

While the Crawfordsville lawyer attained some political experience during these years, he also attained some basic military training through the nineteenth-century militia system. Having been involved in a militia company just before the Mexican War, he now wished to continue that pastime by organizing his own company, based in Crawfordsville. The company captain logically named the militia the Montgomery County Guards, and unlike some other such organizations across the country, this company was not organized merely as a reason to meet with the boys and drink.

Wallace organized the Guards in the summer of 1856, and the state furnished muskets while militiamen provided band instruments, tents, and uniforms. The company initially relied on "Hardee's *Infantry Tactics* for instruction." The Mexican War veteran expanded on this drill when he came across a "magazine containing an article descriptive of the Algerian Zouaves of France," and he "reduced what was there reported to a system, including the bayonet exercises." Wallace eventually enlarged the book of drill to two volumes. The company liked the different set of drills and tactics, eventually purchasing Zouave outfits to complement their unique style. According to their captain, the company impressed many, took part in parades and most celebrations, and regularly challenged other militia companies to compare their skills at drill.[48] None accepted the offer.[49]

No longer a state senator, Wallace concentrated on his lawyerly duties while doing his best to support the Democratic Party. He spent a considerable amount of time defending Stephen Douglas, the Kansas-Nebraska Act, and the Democratic support of the South's right to secure, and possibly expand, slavery. The Republican Party was gaining converts in Indiana, and Wallace felt political winds shifting. He even resorted to a common tactic, once charging Abraham Lincoln "emphatically with being in favor of bringing about the social and political equality of the white and black races."[50] Despite his best efforts, Wallace failed to sufficiently harm Lincoln's candidacy in Indiana.[51]

The recently organized Republican Party gained additional seats in Congress, as well as electing a president, in 1860. In the wake of the secession crisis, Wallace believed that the local Democrats were not loyalists, so he went to the office of the governor, Oliver P. Morton, a man Wallace had resented because he had bolted from the Democratic Party in favor of the new party of Lincoln.[52] The son of a former governor now found himself apologizing to the current governor, as well as offering his services should the South force secession.[53] Unlike Morton, but similar to others over the next few years, Wallace would come to embrace the Republican Party (in 1861, Indianans and others called it the Union Party to entice pro-war Democrats to the fold) because he came to see it as the party that more strongly supported the Union.[54] His views on slavery seemed to remain unchanged, or at least were left conveniently vague for the moment. And of course, based on his earlier newspaper comments on equality, he could fit in with numerous conservative Republicans who were not fond of slavery, but also abhorred the possibility of equality between the races.

Wallace made a wise move, one that instantly gave him another political ally. Remarkably, he had secured Morton's approval and Henry Lane's attention and backing. On 6 April 1861, Wallace sent a letter to Lane, asking for one thousand rifles from the federal government to supply an Indiana regiment. A national crisis loomed, and Wallace hoped to handpick and train a regiment that would agree to serve for the duration of the war. The proposal impressed Senator Lane, and he forwarded it to Secretary of War Simon Cameron, further suggesting that the writer of the proposal "is one of our best military men and entirely reliable in his devotion to the Union." One might have assumed, and many would during the nineteenth century, that he had a special knack, or genius, for military matters. Lane urged Cameron to provide the arms if possible.[55] Wallace's assertiveness likely secured him a position as adjutant general of Indiana, a definite stepping stone to even higher rank.

Once the Civil War began, Wallace owed his commission as colonel of the 11th Indiana Infantry Regiment to his budding relationship with his state's top politician, Republican governor Morton. Senator Lane and Morton would later provide the young convert a commission as a brigadier general and eventually as a major general. Wallace's pre–Civil War military career also helped him get these commissions. He was involved with local, county, and state militias from the 1840s through the 1850s. Forming a company of recruits in Indiana and becoming a second lieutenant during the Mexican-American War helped. These early experiences were beneficial to Wallace's informal education as a volunteer soldier and officer. His background satisfactorily prepared him to be a colonel for the 11th Indiana Infantry Regiment during the Civil War.

Being a colonel was a natural stepping stone to brigade and even division command. Headstrong, politically active, opinionated, and identifying with a more martial definition of manhood, Lew Wallace took his place as one of dozens of hopeful officers, from the North and the South, who aspired to lead thousands of men into glorious battle. In this competition to become a general, the Indiana lawyer held some advantages. His veteran status and connections allowed him to attain the commission as colonel, and his abilities as a writer and speaker provided leverage in the beginning and helped support his start as a political general, even though his military experience may not have furnished Wallace with the knowledge necessary to command a brigade or division. Unfortunately for Wallace, ambition, ill-conceived aggression, pride, and an inability to communicate and get along with superiors would often overshadow his advantages.

TWO

═══════════════════════════

"The Fruits of Victory"

Wallace served with local, county, and state militias from the 1840s through the 1850s, and he became a second lieutenant of volunteers during the Mexican-American War. These experiences benefited Wallace's reputation, educated him as a volunteer officer, and prepared him to be a volunteer colonel during the Civil War.

On 13 April 1861, the disgruntled Democrat addressed a jury in Clinton County, Indiana. While he was speaking, a local telegraph operator approached Wallace with a message. The Mexican War veteran had pledged his unconditional assistance to Governor Oliver P. Morton if a war between the states began, and Indiana's chief executive intended to hold him to his word. Fort Sumter, in South Carolina, had "been fired upon" by rebels, leading Morton to request that Wallace come "immediately."[1] Riding a fast horse and taking a late Saturday train, the lawyer reached Indianapolis early the next morning.

Wallace called on the governor at his home, finding that Morton had already left for the office. The governor informed Wallace that he wanted the militia captain to be Indiana's adjutant general. Morton believed that the current adjutant was a rebel sympathizer, and the Crawfordsville lawyer had more military experience than most Indianans. Wallace accepted the appointment but asked that he be given command of a regiment in return for such service. The Mexican War veteran was determined to take part in some combat during this next conflict. He still blamed, and hated, the now-dead Zachary Taylor for not sending the old 1st Indiana into honorable combat, and he was determined that no one would get in his way in 1861.[2]

Morton gave Wallace an office adjoining his and told him that the law provided little on the duties of the state's adjutant general. Furthermore, there were no books to go with the position. Such a lack of organization offered little guidance, but it also allowed leeway in filling Indiana's quota for volunteer soldiers, six thousand men. Wallace asked that he have an assistant, recommending a friend, Fred Kneffler of the Marion County Clerk's Office; Morton knew the gentleman and agreed. The governor then added that he needed the new adjutant and assistant to work quickly since he wanted "the credit of reporting Indiana's quota full, first of the states."[3]

Years later, Wallace praised the experience he gained working under Morton as an adjutant general, commenting that "he gave me lessons which, had I been a politician, selfishly watchful of my own advancement, would have been profitable in the highest degree."[4] It was an odd statement for someone who had held political offices, attended some conventions, and was often obsessed with his own political rise. Wallace's father had been a governor. Wallace himself had held political offices after the Mexican War and yearned for more, and political connections largely contributed to his appointment as adjutant general. Nevertheless, he viewed himself primarily as a veteran of the Mexican War, not as a politician who might be asked to give recruiting speeches, take on various administrative duties, or supervise the occupation of a city or county.

He was, in fact, a veteran of modest experience, even when factoring in his involvement in the militia. Furthermore, his service in the Mexican War lessened in value as the Civil War progressed; instead, Wallace's actions as a Union officer were more important after 1861. Historian Carol Reardon, among others, has asserted that many politically appointed officers believed that they were just as qualified as most professional soldiers. Wallace certainly thought so, and he demanded to be treated as an equal, encouraging an aggressive and sometimes arrogant personality.[5] His embrace of a more martial manhood would show in the months to come.

Wallace and Kneffler quickly recruited Hoosiers for the Federal cause. On 15 April, one day after accepting the position, the adjutant issued his first general order, outlining the manner for companies to be organized and arranged into regiments in Indianapolis. He sent letters to newspapers throughout the state asking for companies to join a regiment of Zouaves, a unit that he planned to train in the "peculiar tactics" of those flamboyant units.[6] Consequently, young men, some already members of militia companies throughout the state, converged on Camp Morton, just a few blocks away from the capitol building. The adjutant general and his assistant created the camp in just a few days, and new recruits flooded into the capital city. Prospective troops "were met at the [railroad] depot by a string band which furnished martial music for us to march by, to the State House" where Wallace administered the oath.[7] As a result, Camp Morton was soon overwhelmed by the tents and booths needed to house and supply so many recruits. Amazingly, five days after Wallace accepted his position, the camp contained as many as 130 companies. Indiana only needed sixty to fill the six regiments required by the Federal government. Having seventy extra companies, Morton telegraphed Washington asking to retain the surplus of men.[8]

Morton and Wallace held an important meeting on that Friday. The adjutant officially reported that the state's quota had been met, greatly pleasing the governor. Wallace then recommended that the Indiana regiments start with the number six. The governor was initially confused, but the adjutant explained that the state should honor the five regiments that served in the Mexican War by retiring the designations. Morton agreed, and then logically asked Wallace to stay on as the adjutant general.[9] He had done a superb job, and the governor would ask him to help recruit again.[10] Despite Morton's pleading, Wallace could not be turned from his goal, to lead a regiment in the field. Regimental command potentially led to honor and glory; a recruiter would not attain that fame. As historian Lorien Foote has noted, the concept of honor was more important to northern men and their manhood than past scholars suggested. Foote states that honor "is when a man's self-worth is based on public reputation and the respect of others. An insult to such a man is a shaming that requires public vindication of worth."[11] Thus, Morton let Wallace choose his unit, and he chose the 11th, the last of the recently organized regiments. He would have the opportunity to attain the honor desired; and, when anything appeared to get in the way of that drive, the Indianan would react.

On 26 April 1861, the governor commissioned officers for Indiana's first six Civil War regiments, including Wallace as a colonel.[12] All six regiments enlisted for a term of three months, and the 11th, at least, received its arms on that same day.[13] Morton forwarded the appropriate paperwork to President Lincoln, who was "greatly gratified" to accept the officers and soldiers from the Hoosier state.[14] Wallace's regiment, to his great joy, included his own militia company, the Montgomery Guards.

Wallace devoted time, before and after leaving Indianapolis, to the training of the regiment in the Zouave tactics with the help of his subordinates, including Lt. Col. George McGinnis. The Guards were the only ones who knew the system, one relying on bugles and a few unique maneuvers that, among other things, allowed the men to more easily fight while on their bellies. Thus, Wallace spent much time just teaching the officers to train the privates. In addition, the colonel ordered uniforms in the appropriate style.[15] But the uniforms of the 11th were not quite what one might expect of Zouaves; they were short on color. In fact, the outfits were "of the tamest gray twilled goods, not unlike home-made jeans—a visor cap, French in pattern, its top of red cloth not larger than the palm of one's hand; a blue flannel shirt with open neck; a jacket Greekish in form, edged with narrow binding, the red scarcely noticeable; breeches baggy, but not petticoated; button gaiters connecting below the knees with the breeches, and strapped over the shoe." Wallace complained that "in line two thousand yards off they looked like a smoky ribbon long-drawn out."[16]

The drill and outfits made for a splendid departure ceremony.[17] At the capitol, the 11th Indiana received two flags from the patriotic ladies of Terre Haute and Indianapolis. Wallace spoke at the celebration, intent on reminding everyone of the Battle of Buena Vista and still smarting over the 2nd Indiana's ill-treatment during the Mexican War. He suggested that Hoosiers should fight for the Union, and also to avenge the slandering by Jefferson Davis and Taylor during the war with Mexico. The colonel then asked his regiment to kneel and repeat that they would "Remember Buena Vista."[18] The speech concluded a tearful ceremony at which Wallace had done his part to keep spirits high and encourage others to do the patriotic thing, join the Union army.[19]

The 11th Indiana's first order came from U.S. Adj. Gen. Lorenzo Thomas. He told Wallace to take his regiment to Evansville, in southeast Indiana. There were secessionists in the town, and across the Ohio River in Kentucky, though that state remained in the Union. Thomas ordered the 11th to search all vessels floating past towns on the Ohio River.[20] Few boat captains presented problems, so the boring assignment allowed Wallace and his officers valuable time for tactical training, four hours a day for company drill and another four hours a day for battalion drill. The colonel understood the importance of training—a sign of a good regimental commander—but the demanding schedule aggravated the men of the 11th Indiana. The soldiers failed to understand that the combat training might soon be put to good use.[21]

In addition to searching boats and drilling, Wallace believed that the regiment provided a great service for a town afraid of supporting the Union. Upon their arrival in Evansville, the colonel was astonished to see "but one flag flying." The number had increased dramatically by the end of the regiment's stay. Wallace concluded that "before our arrival the Union people were afraid to show their colors . . . but now they develop boldly and rapidly."[22] His recognition of such liberties, and the willingness to staunchly address Union citizens' concerns, made him a potential departmental administrator later in the war.

Wallace and his men were eager to leave Indiana, and they eventually got their wish. While in the Ohio River town, the Hoosier lamented to his wife that he was "not yet able to see a fight ahead."[23] The comment was supposed to assuage her fears, but she knew that her husband was desperately trying to find a battle. In the meantime, political allies, including his brother-in-law Senator Henry S. Lane, sought meetings with the president and Gen. Winfield Scott to find the 11th Indiana a different assignment.[24] Thus, in early June, the prospects for action increased as General Scott personally ordered the Indianans to proceed by rail to Cumberland, Maryland, reporting to Maj. Gen. Robert Patterson.[25] Being recognized by Scott encouraged Wallace's desire to find a good fight.

The Zouaves left Evansville on 6 June, eager to see action.[26] The regiment went by train to Indianapolis, then to Cincinnati, and finally to Grafton, Virginia.[27] Cumberland was on the B&O Railroad between Grafton and Hagerstown, Maryland. Patterson was camped at Chambersburg, Pennsylvania, while Gen. Thomas Morris, Wallace's old friend, was at Grafton.[28] Cumberland was a bit isolated from the protection of either general, especially since the town of Romney, Virginia, was close by, and possibly occupied by rebels.

At Grafton, Wallace renewed his acquaintance with Morris, and the general told him that there were 1,300 to 2,000 rebels at Romney, a day's march from Cumberland. Furthermore, the railroad east of Cumberland was not reliable. Morris wondered why Confederates occupied Romney, thinking that perhaps they acted as guards for a movement by Confederate major general Joseph Johnston from Harpers Ferry to the east, or maybe to better threaten the B&O Railroad. The discussion caused Wallace to supposedly ask: "[I]f I were to give Romney a shaking up, it would disturb Johnston some?" Morris laughed and told him to make "sure before you try that."[29] The commander at Grafton, however, was not the only officer to which Wallace must answer. The 11th Indiana was to report to Patterson, who never gave Wallace explicit permission to make any sort of raid on Romney. The plan was bold and aggressive, befitting his personal thoughts on how a man should act, and representative of traits the colonel wanted associated with his leadership.

In the meantime, Wallace received a message from Col. Fitz John Porter, Patterson's adjutant. Porter asserted that the commanding general wished for the colonel to secure the town of Cumberland and gather as much information as possible, being certain to get along with the loyal citizens. But, should the

Indianan "gain information after the gathering for offensive movement of armed bodies of men not too powerful to overcome by a force you can safely detach, capture and rout them, by surprise if possible, and seize and hold" prisoners.[30] The plan to attack forces at Romney did not meet any of the qualifications. The rebels outnumbered the 11th Indiana, and Wallace's march to the Virginia town would leave Cumberland susceptible to an attack. Nevertheless, the Hoosier proceeded to carry out his designs.

Wallace found two guides through the train engineer, and they helped him to map out the region between Cumberland and Romney. They told him that the strength at Romney was between 1,200 and 1,500 men. It appeared that the best route for attacking Romney would be the unwatched New Creek road, possibly allowing the bluecoats to catch the graycoats off guard.[31] The venture would involve forty-six miles of marching. In the end, Wallace decided to retire to Cumberland first, so that a quick attack would be all the more surprising. Once the Indianans arrived, he would look for a camp. Pretending not to find one that was satisfactory, the regiment would get on the train and proceed west as though going back to the last night's camp. Such information would likely get back to the enemy. Once the regiment reached New Creek, they would march from there to Romney, surprising the rebels who held that town.[32]

In the meantime, Wallace urged Patterson to not leave him behind in the event of a major movement against Johnston or Brig. Gen. P. G. T. Beauregard. He also relayed the plan to threaten Romney. On 11 June, the Indianan received a reply from headquarters urging caution and patience. Patterson's adjutant asserted that the "Commanding General will not forget you and would be pleased to have you, but unless a force strong enough to maintain itself comes to take your place he cannot call you from your present position now daily becoming more and more important and essential to be held, for the security of this force." Headquarters received "reports that the bridges which it was desired you should guard, are destroyed." Thus, it was important to Patterson that Wallace and his men "cause them to be repaired and the road in your reach made practicable." Talk of a raid to the south worried the general, so he urged Wallace "to be cautious, very cautious that our forces shall receive no check or reverse" because either would "swell the ranks of the enemy, fill their store houses and dispirit our own forces."[33] The response failed to endorse Wallace's plan, but it did not forbid it either, and that was good enough for the colonel; Patterson's plea for caution fell on deaf ears.

Again, Wallace's bold plan made sense for someone so concerned with honor and proving his place as a man in nineteenth-century America. However, the

Indianan would fail to understand that West Pointers expected subordinates to more carefully follow orders, and they did not tend to define manhood in the same way. A few scholars have mentioned that career army officers often embraced a "communal manhood" in which they defined worth by what one could do for the community. They were concerned with "persistence, character, and rationally self-disciplined restraint. . . . Regular soldiers learned and espoused genteel values of hierarchy and social distance." They aspired to fame, but also "upheld tradition, cohesion, national service, and disinterestedness as ideals, despite frequent deviations from them as individuals."[34] The United States Military Academy, West Point, instilled such ideals in its cadets. Most importantly, every "aspect of the academy, both inside and outside the classroom, was governed by a strict system of regulations and procedures that imposed order and discipline on cadet life."[35] Such officers expected discipline from subordinates, and politically appointed civilians, like Wallace, often became frustrated under such circumstances, as though their rights as American citizens were at stake.

So, despite recommended restraint, the colonel put his plan into action. The regiment reached Cumberland at daybreak. Wallace talked to the mayor, who showed him some possible campsites. The colonel acted dissatisfied, and the men took the train twenty-one miles back to New Creek starting at 10:00 P.M., leaving two companies to guard Cumberland. Then the colonel started his "men across the mountains, twenty-three miles off, intending to reach the town [of Romney] by 6 o'clock in the morning." But, the regiment did not approach the small Virginia town until 8:00 A.M. They were late because the road was rough, "leading along high bluffs and narrow passes, which required great caution in passing."[36]

As it turned out, the rebels received a warning of the bluecoats' approach a full hour before their arrival. The troops drew within two miles of Romney by dawn when some horsemen fired on the advance guard. Wallace could now see the town, which was on a high hill on the other side of the south branch of the Potomac River. Immediately in front of the regiment was the Potomac, crossed by a wooden bridge that had a two-story brick house on the exit side. The colonel could see 1,000 to 1,200 men guarding the town, in addition to two field pieces. Despite the opposition, he decided to proceed as planned.[37]

The colonel ordered his advance guard to rush the bridge. As they exited the bridge and ran down an embankment, the rebels in the brick house opened fire. The Yankees, with the help of a second company, eventually took the bridge and the house, Wallace deciding to burn the home. He left one company in charge of the bridge to cover his getaway, along with the responsibility for destroying the brick residence.[38]

Wallace surprised the rebels by not marching straight up the steep road to the town. "Instead of following the road, as the rebels expected," the colonel "pushed five companies in skirmishing order, and at double-quick time, up a hill to the right, intending to get around the left flank of the enemy, and cut off their retreat."[39] By veering to the right, it was not as steep closer to the top, and the Union men more easily made the summit despite the absence of a road and the presence of a rocky gorge.[40] Wallace hoped that this plan would confuse the rebels because the steep hill made it difficult for them to turn to face an attack on their left flank. It worked.

The Confederates quickly decided to avoid a significant conflict. The Indianans had barely "deployed and started forward, and got within rifle range" before the rebel artillery "limbered up and put off over the bluff in hottest haste." Wallace and his men soon reached the "deep, precipitous gorge, the crossing of which occupied about ten minutes."[41] The rebels fled while the Federals struggled through the ravine.[42] Wallace turned his men left once they reached the hill's summit but found only townspeople and stragglers fleeing to the south. The 11th Indiana's only loss was the broken suspender buckle of a sergeant; it had been hit by a musket ball during the rush across the bridge. As best as the commander could surmise, the regiment had killed maybe two or three rebels owing to their quick flight, and Wallace was able to capture one southern major.[43]

After the Hoosiers secured the town, the black servants of those who fled met the Union soldiers "with the cheeriest welcome, and in time incredibly short there was not a hungry man in the regiment." In addition to being fed, the bluecoats impressed three wagons and their horses, arms, tents, and medical stores.[44] A column formed to depart at 3:00 P.M. that afternoon. From Romney, the troops took the same route back to Cumberland, reaching camp late that night.[45] A dress parade was held the next afternoon, and the Indiana unit seemed to be in fair condition after a forty-six-mile trek and a skirmish.

With some risky endeavors, especially those attempted with little encouragement, one might receive great praise if there is success. In this case, Wallace and his men were victorious, and newspapers, politicians, and generals gave thanks. Patterson received news of the "gallant movement on Romney with the greatest pleasure and satisfaction and returns his thanks to you and your command."[46] The successful rout of rebel forces at Romney gained the colonel positive acknowledgments and fame never before experienced by the young officer. But it also helped to instill that one problematic mindset: the best way to attain acclaim or get out of a jam is to act boldly, with or without permission. Wallace had the ability to think for himself on military matters, and a wonderful willingness to fight, but his yearning for fame and glory soon caused him to misuse those assets. The urge for military glory consumed the man, to the point that he sometimes tried to take matters into his own hands. When risky actions, with little support or knowledge on the part of superiors, fail, the consequences can be severe, but Wallace was not thinking about failure. He anticipated glory and accolades in June 1861.

In his report of the Romney affair to Patterson, Wallace showed a true understanding of the political ramifications of his actions. He believed that one "good result has come of it: the loyal men in that region have taken heart." So much so, the Hoosier believed, that very "shortly I think you will hear of another Union company from that district." The colonel thanked Patterson for his approval of the regiment's actions, despite the general not having ordered the attack, asserting that the enterprise had "brought home to the insolent 'chivalry' a wholesome respect for Northern prowess."[47] These reflections came from a politician who understood how such actions could induce some Virginians to fight for the Union while causing supporters of the Confederacy to lose heart. At the same time, the affair demonstrated that northerners would, and could, fight. Although actions at Romney only involved 1,500 to 2,000 men, the skirmishing raised eyebrows among officers and newspaper writers.

The *New York Times* stated that the Confederacy still claimed that southern soldiers were better fighters, despite losses at Grafton, "Phillippa," Romney, and Harpers Ferry. The setbacks, according to the sarcastic editorial, demonstrated that the rebel soldiers were "so much better at retreating than the Federal troops are at marching as not to afford an opportunity for a 'fair field and open fight.'"[48] Wallace even sent a note to the *Indianapolis Journal* when he learned of false rebel reports of a Union retreat from Romney. He was concerned for the honor of the regiment and its colonel, and the Hoosiers' desire to avenge the ghosts of Buena Vista.[49] He had little to worry about, however, since almost all reports reflected positively on the 11th Indiana's efforts.[50]

According to the victorious colonel, *Frank Leslie's Illustrated Weekly* even asked if it could send a reporter to the Indianans' camp. Wallace also received a signed note of congratulations from Scott because the raid had caused Joseph Johnston to evacuate Harpers Ferry.[51] The Confederate general evidently thought that the bluecoats presented a serious threat from the west. In addition to all of this fanfare, the raid seemed to clear up control of the B&O Railroad for at least a short time. According to one private, all the men were proud, and they "thought it a very large affair at the time but found out later on that it was not so large as it appeared to us then."[52]

Wallace soon learned that Confederate cavalry, artillery, and infantry had arrived in Romney, and he feared that the rebels would attempt to avenge the late skirmish with an attack on Cumberland, this time confronting the Hoosiers with a far superior force. As a result, the Indianan asked Patterson for more men. The general could not afford to send any to Cumberland but suggested that he would ask Maj. Gen. George McClellan to send aid.[53] Unfortunately for the Hoosier, the cautious general could not offer any troops to Patterson. In addition, an earlier note from Wallace suggesting the absence of the enemy, and preparations for a major battle, discouraged Patterson and his assistant adjutant general.[54] The bold actions of the young officer had won him some acclaim, but now he was forced to deal with the consequences of an aggressive affair not fully endorsed by his superiors.

The communication from Patterson's adjutant, Fitz John Porter, particularly worried Wallace. The colonel's bold action convinced his superiors to keep the Indiana regiment in Cumberland, but without reinforcements. Since the apparent buildup at Romney meant that someone needed to stay and hold Cumberland and that portion of the B&O Railroad, the ambitious Hoosier might not be able to join Patterson in the event of a major action against Confederates under Johnston or Beauregard. Wallace agonized over this turn of events and wrote to Porter asserting that there was now no enemy in sight. Under such circumstances, he begged "the general for God's sake not to leave me behind when he marches." After all, the Indianan wanted "to show him how we can fight," even suggesting that maybe his unit could be relieved at Cumberland by "one of the idle Indiana or Ohio regiments."[55]

Soon Wallace applied for assistance from Governor Andrew Curtin, a Republican from Pennsylvania. He told the governor that he would have to retreat through Pennsylvania if forced from Cumberland. The thought of rebels invading his state convinced Curtin to send two regiments of "State Reserves" and a battery of six guns, all under Col. Charles Biddle. Oddly enough, the men were ordered to go no farther than the state line, greatly frustrating Wallace and the commanders of the Keystone State units.[56] The irritated colonel would have to improvise in order to secure his position.

In order to better protect Cumberland and the railway, Wallace impressed thirteen horses to mount some scouts to be on the lookout for rebels; he gave the command of these thirteen soldiers to Cpl. David Hay. This makeshift cavalry could alert the commander to any potential dangers. In the meantime, rebels burned the bridge at New Creek, and communications were cut off with Grafton. Luckily, the town helped supply food and ammunition, and the banker forwarded a month's pay to all commissioned officers. One rebel column approached Cumberland in force, but the scouts detected the movement. As a result, Wallace marched most of his men out of town to meet the Confederates, who turned away when they realized that they faced resistance.[57]

On 24 June, Patterson decided to grant Wallace's greatest wish, asking him to join the growing army then at Hagerstown.[58] But the department commander rescinded the order two days later, further frustrating the battle-hungry officer.[59] While dealing with this irritating development, the colonel became increasingly nervous for the whereabouts of the rebel reinforcements at or near Romney. Little news was coming in with regard to the graycoats, so on 26 June the Hoosier sent his thirteen scouts out on a turnpike toward Romney. Wallace's apprehension was validated when the men discovered rebel infantry and cavalry at the small town of Frankfort, Virginia.[60]

Wallace's following account may exaggerate, in terms of the number of Confederates present and killed, but otherwise tells the correct story. According to the Indianan, Hay decided to try to get around the town via another road, but the bluecoats soon caught up with forty-one Confederate cavalrymen. The rebels could not easily turn around on the narrow road, so the Union scouts charged, and the southerners tried to evade. They eventually all came to a more open area where the rebels could turn around, and a desperate fight ensued. According to Wallace, however, the ferocity of the Union men overwhelmed the Confederates, who soon fled over a railroad track that hid a large culvert. Maybe eight died in the deep crevasse. Once the last of the rebels had fled, the scouts collected seventeen horses and equipment, and they discovered eleven dead graycoats.[61]

Corporal Hay was badly wounded in the affair, so the victors headed back to Cumberland. While two of the men looked for a wagon to carry the wounded corporal, some rebels fired from the west side of the road at about 2:00 P.M., causing Hay to ride on to Cumberland despite the injury. The remaining ten stayed to confront the rebels because they wanted to hold on to the spoils, mostly consisting of horses. Since the Confederate force numbered seventy-five men, the scouts rushed for the other side of a creek where they could take cover among some large rocks and logs, a spot referred to as Kelly's Island. The opposition followed.[62] The Union soldiers repelled at least two charges. Quite a few Confederates were killed, with only one Union death. Hay's men eventually returned to Cumberland with news of the successful skirmishes, as well as the seventeen horses.[63]

Wallace sent three companies out to the battlefields on the following morning, and they discovered that the Confederates "laid out twenty-three [dead] on the porch of a neighboring farm house," quite a tally for the thirteen scouts. On that same day, the colonel also received "positive information . . . that there are four regiments of rebels in and about Romney, under a Colonel McDonald. What their particular object is I cannot learn." The Hoosier used the incidents to complain that the "two Pennsylvania regiments are in encampment at the State line, about nine miles from here, waiting further orders," and they "have not yet reported to me."[64] Wallace's superiors did not, however, encourage Curtin to send the Pennsylvania units to Cumberland.

The colonel sent almost identical reports of the adventure to Patterson and McClellan, and the latter forwarded his copy to Scott.[65] The news pleased Patterson to such a degree that he announced the "second victory over the insurgents by a small party of Indiana Volunteers, under Colonel Wallace," to all under his command as a general order. The news was meant to be motivation, as the commander desired "to bring to the attention of the officers and men of his command the courage and conduct with which this gallant little band of comparatively raw troops met the emergency." The scouts' success further amazed Patterson since the Hoosiers had turned "on an enemy so largely superior in numbers . . . chastising him severely, and gathering the fruits of victory."[66]

The scouts' aggressiveness also impressed McClellan, who honored the Zouaves' "heroic courage, worthy of their French namesakes." The general regretted "more than ever . . . that you are not under my command." Furthermore, he pledged to press Scott to order the Pennsylvania regiments to proceed to Cumberland. The regiments eventually went to Cumberland, but only after the Indianans were ordered to leave the town. McClellan, however, was not worried about the Hoosiers, confessing that he began "to doubt if the Eleventh Indiana needs reinforcements."[67] Such a reply only reinforced Wallace's aggressive and sometimes uncooperative personality. He was receiving acknowledgements worthy of the manliness he desired to demonstrate to Indianans and to Americans at large.

A fellow Indianan, U.S. congressman Schuyler Colfax, also sent his compliments to the colonel, suggesting that Washington "was ringing with the magnificent news from your scouting party, though it seems too splendid to be true." Moreover, he asserted that "Indianans, I need not tell you, feel prouder than ever of our volunteers, and I only hope it may be confirmed." Such good news could only help recruiting in the home state. In fact, according to Colfax, the president was particularly impressed, commenting that "Indiana had won nearly all the glory so far, and taken about all the scalps." Lincoln also "alluded especially to your splendid dash on Romney."[68] Again, these compliments greatly inflated the colonel's ego, and validated his aggressive actions.[69]

The good press eventually encouraged Patterson to include the Hoosiers in plans for a major offensive.[70] The general ordered Wallace, on 7 July, to move his men to Martinsburg, Virginia.[71] Colonel Biddle, from Pennsylvania, took his place in Cumberland, since Governor Curtin now feared the possibility of rebels marching straight through Maryland into the Keystone State. When the Indianans arrived in Martinsburg, the regiment had a train of sixty-two wheeled vehicles, carrying mostly booty from Romney. The colonel was too willing to bog down the unit with the excess supplies, much of which could have been left in Cumberland.

Once the troops arrived and chose a campsite, Wallace met with General Patterson and Porter for the first time. He also met Col. John J. Abercrombie, in whose brigade the 11th Indiana would serve. The brigade commander, as it turned out, had been a classmate of Wallace's father at West Point, greatly increasing the Hoosier's desire to serve under him in battle.[72] While in camp at Martinsburg, it became clear to the colonel that Patterson's command would soon be involved in some action against either of the rebel generals, Beauregard or Joseph Johnston. Wallace told his wife that in "the event of our being thus advanced, you may look to our being in front bringing on the great battle that is now in hourly expectation." He continued, stating that such "a fight you know, will realize my life-long wish. I would not miss it on any account."[73]

As the Yankees waited to march, an episode demonstrated Wallace's willingness to confront colleagues. While in camp, a Massachusetts regiment, engaged in drill, ridiculed the Zouaves' dirty uniforms and western heritage. Thus, on the afternoon of the next day, Wallace rushed his regiment out to challenge them at competitive drill. The Hoosiers outclassed them in combat maneuvers, and the colonel called the Indianans back by bugle in good order. Wallace believed that this stunt ended some bias against westerners.[74] It certainly demonstrated his fear of being dishonored, even in relation to a trifling event.

Just two days after the 11th Indiana arrived in Martinsburg, on 13 July, Scott ordered Patterson to move toward Johnston's force in order to keep the Confederates from leaving the proximity of Winchester. The march began on 15 July, but Patterson failed to follow the orders as Scott intended.[75] The army soon came within six miles of Winchester, but then they stopped at a place called Bunker Hill. Patterson considered this movement toward Winchester to be a suitable demonstration. Abercrombie told Wallace to be ready for an alarm, but none came, and the troops were soon marching away from Johnston.

Patterson's army eventually rested in Charlestown, about eighteen miles from Winchester, possibly giving the appearance of a retreat.[76] While there, the separate regiments were asked to vote on reenlistment since the three-month terms were about to expire. Patterson had already asked the regiments to stay a few days beyond their terms, until recently recruited units could replace them, but long-term reenlistments could greatly aid in an effort to destroy Johnston's army.[77] Only two regiments voted to reenlist, the 11th Indiana and the 2nd Wisconsin.[78]

While Patterson's men voted for or against reenlisting, an army under Maj. Gen. Irvin McDowell moved to attack Beauregard near Bull Run Creek. On 21 July, McDowell attacked the rebel left, not knowing that Johnston was there. Patterson's feeble demonstration had not induced Johnston to remain at Winchester. In fact, on the day the Battle of Bull Run began, Patterson's men were quietly marching from Charlestown to Harpers Ferry, another twelve miles away from Winchester.[79] Patterson's and McDowell's reputations both suffered greatly due to the failed Bull Run campaign.[80] The former took much of the blame for not making a more concerted effort to occupy the interests of Johnston. Wallace, years later, was uncharacteristically objective in his account of the whole affair, not wanting to speak badly of an old friend in Patterson, but still understanding that more of an effort should have been made. While the Union force, in Wallace's opinion, should have exerted more pressure on Johnston, the colonel later acknowledged that the unwillingness of eighteen of Patterson's regiments to reenlist might have made pursuit of the Confederates more difficult.[81]

The 11th Indiana returned to Indianapolis from Harpers Ferry; their initial three-month service had expired.[82] They arrived in the city on 29 July, where the governor and citizens applauded them. The men were mustered out a few days later. The 11th was again mustered in, this time for three years' service, on 31 August 1861.[83] Many in the regiment reenlisted, and, according to one newspaper, Wallace was already "spoiling for a fight."[84] The hero of Romney supposedly asked Morton to order the regiment to Missouri because he thought he might see quick action there. By 6 September, the unit was marching to St. Louis in order to report to Maj. Gen. John C. Fremont.[85]

Wallace arrived in St. Louis on 8 September and went to Fremont's headquarters.[86] In retrospect, he was not impressed with the "Path Finder," stating that

"Frémont garrisoned Cairo and partially fortified St. Louis; but the achievements seemed to have exhausted him for military performances, and he surrendered himself to politics." Instead of engineering great victories in the West, Fremont was ignoring the policies of the "general government in Washington." Wallace asserted that "he assumed dictatorial control of his department, took possession of public moneys, levied forced loans on what he apologetically called secession banks, and gathered about him a staff disproportionate in numbers, if not of his own choosing."[87]

The Hoosier developed the negative opinion partially due to his inability to meet the general. His headquarters appeared to be full of politicians. Again, the Indianan demonstrated his desire to be seen as a military officer, not as a politician. The jobs of men like Morton and Lincoln did not appeal to him like those of Scott and a younger William Henry Harrison. This may explain why, when opportunities arose for Wallace to make amends for military blunders by political means, he sometimes refused, and sometimes completed such tasks without zeal.[88]

Wallace tried to personally deliver a report to Fremont twice in one day, and then to the adjutant, but the sentinel at the headquarters would not allow it. The colonel left the report with the guard. Wallace quickly became frustrated with what seemed to be the office of a politician, not a general, and so he telegraphed Morton, begging the governor to have him ordered to Cairo, Illinois, or Paducah, Kentucky. A day later, the governor ordered him to put the regiment on a steamboat for Paducah. The 11th Indiana transferred to serve under Gen. Charles F. Smith. The son of a former governor was now greatly relieved to be done with Fremont the politician.[89] The colonel refused to be referred to as a politician, and he came to grudgingly perform tasks more suited to a politician, even though he was willing to use political connections to secure the positions or commands that he desired.

That summer's exploits garnered favorable publicity for Wallace and his regiment. In 1861, he managed to please Patterson, McClellan, Scott, Lincoln, Lane, Morton, and the citizens of Indiana, and he did it his way. His aggressive, uncompromising style led to small but widely known victories. Newspapers across the North recounted the successes. And with his aggressive attitude confirmed by success, Wallace sought more opportunities for combat—and the prospect of glory that it could bring.

THREE

Forts Henry and Donelson

Wallace's successes in the East led him to seek greater glory and fame in the West. Considering this goal, he disliked his first assignment under a political general, John C. Fremont, and desired to work with West Point graduates. The Indianan naively expected that his aggressive, bold attitude, characterized by an unwillingness to shy away from a fight, would impress his new commanders, generals Charles F. Smith and Ulysses S. Grant. Developing a good relationship with, and learning from, these men would be crucial for the Hoosier to attain higher field command as the war progressed.

In St. Louis, the 11th Indiana boarded a steamboat for Paducah, Kentucky, on approximately 10 September 1861. They arrived at the Ohio River town shortly thereafter. The regiment received a welcome unlike the lackluster greeting in Missouri. Upon docking, a crowd of soldiers and a wagon train to haul equipment met the 11th Indiana, greeting the newcomers with "cheering in reply to cheering, and thunderous applause" for the tunes of the Hoosiers' band. Wallace believed that such a welcome signified that there was "a real soldier somewhere about in command of the place," again demonstrating his disdain for political generals like Fremont, who he continued to criticize for mismanaging affairs in Missouri.[1]

The colonel believed that he could do a better job than Fremont handling affairs in Missouri. Wallace egotistically asserted to his wife that, if he were Fremont, he would select "a point, say St. Louis or Paducah, concentrate a hundred thousand men, and, when my stores were ready, [move] forward in a grand column toward Memphis." In this manner, methodically and "leisurely, I could pick up the secession fragments" and "draw from before Washington fifty . . . thousand rebels." The great advance would allow McClellan to "reach Richmond," and "the great rebellion of the century would be at an end."[2] The plan was reasonable, but Wallace certainly failed to understand the logistical difficulties involved in collecting and supporting so many men in a march south. Moreover, he exhibited an overconfidence that could get him in trouble, especially considering the low probability that an officer of his limited experience would be given such a large army.

Wallace next reported to his new commander, Brig. Gen. Charles F. Smith, a former commandant at West Point and a veteran of the Mexican-American War. This time, unlike the affair in St. Louis, the superior was willing to meet the Indianan. Although the initial meeting lasted but a few minutes, Smith, who did not even shake the newcomer's hand, impressed the colonel as a "soldier without a tincture of the politician." The general invited the Hoosier to come back that evening for supper, at which they discussed Wallace's soldierly skills and experience. The two officers spent the following afternoon and evening looking at a map as Smith made some vague hints about the importance of the Cumberland and Tennessee Rivers.[3] Wallace was content and happy with Smith after the early meetings, but he soon began to chafe under perceived monotony as other men began receiving opportunities to see action.

Once the Indianans settled into their new camp near Paducah, Wallace came to despise the town. He decided that Romney was "only a little viler than Paducah, concerning which last I never hear a bell without listening in hope that it is the signal for a universal conflagration." The colonel observed that it abounded "with traitors." Sneaky spies, "hypocrites, liars and perjurers, compound its citizenship."[4] In the shadow of the Kentucky town, Wallace's regiment spent most of its time drilling. Confederate general Leonidas Polk also sent graycoats northeast from Columbus to challenge Union pickets on occasion, and Smith often dispatched Union patrols to check on Polk. All of this drilling and picketing frustrated Wallace, but an official communication relieved his boredom with pride and fear come late September of 1861.[5] He had been promoted to the rank of brigadier general, soon to be in charge of an entire brigade, maybe two to four regiments totaling as many as four thousand troops. The man's ambition and ego cherished the opportunity, but he knew little about commanding that many men.

Wallace proceeded to Smith's office and explained his fears and, according to the ambitious colonel, asserted that he might not accept the promotion. The Hoosier later asserted that he seriously considered turning down the commission, but such commentary is hard to believe. He may have informed Smith of his inexperience, and he may have openly considered rejecting the position, but it could only have been for show. The prideful colonel needed Smith's guidance and acceptance to excel in the new rank; that is why he presented his fears to his superior. Wallace's behavior, up through September 1861, contradicts his account of the incident. Years later, he liked to recall that he humbly and reluctantly accepted the title of brigadier general even though such an elevation in rank could provide the greater chances for glory and fame that he desperately desired. Smith, the Hoosier recollected, was impressed with the show of ignorance and humility, proceeding to tell the thirty-four-year-old colonel what he could about the duties of a brigadier general. Oddly enough, Wallace remembered that Smith stressed, among other things, that his duties would include obedience "to his immediate superiors," an obvious obligation not easily carried out by the new, and somewhat "rough," brigade commander.[6]

The brigadier general's substantial command included three regiments, the 11th Indiana under Col. George McGinnis, the 8th Missouri under Col. Morgan Smith, and the 23rd Indiana under Col. W. C. Sanderson. The brigade also included an artillery battery from Illinois and some regulars, Company I of the 4th United States Cavalry.[7] In this new position, Wallace still spent most of his time supervising pickets and finding out if Polk would launch an attack on Paducah from Columbus. The routine seldom varied.

Even before receiving official notice of his commission, Wallace complained of inaction to Governor Morton. Indiana regiments stood idle in Kentucky, and he wanted the governor to help. The colonel begged Morton to "get me a command, and let me [go] to work" if appointed general of volunteers. Wallace argued that "lying here while work is doing everywhere, and while we are every where [sic] unlucky, is intolerable." He asked for only "a chance" to lead a few Indiana regiments into battle.[8] Five weeks later, the general further aired his grievances to the governor. He proposed raising a regiment of cavalry to help with scouting toward Columbus. In Wallace's opinion, Smith failed to provide him with adequate cavalry, possibly because the two men did not "exactly suit each other." Wallace found the whole situation to be dull, especially since the bluecoats would "never find an enemy until we go after them."[9] The boredom and the thirst for glory grew frustrating.

In late November or early December, an incident involving the Indianan's troops created tension between him and his superiors, Smith and U. S. Grant. Wallace's typically aggressive attitude again led to problems; but, according to him, he did not order the resulting action.[10] While the brigadier visited Smith's headquarters, men from Wallace's brigade, including the 11th Indiana, were taking the liberty to remove a rebel flag from a residence in Paducah.[11] An assistant adjutant general went outside to clear away the crowd, but not long thereafter a soldier reported that Wallace's brigade was causing the excitement. Smith believed this to be an unfortunate use of the military, infringing on a citizen's right to free speech.

Historian Steven J. Ramold has argued that volunteer officers often had difficulty disciplining troops in such circumstances. "Between their temporary but current obligations as officers and their long-term but remote status as civilians, volunteer officers found themselves caught in the battle between two opposing cultures."[12] In this case, Smith, the West Pointer, wanted to stay out of politics and maintain discipline. Wallace, the civilian volunteer, had trouble urging his men to do the same. As a result, the brigade commander practically disobeyed his commander while acquiescing in his troop's desire to make a pro-Union statement.

Considering the troops involved, Wallace quickly went across the street, intending to quiet his soldiers. Arriving on the scene, he found his own assistant adjutant general in a fistfight with one of Smith's staff. Once he broke up the fight, Wallace's soldiers began to throw rocks at the staff officer sent to disperse the troops. The Indianan saved Smith's adjutant from harm while the troops continued to pull down the Confederate flag, replacing it with the Stars and Stripes. Of course, Wallace sided with his troops and could not bring himself to allow the homeowner to fly a rebel flag. His decision put him at odds with his superior's wishes. His command greatly cheered, and Wallace the soldier-politician relished the moment. The infantrymen happily returned to their quarters, but Smith was irate.[13]

When the brigade commander returned to Smith's headquarters, he found his superior indignant and intent on severely punishing the officers involved in the incident. Calming the general, Wallace agreed to pen an order to the division that would insist on greater discipline. The political general understood the delicacies of the situation, at least knowing how the northern press might look at the affair. Smith's order, written by Wallace, led to numerous newspaper editorials.[14] The papers lauded Wallace for the demonstration of patriotism, giving him credit for instigating the exchange of flags. At the same time, according to the Indianan, the periodicals "denounced General Smith. Nobody but a traitor, they proclaimed, would have found fault with the substitution of the flags."[15]

Wallace later believed that the flag incident signaled the beginning of his troubles with superior officers. He recollected that "the story passed to headquarters at Cairo, thence to headquarters at St. Louis, in both of which the military offence was seen and discussed as of my incitement and I incontinently set down for a political demagogue." While Smith did not appear to be upset with the brigade commander, Wallace suggested that the West Pointer's friends, such as U. S. Grant and Henry Halleck, pegged the brigade commander as a troublemaker.[16] The Paducah incident, however, did not alone convince Grant or Halleck to mistrust Wallace. More substantive matters, including a continued lack of discipline, soured his relationships with superiors.

In retrospect, Wallace mistakenly asserted that another unfortunate happenstance combined with the altercation over the flag to result in diminishing his career. Earlier, in late October, Grant and his adjutant general, John Rawlins, had stayed with the Hoosier while visiting Paducah. Grant had come to the Kentucky town to discuss campaign plans with Smith. At the Indianan's headquarters, Smith, Wallace, and Grant spent a long evening smoking, drinking, and singing. Wallace later insisted that nobody was drunk, and that the revelry involved only singing and good conversation. Unfortunately for the officers, local newspapers received contrary information. A regimental chaplain reported the meeting to papers, and editorials described a night-long round of drinking. In truth, rumors circulated that Grant had resigned from the army in 1854 to avoid formal charges for drunkenness and dereliction of duty, and his history led editors to believe the accusation.[17]

Wallace, on the other hand, worried that a group of West Pointers blamed the rumors of Grant's drunkenness on the Indianan. As a result, he feared that the professional soldiers hindered his efforts to see more active service later during the war. Again, just like the flag raising in Paducah, he exaggerated the importance of the incident to his future relationships with superiors. The two events began to hurt Wallace's relationships with Smith, Grant, and later Halleck. Had the brigade commander resisted his tendencies to be too bold, aggressive, and concerned with his honor, the friction could have ended quickly. For example, his current assignment offered little hope of major combat, in Wallace's opinion, again causing him to complain.

The next few months brought little more than picketing and an occasional skirmish for Wallace's brigade, and the general grew increasingly restless as a result. On 6 November, Grant fought the Battle of Belmont in Missouri, on the other side of the Mississippi River from Columbus. As Smith orchestrated some feints to assist Grant's assault on Belmont, Wallace remained behind to guard the headquarters at Paducah.[18] The inaction made him bitter. After the battle, the political general heard that Grant's men pillaged and plundered once they took Belmont. While doing so, the bluecoats supposedly "were in turn attacked

by re-inforcements from Columbus, and driven with heavy loss to their boats."
Already unimpressed with Grant, Wallace believed that this rumor supported his
opinion. He contended that such "conduct proves, that after all, our army is not
an army."[19] He wanted to show that he could do better than either Smith or Grant.

Indicating his aggressive nature, Wallace made a personal reconnaissance
toward Viola, Kentucky, in late December. With two hundred volunteer horsemen and two companies of regular cavalry, the general approached "Camp
Beauregard, for the purpose of reconnoitering that camp, gaining information
as to the strength of the enemy and their whereabouts, and ascertaining whether
or not re-enforcements had left Camp Beauregard for Bowling Green." Wallace
discovered that troops from the camp had been sent to Bowling Green, but new
regiments would soon replace them. He soon encountered rebel reinforcements
outnumbering his detachment, but the Confederates fled before the Indianan
could bring up the men needed to support an attack. The general accomplished
his mission, also managing to destroy the camp, but he wanted more. He yearned
to play a part in a significant battle.[20]

Late January brought Wallace a great hint of Grant and Smith's plan for a
future action. The commander of the *Conestoga*, a "tin-clad" gunboat, asked
the general if he might wish to accompany him on an excursion to investigate
the status of Fort Henry, on the Tennessee River near the southern border of
Kentucky. The river emptied into the Ohio at Paducah. During the voyage up the
river to the fort, the general claimed to have experienced one of his first looks
into the evils of slavery. While on the water, shortly before sundown, the crew
observed men with bloodhounds chasing what they initially believed to be a fox.
Someone soon made out the image of a man, a slave, fleeing from the patrol. The
captain and Wallace had no interest in seeing the hunters catch their prey, so they
sent a small boat out to fetch the black man while the officers shot at the patrol in
hopes of forcing it back into the woods. Just in the nick of time, the *Conestoga*'s
crewmen were able to rescue the runaway, who told them his story of slavery,
as well as his longing for freedom. Though a recent convert to Republicanism
who had shown little sympathy with the black race early in the war, Wallace was
deeply impressed with the event and the runaway's tale of troubles.[21]

Politically, Wallace's switch to the Republican Party led him to examine
his thoughts on slavery, and those views gradually began to change. The issue
apparently was not a concern for him before the war, and he likely opposed
the expansion of slavery to new territories upon first joining his new party, but
nothing more egalitarian. The general's evolving views appear to coincide with

the war's gradual change from a war for Union to also a war of emancipation. The beginning of that evolution can be traced to his service in Kentucky and Tennessee in the winter of 1861–62, personally observing the horrors of the "peculiar institution." Wallace's conversion to the antislavery cause may have been the most useful political asset attained by the general in late 1861 and early 1862.

Wallace also witnessed the peculiar institution during the months prior to that excursion down the river, and these initial views led him to believe that slavery was, as he wrote, "more awful than any imagination of it." Well before Lincoln's Emancipation Proclamation, Wallace determined that however "we may go into the war, we shall come out of it abolitionists."[22] He had joined the Republican Party for the Union, but like many others, he gradually began to sympathize with the antislavery rhetoric of the abolitionists. The Indianan grew to hate slavery but, as the war progressed, failed to see the need to guarantee political rights for blacks, making him an ideal political ally for President Lincoln.

Finally, in February, Wallace got his first chance to distinguish himself as a brigade commander. Grant planned an offensive into Tennessee via the Cumberland and Tennessee Rivers. The two waterways could be used to carry troops into the state by boat, making operations against Nashville and Corinth, Mississippi, manageable. In order to open up Tennessee to Federal control, Grant, the commander of the District of Cairo, desired to capture three strongholds that guarded a region in northern Tennessee where the two rivers came within a few miles of each other as they flowed northwest to the Ohio River. Fort Henry, and a minor post, Fort Heiman, overlooked the Tennessee, while the larger Fort Donelson guarded the Cumberland. Grant decided to leave the more formidable stronghold to last.

The opportunity excited Wallace, who exclaimed that for "the first time in my life I write you [Susan Wallace] on the eve of battle." He dramatically asserted that tomorrow "morning we attack." The general relished the chance to show his worth as a man and hoped that he would satisfactorily do his duty, "so that, if I come back to you, as I hope and believe I will, it will be in honor."[23] He voiced these feelings even at the expense of worrying his wife, who eagerly waited for word of the results of this movement into Tennessee.

Later that night, 5 February 1862, General Smith's division arrived near Forts Henry and Heiman, transported by boats. Wallace's and Col. John McArthur's brigades landed on the west bank, opposite troops under Brig. Gen. John A. McClernand.[24] Wallace and McArthur were ordered to secure Fort Heiman while McClernand's division, along with one brigade from Smith's command, were

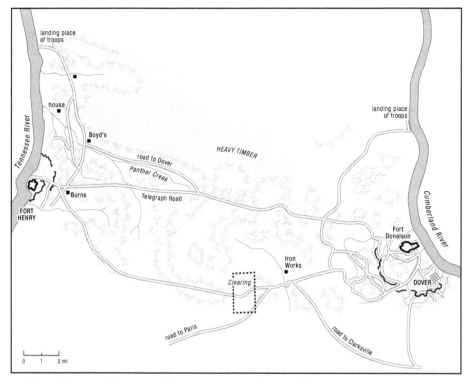

Forts Henry and Donelson, February 1862. *Map by Erin Greb Cartography.*

awarded the task of seizing Fort Henry on the east bank of the river.[25] Commo.
Andrew Foote supported the expedition with a flotilla of gunboats that convinced
the rebels at both forts to flee without a major fight on either side of the river,
stealing the Indianan's chance to garner fame and glory since the "land forces
had nothing to do."[26] Wallace and his brigade entered a burning stronghold
taken chiefly by the navy. The command of Fort Heiman fell to the Hoosier.[27]

All officers understood that the next step might be to move against Fort
Donelson on the Cumberland River, just a few miles away. On 10 February, Grant
invited five or six officers, including Wallace, to his headquarters to discuss the
possibility of attacking Donelson. He asked the subordinates to give their views
of the current situation. As Wallace remembered, Grant first asked Smith, who
energetically declared that they should march "without the loss of a day." The
Indianan then recalled that McClernand, a Democrat from Illinois, irritated
the West Pointers present by drawing out a paper and reading it, entering "into

details of performance; we should do this going and that when we were to come." The Hoosier thought that the speech "smacked of a political caucus." Again, Wallace noted his desire to distance himself from a political general, and he demonstrated an understanding that McClernand had presumed too much clout, seemingly ignoring his own ability to irritate superiors. When finally asked for his opinion, he merely agreed with Smith, asserting that the army should go quickly, "the sooner the better."[28]

On that same day, Grant issued an order for the forces gathered at Forts Heiman and Henry to be ready to move on 12 February "at as early an hour as practicable." He further specified that the troops should carry no more baggage than the men could carry, as well as rations for only two days. Food for three more days might be carried in wagons that would follow the columns, not impeding the progress of the fighting force. Grant concluded by stating that he wanted two regiments from McClernand's division to stay behind to guard Fort Henry, as well as one brigade from Smith's division to look after Fort Heiman.[29]

To Wallace's chagrin, Smith, on 11 February, designated his brigade "to remain at Fort Hieman [sic], [and] he was placed in command of both Forts Hieman [sic] and Henry."[30] In that capacity, the Indianan was "directed to cause the first troops arriving, to debark on the Kentucky side of the river, until three regiments of infantry and at least one company of artillery were there, and that all other troops should be debarked at Fort Henry."[31]

Not happy with the arrangement, the Hoosier told his wife that "I have been sick with rage ever since the order came" through "old Smith." He had endured enough inactivity and disrespect, in his mind, and asserted that his patience was now "played out." Wallace argued that he had "been too modest and patient" with Smith, who had "abused both" qualities. Thus, the political general decided to "change policy—in fact, have done so."[32] There is little evidence that the Indianan truly exhibited patience and modesty before this time, excepting the later claims of his autobiography, and the disappointing news meant that he would try even less to hold back his overconfidence and aggressiveness. West Pointers expected junior officers to dutifully and quietly follow their leaders, but Wallace was not part of that culture. Thankfully for the irritated general, orders to move, as well as a promotion, soon came. Grant instructed him to keep his brigade ready to follow the advancing bluecoats to Fort Donelson, where he would command a division consisting of newly arriving regiments.[33]

In the meantime, Wallace could only wait and hope for an order that would send him to Donelson. His primary duty was to hold the forts and make sure that rebels could not threaten the main Union force from the west, or the rear. After Wallace had been ordered to proceed to Fort Donelson, Grant commanded the general to send cavalry to destroy bridges that might bring rebel reinforcements or serve as avenues of escape for Confederates occupying Fort Donelson. He believed that "the district of country into which they are going is strongly Union, and they should be on their good behavior, and disprove the lying reports made against our forces by the secessionists." Grant, apparently not confident in the Hoosier's abilities, or maybe his attitude, demanded "to hear a good report from this expedition, not only of the favorable impression made, but work done."[34]

Late on 13 February, Wallace received an order calling him to the front. The notice led him to believe that Grant was in a desperate fight. If the Union won the battle, the Hoosier asserted that "the rebellion goes under at once, and there shall be no such word as fail."[35] Already near Fort Donelson, McClernand commanded the 1st Division and Smith commanded the 2nd Division. Wallace commanded the newly formed 3rd Division. The 1st Brigade of his division, under Col. Charles Cruft, included the 31st and 44th Indiana, as well as the 17th and 25th Kentucky Infantry. The 2nd Brigade of his division, which did not entirely arrive until 16 February and was attached to the 3rd Brigade for lack of time to designate a brigade commander, included the 46th, 57th, and 58th Illinois Infantry. The 3rd Brigade, under John M. Thayer, included the 1st Nebraska and the 58th, 68th, and 76th Ohio Infantry. Wallace's division also included Company A of the 32nd Illinois, and Battery A of the Illinois (Chicago) Light Artillery. Six to eight iron- and timber-clad gunboats under Andrew Foote would be available to supplement the land forces.[36]

Wallace arrived with the 8th Missouri and 11th Indiana Infantry, as well as one battery of artillery. He left the rest of his brigade at Fort Heiman to wait for replacements. However, annoying the Indianan more than it should have, Grant forbade him to keep his old regiment as part of his new division. Instead, the regiment was to remain under Smith while "Wallace's Division was assigned a position in our centre" between Smith, on the left, and McClernand on the right.[37] At about noon on 14 February, Grant stressed that the Indianan should concentrate on holding "the centre, and resist[ing] all attempts of the enemy to break through." According to Wallace's memoir, under these circumstances, Grant ordered that he "must not assume the aggressive."[38]

The 3rd Division found its place in the center of the line during the afternoon of 14 February. Fighting occurred during the preceding day, but Smith and McClernand were not able to break through the Confederate lines. Foote's gunboats

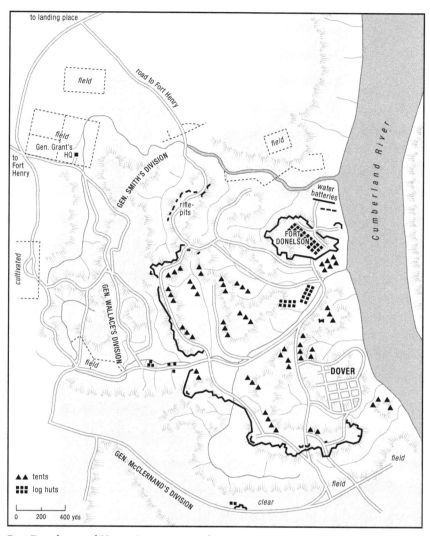

Fort Donelson and Union Divisions, 15 February 1862. *Map by Erin Greb Cartography.*

took their turn in the afternoon and early evening of the 14th while Wallace and his brigades positioned themselves between the 1st and 2nd Divisions. Grant wanted the flotilla to destroy the main rebel battery on Fort Donelson, blocking the retreat of the graycoats across the river to the rear.

Four ironclads and two wooden gunboats soon encountered an array of rebel artillery. Foote tried to close in on the fort, but all four ironclads endured significant damage. The Confederates managed to hit each vessel fifty to sixty times, and Union sailors suffered fifty-four casualties. The guns forced the flotilla to withdraw, the Union navy failing to complete its mission. Grant wondered whether a siege might be needed to capture the fort and its defenders.[39]

The retreat of Foote's gunboats led the commander of Fort Donelson, Brig. Gen. John B. Floyd, to consider the possibility of counterattacking the Union lines. He wished to withdraw his men to Nashville, joining Albert S. Johnston. Floyd consulted with his two chief subordinates, Gen. Simon B. Buckner and Gen. Gideon Pillow. The two generals, however, hated each other and held different opinions on the immediate issue, so the conference ended in discord. The commanding general eventually calmed the two officers and decided to attempt to break through the Federal line early the next morning, 15 February.[40]

At 5:00 A.M., Wallace heard the sound of gunfire to his right, but out of his sight. McClernand's division quickly felt the full force of ten thousand rebel infantry, as well as Lt. Col. Nathan B. Forrest's cavalry, rebel horsemen engaging the Union division on its right flank. McClernand and his troops held their own for three hours until they ran low on ammunition and fell back. The political general from Illinois had no choice but to beg for the assistance of his counterpart from Indiana.

Wallace received McClernand's request sometime around 8:00 A.M., but he failed to comply. Grant had told the Hoosier that he "must not assume the aggressive" while holding "the centre." The general believed that those orders forbade him from assisting McClernand. On the other hand, by Wallace's own admission, the commanding general also directed that the division commander "resist all attempts of the enemy to break through." At this moment, the Indianan demonstrated an uncharacteristic lack of initiative. Assisting McClernand logically meant sending reinforcements. Wallace could have offered one brigade after the first request in order to shore up the broken lines and dispatching it would not have been construed as assuming the aggressive.[41]

In Grant's opinion, Wallace violated his orders by waiting to reinforce the crumbling right flank. After the battle, Grant maintained that at about "8 o'clock, Colonel [W. S.] Hillyer, who had delivered to Generals McClernand and Wallace, my orders as directed, finding that General Wallace under those orders had declined to send support to General McClernand as the latter officer had requested, Colonel Hillyer positively ordered him to do so, saying at the same time that I had contemplated, when orders of the morning were issued, no such condition of things as then existed."[42] Grant certainly made a mistake by leaving the battlefield at daybreak for an extended time to consult with Foote, six miles away, but Wallace's interpretation of earlier orders turned an unfortunate situation into a momentary crisis.

Wallace, contrary to Grant's account, later indicated that he violated orders by sending reinforcements after a second request from McClernand, not because one of Grant's aides ordered him to provide assistance.[43] If that was true, Grant still would have found fault in Wallace's reluctance to resist a breakthrough by the enemy. Finally, and much later than the commanding general expected, the Indianan worked to relieve the pressure on McClernand. At approximately 8:30 A.M., Wallace ordered Cruft's brigade to reinforce McClernand, so the colonel moved all four of his regiments to the extreme right of the Union line.[44]

In the meantime, Wallace personally kept charge of Thayer's brigade, using it to block the rebels' path to the south on Wynn's Ferry Road, a thoroughfare leading southwest from the original center of the 1st Division. The Hoosier encountered fleeing bluecoats, and soon met Col. William H. L. Wallace of McClernand's division. Telling the brigade commander where he could find some surplus ammunition, Wallace positioned artillery on the road to slow the Confederate advance. The general initially supported the battery with the 1st Nebraska Infantry on the right, and a company of the 32nd Illinois on the left. The rest of Thayer's brigade, and the recently arrived 2nd Brigade, soon supported these units.[45]

In place, and just in time to meet charging rebels, the general's first line of defense, from right to left, included the 58th Illinois, 1st Nebraska, Battery A of the 1st Illinois Light Artillery, Company A of the 32nd Illinois, and the 58th Ohio. Wallace placed the 76th Ohio behind the 1st Nebraska, which received the brunt of the Confederate attack. The 46th and 57th Illinois remained in reserve. Guarding Pinery Road, near the center of the Union line, the 68th Ohio waited just in case some rebels tried to sneak around Thayer and Wallace's new left flank. Union generals barely had secured their "position when the enemy advanced up the road with infantry and artillery to attack." Led chiefly by the 1st Nebraska and Battery A, the two brigades responded with a "heavy fire of musketry and artillery," which they "poured into the enemy's advancing columns." Rebels "returned the fire, but so heavy and continuous was that of Thayers [sic] that the enemy could not withstand it." Before long, the graycoats "fell back in disorder and confusion in the direction of" their "intrenchments."[46]

With Wallace's guidance, the defense of Wynn's Ferry Road held, but Cruft's brigade did not fare as well. The brigade came to the aid of the retreating 1st

Division by "forming in line of battle from right to left, to the right and rear of General McClernand's position." While "getting in position, his [Cruft's] advance was opened upon by the enemy who had passed the right of McClernand's line, whose troops were then giving way, which threw it into some confusion, and some of the men unfortunately fired into" the right side of McClernand's force. As the retreating troops "gave way and fell to the rear, [they] passed through the line of the 25th Kentucky and 31st Indiana carrying away some of the men." This clutter "increased the confusion, but it was soon quieted." Cruft's brigade continued to engage in spirited fighting, eventually securing the far right flank of the Union army.[47]

Partially successful, the Confederate attack managed to open an avenue for escape via Forge Road, running to the southeast toward Charlotte, Tennessee. After the war, Wallace wrote that Grant failed to understand the situation, so he and McClernand began to explain the possibility for a rebel evacuation in the middle of the night. Their explanation supposedly turned Grant's face red.[48] More likely, the commanding general was irritated with Wallace's delay in providing support on the right. Grant never reported such an exchange with the two subordinates. He merely stated that the late events convinced him to launch an attack on the left and right in order to secure the road to the southeast and prevent a breakout in the middle of the night.[49] In fact, in Wallace's own post-battle report, he only asserted that at approximately 3:00 P.M. Grant met with him and McClernand, ordering that they advance on the rebel left while Smith was to attack the right. Thus, starting in the late afternoon, Smith's division moved forward while Wallace took command of the situation on the right; McClernand's division had been devastated by the earlier fighting.[50]

Wallace quickly prepared to attack. He placed a brigade under the command of Colonel Smith, consisting of the 8th Missouri and the 11th Indiana, in the front. He borrowed the two regiments from General Smith. Cruft's battered "brigade completed the column," supporting Smith's brigade on the right. Two of McClernand's regiments "were moved up and well advanced on the left flank of the assailing force, but held in reserve." The Indianan's "directions as to the mode of attack were general, merely to form columns of regiments, march up the hill which was the point of assault, and deploy as occasion should require," the goal being to retake the ground lost earlier in the day.[51]

Colonel Smith attacked with his regiments organized into columns as Wallace had ordered, with the 8th Missouri in front. Cruft, on the other hand, "formed line of battle at the foot of the hill [to be taken], extending his regiments around to the right."[52] Both commands acted admirably, slowly forcing the rebels to relinquish their hold on the road to Charlotte and the hill that commanded it. Smith's brigade "moved by bounds." Using the tactics that Wallace taught him, the colonel ordered his troops to "lie prone and fire from that position." Next, when the Confederates' "fire slackened, he ordered his regiments to rise up, charge, and then lie prone again before return fire could do much damage."[53]

By the late afternoon, Wallace and his troops had done their job on the right, forcing the Confederates to retire toward the river. General Smith's division had more success on the Union left, forcing the rebels from their breastworks and into the fort. All had gone well, and the rebels were in a horrible spot with no means of escape when Wallace received an order through one of Grant's aides "to retire my column, as a new plan of operations was in contemplation for the next day." But, if the division commander carried out the order, he would have "to give up the hill so hardly recaptured," leaving the rebels a means to escape on the Forge Road leading southeast from Dover, Tennessee.[54]

Wallace, for maybe the first time in his life, had taken a timid, cautious approach in reinforcing McClernand earlier that day, and he regretted it. Grant considered that the lack of initiative, and the misunderstanding of the situation, demonstrated weakness and a lack of sufficient military training in the new division commander. The Hoosier, irritated by the earlier miscommunication and eager to demonstrate his willingness to think for himself, decided that Grant "did not know of our success when he issued the direction, [so] I assumed the responsibility of disobeying it, and held the battle ground that night."[55] This time, the political general's decision made sense. If Grant knew that Wallace's troops had taken the hill commanding the escape route, he may not have issued the order.

The commanding general likely would have understood and approved of the Indianan's actions had the division commander merely delayed carrying out the order, sending Grant an apologetic note informing him of the situation. Wallace, however, failed to acknowledge the order in a professional manner expected by a West Pointer. Instead, when the aide told him that Grant did not know that he had retaken the hill and road, the division commander haughtily replied "Oh, well! Give him my compliments, colonel, and tell him *I have received the order*."[56] The response failed to convey either respect or regret at not being able to carry out the order. Maybe the Hoosier believed that it would impress Grant or make up for his lack of initiative in the morning, but it did neither. Frustration over the earlier crisis on the Union right, and his own uncharacteristic lack of initiative, led him to revert to his old self. He wanted people to view him as an aggressive fighter, and the reply to Grant might help, in his mind, save the reputation partially lost on the morning of 15 February. Instead, contrary to Wallace's wishes, the return message added to the division between the political general and West Pointers who expected subordinates to show more respect and restraint.

As the sun set, the Union line was in a different order than at daybreak. Rather than guarding the middle, Wallace's division was "on the right." McClernand, on the other hand, was in the center, likely to be used in more of a supporting role on the following day. Smith remained "on the left," but now camped in "the enemy's advanced works."[57] The positions of Wallace and Smith, as well as Foote's gunboats, meant that the rebels had little hope of leaving the town of Dover and the fort during the night.

In the early hours of 16 February, Confederate generals Floyd and Pillow gave Buckner command of the fort while they escaped to join Albert Johnston at Nashville, thinking that their capture would be injurious to the South's cause. Buckner, a friend of Grant's and his former classmate at West Point, decided to remain at the fort and accept the same fate as the garrison.[58] Thus, after the senior officers fled, he sent word to Grant that he was interested in hearing the Union commander's terms for surrender. Grant's reply came as a surprise to the rebel general. The bluecoat acknowledged Buckner's letter "proposing armistice and appointing commissioners to settle terms of capitulation." But he regretted to inform the commander of Fort Donelson that no "terms except unconditional and immediate surrender can be accepted," directly adding that he proposed "to move immediately upon your works."[59]

Wallace anticipated that Grant would order an attack in the morning, and he mandated that an aide bring "Colonel Thayer's brigade to the foot of the hill. Lieutenant Wood's battery was also ordered to the same point." After the forts surrendered, the Indianan claimed that he intended "to storm the intrenchments about breakfast time," even though the commanding general had given no such official order at that point. But, while "making disposition for that purpose a white flag made its appearance." As a result, Wallace rode to "General Buckner's quarters, sending Lieutenant Ross with Major Rogers, of the Third Mississippi (rebel) Regiment, to inform General Grant that the place was surrendered and my troops in possession of the town and all the works on the right."[60]

Wallace had taken part in much of the fighting around the river forts, eventually offering sufficient aid to McClernand, and he launched a fruitful attack in the late afternoon of 15 February. However, in Grant's mind, this service did not give the division commander the right to ride into Buckner's headquarters as though he had the authority to accept the surrender of thousands of troops. In his memoirs, Grant gave Wallace the benefit of the doubt; he presumed "that, seeing white flags exposed in his front, he rode up to see what they meant and, not being fired upon or halted, he kept on until he found himself at the headquarters of General Buckner."[61] Even though Wallace later felt that he had done his superior a favor by preventing the navy from accepting the official surrender of so many troops, the Hoosier's action more likely irritated the usually patient and understanding Grant.[62] The regular's West Point training encouraged discipline and respect for proper procedure.[63] Wallace had not grown to embrace such ideals.

Due to his lack of initiative on the morning of 15 February, as well as his unprofessional response to Grant's late order of the same day, Wallace found himself receiving fewer congratulations than he had hoped. In fact, once Buckner surrendered, Grant ordered the division commander to return to Fort Henry with two brigades, two batteries, and some cavalry in order to defend it from any possible outside attacks.[64] Smith's and McClernand's divisions remained at Donelson and would later be sent forward, while the Indianan's would remain in the rear.

Due to an incident occurring on the return to Fort Henry, Wallace believed that he fostered distrust between him, Grant, and Smith. While forming his brigades to march west to the Tennessee River, the general noticed that Morgan Smith's brigade had joined his division. The brigade included the 8th Missouri and his beloved 11th Indiana, which now rightfully belonged to Charles Smith's division. The Hoosier later argued that he "had doubts of the propriety of the thing, but they were anxious to stay with me as I was to have them, and . . . it was not in my heart to order them out."[65] The brigade had served him during the recent fighting, borrowed from General Smith, but Wallace failed to return it. Once the 3rd Division, and its extra brigade, arrived at Fort Henry, the Indianan received an order from Grant's adjutant, on behalf of the commanding general, stating "that the 8th Missouri and 11th Indiana are not of your Division. They will remain at this place [Donelson]."[66] According to the recipient, the "intimation was of a new kind of larceny, and that I had been guilty of it."[67]

Wallace returned the regiments immediately; but, had he dutifully done so before leaving Donelson, Grant would not have one more reason to distrust the general. Even as he sent the regiments back, Wallace tried to persuade John Rawlins and Grant to let them stay. He even offered to give up Thayer's brigade, which had not rejoined him.[68] The tense situation may have led the Hoosier to write to Grant's aide, Captain Hillyer, begging him to convince the commanding general not to leave him behind when the army moved south. Pushing the edge of decorum, Hillyer dryly assured him that Grant "intends to give you a chance to be shot in every important move." The aide declared that Wallace would "not be left at Ft. Henry unless it be to defend against a threatened attack." After all, "God bless you; you did save the day on the right."[69]

As Wallace expected, Grant left his division at Fort Henry for two or three weeks. The circumstances aggravated the Hoosier, though there was good news. He could tell his wife that her husband now commanded an entire division. Moreover, according to the Indianan, that was "not so satisfactory as the happy riddance of Gen. Smith, which is at last accomplished." The political general now truly hated Smith, who "left me behind on the marching of the troops, thro' jealousy."[70] He failed to earn the trust and respect of Smith and Grant while also managing to frustrate the commanding general's aides.

A week later, another incident led Wallace to wonder whether he would ever get another chance to demonstrate his abilities. Captain Hillyer came to Fort Henry to ask the Indianan to make an amendment to his official report on the Battle of Fort Donelson. Hillyer wanted the Hoosier to acknowledge that he had seen the aide, and his associate, delivering orders sometime during the battle. Wallace asked the gentleman to leave the report with him, so he could make any necessary changes; however, he reportedly could not remember ever seeing the aides during the battle. In fact, he later claimed that Rawlins was the aide who encouraged him to assist McClernand on the 15th, contrary to Grant's recollection. The general then noted that he asked his staff if they had seen the men, but they had not. When Hillyer returned, the Indianan informed the aide that he regretfully could not amend the report, so the captain left unhappy. Wallace later discussed the incident as though it turned Grant's aides, and thus the commanding general, against him.[71] Grant could think for himself, however, and it is likely that the commandeering of Smith's brigade and Wallace's unprofessional actions during the battle had a greater effect.

Grant soon reorganized the Army of the Tennessee, with Wallace continuing to command the 3rd Division, which included twelve infantry regiments.[72] For the moment, Grant was at least publicly pleased with the Hoosier's performance, vaguely commenting in his post-battle report that "Generals McClernand, Smith, and Wallace . . . were with their commands in the midst of danger, and were always ready to execute all orders, no matter what the exposure to themselves."[73] In addition, the citizens of Crawfordsville, Indiana, sent their favorite son a sword and scabbard "in recognition of his gallantry at Fort Donelson."[74]

In reality, due to a series of missteps, Wallace's relationship with Grant had been damaged. The commanding general had begun to lose trust in the general who delayed in supporting McClernand during the last battle, and who practically stole two regiments from Smith's division. Another minor matter added to the friction. Wallace continued to undermine his commander's trust after the battle when Grant ordered the Indianan to destroy a portion of a railroad bridge running across the Tennessee River. In carrying out this order, at least in Grant's mind, Wallace again neglected to follow directions. The army commander believed "that much more destruction has been done the railroad bridge . . . than was authorized by my order." He wanted "the officers who had charge of the job to make a written report of what was done, and forward it to me."[75] This miscommunication, or inability to follow orders and respect protocol, was yet another in a lengthening list of frictions between Grant and his division head.

While Wallace made mistakes during the Battle of Fort Donelson, and continued to be his troublesome self, he still confirmed his ability to think in the midst of enemy fire while demonstrating a willingness to risk his own life. Thus, shortly thereafter, Wallace, McClernand, Smith, and Grant were promoted to major generals. The Indianan was particularly proud of his accomplishments, and he yearned for an opportunity to attain more fame and prove himself again on the battlefield.

But, at the same time that Wallace rejoiced over his promotion, he fretted that "the war looks over to me" since Grant had just destroyed "the centre of the rebellion." He wondered whether he might be coming home soon.[76] Such a thought was premature. He soon received orders to move by boat to Savannah, a town up the Tennessee River, and not too far north of the strategically important town of Corinth, Mississippi. Fortunately for the Hoosier, the campaign continued, and he had a part to play in upcoming operations.

During the last few months of 1861, Wallace's successes as a colonel had quickly led to a promotion, but his inability to get along with superiors and to exhibit the qualities they expected in an officer raised questions and caused doubts among his colleagues in early 1862.[77] As a general, he soured relationships with both Generals Smith and Grant. The seeds of distrust between Wallace and Grant had been planted almost two months before the Battle of Shiloh, before, during, and after the battles for Forts Henry and Donelson.

FOUR

━━━━━━━

Shiloh

In 1861, Wallace's successes as a colonel quickly led to promotion, but his inability to get along with superiors and follow their orders sans complaint eventually resulted in sour relationships with both generals Charles F. Smith and Ulysses S. Grant. In fact, the seeds of distrust between Wallace and Grant took root before and during the battles for Forts Henry and Donelson.

Now a major general of volunteers, Wallace took control of his reorganized division, hoping to lead it into battle soon. He was "just as anxious to go forward as ever." Despite the death and destruction that accompanied the latest combat experience, he found that his "interest in battles rather increased than otherwise." In fact, the Hoosier liked "the excitement, and in . . . truth, I never heard music as fascinating and grand as that of battle."[1] But unfortunately for the general, he found himself again guarding Fort Henry after Donelson fell while other divisions prepared to move south, adding to his usual frustration.

Thankfully for Wallace, a promising order soon came from Grant. On 5 March, the army commander ordered the Indianan to load all troops available, except a small garrison for Fort Donelson, onto transports in order to bring them upriver.[2] The movement south briefly excited Wallace, and his brigades proceeded up the Tennessee River by 10 March.[3] A few days later, the 3rd Division camped at Crump's Landing, a spot on the west side of the river. The position was across the waterway from Savannah, a town with approximately eight hundred residents, most of them pro-Union.[4]

In the meantime, Grant and Henry Halleck were not getting along. Grant failed, according to Halleck, to satisfactorily report the strength of his command. Furthermore, "Old Brains" (as Halleck was nicknamed) claimed that Grant neglected to regularly communicate with the departmental commander while resorting to "his former bad habits." Because of unsubstantiated rumors that Grant was again drinking heavily, Halleck placed Smith in command of the expedition up the Tennessee River.[5] These charges may have resulted from jealousy on the part of Halleck, due to Grant's newfound fame as the hero of Fort Donelson, but the implications for Wallace were the same no matter why Grant had been relieved. While establishing his command near Savannah, the Indianan had to answer directly to Charles Smith, a man that he longed to get away from.

Sometime on the evening of 12 March, Smith visited Wallace, whose headquarters were on a large boat, packed with troops, called the *John J. Roe*. The visitor ordered the Indianan to debark his troops at Crump's Landing, just a few miles upstream. From this new base, Smith entrusted the Hoosier with the job of sending cavalry to the west in order to destroy a railroad connection leading to Purdy, Tennessee, and beyond to Columbus, Kentucky. The assignment meant some danger, considering that Confederate major general Benjamin F. Cheatham was camped six miles south of Crump's, and with manpower likely greater than that of the 3rd Division.[6] The glory-seeking general, however, wanted more action than this task promised, remarking to his wife that the "errand is considered hazardous, tho' I do not consider it so."[7]

According to Wallace, the expedition's interim commander spent much time explaining the particulars of the mission, stressing that the Confederates could not easily reach the Indianan's command unless they rebuilt a bridge over Snake Creek. That waterway overflowed because of heavy rain, and the structure, coincidentally called Wallace's Bridge, could not be easily rebuilt. The meeting was probably not as pleasant as the Hoosier later recounted, but the two men got along well enough to devise and agree upon a plan of action. In a conclusion to the story that is difficult to corroborate, Smith bid goodbye to Wallace at the edge of the boat and "stooped to get into the yawl drawn up to receive him." Since darkness had fallen and vision was limited, "he lost balance and fell forward, raking the sharp edge of a seat, and skinning one of his shins from the ankle to the knee—a frightful hurt."[8] The general left the boat in much pain, but he continued his immediate business. Before long, however, Smith became ill. He rested in bed, developed an infection, and his condition worsened. In the meantime, "Unconditional Surrender" Grant retained his command since the American press, public, and president refused to demote the man who had achieved the greatest Union victory of the war to date.

After meeting with Smith, Wallace proceeded to land cavalry and infantry in order to carry out his mission. At 4:30 P.M. on the 13th, he reported that Cheatham

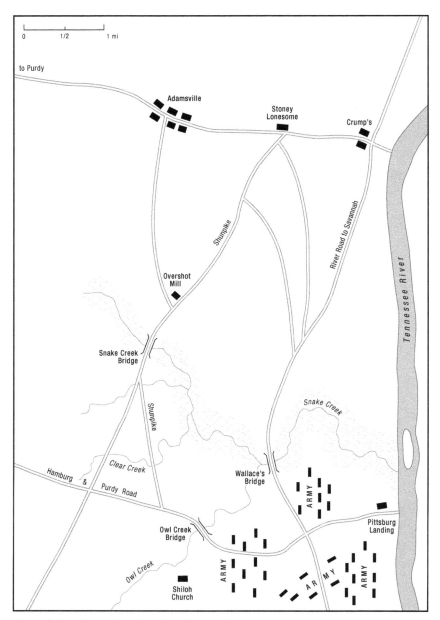

Crump's Landing to Pittsburg Landing, April 1862. *Map by Erin Greb Cartography.*

"encamped across a [Snake] creek now very full from backwater, and last night or this morning destroyed the bridge." Local men told the bluecoats that the Confederates originally intended to hold Crump's Landing, but the 3rd Division beat them to it.[9] Wondering if the rebel general commanded more men, Wallace soon decided that the graycoat was "more afraid of me with exaggerated numbers than I am of him." Once he secured the landing, the division commander sent cavalry north to destroy part of the railroad. Wallace recounted that Col. John M. Thayer's brigade proceeded to Adamsville, four or five miles from Crump's, to watch the rebels near Purdy. The division commander took charge of a brigade near Stoney Lonesome, at an intersection two miles closer to the river, and he believed that both brigades were in position to aid the Union cavalry if necessary.[10]

Eventually, the cavalry "returned safely and successfully" and the major in charge "extended his orders by cutting away about half a mile of trestle-work over a swamp, now impassable, on the north side of Purdy." Rebel cavalry briefly threatened the endeavor, but to no avail.[11] The success of the mission, to Wallace's chagrin, did not bring great praise or more demanding duties. Grant kept the 3rd Division in reserve, still based at Crump's Landing, while the rest of the army proceeded south to Pittsburg Landing, about six miles upriver.

On the 19th, in a message to Halleck, Grant reported that Sherman informed him "the enemy cannot be over 20,000 strong at Corinth, but has troops scattered at all stations and important points." While some "heavy artillery arrived at Corinth on Monday . . . the informant saw no signs of fortification," likely encouraging Grant to plan an attack. He believed that his movement might be a surprise since Maj. Gen. Don Carlos Buell "seems to be the party most expected by the rebels. They estimate his strength all the way from 20 to 50 thousand."[12] The information did not lead Grant to call for Wallace to come to Pittsburg Landing. Although staying at Crump's, the Indianan had to be ready to move south if the opportunity for action presented itself.[13]

Meanwhile, the main force was based on the opposite side of Snake Creek, and the Hoosier wisely decided to inspect the roads in case his division needed to move south. Two roads led toward the front lines, one named the Shunpike and another called the River (or Pittsburg) Road; both needed repair. The River Road included the coincidentally named Wallace's Bridge, which had been dismantled, and it offered a more direct route to Pittsburg Landing, Grant's base of operations. The Shunpike led more directly to the right of the front lines, where William T. Sherman's division camped, and it required the crossing of two bridges to eventually reach the front or the base on the river. The second bridge was on the Hamburg

& Purdy Road that intersected the Shunpike. That path took travelers the rest of the way to the main army, and over Owl Creek, which flowed into Snake Creek.[14]

Deciding to repair only one of the roadways, Wallace chose the Shunpike. The general, in retrospect, asserted that he chose the Shunpike because "if the enemy succeeded in driving my brigades back to Crump's, the exposure of his flank and rear must be fatal to him." In any case, the 3rd Division could reach the army if needed, and vice versa. To protect the repairmen, the general moved Thayer's 2nd Brigade to Stoney Lonesome. In order to secure the road after the completion of repairs, he sent the 3rd Brigade to Adamsville. According to Wallace's maps, Stoney Lonesome was about two and a half miles from Crump's while Adamsville was five miles away from the landing.[15]

Come early April, the brigades were still camped at those locations, and a skirmish at Adamsville between Union pickets and "a small body of the rebels" led the division commander to increasingly believe that the rebels might threaten Grant's rearguard at Crump's Landing, making the reconstruction of the Shunpike a good idea.[16] Why Wallace initially neglected to take an added precaution by also fixing Wallace's Bridge is unclear, considering that the River Road offered the most direct route to Grant's base. In any event, the political general failed to see the need to repair a road and bridge that would more easily bring his 3rd Division to the left or center of the Union front line, as well as to the commanding general's headquarters. Some of the Indianan's troops later helped to fix Wallace's Bridge, but only because Grant ordered the repairs.

During the last week of March, Wallace received his official commission as major general, a promotion that newspapers had already relayed to the recipient a few weeks earlier. The division commander later claimed that "so absorbed was I in the conditions, and in struggling to get ready for the trial so manifestly right at hand, that after qualifying I dropped the precious sheepskin into my mess-chest." At the same time, he admitted to thinking that it was "the last round. I can't get higher." The political general further asserted, without proof, that "the promotion had its initiative in General Grant's recommendation, not in any striving of mine."[17] In truth, however, Wallace did not toss the official paper aside, and he was fiercely proud of the promotion; his status as an honorable man, by his definition, had received validation. At the same time, the news may have irritated Grant since the Indianan had been difficult to deal with in northern Tennessee.

Grant was not the only one frustrated with Wallace. John Hardin, a company orderly in the 23rd Indiana, believed that his regiment was "the best in the service," but he could not prove it because the unit served under the former colonel of the

11th Indiana. The latter regiment was finally, for Wallace, a part of his division. Hardin claimed that Wallace was "the most partial man I ever saw." The commander seemed to have "a pet *regiment* or two that he devotes his whole attention to," so the "men and officers are all down on him and remain so unles[s] he changes his way doing." Even though he was from Indiana, Hardin complemented Halleck, Grant, and Smith at the expense of his own division commander.[18]

Besides contending that Wallace favored the 11th Indiana, and quite possibly the 8th Missouri of Morgan Smith's brigade, Hardin asserted that Wallace's promotion had gone to his head, even before it had been officially received. According to the orderly, the politician "assigns his name Major General when he sends an order to any of his division but when to another he is a General." Some officers took this inconsistent approach for arrogance. As it turned out, "Grant and the rest of the *Gen*[s] have got hold of" orders with the former signature. And, according to Hardin, they were having "some sport over it," saying that "he is not commission[ed] as such yet."[19] Shortly after the Battle of Fort Donelson, John McClernand, Charles Smith, Wallace, and Grant were promoted to major generals. All, except for the Indianan, refrained from using the title until they received official notice. To West Pointers, especially, Wallace's reaction to promotion would have seemed unmanly, exhibiting too much focus on self and too little restraint.[20] Despite all of the earlier problems, Wallace managed to find one more way to foster irritation between himself and superiors.

On 4 April, General Smith turned over command of his division to Brig. Gen. William H. L. Wallace. He was suffering from his terrible scrape of 12 March. According to Grant, the West Pointer's injury was so severe that no "advice or entreaty could induce him to go further than Savanna [*sic*]."[21] His eventual death, on 25 April due to infection and dysentery, may have increased the tension described by Hardin.[22]

Once Smith relinquished his position, Grant's Army of the Tennessee included six divisions, commanded by John McClernand, William H. L. Wallace, Lew Wallace, Stephen A. Hurlbut, William T. Sherman, and Benjamin M. Prentiss. The Hoosier and fellow political general McClernand were major generals, outranking the other four brigadiers.[23] The army, along with detachments at Forts Henry and Donelson and another at Savannah, made up the District of West Tennessee, which numbered 56,336 men and officers present for duty in late March. The Indianan's division included 8,960 men and officers fit for battle.[24] With this force, Grant prepared to move against a Confederate army, under Gen. Albert Sidney Johnston, camped near Corinth, Mississippi.

As the Union commanders organized for offensive action, Wallace sent a message to Grant, "confirmatory of a previous report that the rebels were reinforcing Purdy." He believed "that there were eight regiments of infantry and 1200 cavalry at that place, with an equal, if not larger, number at Bethel four miles back of it." The Hoosier could not discover "the object of this movement of the enemy . . . but as a measure of precaution," he requested that some extra artillery be sent to him at Crump's Landing. Grant sent the guns, and he ordered W. H. L. Wallace to temporarily reinforce the Indianan. He also ordered Sherman to send out pickets and be ready in case rebels attacked the rearguard division.[25] While Grant took these precautionary measures, he failed to seriously consider the possibility that the rebels might attack the main force near Pittsburg Landing.[26]

And that was exactly what Johnston, with prodding from P. G. T. Beauregard, decided to do in early April. Confederate forces throughout Tennessee had fallen back south after Grant's impressive victories at Henry and Donelson. As a result, the Union forces now threatened the strategically important railroad junction of Corinth, Mississippi, just south of the Tennessee border. The Memphis & Charleston Railroad and the Mobile & Ohio Railroad crossed at Corinth. If the Army of the Tennessee captured that junction, the city of Memphis would be more difficult to defend, and its fall might mean Union control of the Mississippi River as far south as Vicksburg, Mississippi. Moreover, the railroad allowed the rebels to more easily move troops and supplies from one region to the other, depending on where they were needed most. If Grant could capture Corinth, the Union would stop this traffic, and possibly use the same line to carry troops west to Memphis and east toward Chattanooga, Tennessee. Furthermore, if Federals broke the line at the Mississippi town, rebel communications to the east and west would be severed. Grant could force the Confederacy to rely on more complicated lines of communication and transportation.[27]

Rebel regiments from nine states converged on Corinth for a desperate effort to halt the bluecoats in the West.[28] The gravity of the situation convinced Johnston and Beauregard to act decisively—to assault an unsuspecting Union army at Pittsburg Landing. Their Army of the Mississippi was organized into four separate corps under Leonidas Polk, Braxton Bragg, William J. Hardee, and John C. Breckinridge, the former vice president of the United States. When this army finally approached Shiloh Church, on the far right of the Union front line, it numbered at least 40,000. The Union force, stretching from the church to the river, consisted of approximately 35,000 men. This number did not include Wallace's division of 7,564 effectives camped at Crump's Landing.[29]

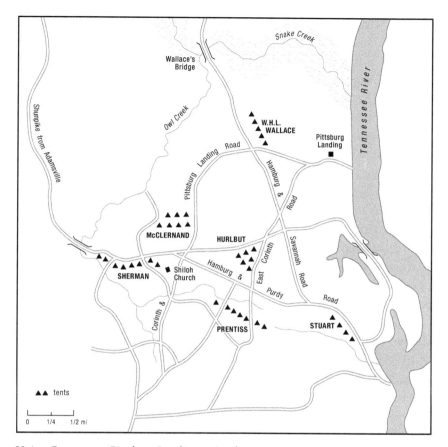

Union Camps near Pittsburg Landing, 6 April 1862. *Map by Erin Greb Cartography.*

In the meantime, Wallace and Grant worried that the Confederates might attack the partially isolated 3rd Division. The possibility of such a move seemed more likely, in the Hoosier's view, as his troops seemed to be in constant contact with the rebels. On 3 April, he reported that "the enemy's pickets and mine eat their dinners in sight of each other, and at night amuse themselves by exchanging shots."[30] According to the Indianan, however, this opinion changed when his troops brought him some new information on the following day.

Wallace later claimed that he received good intelligence of the Confederate march toward Pittsburg Landing on 4 April. Two scouts told the division commander that Johnston meant to attack Grant's front line as soon as possible. In response, the Hoosier asserted that he sent an orderly to Pittsburg Landing with a note for Grant. If the commanding general was not there, the messenger was to give the note to the army postmaster with special directions.[31]

The story is hard to credit, considering that no material evidence exists to verify the political general's statements. If the claim is true, Grant never received the note, or he failed to acknowledge it. Even if the Indianan sent such a note, he committed two errors. The intelligence was significant; the possibility of a rebel attack on the front line should have caused the commander of the 3rd Division to take all precautions in getting that information directly to his commanding officer. Certainly, Wallace should have entrusted such vital intelligence to an officer, not an enlisted orderly.[32] And furthermore, he did not verify the delivery of the ghost letter on the 5th.

The orderly discovered, in delivering the letter to the postmaster, that Wallace's Bridge over Snake Creek was intact, though some backwater covered the approaches. In addition, the Hoosier decided to send cavalry down the Shunpike to make sure that it was passable all of the way to the front.[33] Such an order proved important as pickets in front of Sherman's headquarters near Shiloh Church reported more enemy activity than usual on 5 and 6 April. The increased commotion proved to be the beginnings of a major battle.

At about sunrise on Sunday, 6 April, 40,000 Confederates approached Union camps from the southwest, less than one thousand yards from Sherman's headquarters and approximately four miles from Pittsburg Landing.[34] By 8:00 A.M., the rebels were overwhelming Sherman's and Prentiss's divisions while Grant had not yet reached the battlefield. The commanding general, eating breakfast in Savannah, heard the gunfire and quickly decided that the Confederates had forced a general engagement.

Quitting his morning meal, Grant wrote a note to Don Carlos Buell, who slowly approached Savannah from the east with Union reinforcements. The commander of the Army of the Tennessee told Buell that he had hoped to meet with the general later that day, but now had to board a boat for Pittsburg Landing. Moreover, Grant directed Brig. Gen. William Nelson to move his recently arrived division south, marching his brigades upriver until they were just opposite of the landing. Then the Illinoisan boarded the *Tigress* and headed upriver.[35]

Wallace also heard the fire of muskets and artillery. As a result, he ordered his brigades to prepare to meet at Stoney Lonesome. From there, the division could take the Shunpike to the right of the front line, or the road to the main landing.[36] Eventually, a little after 8:00 A.M., the Indianan recognized the *Tigress* as it chugged upstream. Grant's boat pulled up alongside the steamer that served as the Hoosier's headquarters, and the two men briefly discussed the situation. Wallace told the commander that he had already sent scouts to discern whether Crump's Landing might be threatened as Grant worried that the gunfire might constitute a feint to cover up an attack on the army's rearguard. The senior officer later claimed that he concluded the meeting by ordering Wallace to be ready "*to move to Pittsburg landing* on receipt of orders."[37] Such a plan made sense, considering that the two generals had little knowledge of the current events at the front. Planning for reinforcements to go directly to the headquarters, the commanding general could route the Indianan's troops to any portion of the battle line.

When Grant left the steamboat at Pittsburg Landing, he witnessed a discouraging sight; hundreds, maybe thousands, of men had retreated to the landing, many expecting to cross the river as soon as possible.[38] The Confederates had pushed the Union divisions back behind the Hamburg & Purdy Road, the second trail that Wallace would use to take his division to the main landing if he decided to use the Shunpike south to the front. As a result of the dire situation, Grant worked to halt the stragglers and organize a reserve. After talking with W. H. L. Wallace, he sent a message to Nelson asking that the general hurriedly bring his division from Savannah.[39]

Events also convinced Grant that the rebels no longer intended to attack Crump's Landing. After the battle, the commanding general stated that he then "sent orders to General Lew Wallace at Crumps [*sic*] Landing, to move his Division, detaching a sufficient force to guard the property at Crump's Landing, by the road nearest to, or parallel with, the river to Pittsburg Landing until he reached the rear of the camps of C. F. Smith's Division, where he would form in line at right angles to the river and await further orders." John A. Rawlins, Grant's adjutant, likely relayed the command to Capt. A. S. Baxter. According to the general, the "order to General Wallace was verbal and conveyed by Captain Baxter, who before starting made a correct memoranda of the order, which memoranda, after delivering the order, he handed to General Wallace."[40] However, if Grant in fact phrased the order as above, what seemed clear to the army commander was vague to Wallace.

In the meantime, the Indianan and his division spent most of the morning waiting at Stoney Lonesome for word from Grant. Finally, at approximately 11:30 A.M., maybe earlier, one of Wallace's staff officers arrived with Baxter, who was riding a horse left at Crump's Landing for such a messenger.[41] The Hoosier later claimed that his orders from Grant were worded a bit differently than the commanding general remembered. In fact, years later, the two men still disagreed about the contents of the note when writing their memoirs.

Wallace, in his *Autobiography*, asserted that Captain Baxter's note ordered him to "leave a sufficient force at Crump's Landing to guard the public property there; with the rest of the division march and form junction with the right of the army. Form line of battle at right angle with the river, and be governed by circumstances." He further claimed that Baxter told him that the army was "repulsing the enemy." This information convinced the Indianan to take the Shunpike to more quickly get to the right of the army in order to assist Sherman. The order, in Wallace's recollection, contained no mention of the division proceeding to Pittsburg Landing.[42] The political general's post-battle report mirrored the later memoir in its description of Baxter's letter, possibly serving as the source for that portion of the book.[43]

On the other hand, Wallace did not always remember the order in the same way. In 1896, he relayed a slightly different story in his letter to a colonel who served at Shiloh. He failed to emphasize an ordered junction with the right of Sherman's division. Instead, the Indianan believed that Grant intended for him to take the River Road to the Landing, but Baxter did not include such a suggestion on the penciled memorandum, a note that the captain scribbled because he was uneasy with merely delivering a verbal order. Wallace then mentioned Baxter's statement that the Union was "repulsing them all along the line," supporting the political general's view that he should take the far road in order to get to the far right of Sherman. In this version, he acknowledged that Grant likely wanted the 3rd Division to go to Pittsburg Landing, not the west end of the front, greatly contradicting his later autobiography.[44]

Grant's memoir seemed to verify the letter from 1896, and it echoed the commanding general's post-battle report with respect to the content of Baxter's note. Grant further stated that he "never could see and do not now see why any order was necessary further than to direct him [Wallace] to come to Pittsburg landing, without specifying by what route." Considering that the Shunpike route added distance to the march, while the River Road came almost directly to the landing, the division commander's decision to take the former still confused Grant. He kindly observed that the Indianan "would not have made the mistake" in the final years of the war.[45]

But the next sentence of Grant's memoir, despite the gracious tone, portrays Wallace's action as something other than a mistake. Grant, considering the circumstances, presumed that the fellow general's "idea was that by taking the route he did he would be able to come around on the flank or rear of the enemy, and thus perform an act of heroism that would redound to the credit of his command, as well as to the benefit of his country."[46] This assumption, on the part of the army commander, was meant to be a conciliatory explanation of Wallace's actions on 6 April. The two men were fixtures of the Republican Party during the postwar years, and neither wished to alienate the other. But, at the same time, Grant offered a subtle and logical description of the Indianan's decision to take the Shunpike.

Considering Wallace's actions and desires up to that point, Grant's theory makes some sense. The Hoosier had yearned for glory and fame since he was a boy. He had hoped to join the Texas Navy as a young man and volunteered to serve in the Mexican War in 1846, both in order to attain fame. Once the Civil War began, the son of a former governor wished to be part of the war in any way possible, starting with his first position as Indiana's adjutant general. However, Wallace quickly demanded to be a colonel because such an appointment might bring him closer to a glorious battle and the honor so important to one embracing a more martial understanding of manhood. Once he received a taste of fame at Romney, Virginia, he thirsted for more, actively urging Governor Morton to find him a place in the West where the 11th Indiana would likely see action.

Wallace eventually found himself in Kentucky under Gen. Charles F. Smith. Picket duty and scouting could not satisfy Wallace's hunger for success in battle. The political general complained that Smith refused to provide him with the opportunity to prove himself as a warrior, as he saw very little action in relation to the Battle of Belmont. He chafed at not being included in the initial movements toward Fort Donelson. And, once the general commanded an entire division at the battle for the fort, he refused to politely cooperate with Grant when doing so might, in Wallace's mind, get in the way of proving his worth as a military commander. Nothing would be allowed to ruin his quest for glory on the battlefield. After the Battle of Fort Donelson, the uncooperative general realized that Grant and Smith were not inclined to include him in the initial thrust toward Corinth.

Once the commanding general called on Wallace to come to the aid of Union divisions besieged by a Confederate force under Albert Sidney Johnston, the Hoosier wanted to take part in the Battle of Shiloh on his own terms. If he went directly to Pittsburg Landing as Grant logically expected, the 3rd Division might be divided in order to plug numerous holes in the Union front. In the end, the contents of the note carried by Baxter meant little to the division commander. Wallace felt compelled to go where he might claim the glory and fame that he thought he deserved. Maybe the note said that he should go to the landing. Maybe it directed him to take the River Road. Maybe the directions were even vaguer than that. At any rate, Wallace proceeded to take his division toward the left of the Confederate line where he might become famous if he helped to save the day by turning the rebel flank.[47] This explanation would have at least made sense to a West Pointer convinced that political generals had trouble following orders and respecting superiors.[48]

In 1868, the year Grant ran for president, Wallace sent a letter to the candidate explaining that several of the Indianan's subordinates at the Battle of Shiloh remembered that the written orders were as interpreted by the Hoosier. Thus, Wallace argued, there must have been some sort of miscommunication since Grant had not been able to give the division commander his orders directly. In other words, Baxter's note failed to accurately convey the commanding general's instructions. As a result, Wallace asserted that if the note "was not received in a form to convey your true design, but was promptly executed, neither of us is responsible for the result—it was not your mistake, nor was it mine."[49] Grant's gracious reply stated that Wallace's evidence seemed "to exonerate you from the great point of blame."[50] But this exchange occurred during a time in which both men were interested in solidifying political alliances, especially Grant. Even if there was miscommunication, Baxter's note did not likely tell Wallace to take his division directly to the right of Sherman's division, or on a movement to outflank the enemy. The note's recipient probably made that decision through a loose interpretation of the order—an interpretation that suited what the commander of the 3rd Division really wanted to accomplish.

Unfortunately, whatever the true wording of Grant's order to the division commander, Wallace erred by neglecting to send a message once he departed Crump's Landing, advising Grant on his movements. Indeed, neither general exhibited great communication skills on the 6th. Communications were exchanged, but without any specifics, leading to a bizarre set of events that combined to prevent the 3rd Division from reaching the battlefield until approximately 7:00 P.M. on that Sunday, *seven to eight hours* after Wallace received Baxter's note, and eleven hours after Grant and the Hoosier exchanged words at Crump's Landing.

Inexplicably, with the battle under way, and considering the importance of the impending march south, Wallace allowed his brigades to pause thirty minutes for lunch. Then, at about 12:00 P.M., the division set off down the Shunpike, toward the right of the Army of the Tennessee.[51] The troops swiftly crossed Snake Creek and Clear Creek. The only bridge left to cross was that over Owl Creek, which, by this time, was in the rear of the Confederates. At 1:30 P.M., a lieutenant overtook the division. The Indianan later claimed that the young man merely stated, "General Grant sends his compliments. He would like you to hurry up."[52]

The message failed to alter the general's thinking, and he proceeded to push his division toward the Owl Creek Bridge. Then, a little after 2:00 P.M., an excited captain from Grant's staff confronted the Indianan. The officer proclaimed that he "had a devil of a time in finding you," and that he had "been sent to hurry you up." The Hoosier shocked the captain when he stated that his division was going to join Sherman on the right flank of the army. The staff officer informed him that the army had been pushed back toward Pittsburg Landing, and the division commander now realized that his troops were *behind* the entire rebel army. The 3rd Brigade had not yet caught up with the other two in the march to the south, and Wallace later confessed that he considered waiting for the tardy unit, so the whole division might proceed on the current path to the rear of the Confederates. He admitted that such a move "was my impulse. The advantage of an attack in the rear would be mine; and, though more might not have been in my power, I could at least have distracted the enemy and compelled him to notice me." Ideally, "such a course might have been their salvation, and I would have tried it had I been left to myself."[53]

It is possible that Wallace intended such a heroic movement all along. "*Unfortunately*," the general later noted, "in that moment of suspense I received from General Grant his *third order* to me since morning." The captain explained that the commanding general "wants you at Pittsburg Landing—and he wants you there like hell." The directive bluntly and effectively destroyed the opportunity to assault the left flank of the rebel army from the rear.[54]

The Indianan then proceeded to order "a countermarch by brigades," the general meaning that the whole column would back out of the current position, and then make a U-turn within the confined space offered by the road. The division's commander could have directed the individual men to make the 180-degree turn to the north, or an about-face, allowing the entire unit to quickly march in the other direction. But, for reasons of his own, the Hoosier wanted the brigades and their artillery to be marching in the same order when they finally approached Pittsburg Landing; the general had more confidence in the fighting ability of some regiments than others.[55] In the end, it was for the best that the 3rd Division failed to get to the Owl Creek Bridge, for a Confederate artillery battery and two infantry regiments had established defensive positions there.[56]

The column retraced its route for roughly two miles to the north on the Shunpike, where the 3rd Brigade finally caught up to the other two.[57] The division then "bore off to the right, taking a shortcut toward the River road." As the troops began marching along the muddy path, Capt. John Rawlins, Col. James McPherson, "and two aides, finally galloped up to the lost column and accompanied it to Pittsburg Landing." They later claimed to have found Wallace at about 3:30 P.M.[58]

According to Wallace, the progress on the shortcut "was toilsome and intolerably slow." Captain Rawlins soon became frustrated with the pace. The Indianan later admitted that Grant's aide soon "insisted that the batteries should be abandoned—they were hampering the infantry," but the division's commander rejected the idea. Rawlins's "next proposal was to send the regiments forward as fast as each one arrived." The Hoosier also disliked that advice, and eventually "announced that there should be no forward movement until the column closed up." To Grant's staff officers, who had witnessed the chaos back at the landing, Wallace's lack of urgency was most distressing. Rawlins even "privately suggested arresting" the general, but McPherson discouraged such talk. The political general understandably did not want to send his men into battle piecemeal, and he dreaded the thought of leaving his artillery behind. So men, wagons, and cannon slowly ground along through numerous muddy lowlands or bogs, especially when the division neared Snake Creek and Wallace's Bridge.[59]

Wallace and all of his troops finally crossed the bridge over Snake Creek at approximately 7:00 P.M. By that time, it was almost dark, and the fighting had stopped. The division then positioned itself behind Tilghman Creek, on the right flank of Sherman's division, which by evening had fallen back two to three miles north of the morning's camp.[60] Instead of traveling five to six miles to get to a point close to the landing, Wallace's division marched sixteen to seventeen miles, taking at least seven hours. After midnight, Wallace reported that at about "1 o'clock at night my brigades and batteries were disposed, forming the extreme right, and ready for battle."[61] As a result, after marching and countermarching most of the day, his troops would have to wait until morning to demonstrate their eagerness to fight.

As Wallace prepared to engage the enemy in the morning, "General Grant came up and gave me my direction of attack, which was forward at a right angle with the river, with which at the time my line ran almost parallel."[62] The army commander told him to advance once supported on his left, but there was no talk of the previous day's events.[63] For all the Indianan knew, the commanding general was either satisfied with or did not have time to discuss his performance on 6 April. Once Grant left his sight, the Hoosier pressed his brigades to challenge the rebels in front of them.

Wallace's actions on 7 April elicited much less controversy than those of the 6th. By all accounts, the commander and his division performed well as Grant's army, now supported by Buell's Army of the Ohio, which had begun crossing the Tennessee River during the evening hours of 6 April, steadily pushed the

Confederates back across Shiloh battlefield and on toward Corinth. The rebels were exhausted from the heavy fighting on Sunday, and without reinforcements could not gain a victory. Moreover, Albert Sidney Johnston had received a mortal wound at approximately 2:00 P.M. on the 6th, leaving Beauregard in command, and he declined to order other attacks after nightfall. By the next morning, the bluecoats seriously outnumbered the rebels. The graycoats consistently exhibited bravery and determination, but their efforts could only stall the advance of a much more powerful foe.[64] As a Confederate regiment would retreat under the pressure, those near it were forced to fall back. By evening, the Union had reclaimed the ground lost on the 6th, and more besides. With Buell's army on the Union left and Grant's on the right, the Confederate Army of the Mississippi could not stop their advance.

Wallace's 3rd Division represented the far right of the Union line on 7 April, and their fight began at daybreak with an artillery duel. The general correctly deduced that rebel cannon on a bluff in front of the Union division could make an advance extremely difficult, so he ordered that two batteries of artillery cooperate in shelling the Confederate guns. The bombardment was successful, so the Indianan moved his entire command "forward, the brigades in echelon—the First in front, and the whole preceded by skirmishers." A hollow and Tilghman Creek lay before the bluff, and the Union soldiers soon crossed the obstacles, "the hill gained almost without opposition."[65]

In his post-battle report, Wallace observed that since "Sherman's division, next on my left, had not made its appearance to support my advance, a halt was ordered for it to come up." Once the West Pointer's unit arrived next to Wallace's, both moved forward, steadily pushing back the rebels. All went so well that the Hoosier tried to turn the left flank of the Confederate army, which positioned itself along the far edge of some fields, sheltered by woods, and anchored by another bluff on the far left.[66] The Indianan's troops could not quite turn the flank, however, because the enemy fell back too quickly. The rebels offered some resistance in the form of countercharges and artillery fire, but such efforts could not stop the fresh Union troops. Sometime around 12:00 P.M., Union soldiers charged into the trees at the far side of the clearings. According to Wallace, from "the time the wood was entered 'Forward' was the only order; and step by step, from tree to tree, position to position, the rebel lines went back, never stopping again. Infantry, horse, and artillery—all went back."[67] This steady reverse of the graycoats continued for roughly four hours.

Wallace took great pride in the 3rd Division's constant pressure on the Confederate army's left flank. The steady push by all Federal divisions led to success. Wallace proudly stated that at about "4 o'clock the enemy to my front broke into rout and ran through the camps occupied by General Sherman on Sunday morning." The rebels then proceeded to their own camps, which "had been established about 2 miles beyond. There, without halting, they fired tents, stores, &c." In a great hurry, the retreating graycoats abandoned hundreds of wounded men while they "filled their wagons full of arms (Springfield muskets and Enfield rifles) ingloriously thrown away by some of our troops the day before, and hurried on." Wallace further insisted that after "following them until nearly nightfall I brought my division back to Owl Creek and bivouacked it."[68] By the end of the day, the 3rd Division suffered 305 casualties, most wounded.[69] These losses were far less than those incurred by other divisions on the day before, but such numbers still helped Wallace to feel as though he did his duty during the bloody battle near Pittsburg Landing.

In a letter to Susan Wallace, the husband glowingly recounted how his division valiantly confronted the Confederates on the 7th. During the day, "step by step, I drove them before us; turning their left flank. The fight was indescribably grand." He further acknowledged that the "dead are numberless," but not in vain, since the "victory on Monday was complete." The rebels were fortunate to get away as muddy roads made it "impossible to follow up the enemy." The general neglected to mention the miscommunications and countermarching of the first day, merely stating that on Sunday "evening my Division got up."[70] Susan later heard about the problems from newspapers, not her husband.

Courage, intelligence, and luck allowed the most able volunteers to assume many obligations, including "the intelligent employment of the army's combat power . . . transportation and supply; rapid and secure communications; the gathering of intelligence; [and] the need for accurate maps."[71] In the case of Shiloh, Wallace demonstrated courage, but he did not always use information about the enemy to his advantage. Moreover, he failed, for one reason or the other, to satisfactorily communicate with his superior or intelligently employ his troops on the first day of the battle. These faults nearly derailed his career. Grant, his staff, other officers, and eventually the media proceeded to criticize the Hoosier's actions on 6 April 1862. The manner in which Wallace handled such criticism reflected his views on honor and manliness and would have a lasting effect on his service to the Union. His relations with General Grant suffered as emerging problems induced him to blame others for his own faults, and he sometimes made hasty decisions that could have led to his dismissal from the army.

FIVE

"On the Shelf" and Off to Cincinnati

Despite his uneven performance at Shiloh, Wallace still had the opportunity to redeem himself for his earlier mistakes. Notably, Governor Oliver Morton and Senator Henry Lane continued to support him. If he mended fences with fellow army officers and calmly relied on long-standing connections, the general was capable of contributing to the Union war effort through political as well as military means.

Wallace expected the Army of the Tennessee to actively pursue the Confederates into Mississippi, and then quickly attack them under the unflappable command of Grant. Shiloh's bloodletting, however, exhausted both armies, the roads were flooded, and there were insufficient supplies.[1] As a result, and largely due to the concerns of the departmental commander, Henry Halleck, the Union force slowly regrouped and methodically moved toward Corinth's rail junction.

Waiting for the next opportunity to engage in battle, Wallace received word that Halleck had arrived to personally take command of the collection of Union armies that were now in position to overrun Corinth. The Hoosier had not met the West Pointer and decided to call on him after a few days. He found Halleck surrounded by staff officers and orderlies, along with new tents and furniture. The departmental commander greeted Wallace and offered much encouragement. Halleck "asked no questions of me, but indulged in very positive speech of the great things he would now give me to see."[2] Wallace gathered that the older general wished to inspire his subordinates, especially considering the exhausting two days near Shiloh. Most importantly for Wallace, the allusions to future action led him to believe that he may receive another chance to attain glory, this time in northern Mississippi.

A great assault on Corinth never materialized, to Wallace's dismay, as the Union army methodically approached the town. The Army of the Ohio, as well as the Army of the Mississippi, now joined with the Army of the Tennessee. But under Halleck's cautious direction, the bluecoats built numerous earthworks as they began to put themselves in position to lay siege to Corinth. Leading a great force, Halleck decided on a slow pace and avoided any meaningful engagements.[3]

As a result, Wallace used his spare time to begin writing a book on tactics. He later claimed that his first glimpse of a Henry repeating rifle inspired him to begin a manual that might compensate for the new technology. Differing from earlier books, the Indianan's would "replace the company unit of four by a three," as well as provide "a corporal as one of every doubled three." The bugle would deliver all commands, and "it was the corporal's duty to listen for the calls and see to their instant execution." He believed that the use of the bugle might make it easier to direct troops scattered over a mile or more of hills and woods.[4]

Using his typically bold rhetoric, the general concluded "that the government would make haste to supply the whole national army with it, and then farewell to [books by] Scott, Casey, and Hardee." Shortly after the war's end, Wallace submitted his *Light Infantry Tactics* to Stanton. The secretary of war created a board of three officers to report on the book, but the members postponed considering it after some discussion. They may have refused to take seriously a book of tactics that had not been written by a professionally trained officer with a sterling reputation. It is difficult to be certain because no copies of the manual remain.[5]

It is also possible that the manual lacked the utility of previous publications, or that the board found little reason to adopt new tactics in the midst of, or immediately after, fighting a war. One should note that numerous officers had tackled the problems apparent in "frontal assaults . . . against defenders armed with rifles and protected by entrenchments" since the 1850s. Wallace was one of many to make the attempt, especially in the years following the Civil War. He was to be commended for trying, especially as his description of the manual suggests that it may have gone beyond mere drill to address actual engagement with the enemy in battle. But, considering the many disagreements army officers would have over tactics and the publication of new manuals after the war, he was too confident.[6] No matter the truth behind the training manual's submission, the whole affair again demonstrated the audacity of an officer recently humiliated by a sub-par performance in a major battle. Someone so audacious seemed to create additional problems for himself at almost every turn.

While the army dug trenches as it went, Wallace fell into his next mistake. He seldom got along well with superiors, and now he found one more way to irritate a senior officer. His division eventually camped halfway between the southernmost Union trenches and Pittsburg Landing. Such a position encouraged many officers to stop by and have lunch or dinner with the Hoosier as they came and went from the front. These visits usually went well, but one meeting led Wallace to make some characteristically unwise remarks.

Late in April, three well-dressed officers came to the camp, and the Hoosier encouraged them to partake of biscuits, whiskey, and cigars. The meeting was not unusual; Wallace had been entertaining travelers for days. On this occasion, however, a question induced the Indianan to unwisely criticize Halleck. One of the visitors asked him about the progress of the siege. The inquiry, certainly a logical one, caused Wallace to deliver a tirade against the commanding general's maneuvers up to that point. Unfortunately, as he later admitted, to "ridicule General Halleck's plan of operations was to ridicule the man himself; and that was what I did." As the general saw the men to their horses, he realized that the men were part of Halleck's staff. To be certain, he asked a member of his own staff to follow the travelers. When the orderly returned, he reported that the officers were indeed members of Halleck's staff, and they had just arrived from St. Louis. The division commander "had made an enemy, and he was in high place and going higher."[7]

Halleck disliked the offering of commissions to politicians, including Wallace, making him an easy person for the Hoosier to blame for current and later troubles. During and after the conflict, it became almost fashionable for officers and historians to blame Halleck for troubles and mistakes. He was an easy target. As T. Harry Williams has noted, many "people disliked Halleck simply because of his appearance and his habits of behavior. In a war in which handsome and impressive generals thrilled an eager public, Halleck had the misfortune to look plain and act ordinary. Forty-seven years of age in 1862, he seemed older."[8] He could be a rather unfriendly person, who, even more so than most West Pointers, did not tolerate mistakes and indiscipline in others.

Still, one should note that Halleck was a legitimate star at the time that Wallace first met the department commander. Halleck, as a young man, attended Union College and West Point, graduating from the latter in 1839. He taught French at the military academy. After a visit to France, he wrote a *Report on the Means of National Defense* as a congressional publication, and eventually the well-regarded *Elements of Military Art and Science*. He even authored a book on the use of asphalt, and then another on international law. Harvard offered him a professorship in 1848. Old Brains was no slouch, and his performance early in the Civil War demonstrated considerable ability.[9]

After John C. Fremont was removed from command in Missouri, Halleck received the duty of cleaning up the financial, logistical, and organizational mess. He succeeded in this endeavor, to the president's delight, and then proceeded to plan offensive operations. These included securing Missouri for the Union, and then the operations up the Tennessee River. While Grant received much of the glory at Donelson and Shiloh, Halleck certainly had a lot to do with managing and supplying the forces in the West, as well as forging a plan for the latest campaign. In such a capacity, it is no wonder that Old Brains could be a problem for Wallace; he was the political general's departmental commander until being promoted to general in chief in July of 1862. While Halleck would not excel in the latter position, he had done good work previously; Wallace's thoughts on Halleck should be carefully considered in this context. And, regardless of successes and failures, Halleck would be one of the Indianan's superiors for the rest of the war.[10]

Even if the above story, from his autobiography, is true, Wallace had already done much to irritate his superiors. His ill-advised tirade was not quite the defining moment that the general believed it to be. This incident was just one more in a series, including the death of Maj. Gen. Charles Smith on 25 April. Wallace admitted that Smith was "as much loved and respected in his dying days as he used to be despised" by the Hoosier.[11] Generals like Grant and Halleck, on the other hand, admired Smith before his death, so Wallace's connection to the older general's accident before Shiloh added to the tension between the men. Importantly for the Indianan, he had managed to irritate Generals Grant and Halleck by May of 1862, not knowing how high the generals' stars would rise.

Shortly thereafter, Grant was temporarily relieved of command of the current expedition.[12] Halleck placed Maj. Gen. George Thomas in charge of most of the Army of the Tennessee while the department's head took control of the operation against Corinth. The commanding general assigned McClernand's and Wallace's divisions to the reserve, with the former overseeing both. Grant later stated that he was designated as second in command of the entire force, supposedly in command of the right wing and the reserve, but Thomas had effectively taken his place, leaving the hero of Fort Donelson with nothing to do.[13] The changes also irritated Wallace, who complained that nobody "but West Pointers have high commands in the front, and some of them are Brigadiers. That 'close corporation' has concluded that McClernand and myself are interlopers."

The result infuriated the Indianan, who deduced that he and McClernand were "undergoing the process of shelving."[14]

The former commander of the Army of the Tennessee had plenty of time to consider his options, as well as defend his actions at Shiloh. Grant spent some of that time looking at the official reports for the battle, one of them written by Wallace. The Hoosier submitted his account of the late battle on 12 April 1862, one day after Halleck took command of operations south of Pittsburg Landing. The division commander's assertion, that at "11.30 o'clock [on 6 April] the anticipated order arrived, directing me to come up and take position on the right of the army and form my line of battle at a right angle with the [Tennessee] river," aggravated Grant. Furthermore, Wallace recounted the countermarching of that day as though it was not his fault; in his mind, Grant's staff prolonged a march that would have otherwise taken less time to get to the appropriate place. Such comments ignored how the Hoosier had been marching to the far-left rear of the Confederate army, where his senior officer likely did not order him to go.[15] Wallace's statements also revealed an inability to take responsibility for mistakes as he consistently found ways to blame his superiors.

When Grant forwarded the report to Halleck, he added an endorsement in which he asserted that he had directed the 3rd Division "at about 8 o'clock A.M. to be held in readiness to move at a moment's warning in any direction it might be ordered." Grant disagreed with Wallace's statement that he did not receive an order until 11:30 A.M., suggesting that certainly "not later than 11 A.M. the order reached General Wallace to march by a flank movement to Pittsburg Landing," not to the right of the entire army. He further asserted that waiting "until I thought he should be here, I sent one of my staff to hurry him, and afterwards sent Colonel McPherson and my assistant adjutant-general." Wallace's account seemed to be so inaccurate, at least to Grant, that he ended his comments by affirming that "in some other particulars I do not fully indorse" the division commander's report.[16]

The response to Wallace's account of the Battle of Shiloh reached Halleck's headquarters, but the Indianan failed to see it until much later in 1863. Some newspapers, officers, and politicians soon looked to place blame on someone for the mistakes and losses on 6 April 1862, but the division commander did not know, at least at first, that one of those accusers was Grant.[17] John A. Rawlins, an adjutant, sent Wallace a reply that seemed to suggest that Grant approved his report. Rawlins was "directed by the General Commanding to say that you [Wallace] have permission to forward your Official Report of the Battle of Shiloh for publication."[18] During the following weeks, Grant's comments likely helped to convince the departmental commander to use Wallace as little as possible in current and future operations. After all, Grant's message spoke ill of a general who had already embarrassed himself by complaining about Halleck to that general's own staff members. Approximately one year later, the favorite son of Indiana discovered Grant's analysis of his report; his reaction to the old note would greatly affect his relationships with not just Grant, but Halleck and Secretary of War Stanton.

Wallace had no knowledge of the response to his report, but he likely understood that Grant was extremely frustrated with his latest actions. After Shiloh, the Indianan's primary duty, besides writing a tactics manual, was to engage in reconnaissance, as well as dismantle railroad lines that might supply Corinth. When Grant ordered him to perform these duties near Stantonville, Tennessee, there seemed to be some confusion over the directions. Wallace had encountered some resistance from rebels and wondered what he should do in response.

Grant reasserted that the "object of the expedition being to cut off the railroad, and you, being with the command to do it, can tell better whether any change from the plan laid down should be made, and will be at liberty to do so." He directed the division commander to still "cut the road, if possible, but do not engage a force that you are not certain of success over, and if possible an engagement should be avoided altogether."[19] A copy of this letter was filed away to be included later in the *Official Records* of the war. On the other hand, Wallace misplaced a copy of an additional endorsement that Grant felt compelled to write after receiving further questions from the division head about the use of additional horsemen in those same endeavors.

The commander of the Army of the Tennessee no longer contained his frustration. Acting on a message received from Wallace, and which he returned, Grant felt compelled to relay his displeasure by asserting that his "instructions are plain. You were not to await the arrival of cavalry but the cavalry was to follow and report." Since the West Pointer had problems with the subordinate in the past, he added that too "often my orders and instructions are misunderstood or totally disregarded by you."[20] It is not clear as to whether the last comment somehow related to Fort Donelson or Shiloh, or both, but it is likely, especially considering Grant's aforementioned comments about Shiloh in his postwar memoir. At any rate, such behavior was not tolerable to regular officers trained at the United States Military Academy.[21]

Even after this uncharacteristically negative note from his superior, Wallace again failed to do the job as well as expected. A day later, Grant ordered Wallace to return "to the railroad and do the work thoroughly," even though the division commander continued to worry about rebel pickets and cavalry.[22] Eventually, that task and others were completed by the 3rd Division as the army slowly pushed south, but occasionally with too much delay or confusion for Grant's liking. Oddly, the rebuke failed to faze the Indianan, and he continued to focus on the prospects for more glory on the field of battle.

For the time being, and not having yet seen Grant's response to his report on Shiloh, Wallace refrained from the overly defensive arguments that later developed. During the following weeks, he thirsted for another great battle, this time for Corinth, but it never came. Halleck spent three weeks organizing and reinforcing, and then he ordered the divisions to slowly move toward the Mississippi town in the form of a protracted siege. The Hoosier complained that he had "nothing to do but drill, and listen to the cannonading in front" while, in his opinion, the rebels would not leave their camps until the Union army forced the issue.[23] Near the end of May, the Union army of 100,000 soldiers and more than two hundred cannon came closer to Corinth. The rebels had half the men of their counterparts, but the Union commander insisted on "a careful investment of the Confederate position." He feared making the same mistake that Grant made at Shiloh, so he sacrificed time. As the entrenchments inched closer, Gen. P. G. T. Beauregard evacuated the town. On 30 May, Halleck's army seized the defenseless town without great celebration or climax, ending a slow and confusing campaign.[24] Wallace certainly noticed the faults of the late movements, increasing his usual frustration, which then turned to astonishment as the overly cautious Halleck was promoted to be commander of all Union armies. The promotion meant that Old Brains would be moving to Washington, and that Grant would again command soldiers without Halleck nearby. This news, though, failed to materialize until 11 July 1862.[25] In the interim, both Wallace and Grant would find themselves leaving Corinth and Halleck for western Tennessee.

After Corinth came under Union control, the political general, who believed that he had natural and proven ability, and his division were ordered to the town of Raleigh, Tennessee, approximately ten miles from Memphis, "left to guard and repair the railroad, while sundry Brigadier Generals go marching on to glory, they being of the regular army."[26] In charge of that position on the Memphis & Ohio Railroad, the general received news that Nathan Bedford Forrest, with up to six thousand cavalry, planned to raid Memphis. As a result, the Indianan occupied the city. The move, along with a corresponding neglect of the railroad, irritated Halleck, but the note of a colonel requesting the Hoosier's assistance in the Mississippi River city eventually satisfied the commander of all Union armies when he questioned Wallace's actions.[27] Commanding the town, the general seized the office of a secessionist newspaper, which had published an anti-Lincoln editorial. For the moment, he seemed to enjoy instituting martial law and getting his picture taken by *Harper's Weekly*.[28] But to Wallace's chagrin, Grant soon arrived to command troops in the city, encouraging the division commander to look for ways out of western Tennessee.

In his memoirs, Grant stated that after the fall of Fort Donelson, he repeatedly asked the War Department "to be relieved from duty under Halleck."[29] He received permission to leave the department after the taking of Corinth, but Maj. Gen. William T. Sherman convinced him to stay. Instead, Grant obtained permission to transfer his headquarters to Memphis, and he headed northwest with his staff on 21 June. He remained in the city until mid-July.[30]

Once Grant arrived, Wallace applied for a two-week leave of absence in order to take care of business and reunite with his wife and son. He had last seen Susan in Paducah in late 1861. In Crawfordsville, the political general received a telegram from Governor Morton asking him to come to Indianapolis, and the general obliged.[31] Indiana's chief executive told Wallace that recruiting was becoming more difficult, so the governor hoped that the political general would agree to address men across Indiana.[32]

The request was not unreasonable. Some political generals attained higher rank and more prestigious commands by energetically agreeing to give recruiting speeches for their governors, or for President Lincoln. Wallace, on the other hand, refused to see the utility in such a favor. He was unwilling to consider that doing something for Morton might ensure his support in receiving another important field command like what he had at Donelson and Shiloh, one in which there was a good possibility to see action in another great battle.

Instead of immediately assenting to give the speeches, Wallace, according to his telling postwar account, begged Morton to find someone else. The governor asserted that he could not find another officer, and the general responded by voicing his fear that he might lose his division since he had made enemies. Wallace's paranoia caused Morton to retrieve a telegram from Secretary of War Stanton. The message ordered the general to report to Indiana's governor as soon as possible. Wallace recalled that his biggest fear had come true; he "stood actually relieved of my command." Wallace's indiscretions, his uncooperative and temperamental nature, and the thirst for manly glory had produced a result that he had not anticipated one year earlier. Most importantly, the general lost his division.[33]

Wallace soon discovered that Morton had asked for the order to be approved, but the governor was unaware of the implications. He asserted that Morton had taken "an unwarranted liberty" in making such a communication with Stanton. This statement puzzled Indiana's leading Republican, who then stated that he could get the general's command back for him. Wallace claimed to have then indiscreetly told Morton that the powerful, angry man who now disliked the Hoosier was Halleck, causing the governor to flinch. He remembered this admission as a mistake, but he refused to admit that the conclusion to the conversation likely had a greater impact on later events.[34]

Wallace told Morton to make arrangements for him to speak, but he wished the governor to understand that he would quit the recruiting "when done with the first district." The general perceived the actions of Morton as some sort of slight on his honor as a man. The meeting ended with ill feelings, as the governor's tone likely soured in reaction to the soldier's. The general later stated that the two men "were never friends again." The volunteer officer correctly understood that he "resented the liberty he [Morton] had taken with me; he resented my resentment." On the other hand, the battle tested officer was so confident in his own interpretation that Morton had wronged him that he concluded his postwar words on the meeting by asserting that "the disinterested [could] judge between us."[35]

Wallace had shown at Romney and Fort Donelson that he could lead men into battle. He had made mistakes at Shiloh, but he could learn from them. The general just needed a chance to command a division in a campaign. The governor of Indiana might have helped to solve this problem if Wallace had energetically assented to assist in recruiting soldiers from his home state. Wallace needed to understand the importance of such duties, which could earn Morton's and the president's trust and favors.

The son of a former governor had political clout and military experience, qualities that made him ideal for the task at hand. He had finetuned his speaking skills as a lawyer and state politician. He had a way with words. The general could speak as he wrote, with a convincing flair that could make listeners forget the counter argument. In this sense, he did his duty as a recruiter, and it earned back some of Morton's trust and respect, but the reaction to the original request to give speeches could not be easily forgotten. Needing the governor to help him get another prestigious field command, Wallace had not earned that assistance, at least not yet.[36]

When Wallace returned to Crawfordsville from his stint as a recruiter, he discovered that his 3rd Division had been broken up, and he was told to wait for further orders. As the Hoosier later put it, he was now "on the shelf." He sent a copy of the directive to Morton, but the governor did not intercede, at least as far as the general knew.[37] If Indiana's chief executive attempted to help, he could not have accomplished much, for Grant and Halleck believed that Wallace had miserably failed at Shiloh. Moreover, the Lincoln administration was not about to come to the Indianan's aid when news of his April march could deflect criticism of Grant, whom the president recognized as a rising star.[38]

Wallace responded by contacting Halleck, evidently asking for the reorganization of the 3rd Division with him in charge, but was told that "no general can be permanently assigned to any command" and "no promise to that effect can be given." Furthermore, "assignments will be made as the good of the service may at the time seem to require."[39] It may be that Halleck had learned that Wallace testified before the congressional Joint Committee on the Conduct of the War (CCW) on 9 July 1862. That committee, created by Congress in late 1861, was heavily influenced by the presence of Republicans like Senators Benjamin F. Wade and Zachariah Chandler, as well as Congressman George W. Julian of Indiana, who wanted the war to move in a more radical direction. According to at least one historian, the CCW seemed to represent "the new, aggressive, acquisitive male of the market economy," favored a less conciliatory approach to warfare, did not understand military matters, distrusted the West Pointers and their supposed expertise in waging war, favored officers who espoused radical views, and consequently sided regularly with politically appointed generals.[40]

As a result, the CCW's reports, some leaked, fostered turmoil within some commands and distrust between civilian officials and military officers.[41] Unfortunately, Wallace agreed to talk to the committee. The Indianan criticized the lack of proper communication and energy in the West, implicitly placing blame on Grant, his staff and junior officers at Shiloh, and Halleck. He also argued that the army should seize slaves while on the march, and he gave a speech, "from a hotel balcony," echoing such thoughts that same evening. However, assuming that Halleck and Grant knew about his testimony, it was the former comments that likely hindered his personal cause to see another fight.[42] The Hoosier had no choice but to retire to Crawfordsville. The situation remained uncertain through July and much of August, as Morton again received permission to send Wallace on the recruiting trail to give speeches.[43] Then the Indianan received a telegram from his governor, again asking him to come to Indianapolis. Proceeding to the state capital, he hoped that Morton's call might mean a field command.[44]

As it turned out, Confederate major general E. Kirby Smith and Gen. Braxton Bragg had marched separate armies into Kentucky, hoping to retake the Cumberland Gap, re-secure central Tennessee and Kentucky, and threaten a Union force under Don Carlos Buell.[45] Morton feared that the thrust endangered Indiana and Ohio. The governor had organized five regiments that were almost ready to send into Kentucky, but colonels had not yet been assigned to each; he asked Wallace to take charge of one of the units for the duration of the current crisis. The major general balked, seeing more risk than opportunity and thinking that colonels "were becoming generals every day, but I had yet to hear of generals dropping back into colonels." The citizen-soldier, who subscribed to a more martial or "rough" understanding of masculinity and honor, had trouble with the arrangement. Still, Wallace was anxious to see action in the field, so he accepted a temporary position as commander of the 66th Indiana Infantry Regiment.[46]

The general arrived in Jeffersonville, Indiana, where the 66th Indiana waited, later that same day. The town lay on the northern bank of the Ohio River, Kentucky in view to the south. Wallace and his regiment then proceeded across the river to Louisville; forces there were led by Brig. Gen. J. T. Boyle, commander of the Military District of Kentucky. On the evening of 17 August 1862, Boyle conferred with Wallace, his regiment waiting outside. The Indianans' arrival had surprised Boyle, who greeted Wallace in a nightshirt. The district commander first agonized over how he would give orders to a major general, so Wallace explained the situation, recounting Morton's concerns. Boyle was not as worried as Indiana's governor about Bragg and Smith, but he understood the situation, writing orders for the 66th and its commander to go to Lexington, Kentucky, as soon as possible.[47]

On the following day, Boyle received word that rebels had massed at Richmond, Kentucky, about twenty miles south of Lexington. As a result, Boyle ordered Wallace to take his regiment to the latter town, where he would "take command of forces there."[48] The assignment included a total of six regiments, more fitting someone of the rank of major general. As Wallace proceeded to Lexington, Bragg and Kirby Smith moved farther north, the latter threatening the Cumberland Gap while the former bypassed Union general Don Carlos Buell and the Gap to march directly into central Kentucky.

Boyle told Wallace that the "enemy, in force not known, has gained the rear of General Morgan at Cumberland Gap, destroyed his trains, cut off all communication, &c." The Indianan was to "prepare and take such portion of the forces at Lexington under your command, and make such reconnaissance, ascertaining the strength of the enemy, and if practicable engage him, and drive him out, and open the route to the gap." Cavalry had been ordered to report to the Hoosier "with such information of the enemy's position and force as they may ascertain." He further warned that feeding his force could be difficult, and that the general should "conduct this movement according to your judgment and in such manner as your knowledge and experience may dictate."[49]

Mirroring his typically bold fashion, and considering the conclusion of Boyle's message, Wallace decided to amend the orders. Pondering reports that Kirby Smith had 21,000 men, far outnumbering his, the Union general found a defensible spot on the north side of the Kentucky River. The rebel general now had passed the Gap and moved north toward Lexington; proceeding south to Cumberland Gap would do little good. Next, Wallace learned that 1,200 rebels under Col. John S. Scott marched well in front of the main southern force. Wallace hoped to trap the regiment in a pincer movement before Kirby Smith could come to its aid. To the Union general's chagrin, however, Buell placed Maj. Gen. William Nelson in command of the regiments at Lexington. This new commander refused to let the Indianan continue with the pincer movement against Scott. Moreover, he seemed to have little use for Wallace in any capacity, so the Hoosier took his dwindling staff with him to Cincinnati, Ohio, where he hoped to tender his services to Maj. Gen. Horatio G. Wright.[50]

Approximately six days after rejecting Wallace's services, Nelson and his command were routed by Kirby Smith, losing 5,353 soldiers.[51] Wright, who headed the Department of the Ohio, acted quickly to find a replacement for the wounded Nelson. As a result, on 1 September by telegraph from Lexington, Kentucky, he asked Wallace to please "come down immediately and take command of the troops in this vicinity."[52] Wright then changed his mind, as Smith was rumored to be approaching Cincinnati. Considering the possibility of a threat to Ohio's largest city, the departmental commander telegraphed Wallace, ordering him to remain in that town of 161,000 to "take command of the troops there and arriving there."[53] The emergency presented a major opportunity to the Hoosier, one in which he might make both a military and a political contribution to the Union war effort.

On 2 September, Wallace issued a proclamation to local newspapers, in which he assumed "command of Cincinnati, Covington, and Newport," the latter two towns on the south side of the river in Kentucky. The general believed that Kirby Smith intended to cross the river into Ohio, so he informed "the citizens that an active, daring, and powerful enemy threatens them with every consequence of war." He could not avert this menace on his own, declaring that "the cities must be defended and their inhabitants must assist in the preparation. Patriotism, duty, honor, and self-preservation call them to the labor, and it must be performed equally by all classes."[54] Wallace the politician and speech maker took over in this crisis, motivating the citizens of the city in a way that most professional army officers would not have been able to do.

Wallace's passionate announcement continued to outline the conditions under which the Ohioans would be required to work during the following days. To ensure that all able-bodied people were helping with the defense of the city, Wallace ordered that all "business must be suspended by 9 o'clock to-day. Every business house must be closed." Furthermore, under "the direction of their mayor, the citizens must, within an hour after the suspension of business (10 A.M.), assemble in their convenient public places ready for orders," so that the residents could be assigned appropriate tasks, whether it be digging or guarding trenches, producing food, or recruiting help. The general inspiringly stated that this "labor ought to be that of love, and the undersigned trusts and believes it will be—anyhow, it must be done." He then promised that the "willing shall be properly credited, the unwilling promptly visited." In other words, the "principle adopted is: Citizens for the labor, soldiers for the battle."[55]

As a precaution, Wallace also proclaimed that ferries could not operate after 4:00 A.M. "until further orders." Then, in closing, the Indianan announced that he had placed Cincinnati, Covington, and Newport under martial law, at the same time conceding that "until they can be relieved by the military the injunction of this proclamation will be executed by the police."[56] The Hoosier appeared to have the full cooperation of the mayor of Cincinnati, George Hatch, who already had declared that his city's residents should suspend normal business and congregate for the purposes of defending the city.[57]

The mayor, in "accordance with the proclamation of Major-General Wallace," gave "public notice that the police force of this city will, until further orders, act as a provost guard, and I order and enjoin upon all good citizens to respect and obey them as such." Consequently, any "disregard of orders from the general commanding through the police will be enforced [sic] strictly."[58] The announcements of the general and the mayor had a positive effect, and the Cincinnati Enquirer noted, one day later, that the "most commendable spirit was displayed by the citizens generally in their disposition to carry out faithfully the orders . . . for the defense of the city against the rebel hordes by who [sic] it is threatened."[59]

Only one newspaper, the *Cincinnati Times*, published an editorial critical of Wallace and his efforts, so the general ordered that the periodical's offices be closed. Once the chief editor proved his loyalty and willingness to volunteer for the defense effort, the Hoosier allowed the paper to reopen.[60]

The high degree of cooperation between Wallace and Hatch represented an important achievement. The mayor could have declined to cooperate, but the general convinced him to do just the opposite. The working relationship allowed the Indianan to make some potentially controversial declarations, understanding that the city's mayor supported him. For example, the military commander's first general order maintained that all "places in the cities of Cincinnati, Covington, and Newport where liquors of any kind are sold must be closed at 4 o'clock this morning. All sales are prohibited. Upon failure or refusal, stocks on hand will be confiscated for sanitary purposes."[61] More directives like this one were enforceable because Wallace understood that he needed the backing of the civil authorities, respecting Hatch's position as mayor.

Wallace needed the support of Cincinnati's mayor, as well as the governor of Ohio, because the city had experienced cultural and political division, making it difficult to unite the "Queen City" of the West in the face of danger. For one, the area was "home to considerable Midwestern opposition to Abraham Lincoln's war policies." Such a political climate further led to "lingering disputes and deeply rooted prejudices" that "rose to the surface and complicated its defense." Nativist whites worried that Irish immigrants were stealing jobs, while the latter feared that free blacks threatened their future employment. Getting these different groups to cooperate in the midst of a crisis was difficult.[62]

Another Confederate threat occurred back in July; rebel John Hunt Morgan and his raiders rode into the region. As Cincinnati prepared to defend against the enemy, disturbances between Irish and black workers caused worried "white leaders" to dread "disorder in the city more than they feared Morgan's advance." Also, wealthy and poor whites could not agree on the proper contributions of each class to the defense effort, those of lesser means feeling as though the rich were not paying their share for their own protection. These issues still plagued Cincinnati in September of 1862, but Wallace already had some knowledge of the city's labor problems when he took command.[63]

Approximately two weeks after Morgan's raid in July, Unionists met in the river city to advocate a tougher war policy. Governor Morton pleaded for all to unite under the American flag. Moreover, the Cincinnati Chamber of Commerce urged young men to volunteer, while businesses were asked to contribute recruitment funds. Wallace also appeared, "calling for a 'terrible, earnest war.'" He further "advocated using Southern 'niggers' to spare white troops the hard work of the war." The latest crisis seemed to have "played into the hands of Unionists who favored a more vigorous war policy," and it certainly helped citizens in Compton, Newport, and Cincinnati to understand that Wallace and others would need undivided support weeks later as rebels again approached the area.[64]

By 8 September, 12,000 soldiers and possibly another 60,000 civilian volunteers manned earthworks, forts, and fordable stretches of the Ohio River. Wallace also commanded his own small navy on the river, including sixteen steamboats with two small cannon apiece and bales of hay for armor.[65] He received support from all types of citizens and officials, even as he attended entertaining dinners and merriment in the evenings. Cincinnatians organized home defense companies under many different categories; for example, one was filled by only school teachers, and another by men of French heritage.[66] But the fun ended on 6 September when a Union officer reported that nine thousand Confederates, a portion of Kirby Smith's army, were just five miles away from Covington.[67] More rumors also put John Hunt Morgan and his raiders in close proximity to the three river towns.[68]

To combat the approaching rebels, Wallace urged the governors of Indiana and Ohio to send help. Morton initially sent four regiments from Indiana, and he intended to send others.[69] David Tod "called upon all the armed Minutemen of the State, requesting each to take two days' cooked rations and a blanket. They will pour in upon you by thousands." He further "ordered ten incomplete regiments to report," numbering approximately eight thousand men.[70] Exaggerating the possible turnout, Tod told Secretary of War Edwin Stanton that he hoped to send "at least 50,000" militiamen to Cincinnati.[71] These "squirrel hunters," as some contemporaries called them, came from all parts of Ohio, carrying a variety of weapons.[72]

The Hoosier also continued to receive the cooperation of most citizens of all three towns, even as his headquarters was moved south across the river to Covington. Wright felt that it was most important that the base be closer to the trenches built there under the general's direction. Key points along the earthworks communicated by telegraph.[73] Even the divisive labor force of Cincinnati caused little trouble. Irish immigrants volunteered to dig and guard trenches, and the "negroes of the city . . . turned out and labored very cheerfully when called on to do so," developments that the Republicans of Ohio certainly appreciated.[74] Volunteer troops of all races, ethnicities, and professions tormented citizens of Covington and Newport, sometimes abusing "the hospitality offered to them" as they guarded nearby trenches, but Wallace did not let the occasional problems interfere with preparations.[75]

Until 12 September, Confederates approached and studied Wallace's well-constructed entrenchments around Covington and Newport. On that day, considering the fortifications prepared to counter their advance, the Confederates marched back toward Louisville. One might suggest that Wallace declined to pursue the rebels "with the heterogeneous force at his disposal," but it appears that the general made no such decision on his own.[76] He usually dared to be bold, and that characteristic reemerged on this occasion. Hearing about the Confederate withdrawal, Wallace told Wright that the "skedaddle is complete. Every sign of a route [sic]." Instead of being content with the successful defense of the river towns, the daring general stated that if Wright said so, he would "organize a column of twenty thousand men to pursue tonight." He further suggested that some gun batteries from the north might be sent after him.[77] The department's commander refused to allow the pursuit, so the Hoosier's latest hope to see combat in the field faded.

Reports over the next few days reassured civilians, as rebel detachments deserted camps and moved south.[78] By 14 September, Wallace was already receiving congratulatory letters and compliments from resigning volunteers. One assistant expressed his "individual admiration of the efficient manner in which you [Wallace] have discharged the responsible duty of delivering our city from fear of rebel invasion."[79] The *Cincinnati Enquirer* declared that the "people of Cincinnati, Covington and Newport, will ever retain a grateful recollection of the services of this distinguished officer," assuming that the threat had passed.[80] In return, the general issued an inspiring statement, concluding that all volunteers had "won much honor; keep your organizations ready to win more. Hereafter be always prepared to defend yourselves."[81]

By the 17th, Wallace finally believed with certainty that forces under Kirby Smith no longer threatened the area. The Union general relayed that a citizen of Georgetown, Kentucky, had "passed through the enemy's column on the full retreat." The "main body" of Confederate troops was reportedly "now beyond Crittenden."[82] The news of Cincinnati's assured safety meant that Wallace's stay in that town would soon come to an end; he hoped that the success might lead to a prestigious field command over a division, or maybe even a corps.

To Wallace's chagrin, his next assignment offered little chance of glory and battle. On 17 September, Halleck relayed an order from the secretary of war, directing the general to "immediately repair to Columbus, Ohio, and organize the paroled prisoners now there and those to be immediately sent to that place into regiments and brigades for service against the Northern Indians." Other officers would be sent to aid the general in this assignment.[83] The Hoosier immediately believed, but without greater evidence, that "the order was intended deliberately and with malice aforethought to put me to shame." The originator of the order, and the intent, seemed clear to the savior of Cincinnati; Halleck meant to injure his pride and honor, or prevent him from enjoying his latest success in Ohio.[84]

Despite the news of another unwanted assignment, Wallace enjoyed the praise he received for a job well done in the Ohio River valley. The day after Halleck informed the Indianan of his immediate future, Wright repeated the order. At the end of the communication, the departmental commander asked the Hoosier to accept his gratitude "for the zeal with which you have labored in the discharge of your many and arduous duties, and the assurance of my warmest wishes for your continued success and welfare."[85] The political general received thanks from many different quarters, something that had not happened since Fort Donelson.

For months, Wallace continued to receive accolades from Ohioans for his work in September of 1862. For example, the Buckeye state's senate and house resolved that the "thanks of the people of this State are due, and are hereby tendered through their General Assembly, to Maj. Gen. Lew. Wallace, for the signal service he has rendered to the country at large in connection with the army during the present war." Ohio especially appreciated "the promptness, energy, and skill exhibited by him in organizing the forces, planning the defense, and executing the movements of soldiers and citizens under his command at Cincinnati in August and September last, which prevented the rebel forces under Kirby Smith from desecrating the free soil of our noble State."[86]

Wallace had faltered near the banks of the Tennessee River, but he partially redeemed himself on the Ohio. He diligently turned a city of almost 200,000 people into a fort, stoutly protected by trenches and citizen militia, discouraging Kirby Smith and his Confederates from even attacking. A rebel attack on a major northern city could have been politically disastrous for the Lincoln administration. Wallace's good work heartened Unionists from Ohio and helped the state to more easily recruit soldiers from the Ohio River valley.[87] Buckeyes thanked him, and Lincoln might have thanked the general for his willingness to use blacks as wartime laborers. It amounted to one small step in preparing

Ohio and the nation for Lincoln's Emancipation Proclamation, announced on 22 September, as well as the eventual recruitment of black troops to the Union army. In other words, as historians David Work and Thomas Goss have asserted with respect to a number of politically appointed officers, Wallace's efforts in Cincinnati confirmed that a general's contribution to the Union war effort could be through political, as well as military, means.[88] Seizing the opportunity to turn back a Confederate offensive, Wallace repositioned himself to gain a major command, one that might lead back to the battlefield.

Lew Wallace at age twenty-one. *Lew Wallace,
Lew Wallace; an Autobiography (New York: Harper
and Brothers, 1906), facing p. 208.*

Gen. Lew Wallace, ca. 1861–65. *Brady-Handy Photograph Collection, Prints
and Photographs Division, Library of Congress, Washington, D.C., LC-BH82–3804.*

Gen. Lew Wallace, ca. 1860–65. *Brady National Photographic Art Gallery, National Archives and Records Administration, College Park, Md., 111-B-4184.*

Governor Oliver P. Morton of Indiana,
ca. 1860–65. *Brady National Photographic
Art Gallery, National Archives and Records
Administration, College Park, Md., 111-B-1772.*

Gen. Charles F. Smith, ca. 1860–65. *Brady National
Photographic Art Gallery, National Archives and Records
Administration, College Park, Md., 111-B-4331.*

Governor Augustus W. Bradford, ca. 1855–65. *Brady-Handy Photograph Collection, Prints and Photographs Division, Library of Congress, Washington, D.C., LC-BH82–5358 C.*

(Opposite, top) Gen. Ulysses S. Grant, ca. 1855–65. *Brady-Handy Photograph Collection, Prints and Photographs Division, Library of Congress, Washington, D.C., LC-BH82–3847.*

(Opposite, middle) Maj. Gen. Henry W. Halleck, ca. 1860–65. *Photograph by John A. Sholten. Prints and Photographs Division, Library of Congress, Washington, D.C., LC-B813–6377 A.*

(Opposite, bottom) Gen. Don Carlos Buell, ca. 1855–65. *Brady-Handy Photograph Collection, Prints and Photographs Division, Library of Congress, Washington, D.C., LC-BH82–4164.*

Members of the military commission called to try those who allegedly conspired to assassinate Abraham Lincoln and other governmental officials (*left to right*), 1865: Thomas M. Harris, David Hunter, August V. Kautz, James A. Ekin, Lew Wallace, and John A. Bingham. *Mathew Brady Photographs of Civil War–Era Personalities and Scenes, National Archives and Records Administration, College Park, Md., 111-B-4273.*

Sketch of the Trial of Capt. Henry Wirz, *Harper's Weekly*, 21 October 1865, by Jos. Hanshew. *Lincoln Foundation Collection; digitizing sponsor: The Institute of Museum and Library Services through an Indiana State Library LSTA Grant.*

(Opposite, top left) Gen. Jubal A. Early, CSA, ca. 1860–70. *Prints and Photographs Division, Library of Congress, Washington, D.C., LC-B813-6408 C.*

(Opposite, top right) Judge Advocate Gen. Joseph Holt, ca. 1855–65. *Brady-Handy Photograph Collection, Library of Congress, Prints and Photographs Division, Washington, D.C., LC-BH82-2355 A.*

SIX

Columbus, Buell, and Morgan

Having organized an impressive defense of Cincinnati, Ohio, Wallace received many congratulations and thanks from Buckeye citizens, politicians, and newspapers. Maj. Gen. Horatio Wright also complimented the Hoosier on his quick organization of the region's manpower and supplies. By contrast, the Lincoln administration and Maj. Gen. Henry Halleck failed to positively acknowledge Wallace's service on the Ohio River. The lack of an impressive battle for the city led many to assume that the threat had not been as dire as Wallace and others believed. Attacking Cincinnati would have been more difficult than assaulting Louisville or Frankfort, Kentucky, due to the natural defense of the Ohio River, though it remained a possibility. The general's hurried and anxious organization seemed to be unnecessary and embarrassing after the Confederate threat receded, but better a hasty defense than a battle that would have been a political nightmare for Lincoln.

As a result of these mixed reactions to his impetuous defensive measures, Wallace received no direct reward for the job well done. Instead of a field command, leading a division against the rebels, the secretary of war, through Halleck, ordered him to proceed to Columbus, Ohio, in order to organize paroled Union prisoners into regiments. Once Wallace completed this task, he was to take the regiments to Minnesota in order to police Indians.[1]

The defender of Cincinnati hoped for a more prestigious command or post, and he dreaded going to Minnesota. The real war was in the South. Unfortunately for Wallace, his image had been damaged, and not just in the eyes of Halleck and Grant. For example, Maj. Gen. William S. Rosecrans, from Ohio, argued that his commission as major general should have been dated earlier since now he found himself "ordered from the command of an army whose confidence I possess—a separate army in the field—to go and take subordinate position in a new and unformed one, where Buell, Granger, Gilbert, Schenck, Lew. Wallace, Tom Crittenden, and Bully Nelson are my seniors." Rosecrans did not want to be a general in the army of less respected officers any more than Wallace, who seemed destined to go "on the shelf" again.[2]

Despite his misgivings, Wallace immediately notified Wright of his intention to go north and packed his belongings for the trip.[3] He felt as though he had little choice but to obey. Still receiving occasional reports of rebel activity to the south in Kentucky, he knew that the main threat had dissipated.[4] He and his staff arrived in Ohio's capital on 19 September and established headquarters in a hotel.[5]

The thought of going to Minnesota to police Native Americans irritated Wallace. He wished that organizing the former prisoners of war into regiments would amount to temporary duty, and in such spirit, he rode to Camp Chase intending to complete the task as soon as possible. To the general's surprise, however, the home for five thousand to six thousand paroled Union soldiers was squalid.[6]

During the first year of the war, the two sides had agreed on "an impromptu system of parole and exchange that was quickly overwhelmed by the influx of hundreds of thousands of prisoners."[7] The Union decided to put most of their own, paroled, men in camps, held there against their will until officially exchanged.[8] Named after the secretary of the treasury, Salmon P. Chase, the Ohio camp overflowed with thousands of men. The barracks consisted of dilapidated shacks with no windows and holes through the roofs, and troops fought over the available space. Lice-infested sheets served as doors in the wintertime. The former prisoners lacked suitable clothing, some were practically naked, and at least dozens died from disease and the cold. Wallace later asserted that Camp Chase was almost as horrible as Andersonville, the supremely detestable prison in Georgia, the main difference being that the rebel camp "was a Confederate hell for the confinement of enemies taken in arms, while Camp Chase was a hell operated by the old government for friends and sworn supporters—its own children."[9]

Hearing about the conditions at the camp from the provost-marshal, Wallace failed to believe the worst until he and his staff arrived at the grounds. Escorted by a company of soldiers to protect them from the former prisoners, the general's staff quickly found the officers in camp and brought them to Wallace. He ordered them to arrange the troops into lines, so that he could talk to them. Addressing the prisoners, he discovered the men to be hairy, filthy, and short on clothing. The general swore that their stench was "pungent and peculiar."[10]

Wallace told the troops that Lincoln recognized their terrible plight, and that the president had sent the general to Columbus to clothe, pay, and organize them, with the understanding that they would be moved to another camp. The new camp commander neglected to mention future duty in Minnesota, correctly thinking that such information would cause a mutiny. But the soldiers still closed in on the general and began to curse, claiming that they had heard similar promises before with no results. A nervous Wallace eventually calmed the men, emphasizing that he intended to put money back in their pockets; many had not been paid for an entire year or more. Next, he asked them to organize into companies, clean up, shave, cut their hair, and march to the statehouse to receive back pay.[11]

Wallace set up tables in the capitol building to distribute the money to the arriving companies, but he soon found that the paymaster refused to provide the cash. The funds were held for some other purpose. The Indianan later claimed that he ordered the paymaster to relinquish the money, and then ordered his staff to forcibly take the keys from the paymaster, ending the predicament. In reality, Wallace appealed to the secretary of war and Ohio's governor for any assistance they could provide in forcing the unwilling officer to perform "this duty immediately." On 22 September, Wallace sent a telegram to Adjutant General Lorenzo Thomas, declaring that the former prisoners were "clamorous and mutinous for pay. No funds here to settle with them. They cannot be controlled until paid."[12]

The paymaster general's office countered these telegrams with one of their own to Thomas, stating that it had "been impossible for the Treasury to furnish funds to meet the heavy payments recently required for advance pay." Still, the office required "no order to make these payments if the money can be obtained." Moreover, the assistant paymaster questioned whether the government owed any of the parolees more than two or three months' worth of back pay. It seemed ridiculous to make these former prisoners a priority when there were "large numbers of regiments now in the field fighting who have four months' or more pay due them." The threat of a possible mutiny, according to Wallace, failed to convince the paymaster that the detainees at Camp Chase should be paid before other more deserving units, but the department promised to pay the parolees "as soon as funds are furnished."[13]

On 23 September, the secretary of war replied with positive news, asserting that efforts "have been made to obtain funds to pay the paroled troops. A special paymaster will leave here to-morrow with money to pay them." On the other hand, Stanton stated that he had "no tents."[14] The general decided to move all of the newly organized companies to a new location, naming it Camp Thomas after the adjutant general.[15] Wallace needed supplies, tents, and arms for the short move, but the secretary of war merely suggested that he "cause temporary sheds to be erected, which can quickly be done. Arms will be supplied as soon as your force is organized. You will issue clothing which you say is on hand and take whatever measures are proper to provide for the comfort and health of your troops." Stanton must have been skeptical about Wallace's report of bad conditions since the "Adjutant-General was recently at Camp Chase but made no report of anything being lacking for the accommodation of the prisoners sent there." In other words, Washington was not in a hurry to send supplies, including tents, but they at least sent some money.[16] Revealingly, Wallace took a more patient or restrained approach to the latest problems than he had in the past. He refrained from physically forcing the paymaster to do his duty, despite later claims in his memoir, and he respectfully addressed Thomas and Stanton without the abrasive air that characterized his earlier correspondence with his political or military superiors. He even resorted to flattery in the naming of the new camp. There was a more restrained or gentlemanly side to Wallace's manliness, but it often lost out to his rougher side.

Wallace eventually got money to pay the galvanized Yankees, but conditions in the camp improved only marginally. He had to tell the men that they would soon be leaving for Minnesota, and the response was not positive. The general selected guards every evening to make certain that no one escaped during the night. Each morning, however, a member of Wallace's staff reported that the guards, and a few others, had disappeared in the night. Such disappointment caused the general to write to Stanton, asking that the War Department "not send any more paroled prisoners here. It is impossible to do anything with those now in Camp Chase," since they had become "a mob already dangerous." Wallace could organize the men to receive back pay, but he was unsuccessful in recruiting them for service to the northwest. He refrained from giving the inspiring recruitment speeches that he was known for, likely because he abhorred the idea of leaving the main theater of war.[17]

Desertion was a significant problem during the war. The army endured at least 400,000 cases during the conflict. The reasons for desertion ranged "from poor officers and late pay to low-quality recruits and war weariness."[18] If such reasons, along with the usual American disdain for rules that seemed to inhibit their independence, led to so many soldiers leaving their units for home or elsewhere, then the major general was bound to fail at encouraging the mistreated parolees to stay put.[19] His own sense of right and wrong and the lack of disciplined guards only made it more difficult.

The duties frustrated Wallace until most of the parolees had fled. On 28 September, he sent a report to the War Department on the status of the first full regiment to have been organized under his command at Chase. After being paid, many deserted, so Wallace counted few remaining officers, musicians, and privates from those companies that had been paid.[20] Reasserting that "it was impossible to force or coax the men into organization," Wallace "concluded to leave the matter to time and adopted the plan of organizing one regiment after another, first giving it out distinctly that no one should receive pay or clothing until he had enrolled himself in a company under designated officers." The Hoosier appointed a paroled officer to create and command the first regiment, and another colonel was at work on organizing a second. But, considering the difficulties experienced to that date, "what will such regiments be worth? Of what profit will they be?" The problems convinced Wallace to "inform the Secretary that all attention, money, clothing, &c., furnished the great body of prisoners now here is idly expended." He added that one company, just after being paid, openly marched away from the statehouse, and provost guards persuaded only fifty of the deserters to return to camp. The camp's condition was so poor that the general believed it "would be far better policy to send such regiments directly to Minnesota, to be armed and re-equipped there," sparing the Union troops from the horrors of living in the wartime prison camp.[21]

Continuing to command Camps Chase and Thomas into October, Wallace failed to inspire most of the parolees to serve the United States as Indian fighters, and thus he had to resort to force. He wanted to guard the camps with Union soldiers, but troops were a valuable commodity that the War Department hesitated to send for duty in central Ohio. Wallace, not getting reinforcements from Stanton, Halleck, or Morton, also begged Wright for some troops. On 8 October, Wright sent five green companies of Ohio volunteers, not enough to keep control, and the camps steadily emptied, eliminating Wallace's command.[22] Again, the general was "on the shelf," looking for ways to attain a position in the field.

Wallace waited no more than a month, when he was ordered back south to the Department of the Tennessee. It appeared, at least for the moment, that new friends in Ohio and Senator Henry S. Lane had successfully urged the Lincoln administration to find Wallace a command.[23] In November, he went south to find Grant, even though he told Morton that he preferred to serve with

John McClernand. Going by train, Wallace proceeded to Cairo, Illinois, where a waiting telegram from Grant told him to go back to Cincinnati to receive a dispatch from Washington.[24] Dissatisfied and worried about being stuck in a backwater, he complained to his wife about being "kicked about from pillar to post." The political general feared that Morton was helping other officers while ignoring his plight, leading him to exclaim: "So much for Gov. Morton's friendship. Will [Senator] Lane doubt any longer? I say Morton is a hypocrit[e] and double dealer."[25]

Once Wallace arrived in Ohio, he received an order from Halleck to head a military commission to investigate the operations of units under the command of Maj. Gen. Don Carlos Buell in Kentucky and Tennessee. Halleck required the commission to meet in Cincinnati on 27 November. Wallace's fellow commissioners included Maj. Gen. Edward O. C. Ord, Brig. Gen. Albin Schoepf, Brig. Gen. N. J. T. Dana, and Brig. Gen. Daniel Tyler; Maj. Donn Piatt was to be the "Aide-de-Camp, Judge-Advocate, and Recorder." Of course, Buell himself would be there to defend his actions during the past year, especially those near Chattanooga, Tennessee. The commission did not constitute a trial, for there were no charges levied against Buell, but it would be asked to report to a congressional committee, possibly the Committee on the Conduct of the War.[26]

After Corinth, Mississippi, came under Union control, Halleck had ordered Buell to take his Army of the Ohio, 40,000 strong, east toward Chattanooga. But Buell, who had slowly made his way to Pittsburg Landing in April, again moved at a snail's pace, allowing mounted Confederate raiders under John Hunt Morgan and Nathan Bedford Forrest to destroy supply lines and railways. The actions of Confederate cavalry slowed the advance of Buell's army even more, allowing rebel generals Braxton Bragg and Edmund Kirby Smith to secure Chattanooga before Buell and his men could get to the small city.[27]

The Confederates then used this opportunity to launch an offensive into Kentucky, forcing Buell to follow them north. Bragg and Kirby Smith attempted to secure the border state for the Confederacy, arranging an inauguration for a rebel governor. Buell eventually disrupted such activities, forcing a battle at Perryville, Kentucky, but there was no clear victor, and the graycoats fell back to Chattanooga. The Army of the Ohio outnumbered the Confederates throughout the summer and fall of 1862, but Buell failed to capitalize on his advantages and track down the mounted raiders.[28] These operations embarrassed the Lincoln administration and led Stanton and Halleck to call for an evaluation of Buell's generalship.

Wallace's role on this commission placed him in an unusual position for a volunteer officer—investigating a West Pointer—but he seemed to be honored to have the opportunity. In the Indianan's own words, the "duty here prescribed was only a little less acceptable than field duty." It is doubtful that Wallace enthusiastically accepted the assignment, but, as he later said, at least it provided him with the opportunity to get away from Camp Chase and be "a student under three officers supposedly as proficient as any of the old army—Charles F. Smith, H. W. Halleck, and Don Carlos Buell."[29]

Considering that Halleck played a major part in creating the commission, along with Stanton, it is puzzling that he assigned Wallace to such duty if he hated the political general as much as that officer believed. Perhaps the hatred came later, or possibly Stanton and Halleck selected Wallace merely because he was available. Possibly they did not want one West Pointer investigating another. One historian suggests that Wallace, along with the other commissioners, advocated a brand of warfare that involved unarmed southerners in the conflict, having little respect for their property rights and civil liberties—something bordering on total war. Buell, on the other hand, disagreed with such a prosecution of the war, leading him to have troubles in Kentucky and Tennessee earlier in 1862.[30]

Buell's views mirrored those of many regular officers. One might argue that West Point's "effort to instill in cadets an attachment to the common sense values of moderation and restraint of passion can also be seen in the . . . efforts of most West Pointers to preserve the distinction between combatants and noncombatants." An officer with Buell's training would often be inclined to set "limits on the level of violence, so that the use of force did not get out of hand, stir up unnecessary passion, and become an end in itself, rather than a means to a logical end."[31] Because of the differing views of the commissioners and Buell, according to the judge advocate, the commission was "organized to convict." Wallace later interpreted this statement to mean "that Secretary Stanton and General Halleck were desirous of getting rid of General Buell, and selected us to do the work."[32]

The prosecutor's assertion irritated Wallace and the other committee members, causing them to be more receptive to Buell's defense, conducted by the general himself. The Hoosier recognized Judge Advocate Piatt to be "a cool, quizzical, sharp man of the world—knows everybody and everything—is witty and Frenchy—is not without talent."[33] Wallace believed that he would have destroyed any other defendant, but Buell presented an impressive defense of his actions in Kentucky and Tennessee. According to the commissioner, Buell became "a professor with daily lectures," wisely explaining the reasons for his army's movements. He "allowed nothing to divert or excite him," not even the famously deadly humor of the judge advocate. The general expertly countered assertions by the prosecutor, and his "examinations of witnesses, cross and original, were masterful, his arguments brief and admirably worded." Furthermore, Buell refused to do anything that might be construed as inappropriately trying to influence the commission. "He never smiled or volunteered a remark not strictly *apropos* the business in hand." Wallace thought that maybe this unsympathetic and unfeeling demeanor, one that made Buell's defense so successful, was the key to his unpopularity with other West Point graduates.[34]

Wallace complained in December that the "commission drags slowly on. . . . Sometimes it seems to me like the slow wearing away of a mountain, which I am doomed to see disappear grain by grain."[35] The hearings finally ended in early May of 1863, having convened in Cincinnati, Louisville, Nashville, and concluded in Cincinnati. In their final decision, Wallace and the commissioners were critical of Buell, but they also blamed Halleck for the failure of the operation against Chattanooga in 1862. They believed that Buell's more conciliatory approach to warfare, one greatly respecting the rights and property of disloyal southerners, including their slaves, caused the general and his Army of the Ohio to take too much time in its attempt to force Confederate general Bragg's army from Chattanooga. As a result, the rebels eventually threatened Kentucky, and Buell eventually confronted them at the Battle of Perryville. Still, the army commander's problems related to a philosophy of warfare that increasingly contradicted that of the Lincoln administration, as well as the Committee on the Conduct of the War, and his actions did not constitute a crime that called for an official hearing before a military commission or a court-martial.[36]

Wallace's role on the commission provided him with valuable procedural experience that could be of use later. And, as he stated, the Indianan learned more about the art of war from a seasoned West Pointer. At the same time, it further soured his relationship with General Halleck, as well as Stanton and Morton; all three disliked Buell. Since the findings were not to Stanton's and Halleck's liking, the court's conclusions were never submitted to Congress. The commissioners sent the transcript to the War Department in Washington, where it likely remained unread for many years.[37]

Most importantly for Wallace, while approaching the end of the commission's duties, he learned about a personal, political, and military matter of the greatest importance to him. On 25 April 1862, Grant had attached a critical note to the former division commander's report on the Battle of Shiloh.[38] Up until that time, the political general believed that his problems in attaining command of a division or corps stemmed solely from his personal conflict with Halleck when, in reality, the situation was far more complicated and deep-seated than he first believed. In fact, back in December while campaigning toward Vicksburg, Mississippi, Grant had told Halleck that it would be "particularly unfortunate to have either McClernand or Wallace sent to me. The latter I could manage if he had less rank, but the former is unmanageable and incompetent."[39] Of course, Wallace did not know about the latter communication, but his sense of honor required him to respond to Grant's increasingly evident concerns.

On 3 March 1863 Wallace completed the first draft of a letter that he eventually sent to Halleck on the 14th, by that time having revised and deleted portions of the original version. The disgruntled general stated that he had "heard of prejudices against me at your headquarters, relative to my failure to participate in the first day's battle at Pittsburg Landing. I have also heard that you yourself entertain them." As a result, and for "very obvious purposes," he sent a long explanation of his actions on 6 April 1862.[40]

Wallace recounted how he heard the noises of battle early on that Sunday morning, causing him to prepare his "command for moving instantly upon receipt of an order from General Grant." He waited through the early morning for a directive to move south. According to Wallace, at approximately "9 o'clock General Grant passed up the river. Instead of an order to march, he merely left me a direction to *hold myself in readiness for orders.*" The claim was a slight exaggeration, as Wallace's brigades were not completely ready to march when they finally received an order to go south, and Grant's steamboat approached Crump's Landing sometime between 8:00 and 8:30 A.M., not 9:00 as the Hoosier now suggested to Halleck.[41]

The rest of the letter mirrored earlier arguments made by Wallace, blaming Grant and his aides for halting the 3rd Division as it approached the rear of the Confederate left where, in his mind, the division could have produced significant rebel losses. Wallace further argued that Grant's order on the morning of 6 April 1862 arrived at approximately 11:30 A.M.; the army's commander believed that it should have arrived much earlier. In receiving the long explanation, Halleck ordered that the document be forwarded to Grant for his comments. In the first draft of the letter, Wallace declared that he would soon "solicit" a command in the field, and that if those in charge refused to help because of the prejudices against him, he planned to ask for a court of inquiry. He wisely restrained himself and neglected to include these statements in the final version sent to Halleck.[42]

Approximately one month later, Grant responded to the request for remarks. However, instead of "making a detailed report myself in answer to said communication I called upon Maj. Gen. J. B. McPherson, Lieut. Col. John A. Rawlins, and Maj. W. R. Rowley, all of whom were members of my staff at that time and were cognizant of the facts, for their statements in reference to the same, and these I herewith respectfully transmit," attached as "inclosures" to the commanding general's reply. As Grant stated in his response, all of "these reports are substantially as I remember the facts. I vouch for their almost entire accuracy; and from these several statements, separate and independent of each other, too, a more correct judgment can be derived than from a single report." Most importantly, the three officers, along with Grant, agreed that Wallace should have received his order to come to the battle front much earlier than 11:30 A.M.[43]

Grant's three aides could not offer accounts that were exactly the same as to the times of units' departure, delivery, and arrival, possibly suggesting no collusion on their parts. But, taken together, they suggested that Wallace should have arrived near Pittsburg Landing long before evening. In summary, Grant verbally gave the order to John Rawlins as early as 8:00 A.M. Rawlins then relayed the order to Capt. A. Baxter, who asked that it be put it in writing. Baxter boarded a steamboat, heading north to Crump's Landing no later than 9:00 A.M. The captain claimed that he then delivered the order to Wallace at approximately 10:00 A.M.; the Indianan had stated that he received the order at 11:30 A.M. when an aide brought Baxter to him a couple of miles away from the landing. The captain then rode back to Crump's and took the boat back to Pittsburg Landing, arriving sometime between 10:30 A.M. and 12:00 P.M. The accounts further explained that Wallace's command at Crump's was approximately five and a half miles from Grant's headquarters, giving it plenty of time to get into the fight on 6 April.[44]

Rawlins also asserted that the memorandum delivered by Baxter instructed Wallace to "move forward your division from Crump's Landing, leaving a sufficient force to protect the public property at that place, to Pittsburg Landing, on the road nearest to and parallel with the river, and form in line at right angles with the river, immediately in rear of the camp of Maj. Gen. C. F. Smith's division on our right, and there await further orders."[45] The aides' version of the order mirrored that of Grant, mentioning right angles and supporting the right of the current line, but at the same time making it clear that the Hoosier should have taken the River Road to the landing, not the Shunpike. In total, the supporting letters, enclosed with his to Halleck, encouraged Grant to declare that had "General Wallace been relieved from duty in the morning, and the same orders communicated to Brig. Gen. Morgan L. Smith (who would have been his successor), I do not doubt but the division would have been on the field of battle and in the engagement before 10 o'clock of that eventful 6th of April. There is no estimating the difference this might have made in our casualties."[46] It was not the result that Wallace had hoped for; his defensive explanation to Halleck, who likely viewed it as a selfish display typical of a politician, had now managed to make things worse. On the other hand, and maybe for the best, it appears that the Indianan did not find out about the staff officers' letters until after the war.

In the meantime, Wallace boldly decided to ask Stanton to work on his behalf to find a field command suitable to his rank. Stanton responded on 25 May, stating that he would endeavor "to have you Placed on the Field as Speedily as Possible."[47] The reply must have been soothing for a short time, but nothing came of the secretary's response. Due to the lack of positive results from his latest communications, the Indianan again resolved, as he had during the summer of 1862, to see Grant in person.

Sometime in middle to late June, Wallace sent a telegram to Halleck, asking whether there might be any "objection to my visiting Vicksburg?"[48] Wallace lost patience when he received no prompt reply. He sent another note from Cincinnati on 24 June, arguing that since he received "no prohibition [from Halleck], I infer your assent, and will leave for Vicksburg tomorrow."[49] Wallace should not have sent the second telegram, as it likely irritated the general overseeing all Union armies, but it at least forced a response. Halleck quickly replied to the message, stating that no "prohibition does not give consent," so the West Pointer declared that Wallace would have to "await orders at Cincinnati & will not leave that place without proper permission."[50]

The discouraging note would have deterred some officers from pushing the matter any further, but Wallace was not the kind of person to easily back down from an obstacle to self-made success, no matter the prestige or power of the adversary. He had heard that Governor Andrew Curtin of Pennsylvania was calling for volunteers, and the politician needed officers to command the few people that responded to his plea for defenders.[51] Robert E. Lee and the Army of Northern Virginia had just defeated Union general Joseph Hooker and the Army of the Potomac in May, and the rebel general now set his eyes on another invasion of the North. Wallace believed that there was a real possibility of experiencing the exhilaration of battle in Maryland or Pennsylvania, so he responded to the latest telegram on the 26th, asking "leave to tender my services to the governor of Pennsylvania."[52]

Halleck replied to this request on the following day. One might suspect that he and Stanton would have been happy to be rid of Wallace, allowing Curtin to deal with a general that Halleck did not respect, but his "application to report to the governor of Penns has been submitted to the Secy of War & is not granted."[53] The result of these exchanges greatly frustrated Wallace, as Halleck and Stanton forbade him to do the two things that mattered most to him. He could not go out, on his own, and offer services to a governor that might consider offering command of thousands of troops, and he could not go home to Crawfordsville to see his wife and child. Despite the great unwillingness to submit to authority, all he could do now was beg to await orders in his hometown. Halleck forwarded this last message to Stanton, who granted the request.[54] Wallace again proceeded to Crawfordsville to take care of personal business.

Since Halleck would not allow him to travel to Vicksburg or Pennsylvania, Wallace decided to write a letter to Grant on 27 June 1863, trying to explain his actions at Shiloh. The more apologetic officer asserted that his previous letters to Halleck and Stanton were written only to salvage his own reputation, not to injure Grant's.[55] The senior general declined to reply, eventually convincing his former subordinate to look for another way to address his grievances. But such actions would have to wait, as Governor Morton telegraphed Crawfordsville for assistance with a new crisis.

Rebel cavalry under John Hunt Morgan had ridden across the Ohio River into Indiana. Almost immediately, the governor's office contacted Wallace, begging him to come to his home state's aid. The political general, though, feared that immediately proceeding to Indianapolis would violate the orders recently received from Halleck. Wallace was told to await orders at Crawfordsville; he was not to leave the town until federal authorities contacted him.

Wallace's response surprised Morton, but the governor eagerly contacted Halleck, telling him that sources revealed that Morgan was now "in Indiana with 5,100 cavalry and six pieces of artillery." The governor desired Wallace's services "at once. I have no officers, and need his services badly."[56] Since Morgan might already be menacing the good citizens of southern Indiana, the governor's office sent a note to Crawfordsville asserting that Morton had telegraphed Halleck. The governor had not yet received a reply from the Union commander, but he needed Wallace immediately. Morton's assistant pleaded with the political general to come now, declaring that Morton would "stand between you and harm." Indiana desperately needed Wallace's services as "Morgan has between (4) four and (8) eight thousand and we have no officers."[57] These rebels were supposedly headed for Indianapolis, making the state government even more nervous. Wallace went to Indianapolis early the next day, arriving before Halleck sent a telegram directing him to report to Morton.[58]

Wallace met with the governor early on 11 July, and at his request took command of a detachment to move against Morgan, who was reported to be near Vernon, Indiana. This initial body of soldiers, numbering more than two thousand strong, consisted of two green regiments. The general proceeded to "the depot of the Madison and Indianapolis Railroad" in order to meet the troops that he planned to take south. Both regiments appeared by 11:00 A.M., but neither had any ammunition. Furthermore, the second to arrive had no rations. To Wallace's surprise, the combined strength of the raw units actually "was about 1,300 effective." Still, no matter the number of soldiers under his command, the general intended to move as soon as he could obtain ammunition. It arrived at approximately 4:00 P.M., making for at least a five-hour delay.[59]

When the train arrived in Columbus, Indiana, Wallace received word "that Morgan had surrounded Vernon; that General [John] Love was in the place with about 1,200 men."[60] The graycoats soon "demanded the surrender of the town," but Love refused, asking for immediate reinforcements.[61] The rebels supposedly numbered "about 8,000 strong, with six pieces of artillery." Wallace also learned at this time that the 15th Indiana Battery was following, ordered to report to him, so he waited for its arrival. This delay meant that Wallace and his command arrived in North Vernon after dark, and "Old" Vernon at about 6:00 A.M.[62] During this trip on the railroad, the general urged all involved to be as quiet as possible, but the locomotive's engineer continued to sound the whistle on occasion, possibly alerting Morgan to their approach. Consequently, the raiders had fled east by the time the Union troops debarked at the town's depot.[63]

The horsemen's movements convinced the political general that Morgan "would not fight if he could help it; also that, as against him, infantry could accomplish nothing more than the defense of towns and railroad bridges." The Hoosier wanted to apprehend the raiders, but he failed. The danger to Indiana soon ended. Wallace later determined that the state needed cavalry ready to face such a threat. He considered forced marches and tried to obtain extra wagons, in addition to using the railroad, but green infantrymen could not keep up with Morgan's raiders.[64]

On 12 July, Wallace received information that Morgan headed south, planning to cross the Ohio River just below the town of Madison, Indiana.[65] The Union general intended to follow the raiders and asked for extra companies to guard

Vernon since its residents were "very uneasy, and the country is full of straggling rebels."[66] The Indianan eventually received more troops, bringing his total to approximately 2,500 soldiers and officers on 13 July.[67] And even more men arrived by some time on the following day; so, on the 14th, Wallace had 4,500 effectives under his command.[68] These men he took to the town of Osgood, northeast of Vernon, instead of south to Madison, as he received information that Morgan was actually headed toward Ohio.

The tired soldiers arrived in Osgood on the 14th, from there marching hard to the town of Sunman, about fifteen miles from the Ohio state line.[69] The governor and Brig. Gen. Orlando Willcox, commanding the military District of Indiana and Michigan, urged Wallace to fall back closer to the capital city, or maybe go to Madison on the Ohio River. Still, the bold, aggressive, and undisciplined officer proceeded northeast toward the Ohio border.[70]

Maj. Gen. Ambrose Burnside, who was then in charge of defending Ohio from invasion, believed that Morgan might already be in Ohio. The former commander of the Army of the Potomac hoped that Wallace and his troops would hold their position at Sunman, a small town with a railroad station where an Indiana regiment already had faced some of Morgan's cavalry. From there, Burnside believed that they could readily assist Ohioans in capturing the rebel raiders.[71]

The next day, however, Burnside told Morton that the emergency had passed, at least for Indiana. After sending numerous telegrams over the last few days due to a fear that Morgan might make a run on Indianapolis, the governor seemed confident that the state was safe, ordering Wallace to come back to Indianapolis, so that militiamen could "be discharged and return to their homes without any unnecessary delay."[72] Willcox echoed the directive, asking whether transportation would be a problem.[73] Wallace was reluctant to give up the command, still hoping to participate in a meaningful fight that would prove his manliness, but he followed the order. He instructed his volunteers to return "impressed horses, wagons, and other property . . . for the purpose of delivering all such property to the proper owners," and then he put the troops on trains bound for the capital.[74]

Twelve days later, and back in Crawfordsville, Wallace defended his inability to catch Morgan by again emphasizing the need for horses in order to mount defending militia. He had tried to impress a number of wagons but could not find enough to quickly follow the rebels with the entire command. Approximately 160 horses allowed a few of his troops to better chase the Confederates, but this small number of cavalrymen could do little against thousands of the enemy. They did manage "quite a skirmish" with some of the graycoats near the town of Harrison on the state line, but the Union general wanted more, lamenting "that the Legion consists so entirely of infantry."[75]

Large conventional battles involving tens of thousands of men on both sides often required little of horsemen, but raids like Morgan's reminded everyone that mounted soldiers retained their offensive capabilities. Wallace certainly agreed, stating that two or "three regiments of cavalry would have stopped Morgan before he passed into Ohio." In conclusion, he "respectfully suggest[ed] attention to the organization of that arm of the service."[76] The political general offered good advice, but horses were in short supply since the entire Union army needed them for transportation. And, unfortunately for Wallace, command of a division or corps in the field did not come his way. After receiving the thanks of the governor, the general once again traveled to Crawfordsville to await orders.

In the meantime, additional repercussions resulted from Wallace's letter to Halleck. Trying to counter criticism of his performance at Shiloh, his letter had achieved nothing but ill will. Compounding this result, the Indianan decided to send a similar explanation of his actions near Pittsburg Landing to Secretary of War Stanton. Just a few days after the scare over Morgan's raid had ended, the Hoosier told Stanton that if Grant's claim that the 3rd Division had been ordered to go directly to Pittsburg Landing was true, "then, in marching to a point so distant from Pittsburg Landing, I was guilty of a disobedience of orders, for which, in the disastrous turn of the battle at the time, there can be but slender apology." Furthermore, if Grant's statement in late April of 1862 was "true, then I am also guilty of making a false report in a very material matter."[77]

Grant's account of how he sent staff, on two separate occasions, to hurry Wallace to the battlefield also irritated the political general, who declared that such "imputations contained in the sentence quoted are of the gravest character. If they are true, I am unfit to hold a commission of any kind in the United States Army." Moreover, the "imputations can be easily shaped into charges of cowardice and treachery, and I regret to say such charges have been made and are yet existing against me in consequence of the time it took me to reach the battle-field from my position at Crump's Landing."[78]

Wallace also bristled over Grant's fifteen-month old statement "that there are some other particulars in my [Wallace's] official report which he cannot fully indorse." Again, the Indianan believed that this "amounts to saying that I have made a false report." He clearly felt that he had been wronged by the statements in Grant's indorsement of late April in 1862. In his opinion, the time had come for a court of inquiry, and "the scope of its investigation may cover my whole conduct in connection with the battle of Pittsburg Landing." Wallace even asked for a particular prosecutor, so that "this investigation may be full and complete."[79] Such comments from Grant were too much for a man bent on self-made, honorable, martial success; it would have been difficult for Wallace to react in any other way. The request must have surprised and irritated Stanton, who was unclear about how to proceed. On 24 July, he forwarded the letter to the general in chief, Halleck.[80]

Refusing to simply wait for answers from Stanton or Halleck, Wallace made an unlikely contact in August; he decided to ask Maj. Gen. William T. Sherman for his advice on how to again secure a major field command. Sherman had been part of Grant's successful siege of Vicksburg, Mississippi, which surrendered to Union forces on 4 July 1863. Wallace congratulated him on his latest achievements and then "asked him to give me some duty, stating if it were under him—he was yet my junior—I would be most happy."[81]

This latest communication, unlike many others Wallace had made to people with clout, must have been well worded. It also surprised Sherman, who was not sure of how to respond. Therefore, he wrote to John Rawlins, Grant's chief of staff. Sherman stated that he had received "a long and very proper letter from General Lew. Wallace, speaking in terms of great respect for General Grant, but evidently restrained from expressing them direct." Asking Rawlins what he thought of "answering him [Wallace] in a kind tone and holding out to him a hope of again serving, with modified notions," Sherman argued that Wallace "was laggard [at Shiloh], but has he no good qualities which, with proper cultivation, might save his honor and be of use to the service?"[82]

Sherman's confidential letter to Rawlins failed to result in a field command for Wallace, but the head of the XV Army Corps did send a gracious reply to the Hoosier on 27 August. Sherman explained his regret that all of the generals who began Grant's grand campaign in the West were not still in command, further stressing that Wallace's good work at Donelson was just as important as the late results at Vicksburg. He promised to talk to Grant on the Indianan's behalf, planning "to convey to him your proper expressions of confidence without in the least compromising your delicate sense of honor." Sherman believed that Grant still held Wallace's soldierly abilities in high regard, and that the hero of Donelson, Shiloh, and Vicksburg "would readily aid you to regain the high position you held in the estimation of the country."[83] The words amounted to less than a promise of a command in the field, but they at least lessened Wallace's fears that Grant hated him.

Stressing the greater good of the country, possibly at the expense of the individual, Sherman wished that every general had "an appropriate command, and that all should learn from our short military career that we can only gain a permanent fame by subordinating ourselves and our peculiar notions to that of the common commander"—Grant in this case. Not wanting to sound too critical, the corps commander declined to say that Wallace had "not always done this, but I do think if I were you I would not press an inquiry into the old matter of the Crump's Landing and Shiloh march, but leave that till war is over." Sherman believed that subsequent "events may sweep that into the forgotten of the past."

For now, the corps commander advised "that as soon as possible you regain command of a division, identify yourself with it, *keep as quiet as possible*, and trust to opportunity for a becoming sequel to the brilliant beginning you had."[84] It was good advice for Wallace, who had a bad habit of aggravating superiors. In fact, the letter outlined the sort of professional, disciplined, dutiful, restrained behavior instilled in West Point graduates.[85] At the same time, the suggestions were designed to eliminate wartime problems for Grant, Sherman's friend.

The rest of Sherman's letter echoed the first half. The corps commander also asserted that he did "not think that General Grant or any other officer has any unkind feelings towards" Wallace, but some may have been jealous of his early successes. Sherman further urged him to be patient, and that in doing so he would eventually have the opportunity to be fully appreciated.[86] The frank letter offered sensible advice, and some hope that the author would find the Hoosier a command. Understanding now that an inquiry into events at Shiloh would make it difficult for Grant or Sherman to help him, Wallace soon asked Stanton to "please suspend action in the matter of my request for a court of inquiry until I communicate with you again on the subject." He was now convinced by Sherman's comments that it might be possible to "satisfy General Grant upon the points involved and thus save further trouble."[87]

In the interim, Wallace respectfully told Stanton that he was "ready and anxious to go to any duty."[88] This concluding sentence to the telegram turned out to be untrue. In mid-September, Governor Morton again asked if the idle general could assist him in recruiting young men to fight for Indiana and the Union, but Wallace still worried about previous orders telling him to stay in Crawfordsville until directed otherwise. More importantly for the general, he disliked the thought of performing duties away from the battlefield, not understanding that such actions might lead to division command.

Despite Wallace's reservations, Morton telegraphed the secretary of war in order to adjust the general's orders, so that he could "speak at such places in Indiana as may be desired."[89] Stanton had no problem with the request, emphasizing that Wallace was "at liberty to render you assistance in any part of the State."[90] After getting this permission from the secretary of war, the governor believed that the general would come to Indianapolis to receive his recruiting assignments. Although the Crawfordsville politician had resisted giving speeches on a previous occasion, Morton's private secretary told Wallace that he had been authorized "to report to the Governor."[91]

Wallace's reaction was even more negative than one might have expected. Writing to Stanton, the general declared that he "never authorized anybody to apply to you to grant me permission to make speeches anywhere." After all, "armies are moving, battles being fought." The temperamental officer further explained that he was "ashamed at being made to stay at home. How much more would I be ashamed to go about making speeches." One might argue that the general could have made a deal in such a situation—deliver speeches in exchange for the governor's aid in obtaining command of at least a brigade, or maybe a division, but the Indianan failed to consider such a strategy. Perhaps the next four or five regiments recruited out of Indiana could serve under Wallace? The political general refused to think about the possibility, even though other officers had made such agreements.[92] In conclusion, he explained that for "months past I have been your respectful beggar for duty in the field. I am so yet, and shall continue. I decline reporting to Governor Morton."[93] The Hoosier general believed that his telegram was satisfactorily respectful, but the secretary of war saw things differently.

Even though Wallace had been difficult to deal with, the governor forgave the general for refusing to give the speeches.[94] Moreover, Morton wrote to Stanton, asking him to allow the idle general to visit Chattanooga, so that he presumably could lobby Union generals there for a command in the field.[95] The secretary, however, declined to answer in the affirmative. He stated that since Wallace "recently, in very curt not to say disrespectful terms, disavowed your [Morton's] authority to make an application for him which was granted by the Department, I must be excused from considering any request not coming from himself in respect to him."[96] Again, the frustrated general had added to his own problems.

On the following day, Wallace found out about Stanton's reply to Morton, so the general sent a quick apology, claiming that he did not mean for his most "recent dispatch to be in the least disrespectful to you or Governor Morton." The Indianan's "design was to say in short telegraph way that I wish to go to duty in the field—not on the stump." Wallace further argued that the "telegram to make speeches was sent to you by the governor, after consultation with my friends, but without consultation with me." In his mind, the governor had mistreated him in arranging for the speechmaking, not getting the general's full permission. On the other hand, the "request to go to Chattanooga was made through his department at my instance."[97]

The secretary of war received and read the telegram but failed to easily forgive the temperamental general for his latest outburst. A new command in the field would not quickly come from Stanton in Washington. Most unfortunately for Wallace, the letter to Sherman also led to nothing. The corps commander, writing from Memphis in October, told Wallace that he had talked to Grant about the possibility of a new command. Neither commander could provide a spot for him without demoting someone else, or at least that was the story. While Sherman offered only bad news, he delivered it with kind words.[98] Maybe the sympathetic general neglected to do as much as he could to help, but he at least handled the matter delicately—in a manner that should have influenced the frustrated officer.

Wallace continued to injure his relationships with superiors like Stanton, Halleck, Morton and Grant. He saw himself as the kind of fighting man that President Lincoln liked, full of courage and the willingness to take the war to the citizenry of the South, but his impatience and temperamental nature routinely got in the way of securing a chance to prove it. Despite serving his country at Camp Chase and as a commissioner investigating Don Carlos Buell, Wallace found no way to turn such service into a significant field command. He served Morton during Morgan's latest raid north, but his aggressive reactions to setbacks and slights seemed to negate any goodwill achieved while assisting his home state. Consequently, the political general spent most of late 1863 and early 1864 in Indiana, finally taking Sherman's advice to wait more patiently for the opportunity he had been looking for. An opportunity eventually came, but it was not quite what Wallace wanted.

SEVEN

"A Command Worthy of His Rank"

The *Crawfordsville Journal*, an organ of the Republican Party in Lew Wallace's hometown, noted on 10 March 1864 that the general had just departed for Washington. The paper speculated, "We trust the time will speedily come when Gen. Wallace will be assigned a command in the field worthy of his rank."[1] The Hoosier would have been thrilled to take command of a division in the field; that was what he had yearned for ever since he left the Army of the Tennessee in June of 1862. But, to his disappointment, Wallace's next assignment was an administrative command of the Middle Department, including Delaware and Eastern Maryland, with headquarters in Baltimore. Wallace would command the VIII Army Corps as well, whose regiments and companies were scattered across the department, attempting to keep order in states populated by numerous rebel sympathizers.[2] Command of the Middle Department offered a chance to redeem himself for the lingering negative impressions after Shiloh.

Lack of professional military training, the impression that he lacked soldierly skills, an absence of restraint, and his uncooperative nature made a field appointment unlikely for Wallace. He had managed to irritate a number of superiors, including Ulysses Grant, Henry Halleck, Edwin Stanton, and Oliver Morton. Luckily for Wallace, President Lincoln refused to hold a grudge. Furthermore, Lincoln understood that there were many critics of his administration in Indiana.[3] Therefore, appointing a friendly Indianan to an important command made political sense, especially during a presidential election year.

There were other good reasons to send Wallace to Baltimore. An election for delegates to a Maryland constitutional convention approached, and the president needed someone with political savvy to take control of the Middle Department. Marylanders were considering a constitutional amendment to abolish slavery

in their state, and residents sympathetic to the Confederacy would likely vote for pro-slavery delegates. Wallace's political experience in the West might aid his efforts in the East, but the legacy of his father, a former governor, and the connections of his brother-in-law, Henry S. Lane, were not guaranteed to work to his advantage in the new position. Could he make use of these political skills and connections in time of war? That remained to be seen. Moreover, the presidential election of 1864 drew near; in a close election every electoral vote could be vital. Winning Maryland could be key to winning the election. Wallace's assignment was predominantly political and making political contributions there could please the president and the secretary of war, leading to a future command in the field.

According to Wallace, Halleck, who was relegated to chief of staff of the U.S. Army in March, protested Lincoln's decision to assign the eager general to command of the Middle Department. Stanton likely informed Lincoln of his negative opinion of Wallace as well, but the president disregarded their advice. [He wanted to see if Wallace could do the job, despite the criticism.]Wallace later recalled that "there was an added sweetness to it [the president's rebuff of Halleck] so strong that my disappointment in not being sent to the field was at once and most agreeably allayed."[4] As this comment reveals, Wallace and Halleck would never again be on friendly terms.[5]

It is likely that Henry Lane, Wallace's brother-in-law and a Republican U.S. senator from Indiana, encouraged the president to give the general a second chance. The senator had used his influence to get his relative a commission as brigadier general in 1861, and now did his best to obtain Wallace a notable command. After arriving in Washington, the general wrote to his wife, stating that he was "delighted to find that Lane stands first in official influence and public esteem." The senator's political standing had contributed to another appointment for Wallace. Nevertheless, the new commander of the Middle Department still worried because his brother-in-law was "powerful against everybody except Halleck."[6]

Receiving his orders, Wallace decided to first pay his respects to President Lincoln, whom he had last met nearly two years earlier. He had called on the president in June 1862, hoping to convince Lincoln to give him a new field command. On the second meeting, according to Wallace, the president cordially greeted him, mentioned the April election in Maryland, and then sent him on his way.[7]

His next stop caused some anxiety. He had to meet with Secretary of War Stanton, whom he had angered in 1863 by rudely denying that Governor Morton had the authority to ask for his services to assist with recruiting and the defense of Indiana from Confederate raiders such as John Morgan.[8] To Wallace's relief, Stanton failed to mention the incident. The secretary of war stressed, as had the president, the importance of the upcoming election for representatives to the constitutional convention, and that any evidence of the Lincoln administration or the army tampering with proceedings would be very unfortunate for the president's reelection campaign. Many Americans, Democrats in particular, worried about the participation of soldiers in any part of the electoral process; the potential danger to the republic seemed apparent to many who feared the power of standing armies. The general understood these points. The two men said a quick goodbye, and Wallace made his way to Baltimore.[9]

Arriving in Baltimore, the general immediately issued an order taking command.[10] Wallace realized, from his conversations with the president and the secretary of war, that the department was "crowded with perplexities, and for that reason I pray all good men residing in it to unite and give me their earnest support, more for their own welfare than for mine."[11] These "perplexities" included a large number of rebel sympathizers, the constant presence of spies, the continual drain of men from the department in order to fill the needs of the Army of the Potomac, and often uncooperative local politicians.

The westerner had an idea of the potential problems in this eastern department, but a full understanding came later. By July, Susan Wallace had determined that the "city is rebel to the core." Furthermore, her husband found it difficult to get Union men in the state to cooperate since the "small Union party is divided into radicals, led by [U.S. Congressman Henry] Winter Davis, & conservatives, headed by [U.S. Senator] Reverdy Johnson." As if all of these handicaps were not enough, Susan asserted later in July that the "authorities at Washington constantly interfere with all Lew does & he really is so harassed and walled in by political influence the poor man is nearly ready to throw up the whole thing."[12] All of these problems presented themselves during the first few months of Wallace's assignment in Maryland. They complicated his efforts to complete his first big task, a secure and uncontroversial election of delegates to a constitutional convention expected to determine the future of slavery in Maryland and possibly the general's chances to resume field command.

Fortunately for President Lincoln, Wallace was just the man to carry out the administration's policies in Maryland. During the war, the recently converted Republican developed a hatred for slavery, especially after observing the institution in Kentucky and Tennessee. Wallace, though, was not a radical. While he advocated abolition, as a politician he was not convinced to condone more controversial measures, such as civil and political rights for freedmen. Earlier in 1864, the general suggested to his brother "that the fanatics of Massachusetts do govern the country. I begin to think that, if they go on at the present rate, white men will be leveled down to equality with the contraband." He believed that the Republican Party might be in danger of splitting or becoming too radical. Wallace asserted "that Old Abe is right after all—Conservatism is a necessity" if the party wished to maintain its hold on Congress and the presidency.[13] Lincoln needed a commander who would carry out his wishes while not grandstanding or overplaying his authority, actions that would fuel Democratic criticisms that the president and his party wished blacks and whites to be equals politically and socially. Historian Thomas J. Goss suggests that Lincoln often gave commands to political generals because he believed that an individual could deliver on a defined mandate and maintain "the impression of Union success." Well, the general now had his mandate.[14]

Wallace soon learned that many Union men had sent requests for troops to guard polling places in the upcoming election.[15] Yet Lincoln and Stanton prohibited the use of the bayonet in such cases. After some thought, the general wondered whether he might get around this restriction with the help of the governor, Augustus W. Bradford. None of his new staff could remember a time in which a past commander had even bothered to call upon the governor; and, furthermore, no one knew for certain whether or not Bradford genuinely supported the Union.[16] The general determined to find out.[17]

Wallace and his entire staff dressed formally, including all regalia, and took the train to Annapolis to call upon the governor in the statehouse. The appearance of the new department commander's staff in their fanciest garb impressed the governor. After introductions, Wallace presented Bradford some of the petitions asking for election guards that the headquarters had received. The general then asked, "If, fast as such petitions come to me, I send them properly endorsed to you, governor, what will you do with them?"[18] After a pause, Bradford stated that he would return the petitions to Wallace with an official request that troops be sent to those districts. This response delighted Wallace, and the governor was equally delighted that the political general acknowledged his authority as the chief executive of Maryland. At least one previous commander had displeased Bradford through the "usurpation of his authority."[19] But it turned out that Bradford was a cautious pro-Union man, taking office in 1862 as a Union party candidate, and this meeting helped forge a decent working relationship.[20] While

Wallace could not always count on the governor to back him up, neither would they be enemies.

The success of the commander's meeting with the governor suggested that Lincoln's assignment of Wallace had been a good one. Nevertheless, the perplexities of the department presented themselves again almost immediately after the cordial meeting in Annapolis. Wallace discovered that Elbridge G. Kilbourne, a conservative politician and formerly a state senator, had been arrested, presumably for openly anti-Union remarks, but then released. Arresting this man a second time might warn others who openly protested the Union. More importantly to Wallace, Kilbourne had announced his candidacy for a seat in the constitutional election; confining him would violate the orders of President Lincoln. While arresting men like Kilbourne tended to quiet the Southern sympathizers in Maryland, jailing a candidate to the convention would raise questions about army interference in the political process—even the validity of the election itself.[21]

The general decided to test his relationship with the governor. On 24 March, Wallace sent Bradford a letter outlining the situation, emphasizing that Kilbourne's election would be "incompatible with loyal interests." The officer hoped that the governor would inform him of the most proper course to take in this case, again drawing attention away from the military authority in the state. In conclusion, Wallace repeated his appreciation for any cooperation that might "advance the interests of the Union and promote the welfare of the noble people who have honored you with their chief magistracy."[22] It does not appear that Wallace received any help from the governor in this case, but the attempt to use the office of the chief executive to his advantage amply demonstrated the commander's new political savvy. In the end, Wallace interrogated Kilbourne, discovering that he had been speaker of the House of Delegates that considered secession for the state of Maryland, and he had voted in favor of leaving the Union. The general convinced the man to withdraw "his name from the canvass," without serious incident.[23]

Governor Bradford answered Wallace's letter with a request that the general investigate an alleged crime that occurred on 9 March.[24] Lt. Col. Joseph G. Perkins, in charge of the 19th Infantry, U.S. Colored Troops, having orders to release some former slaves from a local jail, instead released all ex-slaves and all but one free black man. It may have been considered a humane act, for the conditions of this jail were poor, but it was still illegal. The governor's agent forwarded some testimony in the case, reasserting the state government's willingness to assist Wallace.[25] The general delicately and quietly handled the situation so as to not produce fodder for the Democratic newspapers of Maryland. Perkins likely received no penalty, as Wallace allowed him and his regiment to be transferred to the Army of the Potomac, in which they served through the end of the war.[26]

With other men like Kilbourne still running for seats in the constitutional convention, the future of slavery in Maryland was not certain. It was hard for anyone to gauge the strength of pro-slavery and anti-Union sentiment. Harboring one view did not necessarily mean that a man harbored the other, which further complicated matters. The general, therefore, determined to do what he could to legally assist in an outcome to the election satisfactory to Republicans.

On the 25th, Wallace ordered his adjutant, Lt. Col. Samuel B. Lawrence, to contact four of his senior subordinate officers: Gen. Henry H. Lockwood, Gen. Erastus B. Tyler, and Gen. Daniel Tyler, as well as Col. P. A. Porter. The commanding general hoped, since the release of Lincoln's Emancipation Proclamation, that most Union soldiers were inclined to equate Union victory with a defeat of slavery. As a result, Wallace wished the officers "to inform him whether anything exists making it incompatible with the public interests to grant furloughs to such members of Maryland regiments in your command, as are legal voters and desire to visit their homes for the purpose of exercising the elective franchise, on the 6th of April next."[27] He further requested that the officers give an estimate of the number of soldiers needing furloughs. Republican leaders would use this strategy in several elections in 1864, and they seldom hid "the partisanship behind their furlough decisions," but it was more important for the general to tread carefully.[28]

Wallace followed up this request with thorough directions to the brigade commanders on the 29th. The general commanded that soldiers travel to the polling places "in squads or by companies" with "their arms and accoutrements." Furthermore, men should be sent in the "charge of a commissioned officer," and only to "localities where they are entitled to vote." When the polling places opened, the soldiers had to rendezvous at an agreed-upon location, leave their weapons there under sufficient guard, and then proceed, as a group, to vote. Once the squad or company voted, they were to return and collect their arms. The officer in charge needed to inform the judge of election of this rendezvous. The judge could request military assistance at any point during the voting. Being doubly cautious, Wallace also stipulated that the officer in charge only carry ten rounds of ammunition, only distributing it if absolutely necessary.[29]

Such actions would surely diminish the true strength of the forces needed to guard the polling places, but the mere presence of soldiers voting, even if unarmed, might encourage a secure election with little or no violence. Receiving positive responses from his brigade commanders, Wallace repeatedly requested that Maryland men in different regiments and companies be allowed furloughs in order to vote. It turned out to be a less controversial way to keep order at the polling places, especially at those where officials failed to request direct assistance. Wallace also believed that the soldiers tended to vote for anti-slavery candidates. That conclusion was debatable, as soldiers did not necessarily have such an ideological conversion, but Republican Party men echoed Wallace's thoughts.[30]

It gratified Wallace to learn that the president approved of his actions. During the last week in March, the president asked to meet with him, presumably to discuss the election. When the general arrived in Washington, he explained how he had contacted the governor, arranged for guards at polling places, and ordered furloughs for Marylanders in the department wishing to vote. These decisions pleased the president, and he suggested that "getting Governor Bradford between you and the enemy here in Congress" was a "good thing."[31] He thanked Wallace, and then sent the general to speak with Stanton.

Lincoln sent a note along with the commander stating that Wallace was "getting along with the matter we wished to see him for." It "is a great point which he seems to be effecting, to get Gov. Bradford and Hon. H. Winter Davis together." With Wallace's encouragement, the radical Republican congressman, Davis, and the governor were beginning to work together to further the interests of the administration. The president concluded by stating, "I have told him to be fair, but to give the benefit of all doubts to the emancipationists."[32] The general's political savvy also impressed Stanton. After meeting with his superiors, Wallace made his way back to Baltimore in order to continue preparations for the April election.

In the meantime, Lawrence, Wallace's adjutant, investigated an article printed in the *Baltimore Daily Gazette* titled "Negro Equality," a sarcastic commentary on the upcoming election and the potential emancipation of Maryland's slaves. The article claimed to be the work of anti-slavery candidates in the upcoming election but was obviously an attempt by someone else to ridicule emancipation and those who might support the idea. The article began by urging immediate freedom for all the "poor enslaved negroes, without compensation to their owners." It declared that "when strikes for higher wages, in our mining and manufacturing districts, takes [sic] place on the part of whites, they can be turned adrift and their places filled with free blacks." Moreover, blacks should be able to vote, hold office, sit on juries, and "testify in courts of justice, against whites as well as blacks." The anonymous author claimed his ideas were advocated by all in the Republican Party, and that five men, whose names appeared at the end of the article, would certainly vote for emancipation at the convention if they were indeed elected on 6 April.[33]

The commanding general was likely concerned that such an article would convince some Marylanders to vote for pro-slavery candidates. In most cases, it would have been difficult for Wallace to investigate a political article without causing a political stir against the Lincoln administration. The piece, however, claimed to be the work of someone with direct ties to anti-slavery men seeking election. Such a claim could be seen as libel, so the commander asked Lieutenant Colonel Lawrence to look into the matter.

On the 29th, Wallace sent, via his adjutant, a letter to the editor of the *Gazette* requesting "a report to him of all the circumstances connected" with the article on "Negro Equality." Wallace also demanded to know "by whose authority it was published."[34] The editor of the Democratic organ neglected to send back a satisfactory answer. Highly irritated, the commanding general again demanded to know by "whom was the circular in question left at the Gazette Office."[35] Wallace never received a satisfactory answer, and this confrontation with the editor of the *Gazette* was not the last.

On 30 March, the commander of the Middle Department disclosed to Governor Bradford that disloyal persons were candidates in the upcoming election. Wallace had papers enclosed that he believed would make this case. The commander further worried that disloyal men would attempt to vote for these disloyal candidates. The lawyer-turned-general suggested that the oath of allegiance, taken by men before sitting in any legislative body in Maryland, required that disloyal residents be excluded as candidates. It may, he hoped, also be interpreted as giving judges of election the authority to turn away disloyal voters. Since the governor gave that oath, Wallace believed that Bradford had some say in this matter, and the general strongly encouraged him to offer an opinion. Attuned to his political role, Wallace reasserted his appreciation of their newfound cooperation, and hoped that the governor might assist him in this matter, just as he assisted him with the petitions for guards at the polling places.[36]

During the first five days of April, Wallace spent most of his time answering questions about furloughs, reasserting that men must be sent to the polls in squads or companies, and emphasizing that passes should not be given to anyone except eligible voters unless absolutely necessary.[37] In a letter to his wife, who remained in Crawfordsville with their son, Wallace lamented that "I have had to devote my energy almost exclusively to the election."[38]

Election day, 6 April, proceeded almost as planned. Troops were sent to every precinct requesting them, and in many instances the appearance of what pro-Confederates called "blue-coated hirelings" near the polling places "so enraged the Secessionists they refused to go to the polls." Thus, the convention was eventually held, and an amendment to the state constitution abolished slavery.[39] Wallace had delivered on a presidential mandate; his ability to follow and understand the importance of the president's guidelines, cordial relations with the governor, attention to detail, careful management of furloughs, and judicious stationing of troops at key locations resulted in an orderly election favorable to pro-Union supporters. The soldiers' votes were likely not decisive in this case, but it was the uniformed men's potentially controversial presence that had the desired effect.[40]

The general heard occasional complaints, usually from pro-slavery men. There were the infrequent misunderstandings in which a noncommissioned officer and his squad or company did not carry out their duties to the letter. These problems were to be expected, and they were minor.[41] Only one notable confrontation occurred on election day. The incident happened early in the day; voters of the 14th Maryland Cavalry and Alexander's Battery protested "against marching to the polls in one body." During past elections, the soldiers traveled to the polls as individuals. Since this was the custom, the men requested that they be exempted from this order. Such a request caused a degree of discontent, which was rather late in surfacing; therefore, the commander was not in a mood to bend his rules. Wallace ordered that the squads should go "without arms," and that the order should be carried out "at once."[42] These men were certainly not happy with the reply, but they followed the order, while no other major disturbances presented themselves during the day.

The election was an all-around success for the Lincoln administration. Of the ninety-six delegates elected, sixty-one were emancipationists and only thirty-five opposed freeing Maryland's slaves.[43] The president wanted someone with political astuteness to handle the election in Maryland, and he found that person in Wallace. The Lincoln administration managed to please constituents in Indiana who wanted Wallace to receive a command fitting his rank, and the Federal government managed to come to the support of Republicans in Maryland without giving Democrats numerous chances to argue that the election had been tampered with. The election results thrilled Congressman Davis. The radical Republican lauded Wallace's handling of Governor Bradford, emphasizing that the Indianan pleased a number of important Marylanders. Referring to the happy constituents, Davis asserted that the departmental commander could add his "voice to the Chorus [sic] of their eulogies."[44]

Moreover, according to the general, his handling of the election was received well by many U.S. senators. Senator Willard Saulsbury (D-DE) did accuse the commander of inappropriately interfering in the election, but he could not provide satisfactory proof. As a result, Henry Lane and Reverdy Johnson managed to defend Wallace "handsomely."[45] Senator Saulsbury may have been referring to some reports in the *Baltimore Daily Gazette* during the week following the election. Returns were received daily and published in the various papers. The *Gazette*, basically opposed to the Lincoln administration, asserted that instances of fraud occurred in a few counties. For example, a judge in one district openly challenged a number of dissenting voters in Kent County. Fortunately for Wallace, such problems directly concerned the judges of election and the oath administered to the voters, seldom the soldiers voting or guarding at the polling places.[46] Often, submissions to the *Gazette* insinuated that these problems were directly related to the presence of soldiers, but limited evidence surfaced to suggest inappropriate activity on the part of the army.[47] The general completed this task approximately two weeks into his administration of the Middle Department. Now, with the election behind him, it was time to settle in to the everyday duties of the command.

Wallace's successful management of the election was even more impressive considering that the actions of disloyal persons and the siphoning of troops away from his command preoccupied him. Even though the election was most important to the Lincoln administration, the general could not ignore multiple cases of disloyal activity. Marylanders—men and women—were smuggling, spying, and agitating all on behalf of the Confederacy. He repeatedly ordered the investigation or arrest of suspicious persons in his department, and he often had to deal with the consequences of those arrests.[48]

Wallace also expelled citizens he viewed as disloyal. For example, on 30 March, the general ordered that a woman and her children be expelled from the state, via Fortress Monroe. A day later, he changed the order, stating that the family's departure should be delayed. The change was not out of kindness. Wallace hoped that the extra time would allow the woman to collect materials that his men might find in her luggage before she left for Fortress Monroe.[49]

The realization that women were spying for the Confederacy led Wallace to request that Col. P. A. Porter, commanding the 2nd Brigade, "inform him whether the casemates at Fort Carroll can be fitted up for reception for safe keeping of female prisoners violating the military laws and orders of this Dept."[50] In addition to worrying about what the commander called "the fairer sex," Wallace spent time keeping his troops out of trouble.

Also leading up to 30 March, the general received numerous complaints "against the drinking saloons in the vicinity of the Northern Central Depot" in Baltimore. It appeared that some saloons had become dens of disloyal activities, and the commander could not let them remain in business. Moreover, many complaints had been made against drunken soldiers in the various bars of that area. On the 30th, Wallace ordered that saloons near the depot be closed, and if the directive was disobeyed, soldiers were to arrest the owners.[51] These arrests complicated matters when the disorderly persons were politically connected, especially if they proceeded to beg Stanton or the president for mercy.

As the above incidents, and Wallace's reactions, suggest, occupation duty did not usually lead to the barbaric "hard war" actions of legend. For example, even Benjamin "Beast" Butler in New Orleans strategized "to make a few dramatic examples that would give the citizens of the occupied city pause before trifling with Federal authority. In many respects, his overall policy was temperate. He permitted most New Orleans newspapers to publish with a minimum of censorship, allowed the rabidly secessionist clergy to preach in relative freedom, and took firm steps to ensure that residents of the city received sufficient rations."[52] While the hard-war policy in place by early 1864 led to significant, but discriminate, destruction as Union armies moved across the South, occupation of a border state did not warrant similar actions. The major general needed to be very selective, or pragmatic, in his approach; that was usually the case. But there were instances in which he would do more than the Lincoln administration desired.

Throughout his assignment, Wallace received letters complaining of rebel activities in parts of Maryland or Delaware. For example, on 21 April, the provost marshal forwarded a letter from a resident of the Eastern Shore to Wallace reporting that "Seceshism [sic] is almost intolerable" in the vicinity of Galena, a town on the eastern side of the Chesapeake Bay. The author claimed that local governments in the area were either anti-Union or scared to oppose anti-Union partisans, and disloyal citizens had circulated a "scandalous and infamous work" titled "the Lincoln Catechism," which Union men could do nothing about. The writer feared that such activity would endanger Lincoln's chances for reelection and promote all sorts of disloyal activities.[53] The cumulative effect of spies, agents, and such statements—as well as Wallace's own strong Union views and tendency to overreact—may have driven him to take drastic action.

On 24 April, the commander acknowledged that military commissions in his department had convicted four persons as spies since he took command in March. On that date, the general wrote that a rebel soldier had been convicted of espionage. The military commission sentenced him to death, just like three others before him. One more alleged spy was about "to be tried, with every prospect of a similar finding." The general hoped to hang them all immediately, so he proposed to go to Washington to beg the president for such permission. Wallace was certain that prompt action was "the only means of stopping like intrusions into" the department.[54] President Lincoln's kind heart often produced pardons for such criminals, and the general hoped to prevent such an occurrence in these cases.

On 28 April, more letters from the Eastern Shore of Maryland convinced the general to write to the U.S. Army's adjutant general, E. D. Townsend, suggesting that he would "have to proclaim martial law over" seven different counties east of Chesapeake Bay. Wallace begged Townsend for seven companies of infantry to enforce the law. He hoped that Stanton would understand the situation, and that martial law enforced by non-Maryland infantry was "absolutely essential to enable me to administer to his [Stanton's] satisfaction the affairs of this department."[55]

Up until this point, most of the general's actions pleased the secretary of war and the president. A possible declaration of martial law, on the other hand, was just the sort of action that Lincoln refused to condone in Maryland, especially during a presidential election year. Nevertheless, on 3 May, Wallace again asked for permission to declare martial law.[56] Townsend responded by clearly stating that such a move did not meet with Stanton's approval.[57] Wallace believed that if the department could only be supplied with additional companies or regiments, martial law might not be necessary, but requesting more troops did no good. This refusal forced the commander to take other measures. When rumors abounded that furloughed rebel cavalry were spying on the streets of Baltimore, martial law was not an option. Only significant guerilla activity that endangered numerous lives, as experienced in occupied areas farther south or west, might have warranted such a move.[58]

In the end, Wallace could only encourage the Baltimore Police Department to assist in monitoring disloyal activity in Maryland's largest city. These steps, unfortunately, provided little to suppress anti-Union voices on the Eastern Shore.[59] Furthermore, even the Baltimore police could not handle the smuggling and espionage that occurred in the nighttime. As a quiet compromise, the general allowed the police to secure Maryland's largest city during the day while soldiers patrolled the streets at night. This arrangement provided for martial law without a declaration. It was effective, and the objections were minimal.[60]

Wallace further tried to hinder the secessionists' activity by attacking their pocketbooks. In a general order on 26 April, the commander proclaimed that many people currently residing in, or visiting, the department were encouraging the rebellion. In response, he ordered that the assets of such persons be withheld by banks, railroad companies, factories, and other businesses. These assets would include slaves. Confiscated monies were to be delivered to the quartermaster general of the department. On 1 May, the general issued General Orders No. 33, clarifying policy and demanding that businesses provide the department with names of those suspected to be sympathetic to the rebellion.[61]

The general hoped that the orders would be in line with the president's anti-slavery policy, and that the confiscation of funds would greatly reduce anti-Union activity in Maryland. But the president did not wish to force emancipation on a border state, and he believed that Wallace had assumed too much authority. According to Stanton, "issuing these orders without his instructions you have transcended the power vested in you as a major-general and commander of a department. He instructs me also to say to you that the authority claimed to be exercised by you in these orders is a power vested in him alone, and only to be exercised by a subordinate officer when directed to do so by the President."[62] The commander promptly revoked the orders, but he had once again managed to do something politically damaging for the administration.[63] Wallace handled the election well, but the later miscues with regard to martial law and general orders on 26 April and 1 May again demonstrated his tendency to assume too much, to believe that his bold, manly actions would impress his superiors.

In addition to arranging for furloughs, and numerous dealings with potential criminals and disloyal persons, the commanding general asked his brigade commanders to forward reports that included clear maps with troop posts clearly visible.[64] The politician-turned-general wanted to have a good idea of what regiments currently resided in his department, because demands from the Army of the Potomac were steadily depleting the VIII Army Corps. Wallace worried that he would not have sufficient numbers to defend Maryland and Delaware from rebel raids, much less guard polling places. Beginning in April, he suspected that sorely needed troops would only remain in Maryland and Delaware until field generals called for reinforcements. As Grant's campaign into the Wilderness began, it became clear that the Middle Department would not be a permanent posting for most regiments. Writing to Susan on his thirty-seventh birthday,

Wallace suggested that one "thing is very observable . . . and that is the immensity of the preparation in progress." Countless regiments were traveling across his department, most heading for the Army of the Potomac, and none were to remain in Maryland. He believed that if "Grant fails it will not be for want of means."[65]

On 14 April, Wallace voiced his displeasure with the drawing of men away from his department. Writing to Adjutant General Lorenzo Thomas, he begged that the "3rd Regiment Maryland Veteran Volunteers may be permitted to remain" in their home state. They had just been ordered to serve in the Army of the Cumberland, but the commander of the VIII Army Corps desperately needed them to guard the depot camp. He could no longer use the Veteran Reserve Corps, because it had been withdrawn, and the other troops of his command were scattered all over the state at important points.[66]

Just one week later, Wallace received word that "some gentlemen of this city [Baltimore] have been soliciting the Secretary of War to send off" the 8th New York Heavy Artillery. The commander had no idea who made such a request, but it was in error and without his authorization. According to the general, the 5th New York Artillery had just been ordered to Harpers Ferry, so losing another would "strip free the Defenses of Baltimore." While his superiors often ordered men away from the department, other local "gentlemen" seemed to be interested in removing as many regiments as possible from Maryland.[67]

Such exchanges between Wallace and Thomas, Townsend, Stanton, or Halleck occurred quite often after the election of 6 April. The commander of the Middle Department understood the importance of his department's location, since any assault on Baltimore or Washington would likely come through Maryland. He needed plenty of troops to defend the area, and the commander did not, and would not, ever be granted enough regiments to adequately guard the different localities of the department. Wallace almost never got his way, and likely managed to further irritate Halleck with his protests.

Halleck exhibited distaste for political generals, and particularly Wallace, in an exchange of letters in April. After Grant showed interest in removing Nathaniel Banks from command, Halleck suggested that "the President will consent to the order if you insist upon General Banks' removal as a military necessity, but he will do so very reluctantly, as it would give offense to many of his friends." Even if Banks was removed from his command in Louisiana, he had "many political friends who would probably demand for him a command equal to the one he now has. The result would probably be the same as in the cases of [William] Rosecrans, [Samuel] Curtis, [Franz] Sigel, [Benjamin] Butler, and Lew. Wallace."[68]

Halleck's experience with Wallace after Shiloh led him to further laments in another letter concerning Banks. The chief of staff complained to William T. Sherman that "Banks' operations in the West are about what should have been expected from a general so utterly destitute of military education and military capacity." He declared that it was "little better than murder to give important commands to such men as Banks, Butler, [John] McClernand, Sigel, and Lew. Wallace, and yet it seems impossible to prevent it."[69]

Always concerned about his assignments and personal standing, Wallace believed that Halleck desired to force his removal from the Middle Department, and that belief gained some plausibility on 6 May. On that day, the general received a note, by "direction of Major General Halleck," pertaining to an inspection report for March. According to the report, the department was deficient in a number of ways. The brigades under Wallace's command suffered due to arms, accoutrements, clothing, and equipment deficiencies. Moreover, the Hospital Department of the 1st Separate Brigade was poorly supplied, with contagious diseases being prevalent. Officers and soldiers in one brigade, according to the report, were "not well instructed in guard and picket duty." The report went on to suggest that the same brigade, and other companies and regiments, experienced numerous other problems. The negative report unfairly blamed Wallace for the condition of the department in March, odd since Wallace first assumed command on 22 March.[70]

By June, even though the chief of staff was not happy with Wallace's performance, Lincoln was extremely grateful. The political general had successfully managed a crucial election while enthusiastically supporting the policies of the Lincoln administration; a West Pointer would have been quite reluctant to get so involved in such matters. The commander's tendency to take the initiative in some rather unwise ways did not seem to concern the president. Therefore, Wallace was invited to the Republican Party convention on 7 June, coincidentally meeting in Baltimore.[71] He beheld Lincoln's nomination for a second term, and the commander justifiably could believe that he had provided an important political contribution during a presidential election year.

In the meantime, Grant's Wilderness Campaign depleted the Middle Department's forces, and the general worried that his troops could not defend the approaches to Baltimore and Washington, D.C., if the Confederates mounted a campaign to threaten the cities.[72] Yet, at the same time, if Wallace truly worried about such a possibility, he failed to use all available means to establish a satisfactory defense of the department. The general made certain that key supply stations and railroad junctions had been protected from small rebel forces bent on stealing and destroying resources, but a large Confederate corps or army might march straight to Baltimore or Washington if there was no sufficient warning. Wallace did not go directly to Lincoln with such concerns, and he refused to ask Henry Lane or Oliver Morton for assistance. His sour relationships with Stanton, Halleck, and Grant also made it difficult to communicate effectively.

Up until July, Wallace's most important duties were predominantly political and, especially in the beginning, his political contributions there pleased the president and the secretary of war. Despite a couple of typically bold but ill-considered moves in April and May, the general did his best work of the war while commanding the Middle Department. In fact, Wallace's command in Maryland during a presidential election year could have provided an example for the army in supervising elections in the South during Reconstruction, but postwar officials failed to see the connection. Wallace acquired the experience necessary to be a departmental commander during Reconstruction, but such commands were mostly reserved for West Pointers after the war. Unfortunately, the experience gained over the preceding few months would not prepare Wallace for his next challenge, an invasion of Maryland by an entire Confederate army corps. In fact, the preoccupation with politics may have distracted the general from military matters until it was almost too late.

EIGHT

==========

"A Forlorn Hope"

In July, Lew Wallace attended to politics and various duties in Baltimore when suddenly Confederate general Jubal Early and his army launched a raid toward Washington.[1] Wallace quickly organized a few regiments, bought time for General Grant to reinforce the capital, and stalled the Confederate advance at the Monocacy River. Some historians give the general an enormous amount of credit for "saving" the nation's capital. Certainly, Wallace claimed that distinction. But critics questioned whether the Confederate threat was as serious or as dire as it may have seemed. As a field commander whose capabilities and leadership had been questioned by critics, Wallace faced both a military and political crisis. Early's raid obviously put the Union general in a situation where he needed to display some military skills or be judged a failure. But the Confederate also tested Wallace, the politician. The Hoosier would have to confront a much larger force. Defeating the rebels was a forlorn hope but delaying them might allow the Lincoln administration time to properly defend Washington and Baltimore, averting a morale-sapping embarrassment during a presidential election year.

One of Wallace's chief concerns during his command of the Middle Department was the lack of infantry and cavalry necessary to thwart an attack that might threaten Washington or Baltimore. Additional troops, to the dismay of Wallace, were reserved for Grant's Wilderness Campaign. On 9 June, in fact, the departmental commander was so concerned with reported guerrilla activity near the Monocacy River that he had to beg Henry Halleck for permission to impress a "sufficient number of horses to mount a company of infantry."[2] Halleck granted the request, but permission to impress a few horses did not adequately provide for the protection of two important Union cities. And, by the third day of July, it was becoming increasingly apparent to Wallace that those cities may be in danger.

Earlier, on 12 June, Robert E. Lee, leading the Army of Northern Virginia, revealed a plan to secure the Shenandoah Valley as well as threaten the cities of Washington and Baltimore. He ordered Jubal Early's II Corps to eliminate a Union force under Maj. Gen. David Hunter. Once this order had been carried out and the Shenandoah Valley secured, Lee directed Early to march north of the Potomac to threaten the Northern capital, or return to Petersburg if necessary. According to historian B. F. Cooling, success "would relieve some pressure on the Richmond-Petersburg line" and "protect Lee's invaluable supply base and railroad center at Lynchburg."[3] Complete success might force Grant to abandon his designs on Petersburg and Richmond.

The II Corps soon defeated Hunter on 17 and 18 June, west of Charlottesville. Upon reaching Lynchburg, Early telegraphed the results to Lee. He replied that Grant was now in front of Petersburg, and that it was necessary for "Old Jube" to strike quickly. If the opportunity for success presented itself, Early must "carry out the original plan, or move upon Petersburg without delay."[4] The II Corps pursued Hunter as far as Salem, Virginia, but Early then decided to drop the chase. Hunter and his men had been forced out of the Valley. In fact, they retreated into West Virginia. It was now time to turn north.

Early and his corps proceeded toward the Potomac River, marching eighteen to twenty-four miles a day through small towns such as Strasburg, Middletown, and Kernstown.[5] The rebels maintained a grueling pace in the intense summer heat, until they were delayed. Lee belatedly demanded that Early's troops rip up the Baltimore & Ohio Railroad and damage the Ohio Canal as much as possible before continuing toward the capital. To do this, Early had to cross the Potomac near Harpers Ferry, instead of traveling east through Leesburg. To Early's chagrin, as the rebels approached Harpers Ferry, Maj. Gen. Franz Sigel and Brig. Gen. Max Weber retreated to Maryland Heights, a strong position across the Potomac from Harpers Ferry, blocking Early's advance into Maryland.

Wallace understood that his VIII Corps could not stop a serious effort to invade eastern Maryland, but up until July he was not worried for the safety of his department, even though vague news of activity to the west and south was trickling in. After all, western Maryland was not included in his Middle Department, and Generals Sigel and Weber, as well as Hunter, should have been able to contain any pesky raiders to the west. In fact, the commander demonstrated his lack of concern on 25 June by taking his wife, among others, on a steamer excursion to Fortress Monroe and back. They did not return to Baltimore until Monday, 27 June.[6] Once Wallace arrived back, however, urgent communications made him warier.

By 2 July, Sigel and Weber reported to Washington that the enemy was in force, marching on their position.[7] Sigel, in response to the threat, only garnered four infantry regiments, one thousand dismounted cavalrymen, 1,800 mounted troopers, and a number of artillery batteries, while Weber only added four hundred more men.[8] Considering the situation, the outmanned officers abandoned their position on Maryland Heights. Although Sigel and Weber would only offer sporadic resistance during the next few days, they delayed Early, supplying some time for Wallace to organize a defense.

Becoming increasingly anxious, Wallace, on 3 July, asked Maj. Gen. Darius N. Couch if he had "any information as to the movements of the enemy in the Valley, of the safety of Sigel's trains, or of any engagement he has had with the rebels?"[9] Couch replied that Sigel faced an enemy "movement in force," and that telegraphic communications with that general had now been cut off.[10] The result of this exchange led to a series of confusing, and often contradictory, telegrams involving Wallace, Halleck, Stanton, and officers in the field. Wallace took the warnings seriously while Halleck, Stanton, and Grant only lamented the ineptitude of Hunter, Sigel, and Weber. Grant correctly assumed that the Confederate demonstrations were attempts to draw men away from the Army of the Potomac, but he considered these efforts merely ill-conceived and poorly manned. Furthermore, on the 3rd, Lieutenant General Grant mistakenly concluded that Early and his corps were still with Lee, in the Army of the Potomac's front.[11] Assistant Secretary of War Charles Dana believed the same, only adding that Gen. John C. Breckinridge "has not rejoined Lee's Army," but "he may have with him ten thousand men of all sorts—not more."[12]

Historians have emphasized, many years after this crisis, that there was a flaw in the command system as it pertained to the defense of the nation's capital. Abraham Lincoln finally had a system in which a true and trusted head of the army, Grant, developed a sound strategy for defeating the Confederacy and took charge over the various commands across the country, and the general did this with the help of a very capable chief of staff in Halleck.[13] However, no officer had clear charge over the safety of Washington. Of course, Christopher Augur commanded the trenches around the city, but that was all. No commander, excepting maybe Lincoln, Stanton, Grant, and Halleck in a more general sense, was tasked with confronting threats to the capital and eliminating them.

As a result, all Union officers involved, at least for some time, seemed to be more concerned with how Early's threat related to their command or reputation than how their command related to the defense of Washington. Augur supervised the trenches but had no authority to go beyond them. Hunter concerned himself with the Shenandoah and West Virginia while Sigel and Weber had charge of Harpers Ferry. Erastus Tyler commanded western Maryland, Wallace watched over eastern Maryland and Baltimore, and Darius Couch guarded Pennsylvania. Abraham Lincoln trusted Grant to handle the situation, but the general in chief was more concerned with how the raid was a diversion to draw him away from Richmond and Petersburg. Halleck was now in the best position to do something but assumed only the authority to prod Grant and Lincoln until they would issue an appropriate order. Governmental politics and personalities, especially concerning Halleck, exacerbated this crisis of command.[14]

In the meantime, newspapers reported uneasiness in Baltimore on 3 July. The sighting of large Confederate forces at Martinsburg and Winchester, Virginia, and near the Baltimore & Ohio Railroad, made citizens nervous, and rumors abounded. Worried talk included accounts of generals Sigel, Weber, and Hunter retreating.[15] Despite the increased threat, Marylanders celebrated Independence Day in the usual manner, including cannon, rifled salutes, and fireworks that entertained large crowds.[16] Wallace attended the festivities while continuing to observe the impending threat.

If the ominous news was valid, the commander of the Middle Department needed to put together a force to confront the Confederates. But he might not receive the extra troops that he expected, largely because the size of the rebel force was in doubt. On 6 July, the general forwarded a report from Sigel to the secretary of war. The dispatch claimed that the enemy "forces consist of one corps and three divisions of infantry, 3,000 cavalry."[17] Four years after the war, Jubal Early stated that a late "estimate of the force which advanced on Washington in July, 1864, is considerably more than double its real strength." In one of Early's own narratives, "containing a description of the campaign in the Valley, I have given my force, at the battle of Winchester, at 8,500 infantry, 2,900 cavalry, and three battalions of artillery, making an aggregate force of about 12,000 men. This was larger, by at least 2,000 men, than the force with which the advance on Washington was made."[18] Whether Early reached Washington with eight, sixteen, or thirty thousand men, the raid now presented a major challenge, one to be taken seriously. Even if Early faced Wallace with only eight to ten thousand veterans, as the Confederate and some historians assert, the Union general still confronted a force larger than his own.[19]

Wallace sent other messages seeking troops to combat the threat. He had a lot of experience organizing a defense on short notice, having gathered as many as 72,000 men to defend Cincinnati from rebels in September 1862.[20] He put this experience to good use, encouraging public officials and his subordinates to find any possible ways to raise men.

For example, the commander's adjutant, Lt. Col. Samuel B. Lawrence, quickly convinced Baltimore's Union Leagues to form as many as twelve to fifteen companies for the defense of that city.[21] Wallace directed one officer "to draw arms and equip the stragglers from Sigel's department and use them as guards at Annapolis. As many of his command as are there relieved from duty will be forwarded to" Monocacy Junction as quickly as possible.[22] Furthermore, Wallace ordered that the provost marshal arrest all army officers not authorized to be in Baltimore, and those officers with permission were to register their names with the proper officials in order receive passes.[23] The commander may have issued this order to keep tabs on officers and regiments or companies in the area, just in case they might be needed for the defense of Maryland, or maybe to ensure against desertions.

As the crisis approached, Wallace's superiors seemed preoccupied, and nobody took clear and active command of the situation. For instance, although Sigel's reports and Wallace's reconnaissance suggested danger, Stanton busied himself with other matters. The secretary of war was more concerned about the unlawful arrest of some men in Baltimore.[24] Stanton did not believe General Sigel's report, suggesting to Gen. Darius Couch that there was "nothing to confirm" Sigel's claims that twenty or thirty thousand rebels were crossing the Potomac. The secretary wondered what measures Couch and others had "taken to obtain accurate information of the enemy's movements."[25]

Wallace was not certain of the number of Confederates marching near his department, suggesting to his adjutant, on the 6th from Monocacy, that if "there is a big force of rebels in the Valley it has not developed itself."[26] But, unlike his superiors, the politician-turned-general did his utmost to meet the threat. He planned for the worst while others, such as Halleck and Grant, seemed immune to the possibilities.

On 7 July, Wallace ordered Col. Charles Gilpin to assume command at Frederick and organize the available troops. If the colonel had to evacuate the town, the general wanted him to fall back to the Baltimore Pike and hold the crossing of the Monocacy River at all costs.[27] In the meantime, Lawrence was sending men and ammunition as fast as possible to Wallace's new headquarters near the crossing.[28]

On 7 July, John W. Garrett, president of the Baltimore & Ohio Railroad, was doing his best to arrange for the transport of troops and supplies to Monocacy

Junction, and he continued to encourage the secretary of war to facilitate some sort of serious action.[29] Garrett sent a telegraph to Wallace, with a copy going to Stanton. The message stated that since "General Sigel's force remains on Maryland Heights, you are doubtless aware of the great importance of preserving Monocacy bridge. If it be damaged or destroyed great delay will result in getting forward re-enforcements to General Sigel. I trust you will be able to maintain your position, and protect fully this most important structure." Wallace understood, and he replied that some of his troops were now engaging the enemy near Frederick.[30]

The force under Colonel Gilpin and Lt. Col. David R. Clendenin fought well on 7 July, repulsing the rebels three times. The defense consisted of 250 men of the 3rd Maryland Potomac Home Brigade, some cavalry, three cannon, and several detachments. The force eventually included five squadrons of Clendenin's 8th Illinois Cavalry, which had pulled away from searching for Col. John S. Mosby's raiders and then deployed to Frederick at Wallace's urging. The cavalry, along with a couple of cannon, had hurried over the mountains to the west in order to slow up the advancing Confederates, only to retreat to Frederick, joining Gilpin.[31] Wallace was pleased with their effort, but the Union troops eventually had to fall back to the crossing of the Monocacy.[32]

Another message from Garrett to Stanton suggested three problems that prevented a satisfactory defense of the region. For one, lack of adequate ammunition was partly to blame. Secondly, "some difficulty exists on account of the delicacy of Generals Wallace and Tyler in commanding the troops in action west of the Monocacy, in view of their departmental limits." The Federals hoped that the secretary of war could "issue such order as will relieve this difficulty." Thirdly, "a dispatch from your Department to the officer in command [might] insure more rapid disembarkation" of supposed reinforcements under Gen. James B. Ricketts. His division, and some dismounted cavalry, were ordered by Grant to proceed to western Maryland to eliminate the raiders who were threatening the Baltimore & Ohio Railroad.[33] Finally, Garrett tendered all of the support that his railroad could offer to transport supplies and troops anywhere that was necessary to confront Early's raid, including repairmen to keep the telegraph lines open.[34] Stanton and Halleck now made a more determined effort to assist Wallace.

Later, on 7 July, the secretary of war answered Garrett's letters with an order to Wallace. Stanton simplified matters by allowing the commander of the VIII Army Corps, "in the operations now in progress," to ignore the usual restrictions with regard to "any departmental lines, but do what is proper to be done, with the means at your control; without reference to departmental lines, keeping yourself in communication with General Couch."[35] The order greatly reduced any hesitancy to send pickets west of Frederick. Halleck also seemed to better understand that the situation could become an embarrassing one for the Lincoln administration. The chief of staff ordered Wallace to impress horses "liable to fall into the enemy's hands." He wanted the horses sent to Monocacy Junction in order "to remount dismounted cavalry, which will be sent to that point with equipments."[36] While Halleck's order, and most of his "help," were not effective, it at least showed a growing concern in Washington.

Halleck also ordered Wallace's adjutant in Baltimore, Samuel Lawrence, to send General Ricketts's division "with five days' provisions to mouth of Monocacy or Point of Rocks." He withheld dismounted cavalry, but the rest of the division could be sent west "as fast as it arrives."[37] As was so often the case during this crisis, the chief of staff's effort was late and largely ineffectual. Lawrence had already acted, replying that "General Ricketts' division commenced arriving at 6.30 P.M. Orders were issued at once to proceed to the Monocacy without delay."[38] Lawrence informed Ricketts of the note to confirm the current plans to send the division to the Monocacy River.[39] The order by Wallace's adjutant may have irritated Halleck, but the chief of staff's lack of resolve forced Lawrence and his departmental commander to take the initiative.

The great activity in Maryland was not lost on the constituents in Indiana. With the telegraph, war news traveled faster every month. The *Crawfordsville Journal* declared that news from Baltimore "says there can no longer be any doubt that Lee has sent a considerable portion of his army in this direction." Rejoicing in Wallace's successes, the *Journal* declared that its favorite "has foiled the rebels thus far in all their efforts to drive us" from Frederick.[40] Success by Wallace and Federal forces in Maryland could only help Lincoln's support grow in the important state of Indiana.

Despite having to withdraw from Frederick on the previous day, bluecoats retook the town on 8 July because the rebels withdrew westward to the heights. Union men in Frederick soon came under the command of Gen. Erastus B. Tyler. But rebel reinforcements in that area, as well as movements toward Urbana, convinced Wallace that he might have to abandon Frederick in order to better cover Monocacy Junction and the Washington Pike. That evening at about 8:00 P.M., the Indianan sent a message to Halleck informing him of this decision to move "in position on the road to cover Washington, if necessary."[41] Oddly enough, during that same day, Brig. Gen. Albion Howe urged Wallace to bring his forces to Maryland Heights, instead of defending the Monocacy Junction.

He declined the request because such a maneuver would leave a wide-open road for Early to get to the nation's capital.[42] At times, it seemed as though the commander of the Middle Department was the only Federal official with a clear grasp of the situation.

Sometime that night, General Ricketts and the rest of the 3rd Division of the VI Army Corps arrived at the junction, 3,400 men to augment the 2,800 from the VIII Corps.[43] Greatly relieved, Wallace ordered the division commander "to move your whole command to the left of the railroad, with your front to the Monocacy, with a view of guarding the approaches on the Washington road." This position included the iron railroad bridge and the nearby macadamized wooden bridge leading to Washington. Troops under Tyler were defending the road and stone bridge on the Baltimore Pike, to the north; as a result, the departmental commander wished Ricketts to establish a "picket-line as you may deem best suited to attain this object, connecting on your right . . . with the line of Brig. Gen. E. B. Tyler."[44] Then Tyler's men were ordered to defend a line from the railroad bridge north to the Baltimore Pike, the river always in his front. Ricketts defended a line running south from the same railroad bridge, parallel to the Washington Pike and facing west toward the river. The 3rd Division was expected to endure the roughest fighting because Early would likely try to ford the river to the south, trying to flank the entire force on Wallace's left.

Daylight on 9 July brought the sound of gunfire from skirmishers on both sides. A Confederate division under Maj. Gen. Stephen Ramseur quickly over-matched the Federals at Frederick.[45] Tyler and his troops had retreated from the town back to the river by 8:00 A.M.

While Ramseur and Robert E. Rodes's divisions controlled the Confederate left and center, Generals Breckinridge and John B. Gordon looked for a place to ford the Monocacy south of the junction. Cavalry eventually found such a ford at about 11:00 A.M., and rebels soon threatened Ricketts and the Union left flank. The Confederates charged across a cornfield, with some cover by rebel artillery, not even bothering to fire their muskets. Once the cavalrymen were within 125 yards of the Union line, Ricketts ordered his Yankees to fire from behind a fence line, causing many rebels to disappear beneath the tops of the cornstalks.[46]

Ricketts's infantrymen repulsed the dismounted and outnumbered cavalry by 12:00 P.M. But intense skirmishing ensued, and Early clearly intended to attack the left again, this time with 3,300 veterans under General Gordon.[47] At approximately 2:30 P.M., a sense of certain defeat led the Union commander to beg that a straggling detachment of men from the VI Army Corps be sent

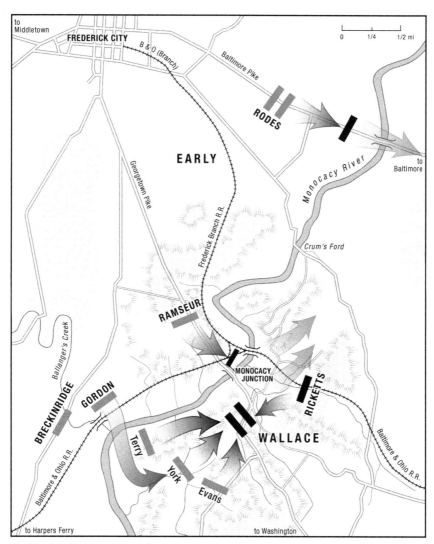

The Battle of Monocacy, 9 July 1864. *Map by Erin Greb Cartography.*

ahead, as soon as possible, by train.[48] The most negative rumors had been true. A large force, quite possibly an entire Confederate army corps, was headed for Washington, and Wallace was the only officer willing to take decisive action.

Unfortunately for Ricketts, Gordon threatened his front while rebel artillery, to the north, fired directly down the Union line. The Confederates soon advanced in force, this time across a wheat field. The two sides delivered a thick and murderous gunfire for approximately forty minutes. The rebels eventually appeared to waiver, attempting to keep order while jumping fences and hiding behind random stacks of grain. Wallace noticed Gordon's troubles, and boldly ordered Ricketts's men to charge, routing the graycoats. Unfortunately for the Federals, Gordon ordered another assault a little before 4:00 P.M.[49]

The intense pressure of the third attack greatly threatened the wooden bridge, leading Ricketts to order skirmishers to come back across the river. The division commander wondered whether he should "merely tear up the planking, or destroy the bridge by fire?"[50] Despite the order, the skirmishers were not able to withdraw over the bridge. The wave of gray uniforms compelled Ricketts and Wallace to burn the bridge early, even though the skirmishers had not yet crossed. These men later, around 4:00 P.M., made a dash across the unfloored railroad bridge, jumping from tie to tie. Rebels shot a few of these men, who fell into the water below. Skirmishers who made it across fired one more round before cheering their escape and returning to their division.[51]

Wallace's troops continued to fight bravely, but fresh rebels under the command of Brig. Gen. William Terry quickly broke through Ricketts's front. Wallace ordered a withdrawal shortly after 4:00 P.M. The politician-turned-general ordered Tyler, with six hundred troops, to secure and hold the stone bridge to the north while the majority of the Union soldiers withdrew along the Baltimore Pike. Tyler held the position until at least 5:00 P.M. when his men were forced to retire toward Baltimore. During the Battle of Monocacy, the Union suffered 1,300 casualties while the Confederacy lost eight hundred soldiers.[52] Based on the numerical losses and the fact that Early forced him to retire from the field, the Hoosier lost the battle.

Moving back to the city, Wallace wrote to Halleck, stating that he had "fought the enemy at Frederick Junction from 9 A.M. till 5 P.M., when they overwhelmed me with numbers. I am retreating with a foot-sore, battered, and half-demoralized column. Forces of the enemy at least 20,000." Luckily, the rebels were just as tired as the Yankees, and did "not seem to be pursuing." Still, they resumed their march in the morning, so, according to Wallace, Halleck would "have to use every exertion to save Baltimore and Washington." As for Wallace, he would "try to get to Baltimore."[53] Halleck, unfortunately, did not receive the telegram until 11:40 P.M., leaving the tired general in doubt as to the safety of the capital.

Sometime during the afternoon, President Lincoln became increasingly anxious due to reports from John Garrett and others. At 5:15 P.M., the president asked Garrett what he had "heard about [the] battle at Monocacy to-day. We have nothing about it here except what you say."[54] The railroad man's response arrived approximately two hours later, stating that Wallace and Ricketts were outnumbered, having to retreat toward Baltimore. This same letter contained a dispatch to the *New York Tribune* that recounted how Wallace intended to defend Frederick and Monocacy Junction. The message also stated that the Confederates had "levied [a ransom of] $20,000 on citizens of Middletown" in order to avoid pillaging.[55] Halleck and Lincoln did not receive corroborating word of a defeat until approximately 9:00 P.M.

At that time, Halleck informed Grant that a letter "to the newspaper press states that they had a severe battle to-day near Monocacy bridge, and that our troops were defeated and are now retreating on the Baltimore road." Such news might have convinced a general to better ensure the safety of the nation's capital, but Halleck's prior history with Wallace led to some doubt. Old Brains was now more interested in the safety of Baltimore, but still unwilling to "withdraw any forces from Harper's Ferry" until Hunter reappeared. He further questioned the validity of the dispatch, stating that knowing "the character of the source, you can judge of its reliability."[56] His unwillingness to prepare for the worst-case scenario, and his great dislike of political generals, could have meant the capture of Washington. Halleck and Grant were both to blame for failing to appreciate the gravity of Early's threat. However, Wallace's injured masculinity was also to blame. Part of the problem included the inability of superiors to trust him. After Shiloh, Wallace had blamed Grant and openly ridiculed Halleck to one of the chief's aides. Moreover, the dishonored general's aggressive note to Stanton in 1863 created another enemy. Now the Indianan's main flaw made it more difficult for his commanders to take him seriously. He did not communicate well with superiors; he sometimes displayed a lack of respect for them. No wonder they were reluctant to trust his information and recommendations during this uneasy time.[57]

After receiving Wallace's aforementioned acknowledgement of defeat at "Frederick Junction," Halleck and President Lincoln feared for the safety of Baltimore. Starting around 9:00 P.M., the administration was more dedicated to ensuring the safety of Baltimore and Washington. The uneasiness was heightened by a letter from leading citizens of Maryland's largest city wailing that "Baltimore is in great peril."[58] Halleck responded to this petition with a telegram to Wallace. According to the chief of staff, he was "directed by the President to say that you will rally your forces and make every possible effort to retard the enemy's march on Baltimore."[59] Halleck and Grant would be able to organize a better defense for Washington, but the security of Baltimore could be more difficult.[60]

Wallace quickly replied to Halleck's order, surveying the path to Baltimore for the best defensible positions. Later, on the 10th, the departmental commander ordered General Ricketts to "detach two regiments of your division temporarily to proceed by rail to the Relay House [near Baltimore], to place that post in a defensible condition. They will find intrenching tools there." But most importantly, the "remainder of your division you will take post for the present" at Ellicott's Mills, "and make every possible effort to retard the enemy should he march upon Baltimore or the Relay House." For support, Wallace would send a battery and four companies under Lt. Col. David Clendenin.[61] Besides defending these points, Samuel Lawrence, who Stanton had placed in command of Baltimore in Wallace's absence, sent notes to a few officers and their commands in the Baltimore area, urging them to be ready to defend the city, even if they were not originally assigned to do so.[62] The organization of force turned out to be more than was necessary since, as the department commander suspected, Early and his corps marched toward Washington.

Nevertheless, the citizens of Baltimore were in a panic by Sunday, 10 July, largely due to the movements of one thousand Confederate cavalrymen around the city.[63] According to Susan Wallace, "the bells rang at daylight for the arming of militia. Cavalry dashed through the streets, drums beat, men collected in crowds and terrified women looked from windows on the crowded streets. About noon Sunday it was supposed the rebels were advancing on the city, in which case it would have to be surrendered." The provost marshal told her to get ready to flee, and Susan "sat a long, long time, waiting, expecting to hear the rattle of musketry every moment." She eventually received a letter from her husband, and at about midnight "Lew came in—as one from the dead—I cannot tell you how I suffered that day & all through my poor distracted mind went the thought of how sister Helen was spending Sunday with husband and child and how I was spending mine."[64] Governor Bradford provided more reason for alarm in a proclamation, signed 9 July but not printed in papers until the 11th, asking all loyal men to come to the city's aid because the "invading enemy is by the last accounts approaching the city." The notice was accompanied by news of Wallace's defeat at Monocacy.[65] Many men, women, and children suffered from fear of attack during the next few days, in Baltimore and Washington, but the panic had largely shifted to the nation's capital by the 12th and 13th.[66]

On 11 July, Wallace wired Halleck, suggesting that the "panic here is heavy and increasing," but he did "not think there is just cause for it." Despite this reassurance, the political general still wished to be prepared, and lamented that he had "not enough cavalry to picket the several approaches or to send out reconnoitering squads, and, therefore, beg you will give attention to a dispatch from me of yesterday, giving a note received from Colonel Clendenin" that asked for the remainder of his men to be sent to the defenses of Baltimore. Wallace wanted to "mount them if you will be kind enough to order them to me."[67]

Halleck responded in the negative, arguing that dismounted "men here have been sent to the field. We cannot give them to you. The main body of the enemy appears to be in our front."[68] Moreover, the late series of events convinced the president to assign Maj. Gen. Edward O. C. Ord "to the command of the Eighth Army Corps and of all troops in the Middle Department."[69] Grant made the recommendation to Halleck the day before, asserting that he "would give more for him [Ord] as a commander in the field than most of the generals now in Maryland." In Grant's opinion, it would be best to send Ord "to Baltimore to command and hold that place."[70] Even though the Indianan did well in slowing down Jubal Early's corps, providing time for the administration to shore up Washington's defenses, his success was not apparent to Lincoln, Stanton, Halleck, or Grant. To everyone outside of the Middle Department, Wallace apparently had blundered, hastily retreating before a force that he should have been able to stop with the help of General Ricketts's 3rd Division.

Wallace was not relieved from duty; he was to report to Ord, "but remain in charge of the administration of the department." Therefore, in "respect to all military operations and movements, whether defensive or aggressive, he [Ord] is by special assignment of the President the superior in command."[71] Demoting Wallace surely seemed like a slap in the face, but it was not surprising, considering the Hoosier's past confrontations with Halleck, Grant, and Stanton. The general's demotion did not cause him to hide in an office while Early's raiders rushed toward Washington. For the next few days, the demoted general continued to correspond with subordinates, organizing the best defense possible for Baltimore, Annapolis, and other important parts of Maryland; only now he had to answer directly to Ord during the crisis.[72]

While Wallace took responsibility and proceeded to make decisions crucial to the defense of the region, the administration made the proper preparations only after word of the Union defeat at Monocacy. According to Assistant Secretary of War Charles Dana, who often criticized Wallace, Early's raid resulted in too much commotion, and President Lincoln seemed unwilling to take responsibility for the situation, being inclined to let Halleck determine whether troops should be "sent out" during critical points of the crisis. Halleck seldom wanted to do so.[73]

On the evening of 12 July, Dana still believed that Washington did not have good intelligence as to the number of Confederates marching before the nation's capital. His quibble over numbers seemed ridiculous, considering that Wallace and others asserted that an entire division, maybe even a corps, menaced Washington. Rather than blaming Wallace, Dana considered much of the confusion to be the fault of generals Christopher Augur and Halleck. The assistant secretary of war proposed that Augur, who was supposed to be in charge of the defenses of the capital city, was shirking his duties. In fact, Augur seemed to know little with regard to the entrenchments, forts, and troops around Washington. Dana intimated that "he knows as little respecting them as I did before I went out" to see them for the first time.[74]

The criticism continued. The assistant secretary also implied that Halleck was useless at that critical time. Dana asserted that Old Brains knew as little about the lines surrounding the capital, and the troops defending them, as General Augur. He judged that Halleck contributed "quite as much as the latter to the prevailing confusion & inefficiency." Furthermore, Dana claimed that there was a not-so-secret reason for this ineptitude. According to the critic, the "testimony of those best informed says that Halleck[']s mind has been seriously impaired by the excessive use of liquor and that as [a] general thing it is regularly muddled after dinner every day."[75] Such a lack of control, on Halleck's part, was unlikely considering his former criticism of Grant for drinking while on duty. Still, one way or the other, the commentary demonstrates the great confusion, the breakdown in the command structure, and the lack of responsibility being exhibited in Washington during the crisis.

The crisis ended despite the confusion among Federal leaders. Jubal Early and his rebels reached the outer defenses of Washington on the 13th, but they arrived too late to make a serious attempt at seizing the city. On 15 July, the *Baltimore Sun* declared that the "invasion of Maryland has at last been brought to a close, and the usual quiet state of affairs in the city [has] been again restored."[76] Wallace's defeat at Monocacy delivered a great warning to Washington. It gave the administration extra time to prepare a better defense, and it provided important proof that this raid indeed presented a substantial threat. In fact, on the 14th, at the conclusion of the crisis, General Ord believed that Wallace showed courage and intelligence. The War Department ordered the temporary commander of Wallace's men back to Washington, and the hero of Monocacy resumed command of all troops in the department. Ord went on to state, to Wallace, that "the readiness with which you have co-operated in arranging the defenses and your desire to meet the enemy under my orders showed a zeal not always found under similar circumstances, and I shall remember it."[77] Those close to the department and the VIII Army Corps came to understand and appreciate Wallace's efforts.

Luckily for Wallace, Lincoln was willing, and needed, to restore the political general to his command once the danger passed. Shortly after the raid, Democratic papers in Indiana used the event to malign Wallace. The *Crawfordville Weekly Review* stated that the rebels put "to flight Major General Lew Wallace, who reported *a la* Hooker that he had the enemy in full retreat, quietly crossed the Potomac on their way to Richmond." Nevertheless, the paper did not place the majority of the blame on Wallace. It charged the blame "upon the lick-spittle organs of Abraham Lincoln."[78] Eventually, even the Democratic papers in the political general's home state were grumbling about Wallace's dismissal from command. The editors of the *Weekly Review*, extremely critical of Wallace before the war, stated that they were "greatly pained to see that our noble Hoosier Gen. Lew. Wallace has been removed from active command in the field and Gen. Ord appointed in his stead." Acknowledging that "Wallace got the worst of the affair at Monocacy Junction," the *Weekly Review* also contended that "the enemy outnumbered him at least ten to one on the sanguinary field." The Democratic organ looked "upon this act of the government as doing great injustice to an officer whom every man, woman, and child in Indiana looks upon as one of the bravest and ablest in the army."[79]

The political general was relieved of his command for only three days, but Wallace's effort continued to be overshadowed by his apparent failure to confront and win against the Confederates.[80] One newspaper reporter underestimated the rebels under Early, contending that they did not constitute a significant force, causing Wallace's defeat to be seen as a great embarrassment at first.[81] Moreover, according to Charles Dana, the command breakdown had become ridiculous. In an extremely sarcastic letter of 11 July, the assistant secretary of war stated that with "Gilmore[,] Couch[,] Wallace[,] McCook[,] and Sigel we only need Milroy[,] McClernand[,] Rosecrans[,] and Kirby Smith to make us safe. If the General [Grant] could spare Butler for the Supreme Command all . . . danger would certainly cease—especially as Hunter is at hand."[82] The proud man from Indiana had become the subject of jokes. But, in this instance, the passing of the crisis and further investigation would lead many to understand that the politician-turned-general had done all he could do to thwart the Confederate raid into Maryland.

The citizens of Baltimore had calmed down by 18 July, and the spreading word of the department commander's good deeds gave him great satisfaction.

Wallace was especially pleased to inform Halleck "that from the report of my patrols and scouts received this morning, the enemy have entirely disappeared from my department."[83] The general then proceeded to thank John Garrett for his railroad's assistance in transporting men to and from Monocacy.[84] Like a true politician, Wallace also thanked the loyal citizens of Baltimore. The city's *Daily Gazette* carried a circular allowing Wallace to express his "desire to return to those citizens who so promptly and cheerfully took up arms to assist the regular forces of the Government my thanks for their courage and loyalty. Their services were really invaluable."[85]

Most importantly, on the same day that President Lincoln called for another 500,000 recruits, Wallace laid the foundation for shoring up the defenses of the city. He knew that more troops would still be hard to come by, so the general asserted, in the same circular, "that the recent experience is a convincing argument in favor of continuing and perfecting the militia organizations. It will not be difficult to do so now, if the loyal zeal already shown continues. If the companies will continue their organization it will be my duty and pleasure to assist the civil authorities to arm and drill them, and form regiments and brigades so as to constitute the National Guard of Baltimore." If the endeavor proved to be successful, "a future invasion will find Baltimore ready and sufficient for its own defence."[86] Wallace effectively drew upon his wealth of experience organizing militia in Montgomery County, Indiana, and he continued to make good use of the knowledge.

In the aftermath of the crisis, Grant also dedicated himself to making sure that a lack of preparedness would not reoccur. Grant could certainly do this by defeating Lee and his army. He might also remove generals he considered ineffective, but Grant did not order the permanent removal of Wallace from command; as the days passed, it appeared that the Hoosier was not actually the problem. The commander of all Union armies became more concerned for Washington's defenses, as well as those of Baltimore. For example, he sent Capt. C. N. Turnbull "to Baltimore to lay out and complete its defenses, and more especially to connect the works constructed by lines of rifle-pits."[87] The general in chief even prepared for the possibility of Early marching "through Western Virginia to Ohio, possibly taking Pittsburg by the way."[88] In future months, Grant would order thousands of men under Gen. Philip Sheridan to the Shenandoah Valley in order to eliminate the most serious threats.

As it so happened, Grant cogently asked for a reorganization of the departments surrounding Washington and Baltimore. "After the late raid into Maryland,"

Grant believed in "the necessity of having the four departments of the 'The Susquehanna,' 'The Middle,' 'Western Va.' and 'Washington' under one head," maybe constituted as a military division. For example, Grant asserted that with "Gen. Meade in command of such a Division, I would have every confidence that all the troops within the Military Division would be used to the very best advantage in case of another invasion. He . . . would station his troops to the best advantage, from a personal examination of the ground, and would adopt means of getting the earliest information of any advance of the enemy and would prepare to meet it."[89] In the end, come August, Sheridan took charge of this division.[90]

Wallace was the only officer to actually do this, and, by the 25th, Grant had come to appreciate his efforts. But the overall chaos during Early's raid led him to argue for a competent man in charge of the region, so that communications breakdowns between different commands would not hinder the effort to protect the capital. During Early's raid, according to the lieutenant general, downed telegraph wires resulted in exchanges that took twelve to twenty-four hours in each direction, further complicating the unorganized attempts to defend Washington. Grant neglected to specifically mention Wallace in the note, but he told Lincoln that many "reasons might be assigned for the change here suggested now of which I would not care to commit to paper but would not hesitate to give verbally." In fact, Grant sent his trusted chief of staff, General Rawlins, to deliver the note and "give more information of the 'situation' than I could give in a letter."[91] These off-the-record comments certainly did not pertain to Wallace alone. Grant may have been more concerned about Halleck's management of the situation. Grant's letter, among others, showed a newfound concern for the safety of Baltimore and the nation's capital, and a reluctance to place the entire blame on Wallace as the commander of the Middle Department.

Grumblings from Indiana and Senator Henry Lane eventually forced the administration to acknowledge the value of Wallace's service. On 28 July, the *Crawfordsville Journal*, lamenting the blame heaped upon the fellow Indianan, contended that the eastern press should be "disposed to do justice [to] this enthusiastic and gallant officer." They wanted more than just a refusal to blame Wallace for Union failures during the late raid. After all, his "heroic stand against the fearful odds that confronted him at Monocacy bridge, has not been surpassed in daring by any contest of the war, nor has any reverse been sustained by our forces where less criticism could be justly indulged in against the behavior of officers or men." According to the editors, papers around the nation, including the *New York Times*, now complimented the performance of young Wallace, who "showed a more thorough appreciation of what the emergency demanded, a more resolute purpose to discover and face the actual danger, whatever it might be, and did more practical service than any other military officer north of the Potomac." Past and current efforts by this general, according to the Republican organ, were "gratifying to us, and should be to all Indianans."[92]

In August, the same paper was relieved to learn that Wallace "retains his command" of the Middle Department and the VIII Army Corps. Moreover, the editors were "assured on undoubted authority, that his conduct in that battle was highly satisfactory to the military authorities at Washington, and has received the warm commendations of General Grant." If not entirely true in August, the statement would be soon. The articles also stated, falsely this time, that Wallace was never actually removed from command after the battle of Monocacy.[93] He was only removed for a few days, but the Lincoln administration, in the aftermath of Early's raid, did its best to persuade Indiana that the brief removal was not a serious matter.

In September, Wallace attempted to publish his report on the Battle of Monocacy, but the secretary of war asserted that such an action was not the normal practice. The War Department usually sent the reports to Congress for publication. But there was nothing objectionable in the report, according to Adjutant General E. D. Townsend.[94] There was little need for such a publication at that time, however; word was spreading that the political general had contributed greatly to the defense of the capital. In fact, Wallace informed his sister-in-law that despite his position being a bit "thorny," he was "now really getting more credit than I deserve." This time, however, he did not let praise inflate his ego, lamenting that "so it always is with our people—the dog they kicked yesterday becomes their hero today—vice versa."[95]

For certain, General Grant was now fully aware of Wallace's militarily and politically important contributions during Early's raid. The two men "had a cordial meeting" in September.[96] The engagement did much to salvage a relationship that was horribly damaged due to the events surrounding the Battle of Shiloh. Remarkably, Grant expressed his gratitude to Wallace in his *Memoirs*. Twenty years after the event, the ex-president asserted that Wallace "moved with commendable promptitude to meet the enemy at the Monocacy. He could hardly have expected to defeat him badly, but he hoped to cripple and delay him until Washington could be put into a state of preparation for his reception."[97]

Grant, in retrospect, believed that Early's repulse was largely "contributed to by General Lew Wallace's leading what might well be considered almost a forlorn hope. If Early had been but one day earlier he might have entered the capital before the arrival of reinforcements I had sent." Wallace's desire to be seen as an honorable, "rough" man led him to be defensive about Shiloh for the rest of his life, but such compliments, even twenty years after Monocacy, helped to salvage the political general's reputation among his contemporaries. Wallace could always respond to criticism by quoting Grant, who stated in his memoir that "by the defeat of the troops under him [Wallace effected] a greater benefit to the cause than often falls to the lot of a commander of an equal force to render by means of victory."[98]

===========================

NINE

Victory and Mexico

In late 1864 and early 1865, the general's military service seemed to be coming to an end. Despite failing to prove manliness and preserve honor to his satisfaction, Wallace relished an end to the brutal conflict, and he yearned to return to Indiana. However, ultimate success under Ulysses S. Grant, William T. Sherman, and Philip Sheridan did not terminate his service. In the months prior to the war's conclusion, Wallace became involved in a new assignment, acquiring arms, supplies, and men for the Mexican liberals who were fighting against the French intervention. The general eventually went to Mexico on behalf of the U.S. government. Somewhat reminiscent of the attempts by American filibusterers to exhibit their martial manhood in Latin America in the antebellum years, the general again hoped that this assignment would bring him glory on the battlefield.[1]

Following the Battle of Monocacy, Lincoln quickly reinstated Wallace as commander of the VIII Army Corps, while the general never lost command of the Middle Department. The general spent the remainder of the election year patrolling for spies and smugglers, as well as investigating other suspected disloyal activities. Along with the occasional effort to argue his effectiveness at Monocacy, the general began necessary preparations for the upcoming presidential election.

In April of 1864, the mere presence of soldiers voting, even if unarmed, encouraged a secure election with little or no violence. Receiving positive responses from his brigade commanders, Wallace repeatedly requested that Maryland men in different regiments and companies be allowed furloughs in order to vote. It turned out to be a less controversial way to keep order at the polling places, especially at those where judges of election failed to request direct assistance. Being pleased with the outcome on 6 April, come October and November Wallace again applied these methods to promote victory for Lincoln in the presidential election of 1864.

On 13 August 1864, in a letter to Wallace, Senator Thomas Hicks, a Unionist from Maryland, lamented that he had not met the man who took such a thankless position on behalf of the Lincoln administration. Hicks stressed that commanding the Middle Department was "a hard position for you, but *in it* a proper commander is of great importance to us—greater difficulty, more perplexing duties and delicate responsibilities is no where devulged [*sic*] upon a commander than is found in your charge." Although, in Hicks's opinion, "the Administration does not understand it yet, *I know* that no where is the proper management of military affairs mixed with civil matters more important to the Govt. than in this Middle Dept. and I have repeatedly urged this at Washington, but without much success I fear."[2]

Hicks further urged Wallace to steer clear of political factions in the department, stressing that the gentleman from Indiana should "be a military and not a Political Genl., that is what we need here, and is what I take you to be."[3] Hicks certainly understood the nature and importance of the department, as well as the feelings of its commander. The "perplexing" department, on the other hand, did not need the military general that Wallace desired to be. As historians David Work and Thomas J. Goss might suggest, it needed a political general, and duties there soon made evident how the delicate sensibilities of a politician-turned-general were crucial to successfully administering the Middle Department.[4]

After Jubal Early's raid, Wallace experienced much political anxiety. He gradually received more credit for actions at Monocacy Junction, but the initial negative reaction to the defeat convinced Wallace to be ever vigilant in securing Maryland and its largest cities from rebel invaders. On 18 July, the department commander asserted to Henry Halleck that "from the report of my patrols and scouts received this morning, the enemy have entirely disappeared from my department."[5] But despite the confidence exhibited by the note to the chief of staff, the good news did not lead to a calm and unconcerned management of the Middle Department.

After Monocacy, the department still contained numerous "perplexities." These problems also frustrated Susan Wallace. As mentioned earlier, she lamented that Baltimore was "rebel to the core." Disloyal residents were difficult to deal with because the "small Union party is divided into radicals, led by [Henry] Winter Davis, & conservatives, headed by Reverdy Johnson." Making things worse, the "authorities at Washington constantly interfere with all Lew does."

The Lincoln administration now was more aware of Wallace's good performance before, during, and after Monocacy, and she believed that her husband's success had "wiped out the foolish lie told after Shiloh." But to Susan's dismay, this new view of her husband failed to produce reinforcements in Maryland, so there was "no reason why the rebels should not come up as easily next week as last. There are very few soldiers here and the rebels know it. All this while the slow butchery goes on before Petersburg."[6] The lack of sufficient troops in Maryland led the department's commander to fear the coming of another Confederate invasion that might influence northern voters during the election year.

Wallace watched with concern in the following weeks. On 25 July, for example, a storm disrupted telegraphic communications between Baltimore and Harpers Ferry. The incident led the general to write to the president of the Baltimore and Ohio Railroad, asking whether "the communication between here and Harper's Ferry [had been] interrupted by the storm or rebels?"[7] Any hints of possible rebel activity received Wallace's full attention in the weeks following Early's raid.

On the 25th and throughout the remainder of July, the Middle Department received numerous reports of rebel threats. Mosby's raiders appeared to be causing trouble in western Maryland and northern Virginia, although few reports professed certainty. Wallace, well into August, spent much of his time sending detachments to positions west of Baltimore, desperately hoping that the latest rumor would not amount to the next grand raid. These weeks frustrated Wallace; he could only do so much. Early's raid had not convinced the administration to send major reinforcements to Baltimore, so the departmental commander continued to draw from the same meager numbers.

In fact, although Grant ordered that the earthworks and forts near Maryland's largest city be improved, Wallace had too few men to fill these works. He wrote to Adjutant General E. D. Townsend, lamenting that when "the guns are mounted on the new defenses of Baltimore, I have neither officers nor men who can serve them."[8] The general could not adequately guard Maryland's waterways, either. He wanted "two small gun-boats for the protection of Gunpowder and Bush River bridges," but none were available.[9] Such problems were important considering that the commander received, almost daily, warnings of another possible large-scale invasion. On the 26th, for example, a captain estimated that a rebel force in northern Virginia, maybe now in Maryland, consisted of 20,000 to 40,000 men.[10] A force of that size could again threaten Baltimore, and possibly the nation's capital. On the same day, the department commander wired Townsend, asserting that if necessary, he could only "concentrate at the Monocacy bridge by to-morrow night 5,000 100-days infantry, 400 cavalry, and one good battery," a force largely devoid of veterans.[11]

In guarding against these potential raids, the general continued to communicate with Secretary of War Stanton, Halleck, and Townsend. Wallace demonstrated professional cordiality in letters to Stanton and Townsend, and they to him. Letters to and from Halleck, on the other hand, ended with little more than the basic signature, no "sincerely" or "your obedient servant." The two generals' correspondence definitely exhibited their lack of respect for each other, at least in the abrupt language and absence of anything resembling a friendly statement. Obligated to communicate with the chief of staff, Wallace continued to keep him abreast of the latest wires from western Maryland.

Such communication was important because the president, in the wake of telegraph problems during Early's raid, directed that all of the military operations for the defense of the Middle Department, as well as the Departments of Susquehanna, Washington, and West Virginia, be placed under Halleck's command. As a result, the chief of staff was "expected to take all military measures necessary for defense against any attack of the enemy and for his capture and destruction."[12] The chief of staff was now responsible for the defense of the nation's capital, though not for long, and Wallace dutifully followed his commands. If another raid in Maryland threatened Washington or Baltimore, Halleck could not justifiably claim that Wallace neglected to relay warnings to him or the secretary of war.

Halleck exhibited his lack of trust and cordiality on the evening of 27 July, one day before Stanton ordered Wallace to resume command of the VIII Army Corps.[13] He received a note from Wallace stating that scouts "from the Monocacy bridge report to-night that they have been to Edwards Ferry, Noland's Ferry, mouth of Monocacy, and Point of Rocks without finding sign or intelligence of enemy" reported to be in western Maryland on the 25th and 26th.[14] The message reported good news, but the chief of staff refused to acknowledge it as such. Without encouragement or cordiality, Halleck responded by merely stating that the "troops at Baltimore, being mostly inexperienced, should be thoroughly drilled, especially at the firings, and kept ready for orders to move at the shortest notice."[15]

While Halleck and others in the administration understood that there was a lack of troops in Maryland, the department commander was compelled to send, on that same day, two detachments of cavalry to the Army of the Potomac, further depleting a force that Halleck expected him to use in defense of Baltimore.[16] Every week, Wallace sent some troops south to reinforce the Army of the Potomac.

On occasion, he was ordered to send men to odd destinations, considering his own need for troops. For instance, on 9 August, Townsend commanded that the general select "three 100-days' Pennsylvania regiments of your command and order one to each of the following points: Johnson's Island, Ohio; Rock Island, Ill.; Chicago, Ill. In addition, send a Massachusetts 10[0]-days' regiment to Indianapolis, Ind." Maj. Gen. Henry Heintzelman, headquartered at Columbus, Ohio, would command the regiments.[17] Consequently, the Middle Department continued to rely on a dwindling force to defend Baltimore and the approaches to the nation's capital.

Due to the regular departures of troops to Virginia, Wallace's command consisted of many green regiments only able to provide a feeble defense of Baltimore. Men enlisting for only one hundred days might go home as soon as the army began to train them. In supplementing these troops, the general demonstrated his willingness to promote the policies of the Lincoln administration. On 28 July, the commander ordered that, under "direction of His Honor Mayor Chapman, the lieutenants and sergeants of the municipal police of the city of Baltimore will proceed immediately to organize the able-bodied negroes in their respective wards into military companies for duty in this city." According to headquarters, the "several companies, as part of the organization, will be permitted to elect their non-commissioned officers, inclusive of first sergeants. Experienced white officers will be appointed by Mayor Chapman." Wallace did not intend for these troops to be glorified ditch diggers, however; after "sufficient rolls are reported, the companies will be organized into regiments by directions from these headquarters. Each regiment will be armed and equipped by orders from these headquarters. Blouses and caps will be provided by the city authorities. Companies will also be furnished with armories for purposes of drill and for the security of their arms. Such armories will be in charge of the police." The special order emphasized that nobody, including employers, could interfere with the recruiting, and prohibiting "a negro from attending the drills or obeying regimental or company orders will be considered an interference."[18] Much like Lincoln, Wallace did not believe in complete equality for blacks in America, but he hated slavery and recognized the utility of ex-slaves in defending Maryland and the Union.

The extra troops were necessary because Jubal Early reportedly remained in Northern Virginia, continuing to threaten a raid into Maryland.[19] Wallace regularly did his duty in supporting Gen. David Hunter and Gen. Philip Sheridan in their pursuit of the Confederates. On 1 August, Grant sent "General Sheridan for temporary duty" in the Shenandoah Valley "whilst the enemy is being expelled from the border." The commander of Union armies wanted "Sheridan put in command of all the troops in the field, with instructions to put himself south of the enemy and follow him to the death."[20] The order was a response to the burning of Chambersburg, Pennsylvania, on 30 July by two brigades of Confederate cavalry under Early.[21]

The destruction of northerners' property irritated a man who received much criticism for actions at Monocacy Junction earlier in July. Wallace showed some bitterness, as well as some satisfaction, in a description of that event to his wife. Writing to Susan on 3 August, he exclaimed that it was "a disgraceful affair . . . to allow Chambersburg to be burnt by 208 robbers!" He took satisfaction in noting that "not a volunteer officer had anything to do with the defense—the thing was very regular." While, in his opinion, West Pointers were botching assignments west and north of the Middle Department, Baltimore newspapers were complimenting the man now known as the hero of Monocacy for "the serenity and order that prevails" in eastern Maryland.[22] As a result of the embarrassing situation, Sheridan's assignment did not turn out to be so temporary, the cavalry general eventually taking command from Hunter. Wallace would be expected to secure Baltimore and the approaches to Washington while Sheridan hounded Early in the Valley, sometimes requiring the departmental commander to send troops to Sheridan that might have been needed in Baltimore.

Stressed by frequent demands for reinforcements from other generals, Wallace received a note from Dublin, Maryland, asking for help. The postmaster wanted troops to aid the loyal residents in protecting the post office's flag and pole, symbol of the Union's authority. Traitorous individuals repeatedly tore down the flag and destroyed the pole while the Union men would raise it again, only to see it destroyed once more. The request irritated the general. He responded by stating that the "military authorities cannot convert every cross-road, or respectable village even, into a garrisoned post." The postmaster had suggested that a lack of response from Wallace would only lead to a belief that the military authorities were unconcerned, or indifferent, to the plight of the Maryland town. The matter, in the general's opinion, was entirely Dublin's responsibility. He believed that the disloyal residents "presume entirely upon your lack of nerve. . . . Fight, and if your enemies are too strong for you, I will send soldiers to your aid." The postman's letter excited Wallace's "indignation; but I confess it is about equally divided between the traitors who do the wrongs, and the citizens who, with such Quaker-like resignation, submit to them." The general suggested that when "next you write me, tell all the particulars of the fight, and give me a list of the rebels killed."[23] At least one of his superiors would have frowned at this response; but, at the same time, it certainly demonstrated Wallace's ability to write and persuade, both qualities of the best politicians.[24]

The ability to create this sort of motivational letter or speech could have aided the general more often during his Civil War career. Governor Oliver Morton valued his assistance in recruiting for that very reason. Never mind his political connections or family name; Wallace was a great writer and speaker who could convince men to enlist in the army for the sake of the Union. This ability may have helped to eventually achieve a significant command in the field if Wallace had realized the potential during the months following Shiloh.[25] His enthusiasm for an opportunity to attain glory on a field of battle was so intense that it prevented him from understanding how he could more easily earn such a command. He seldom grasped the notion that to receive a favor, one should offer a favor in return.

On 7 August, Wallace's department fell under the jurisdiction of the newly created Middle Military Division, commanded by Sheridan, that Grant asked Lincoln to create after the Battle of Monocacy.[26] Reporting to the division's chief of staff, the general documented the small number of men available from the Middle Department. Wallace's command included three separate brigades. These units were scattered throughout Eastern Maryland and Delaware, defending or guarding a number of towns, forts, railroads, hospitals, telegraph lines, prisoners, and "squads of men [sent] to the Army of the Potomac."[27] If the general calculated correctly, as few as 5,585 men under his command were fit for duty on 19 August. Such a condition would only get more frustrating.

Late in August, the general's attempts to organize Baltimore's black men into companies met with some complaints, adding to his frustration. Assistant Secretary of War Charles Dana forwarded "a communication from certain loyal colored men of the city of Baltimore, complaining of grievances to which they are subjected, being forced to drill, &c." Dana wondered whether white recruits were being subjected to the "same drill as is required from the men of color." Wallace replied that "white men have been organized into companies and regiments, and are required to drill," but there were delays in the organization of white units because "Governor Bradford has declined to recognize their organizations and commission their officers." Black units were taking part in more drill because the general was organizing them on his own; since "Governor Bradford declined to have anything to do with the enterprise, the State constitution not recognizing colored men as subject to militia service, I assumed the business myself."[28]

The general further admitted that recruiting was difficult because "it was desirable to enroll all the able-bodied colored men of the city, whether free or slaves." Evidently, some blacks contended that they had been forced to join the militia. Wallace believed that such an error may have been made on occasion because enrolling men "by asking them to volunteer was impossible, as many of them are the slaves or employés [sic] of secession citizens, who would, of course, prohibit such action, hence my measure had to be arbitrary." He refused to allow disloyal slaveowners to prevent their slaves, or former slaves, from enlisting. "That some instances of harshness have ensued is not unlikely, but," according to Wallace, "the sufferers had only to complain to me to have their wrongs redressed." The commander further believed that such complaints emerged because "among the blacks, as with the whites, there are lazy and trifling people who do nothing without compulsion, and complain when it is exerted." In addition, "disaffected whites do not hesitate to fill the minds of the simple and credulous colored men with false ideas of my purposes toward them in this organization."[29]

Wallace concluded by suggesting that he could not "deprive Governor Bradford of his lawful control of the able-bodied whites." But, it "is different, however, with the blacks, whom the Governor repudiates for militia purposes; and as to these latter I will see that they are not abused." Further excelling in pushing Lincoln's wish to encourage the enlistment of blacks, the political general asserted that there would be no complaints if he could answer a couple of questions. Black recruits were asking whether they would be paid, and, "should they be killed or disabled while so engaged, would they or their representatives be placed on the pension list?"[30] Recruits were bound to complain if they did not receive satisfactory answers to these questions.

Wallace had taken a bit too much initiative, in the minds of some locals, as commander of the Middle Department, but in doing so, he supported the wishes of the Lincoln administration. In fact, he told his wife, two weeks later, that his "relations with [the] War office at Washington still continues very cordial." Furthermore, Stanton seemed "satisfied with my management of the Department," also leading Adjutant General E. D. Townsend to suggest that Wallace was giving "them less trouble than any other Department Commander." The general even had a pleasant meeting with Grant, in which the senior officer suggested that he might ask Wallace to be the Army of the Potomac's chief of staff once that army again prepared to go on the offensive.[31] That assignment never materialized, but the cordial meeting demonstrated a growing ability, on Wallace's part, to gain respect and get along with his superiors.

The flow of men out of the department, leading Wallace to recruit the services of blacks in Baltimore and the surrounding area, actually confused the Confederate high command for much of September. Regiments originally assigned to the Middle Department were often sent to Grant at Petersburg, causing rebels to wonder whether Wallace's corps had come south. Confederate intelligence led Robert E. Lee to question the whereabouts of the VIII Army Corps. On 17 September, according to Lee, a deserter confirmed such concerns. The prisoner did not completely convince the general, however, so he asked Early if the report was correct.[32] On the following day, Lee asserted that scouts "confirm report the Eighth Corps, under General Lew. Wallace, from Sheridan, has passed Old Point to Grant; also six steamers with cavalry."[33] Oddly enough, Wallace's woes assisted the Union cause for at least a short time in September of 1864, forcing Lee to consider calling Early back to Petersburg.

For some northerners, Lee's retreat to trenches around Petersburg signaled an eventual Union victory, maybe in the very near future; Wallace agreed. In September, just two months after Monocacy, the political general could see the end of the war, stating, "I can't help feeling the triumph of victory in advance. Ah, when one thinks of our cause, its righteousness, and all the world of consequences it involves, how can he doubt that God is on our side!" The general had come to view victory not only as the preservation of the Union, but as the "righteous" end of slavery. This change in view began in Kentucky and Tennessee in late 1861, leading the general to enthusiastically support Lincoln's emancipation politics by 1864. He further predicted that Gen. John Bell Hood's army would arrive at Petersburg because "it is so clearly the last chance of the great conspirator, that I am sure he will attempt such a concentration."[34] Hood made no attempt to reach Petersburg, and the war did not end as soon as the Indianan believed it would. But the Confederacy had run low on resources, including men, while the Army of the Potomac had a more than adequate supply.

Come October, the impending presidential election overshadowed all of Wallace's duties. Winning Maryland and Delaware might be crucial for President Lincoln. Gen. George McClellan appeared to be a strong candidate who could win the election if majorities in a couple of contested states voted for the Democrat. Thus, the departmental commander wished to be especially vigilant in creating a climate in which Union supporters felt safe going to the polls.

As it turned out, Wallace's plan for the April election in Maryland had garnered the praise of the president, so the political general hoped to use the same plan for the presidential contest. He instructed his adjutant on 4 October that he desired, especially in Baltimore, "to avoid the slightest demonstration looking to military interference. In no case must bodies of armed soldiers be allowed to approach the polls, except to put down an outbreak for which the police are insufficient, and then the mayor must first apply to you for assistance for that purpose." However, in "districts in which the judges of election have formally solicited military protection, by petitions, signed by them, and forwarded to headquarters, do not hesitate to send troops." If the adjutant wondered how many soldiers should be sent to a voting district, Lawrence was to "be governed by the opinion of the judges of election." But, in Wallace's opinion, "it is better, in case of doubt, to send a strong detachment than a weak one."[35]

The commander further asserted that "the object of sending these detachments is purely to protect and support the judges of election in enforcing the law regulating the exercise of the voting privilege." The officers in charge of these detachments needed to declare "themselves and their commands subject to the orders of such judges, by whom they must be governed throughout the two days of the election." Armed detachments must stay clear of the polling places unless needed, so as to not arouse any suspicions about the validity of elections. If some undoubtedly loyal citizens petitioned for help because of a discovered conspiracy to intimidate loyal voters in a district, Lawrence was allowed to send troops he could spare at the last moment.[36]

A couple of disputes in the April election encouraged Wallace to reiterate that officers must clearly understand their purpose and be able to "notify the judges, and all other citizens who may inquire what their orders are, and for what object they have been sent." So the commander ordered that each officer receive written instructions that they were not "to attempt to compel any judge to do his duty or to comply with any requirement of the law, but simply to protect loyal men from violence, injury, or molestation."[37] The hero of Monocacy provided thorough directions, having learned from earlier experience.

Although the election in April resulted in few lasting complaints, he knew that the department could do better. In October, elections for some state offices and a vote on Maryland's "anti-slavery" constitution complicated things. The general was nervous because he would be in Indiana, conducting business and visiting his wife and son, for approximately ten days in October. Lawrence would have to handle most matters while Wallace was away.

The general's role in the election brought the usual criticisms, as well as some extraordinary complaints. In early October, one person, claiming to be "a true American," wrote to Wallace, suggesting that "a scoundrel like you deserves no warning but rest assured that your days are numbered and you [will] never get out of this city a live man." The writer claimed to be from Baltimore, and referenced discussions of Wallace's departmental administration, mostly concerning the upcoming elections, in New York newspapers.[38] The death threat must have created even more anxiety for someone who was trying to concentrate on the task at hand, as well as protect his wife Susan from disloyalists.

As the presidential contest of 8 November approached, the governor of Delaware, William Cannon, made it clear to Wallace that he would need the same military aid as given to the state of Maryland. The chief executive believed that he had "reason to be apprehensive that at the election to be held in this State on the 8th proximo a fair and free expression of the popular will may be prevented." The governor asserted that he had no force of his own to protect loyal voters, so he requested "that as military commander of this department, and as the representative of the authority of the United States, you will cause to be stationed at or near the various voting places in this State during the day and evening of the election a sufficient military force to preserve the peace, to protect loyal and true men, to secure a fair election, and to prevent any violation of the laws."[39]

George McClellan, the Democratic presidential candidate, had strong support in Delaware, and Cannon worried that disloyal elements could easily secure a victory for Lincoln's opponent. The departmental commander had not given Delaware the same attention awarded to Maryland, prompting Cannon to make the request. Realizing his error, the general quickly prepared to meet the request as best he could, also arranging furloughs for regiments from Delaware, so that they could vote in their home state. Securing elections in two states was definitely more taxing, so Wallace begged Halleck for more troops. Eventually, this request made its way to Sheridan, who wrote that he could not send "the five regiments which General Halleck says you ask for." He plainly, and unsympathetically, suggested that Wallace do "the best you can without them."[40]

Such concerns, fortunately for Republicans, did little to injure their cause in October and November. Thankfully, Lawrence successfully handled matters while Wallace was away during the second and third weeks in October, letting his superior know on the 13th, by telegram, that the "election has passed quietly thus far, and matters elsewhere are quiet and all right."[41] The same formula that earned Wallace praise in April also resulted in safe and relatively uneventful elections in October and November.

The voting proceeded as quietly as it had in April, the returns quickly hinting at a victory for Lincoln in the paramount contest. By 10 November, General Grant enthusiastically asserted to Stanton that enough "now seems to be known to say who is to hold the reins of government for the next four years. Congratulate the President for me for the double victory. The election having passed off quietly, no bloodshed or riot throughout the land, is a victory worth more to the country than a battle won. Enemies and Europe will so construe it."[42]

The president won an overwhelming victory in the Electoral College, 212 to 21. The popular vote also went Lincoln's way, 2,213,665 to 1,802,237. The vote was not a landslide, but the incumbent won a healthy 55 percent of the nation's popular vote. New Jersey, Kentucky, and Delaware were the only states McClellan carried. Thankfully, for Wallace's peace of mind, the Democratic majority in Delaware did not cost Lincoln the election. But it justified his furlough arrangements, so that Delaware's soldiers could vote.

Wallace always believed that the soldier vote saved many of the fall contests for the Republican Party, and this was certainly true in one case. The soldiers' votes may not have made a difference in Lincoln's bid for a second term as president of the United States, or in the gubernatorial contests. In fact, one might argue that soldiers were not quite as enthusiastic about Lincoln and emancipation as previously thought, with some officers and enlisted men feeling the need to pressure soldiers to vote Republican.[43] Nevertheless, the uniformed voters were important to the contest on the new Maryland state constitution. According to one historian, the "state's new constitution abolishing slavery would win by a slim 475-vote margin," meaning that the "soldier vote would decide it."[44] The general made a serious political contribution, his efforts being crucial to securing the slim margin of victory for the abolitionist cause. And, while slaveowners later took some "revenge on blacks and black institutions"—a few black churches burned to the ground, and some whites tried to use state apprenticeship laws to claim black children—Wallace would work to subvert such designs.[45]

Although Wallace fared better in Maryland than in previous assignments, he still maintained his propensity to be too assertive in his correspondence with superiors. Thanksgiving brought another occasion for the general to complain to a superior officer. In late November, he came to the mistaken impression that disloyal persons in Baltimore were being allowed to prepare feasts for rebel prisoners in the hospitals. He feared that such "permission will be construed as a license to make manifest once more the disloyalty, now completely cowed, in this city. I beg the sleeping fiend may be let alone." Wallace then made a characteristically unwise statement, complaining that he "was not consulted. Had I been I would have objected to the making [of] such a request."[46]

In this case, Wallace did not seem to anger anyone, but he must have been a bit embarrassed when Townsend informed Wallace that he had misinterpreted the request, thus overreacting in his earlier letter. Townsend talked to Stanton, and then told the departmental commander that the "request which was granted was that [the] Union Ladies' Committee might be authorized to receive contributions for rebel prisoners, as well as for our own men, all to be distributed by the Union Committee." In fact, Stanton saw "no objection to supplies for Thanksgiving being received and distributed to rebel prisoners by our Union Committee, provided our own men receive an equal share of all the contributions with the other prisoners." On the other hand, Townsend understood the concern, stating that no "political demonstration was contemplated, and it is within your power to stop anything which would lead to such demonstration."[47] The letter did not acknowledge that Wallace had any real authority to nullify the granted request. He could only act if one of the feasts turned into an anti-Union demonstration. The general, possibly realizing that he had overreacted, allowed the feasts to take place with little incident. He regularly excited himself in such situations because the actions of disloyal Marylanders caused problems on a daily basis.

The year 1864 closed with no major unresolved conflicts or misunderstandings in the department, and a sense that the long war was approaching a conclusion. In January, the general learned that his old regiment, the 11th Indiana, was temporarily in the department, so he asked that it show off its Zouave uniforms and drill in Baltimore. Many were impressed, and Wallace pressured Grant to allow him to keep the 11th as part of his VIII Army Corps. Surprisingly, considering the constant drain of men from the department, Grant acquiesced.[48] In the last year of the war, the Indianan found himself in charge of the regiment he had commanded as a colonel in 1861.

Although this event greatly gratified Wallace, a completely new endeavor, one befitting the abilities of a political general, came to dominate his time during the first months of 1865. Mexican liberals were fighting against a French puppet government, and the Mexican War veteran soon found himself involved in covert operations to provide arms, supplies, and men to the liberals. The episode began with a visit from an old Indiana schoolmate, S. S. Brown, who had moved to Texas and now lived near Monterrey, Mexico. The friend told Wallace that "Matamoras [Mexico] is to the rebellion west of the Mississippi what New York is to the United States." The town, just across the Rio Grande from Brownsville, Texas, near the most southern tip of that state, was a "commercial and financial center, feeding and clothing the rebellion, arming and equipping, furnishing it materials of war and a specie basis of circulation in Texas that has almost entirely displaced Confederate paper."[49]

Brown believed that the "entire Confederate Government is greatly sustained by resources from this post." The United States might be interested in ending this supply of Confederate war materials. The best way to do that might be to support the Mexican rebels who were fighting against the French. Most people in Monterrey and Matamoras pretended, in Brown's opinion, to be "in favor of the French. But they are, to a man, at heart bitterly opposed to the French, and I am under the impression that by judicious manipulation, and could they be properly approached, they would, in opposition to foreign intervention, rally under the Stars and Stripes." The old friend also offered to provide further information if U.S. government officials decided to use this opportunity to injure the Confederate rebellion while aiding the Mexican rebels.[50]

Brown wrote a letter mirroring their conversation, and Wallace enclosed it with one of his own to Grant. He assured the lieutenant general that the friend was reliable. He further commented that Brown believed that "if overtures were now made to them" the "rebel soldiery in Western Texas, particularly those at Brownsville, would gladly unite with us and cross the river under the Juarez flag. This belief he based upon the great disheartenment that prevailed all through the regions west of the Mississippi." Wallace wondered "if it is not best to let me go and take a look at it and see exactly what obstacles are in the way and how they may be removed, if at all." His longtime fascination with Mexico partly qualified Wallace, and his martial vision of manhood certainly encouraged him, to ask for such an assignment. He hoped that the "adoption of the Juarez flag on the bank of the Rio Grande as the basis of a compromise would stagger the rebellion."[51]

The politician-turned-general did not stop there. He briefly outlined a plan to convince authorities in Texas to support such a mission. Wallace wanted to go to Brazos de Santiago, from where he would "invite the [rebel] commandant of Brownsville to an interview on the old battle-field of Palo Alto. If the man's a soldier I'll wager you a month's pay that I win." In his typically bold manner, the general then mentioned that Grant should "know how to get me there—an order to make an inspection of affairs on the Rio Grande will do so. Such information as Brown's will, I think, fully justify examination."[52]

As with most of Wallace's plans and hopes, the desire to lead an army in the field colored his enthusiasm. If the information proved to be true, he suggested that Grant "may be in position, on report of the facts, to send me troops to smother the Brownsville-Matamoras trade." Thus, if the plan did not work, then "it will be my own fault if I don't get the arms through." He then encouraged Grant's interest by claiming that the "inspection ought not to consume more than a month." Wallace understood that he was being ever so persistent when it came to this "Mexican idea," but he ingeniously blamed the enthusiasm on Grant, immersed in an insightful compliment. After all, "Hold on" was "the lesson you are constantly teaching us. Had Butler served under you as some of the rest of us have he wouldn't have left Fort Fisher."[53] Wallace finally was learning to stroke the egos of his superiors, to use some flattery to get what he wanted, to not just boldly claim that it was his right to take what he wanted from a well-trained superior.

After one week of contemplation, the commander of all Union armies agreed to Wallace's plan. In a special order, Grant mandated that "Maj. Gen. Lew. Wallace, U.S. Volunteers, will proceed, via the Rio Grande, to Western Texas, and inspect the condition of military affairs in that vicinity and on the Rio Grande." He further ordered that all military "authorities will afford him every means in their power to facilitate him in the execution of this order."[54] The approval greatly excited Wallace, and he eagerly made plans for an expedition that would keep him away from the Middle Department for a few months.

In the days that followed, Wallace made many preparations, including suggesting that Gen. Alexander M. McCook take temporary command during his absence.[55] Grant did not agree, and in the end neither got their way; the administration appointed Brig. Gen. William W. Morris as the temporary replacement.[56] This move was one of many during the next few months that would counter Wallace's own wishes. Despite the Hoosier's great efforts to effect such a mission with the Mexican liberals, Grant and the administration often rejected his advice, often placing someone else in a role that Wallace cherished. Although Wallace improved his reputation since Monocacy, the major general had not fully earned back Grant's trust. It was hard to forget the martial or "rough" personality and inconsistent performance of the general at Fort Donelson, Shiloh, and thereafter. The lieutenant general did not want an unpredictable, and sometimes uncontrollable, officer handling such a delicate mission. Wallace talked too much about potential fights and invasion, making his superiors nervous.

The excited general received permission from Sheridan to take Col. John Woolley, his provost marshal, with him to the West, and they departed sometime in early February.[57] Along the way, he determined to find some recruits to fill the ranks of the 11th Indiana, which he hoped might be assigned to him if he took a field command in Texas. Wallace, taking Governor Oliver Morton's advice, convinced the commander at the Union camp in Cairo, Illinois, to allow camp guards there to fill the vacancies in his beloved regiment. In a letter from that town, the Indianan thanked the governor for his advice, and he asserted that Morton's influence could help him secure and succeed in the Mexican "assignment as proposed, and if you will do so, I will recollect it always as a special favor."[58] In addition to such communications, the general occupied much of his travel time in a vain attempt to learn the Spanish language.[59] As it turned out, such knowledge would not be as necessary as he believed.

The Federal contingent arrived in New Orleans no later than 20 February, collecting four thousand dollars in Secret Service funds for the purposes of the delicate mission.[60] A day later, Wallace was reimbursed $520 for earlier "services rendered."[61] He then proceeded to compile a report, sending it to Grant on the 22nd. From information obtained in New Orleans, the general, now turned secret agent, believed that he was "justified in saying now that the statements of Mr. S. S. Brown, forwarded you from Baltimore, are in no wise exaggerated. Mat-amoras [*sic*] is to all intents and purposes a rebel port, free at that, and you can readily imagine the uses they put it to." The general feared that the U.S. consul at Matamoras would inform Secretary of State William H. Seward of Wallace's arrival, and hinted that Grant and himself should act quickly to handle the situation. Seward argued with Lincoln about the merits of such covert activity, fearing that it would encourage the French to declare war on the United States, so Lincoln told Wallace to hide the mission from the State Department.[62]

The major general believed that the Union should delay any serious military action "until it can be seen whether the Mexican Republic cannot be put in position to fight its own and our battles without involving us, an eventuality exactly coincident with Mr. Seward's views." He asserted that the best way to deal with the possibility of Seward finding out about the mission was to approve a vague "arrangement so complete that it will hardly be necessary for the Government to loan me a gun, not even a pistol." But then Wallace audaciously claimed that this "arrangement depends entirely upon your giving me command of Texas as a military department, with orders to report directly to yourself, and upon your sending me a division of infantry and a brigade of cavalry, with the ordinary complement of guns." Grant likely did not trust Wallace enough to issue such orders. The subordinate further suggested that the "main body of these forces acting on the defensive and posted at San Patricio, the lowest ford on the Nueces River, will completely sever communication between the Rio Grande and Middle and Eastern Texas."[63] Such a plan was too bold, considering the current war and the desire to keep France out of it.

Wallace then stated that he would interview Confederate general Edmund Kirby Smith, acting "as if already appointed to the command of the Department of Texas. Conditions will, of course, be subject to approval, and forwarded to you instantly." Wallace further maintained that "if accommodations are impossible, and if, in consequence, it becomes necessary to occupy San Patricio, then, behind that position, and under its cover, I shall initiate the organization of the Territory or new State of Rio Grande." The letter concluded with another request for troops, specifically mentioning the 11th Indiana.[64] The general devised some well-thought-out plans throughout the mission. But the letter was characteristically bold, and unfortunately for Wallace, Grant could not trust him to carry out such plans without creating a major incident.

Grant did not immediately remove Wallace from command, however, and he continued with the mission, meeting with Confederate general James E. Slaughter at Port Isabel in March.[65] The rebel general responded favorably to the proposals, even suggesting that Confederate officers might more honorably get back into the Union if they attacked and annexed some Mexican territory from the French.[66] As a result of the initial meeting, Slaughter and Col. John Ford asked Wallace to draw up some propositions that might satisfy superiors on both sides. The propositions, among other things, asked that "the Confederate military authorities of the Trans-Mississippi States and Territories agree voluntarily to cease opposition, armed and otherwise, to the re-establishment of the authority of the United States Government over all the region above designated." For abandoning the Confederacy, and for any further assistance to the Union armies, ex-rebel officers and soldiers would take "the oath of allegiance to the United States Government, be regarded as citizens of that Government, invested as such with all the rights, privileges, and immunities now enjoyed by the most favored citizens thereof."[67] Slaughter agreed to forward these propositions to Gen. John G. Walker, his superior and Confederate military commander of Texas.

Excited by these meetings, Wallace boasted to his wife that what he aimed "at now is nothing more than bringing Texas, Arkansas and Louisiana voluntarily back into the Union. The business is handsomely begun, and at this time looks promising." The general further remarked that he had to sleep on the same blanket with Slaughter between their secret meetings, jokingly fearing that news of such fraternization between himself and a Confederate officer would lead to a questioning of his "character for loyalty." He "could never get to Congress from the 8th Judicial District," and Susan's "father and Bennett would hail me as the best copperhead in old Montgomery" County.[68] Later correspondence and meetings, by contrast, encouraged less humor in the general's writings.

Such cooperation was not guaranteed from all Confederate officers in the area, and Wallace, in his dealings with Slaughter and Ford, already feared that Gen. Kirby Smith might be negotiating with Emperor Maximilian I.[69] As it turned out, General Walker declined to cooperate with the Union general. On 25 March, he received a copy of the propositions from Slaughter and Ford. Walker chastised Wallace and declared that he never sanctioned such an interview, or any agreement with the delivered propositions. The rebel officer contended that his command was still intent on supporting the Confederacy as an independent nation. He questioned Wallace's methods, "seeking an obscure corner of the Confederacy to inaugurate negotiations."[70] In a pacifying letter, the Hoosier blindly hoped that Walker would still forward the propositions to Kirby Smith.[71]

In the meantime, still hoping for some progress, the Union general wished to contact the Republican forces of Mexico to ascertain whether they would confront Confederate troops that might try to cross over the Rio Grande into Mexico. Wallace needed to find a Republican officer in order to complete the second part of his mission, and eventually he found such a person in General José María Jesús Carvajal.

After the Mexican-American War had ended in 1848, Mexico remained a target of American filibusterers, who looked for adventure and hoped to illegally seize parts of Latin American territory for the United States. Many American and foreign figures attracted the attention of American men looking to prove their manliness and become famous. "The most significant troublemaker based in Texas was the charismatic Tejano veteran of the Mexican Revolution, José María Jesús Carvajal. The light-skinned Carvajal, who spoke English fluently, had little trouble finding Anglos who were willing to follow him into Tamaulipas on three separate occasions in the early 1850s to fight for both freedom and free trade."[72] The seasoned militant quickly made an impression on the Indianan.

The two men soon met, and the Union general was relieved to find out that Carvajal had been educated in the United States, spoke fluent English, and was inclined to agree to Wallace's suggestions. In the middle of their interview, the Mexican "produced a document from his government naming himself as a commissioner with extensive powers for one year." President Benito Juárez authorized the document, dated 12 November 1864. It "empowered Carvajal to purchase 40,000 rifles and other munitions abroad, to enlist up to 10,000 foreigners for service in the Mexican military forces, and to contract for a foreign loan."[73] His hopes raised, Wallace expected that they could do much to aid the Union and Mexican causes. Carvajal assured the Union officer that Juarez's forces would oppose the Confederates, and the American assured the Mexican that he would help him to secure a loan and purchase arms in the United States. Thus, they both went to Washington, Carvajal hiding under the alias of Mr. Joseph Smith.

While Confederate generals Kirby Smith and J. G. Walker did not seem to be interested in negotiating, Wallace had found some hope that the mission would succeed. In the end, however, many things would interfere with his efforts. Grant was not excited to leave him in charge, and the war had ended—at least in the East—by the time Wallace and Carvajal arrived in Washington. Moreover, drastic events caused Wallace, as head of the Middle Department, to place his own plans on hold. On orders from Edwin Stanton, the political general assumed a major role in a process that soon immersed Wallace in controversy.

TEN

Assassination and Andersonville

A t this stage of his military service, Lew Wallace was uncertain how much longer he would be in uniform or in what other capacities he might serve. Therefore, the general left the Mexican border for Washington, hoping to make additional contributions to the Union war effort. In early April, during a brief stay in New Orleans, Wallace wrote to the commander of the Department of the Gulf, Maj. Gen. Stephen A. Hurlbut, before continuing on to the U.S. capital. The Indianan told Hurlbut that he feared that Confederate major general John Walker might be of little help in contacting Lt. Gen. Edmund Kirby Smith. Still, if Smith agreed to meet, the Hoosier wanted Hurlbut to take the matter into his hands, since Wallace planned to escort Mexican general José María Jesús Carvajal to the U.S. capital in order to arrange for cooperation against Confederate and French forces near the Mexico-U.S. border.[1]

Wallace was confident about making an early peace with rebel officers in Texas, possibly hastening an end to the war, but his hopes became practically irrelevant when he learned by telegraph that the Army of the Potomac had Lee's Army of Northern Virginia on the run. En route to Washington, he heard that Lee had surrendered to Lt. Gen. Ulysses Grant at Appomattox Courthouse, Virginia, on 9 April. Wallace still intended to make a report on the Mexico mission to Grant, and he further wished to take credit for arranging the surrender of rebel forces in Texas. Those were his designs, but a catastrophe forestalled the plans.

Just before Wallace arrived in Baltimore, he learned of traumatic events. Seeking an entertaining diversion, President Lincoln and his wife decided to see a play at Ford's Theater in Washington. Grant and his wife were going to join them, but they cancelled. The president and guests were watching the play, titled

Our American Cousin, from an upstairs box when a Confederate sympathizer and actor named John Wilkes Booth entered the theater. Evading the one or two guards present, Booth entered the president's box and shot Lincoln in the back of his head with a small pistol. The president was carried to a house across the street for medical care, and doctors unsuccessfully attempted to save him. Lincoln died early on the morning of 15 April 1865. In conjunction with Booth's attack, another man assaulted Secretary of State William H. Seward and his household, stabbing the cabinet member's son. Vice President Andrew Johnson was also a target, but his would-be assassin had second thoughts and failed to strike.

The latest good news of Lee's defeat and the sad news of Lincoln's death combined to drastically change Wallace's plans to create a deal with Carvajal and meet with Grant. Arriving in Baltimore just a few days after the president's assassination, Wallace resumed command of the Middle Department.[2] He sat down to weed through the mail and paperwork, noticing a letter from the War Department in reference to transporting the dead president to Illinois. Wallace was to prepare to "receive the remains of the late President Abraham Lincoln upon their entry within your lines and take charge of them under the orders of this Department while they remain in your command."[3]

Stanton and the new president, Johnson, decided to have Lincoln's remains carried on an extensive train trip through several eastern cities and on to Springfield.[4] It was an important task, one requiring tight security, so Wallace wasted no time in making arrangements for escorting Lincoln's body to Baltimore. He contacted Governor Bradford immediately, asking him to send instructions or come to the state's largest city as soon as possible.[5] There were no major problems, and thousands met the locomotive to mourn Lincoln's body on its way to Illinois. The funeral train safely arrived at Springfield on 3 May 1865, and the burial ceremony began at 12:00 P.M. the next day.[6]

Meanwhile, Wallace also inherited a dilemma from General Morris, the interim departmental commander. After Lee's defeat, many rebel prisoners, whether recently captured or having served months or years in prison camps, needed help in order to go home. Many of these former Confederates found their way to Baltimore, so Wallace contacted the War Department "respecting transportation for paroled rebel prisoners." He further lamented that "there are a considerable number of paroled rebel officers and enlisted men here, and the number is increasing rapidly, and their presence is exceedingly obnoxious to the loyal citizens."[7] He continued to deal with this matter, through April and into May, telling Townsend on 23 April that he still had "about 100 rebel officers and enlisted men (paroled prisoners of Lee's army) under guard here" in Baltimore. They had "no money or means of getting away."[8]

After organizing guards for the transportation of Lincoln's body through his department, Wallace continued to struggle with the movements of ex-Confederate soldiers through Maryland, complaining to Washington that he was "at a loss to know what to do with the paroled rebel officers, soldiers, and citizens who have been permitted to enter the department for the purpose of returning to their homes." Having no concrete instructions, the Union general planned to confine the former rebels until the government arranged for transportation, usually by train. Wanting some guidance from the War Department, Wallace explained that if he retained the graycoats "in custody they will have to be fed, and to get them away I must furnish them transportation, which I have no authority to do, nor do I know whether to send them back to the South or let them go North."[9]

Besides the lack of food, money, and transportation for these refugees, postwar tension in Maryland made matters worse. Many of the Marylanders who had served the Confederacy wanted to take the oath of allegiance to the United States, declaring that they should thus "regain their residence in this State." Wallace suspected that this was true but was uncertain. Moreover, the "feeling here [in Maryland] against returning rebels is so bitter that to avoid collisions and bloodshed I am compelled to act cautiously and arrest rather than let them run loose while waiting your instructions." Wallace even reminded Washington that his latest telegram of 26 April had been preceded by one three days earlier on the same subject, but to no avail.[10] The problem continued into May, as defeated rebels were "constantly being sent here from Richmond and other points in that vicinity who desire transportation to their homes in Georgia, Tennessee, Missouri, and other distant points." The general found transportation for some, but he still waited for orders authorizing such for all who needed rides home.[11]

Despite several time-consuming duties, Wallace found a few minutes to send a letter to an even busier Grant and arrange a short meeting. The lieutenant general had little time to discuss Wallace's trip to Texas but wanted to invite him to a longer meeting soon. Afterward, waiting for maybe a day or two, an impatient Wallace believed it necessary to explain his plans on paper since Grant neglected to call him south to the Petersburg trenches.[12]

Wallace stated that he had written a long, formal report on his mission to Mexico, and that he would be sending it to Grant as soon as possible since aides were now copying all documents included.[13] He decided that it "may be of importance, however, to sum it up briefly for your immediate information." He explained his trip to Galveston to see Confederates Slaughter and Ford, as well as the abrasive correspondence between himself and General Walker. Walker's negative reaction induced Wallace to proceed to New Orleans where he "arranged with General Hurlbut to open communication direct with Kirby Smith upon the subject" of surrender. Hurlbut "also agreed to send Mr. [Charles] Worthington to Matamoras for the purpose of sounding Slaughter and Ford as to whether they were willing to act independently—a result not at all improbable."[14]

Wallace offered a good summary of earlier events, only leaving out his dealings with Carvajal, whom he may have already introduced to Grant. He had recounted his meetings with the Mexican general in previous reports to the general in chief. Concluding the explanation, Wallace admitted that "an arrangement with Kirby Smith," for the surrender of rebels in the West, "now is practicable I don't doubt at all. I feel sure he will surrender without a shot fired." In a sense, much of the mission had been for naught. But, at the same time, the government might still be interested in aiding Carvajal and Juarez in expelling the French from Mexico. The political general could yet feel that he had done a great service for his country. Wallace ended his letter to Grant by again offering to forward the full report, but he preferred to deliver it in person in order to more easily address any of his superior's concerns or questions.[15] He waited until 16 May to forward a formal report to Grant, hoping until then for a personal meeting.[16]

In the meantime, on 23 April, Wallace's provost marshal received a telegram, supposedly by Stanton's authority, ordering "all vessels trading to Western Shore [Maryland] to be stopped and steam-boats searched." The departmental commander quickly asked the secretary of war if the directive was in fact his, for such an order did not seem necessary any more, at least in the general's opinion.[17] The instructions, however, likely had more to do with the search for the escaped assassins, John Wilkes Booth and the man who attacked Seward, as well as other rebels and spies refusing to submit to Federal authority. Instead of taking the question as a logical one considering that the war was largely over, Stanton became irritated, wondering whether Wallace was doing everything possible to catch Booth and other conspirators. The war secretary responded to the inquiry by stating that he wanted all relevant officers "to procure the information and give the directions mentioned in his telegram, and if it is not furnished officers will be placed in command who will do so."[18]

Wallace still had a reputation for troublesomeness, and Stanton may have feared that the general was up to his old antics. At the same time, the secretary of war was just his usual blunt, coarse self, especially now during the days following the death of his president.[19] Some officers received reports that Booth and his accomplice were headed into Maryland, most likely coming through Baltimore, and Stanton logically wished to do everything possible to catch the felons.[20] Secretary of the Navy Gideon Welles was equally vigilant in his efforts to secure waterways in and around Maryland.[21]

To his credit, Wallace soon let Stanton know that the "Patuxent River is already blockaded, not a vessel allowed to come out, and that there is a perfect chain of picket-boats from Washington around to Baltimore."[22] The general made it particularly difficult for anyone to get out of Baltimore and Annapolis by boat, placing guards and patrols in many locations and ordering officers "to carefully observe all persons and arrest all suspicious characters."[23]

These preparations failed to directly result in the capture of Booth or other conspirators in Maryland, but they may have limited the number of possible escape routes, maybe even forcing Booth to go south. Lincoln's assassin was soon cornered in a barn near Bowling Green, Virginia, where soldiers shot him. Others had conspired with the actor to assassinate Lincoln, Seward, and Andrew Johnson. Suspects captured and prepared for trial included David E. Herold, Mary E. Surratt, George A. Atzerodt, and Lewis Payne. Dr. Samuel A. Mudd, Edward Spangler, Samuel Arnold, and Michael O'Laughlin were alleged to be accessories in the plot or in the escape. Mary Surratt's son, John, actually managed to escape, fleeing to Egypt where he was captured in 1866.[24]

When the search for conspirators ended, President Johnson called Wallace to Washington to serve on the commission, or military court, to try the suspects and accessories in the assassination plots. The tribunal was eventually scheduled to convene on 10 May 1865. The president named Maj. Gen. David Hunter to be president of the military trial, ranking Wallace as second in command of the proceedings.[25]

Trying the suspects through a military commission certainly troubled some Americans. However, one scholar argues that despite "all the stereotypes of inflexible military law, the reality of Civil War military justice is one of flexibility, leniency, and individuality. Far from the rigid and stern administrators of harsh justice, the Union officers who sat on Civil War courts-martial took circumstances into account, listened to both sides of the issue, and operated a system that administered proper justice in the vast majority of cases. While the courts operated by a procedure very different than civil courts, the differences did not amount to an abuse of liberty or the rights of citizens. Military law had its own means of ensuring a fair trial, with objective judges, fair representation, and a limited appeals mechanism."[26] Whether proper justice could be attained in such a politically charged case remained to be seen.

Wallace had experience that made him well qualified to continue his service by sitting on a special military commission. Again, many had discussed whether the proceedings should constitute a civil or military trial, the nation's attorney general soon deciding "that the assassins of a president were public enemies, and as such should be tried before a military tribunal."[27] A man with a military background and service as a lawyer and state senator seemed to be perfect for the position, considering the emotions surfacing due to the death of the nation's leader.

Those emotions gave the general an excellent opportunity to contribute to peacefully reuniting the nation. In a sense, the country now entered a second phase of the sectional struggle, a less conventional one in which Wallace still might serve his country in his capacity as a Union officer, but by political means. Lincoln's death had a heartrending effect on many citizens and soldiers throughout the country, making a prompt and judicious conclusion to the episode all the more important.

In Tennessee, for example, Union troops under Maj. Gen. George H. Thomas were about to celebrate the capture of Richmond and Lee's surrender when they learned of Lincoln's assassination. Thomas told Stanton that the "whole community, military and civic, is profoundly affected at this terrible national calamity. The flags displayed at the different military offices have been draped in mourning, and minute guns will be fired until sundown."[28] Bvt. Maj. Gen. John W. Geary, commanding the 2nd Division of the XX Army Corps, recounted that the news of Robert E. Lee's surrender was received in mid-April "and read to our troops, who received them with unbounded enthusiasm." But, as in Thomas's case, the joyous news was quickly ruined by that of the president's death. Geary recounted how "the news produced the deepest grief and indignation throughout the command."[29]

Citizens and soldiers across the country agonized over the ease with which Booth took Lincoln's life.[30] As a result, Stanton and the new president offered substantial rewards for the capture of the assassination conspirators or information leading to arrests.[31] Johnson even offered $100,000 for the arrest of former Confederate president Jefferson Davis, because many officials came to believe that the rebel leader was a key part of the plot to kill Lincoln.[32]

While northerners cried for their fallen executive, Confederate president Jefferson Davis adamantly declared that he had no knowledge of the plot, and most former rebel officers expressed their regret for the assassination. The murder had led to wild suspicions and hysteria, as Union men were accusing Davis, Robert E. Lee, and other high-ranking Confederates of involvement in the conspiracy.[33] Such bitter assertions aggravated ill will in a country that needed to heal its wounds. A well-conducted trial led by Hunter and Wallace might settle some of the hard feelings expressed in April and May of 1865.

The Federal government soon claimed that it had evidence that Davis and Confederate secret service agents working in Canada played a part in Lincoln's murder, but the judge advocate declined to put them on trial with eight defendants. The former rebel president and his agents assumed the status of unindicted co-conspirators, never tried for treason or complicity in the assassination. Evidence against these southern officials, coming to light during the upcoming trial, amounted chiefly to three witnesses whose testimonies soon appeared to have been perjured. While bits of circumstantial information suggested a connection between Confederate leaders and Booth's plot to kill Lincoln, the Federal government opted not to pursue the matter further once key witnesses had been proven to be perjurers.[34]

These proceedings had begun in the second week of May as scheduled, delaying Wallace's Mexico mission. Consequently, the general merely sent his more detailed report on the western activities to Grant with no chance of going west in the near future.[35] For the next two months, Wallace left most of his other duties to subordinates as he settled in for a lengthy trial.[36]

In addition to Hunter and Wallace, the military court consisted of nine other officers, seven of them generals, with three non-voting members as prosecutors. The accused conspirators and accessories selected their own defense counselors, seven in all.[37] Of the seven generals serving as both judges and jurors, three had graduated from West Point. These generals all had combat experience that was "creditable to a degree."[38] Some had more success than others. For example, Hunter's combat record was lackluster while Brig. Gen. Robert Foster had served gallantly near Petersburg, and Brig. Gen. Thomas Harris had distinguished himself under Sheridan in the Shenandoah Valley in 1864. Bvt. Maj. Gen. August Kautz had performed admirably during George McClellan's Peninsula Campaign. Some, like Wallace, had non-combat experience that may have led to their appointment. Hunter had served on the court-martial of Maj. Gen. Fitz John Porter, and Brig. Gen. Albion Howe was a medical doctor. Bvt. Brig. Gen. James Ekin may have merely been available, as he was a last-minute replacement.[39]

Wallace and his colleagues devoted the next fifty-three days to hearing testimony from 361 witnesses out of the 483 subpoenaed by the court.[40] Judge

Advocate General Joseph Holt later admitted that the "inevitable result of this trial had been generally anticipated throughout the country," with little doubt that the court would convict all of the accused.[41]

The hearings were initially held behind closed doors, but newspapers criticized the secrecy, demanding that the public had a right to observe the proceedings in such a public matter. Consequently, the makeshift courtroom was soon packed with onlookers who whispered constantly, annoying the commissioners and lawyers.[42] Newspapers around the country, most notably Washington's *Daily National Intelligencer*, then printed partial transcripts of the hearings.[43] For example, the *Intelligencer* reproduced portions of the testimony "to which the injunction of secrecy need not be applied" in order "to gratify the natural desire of the public to learn all that is proved against the prisoners on trial." The periodical sold out most of its editions.[44]

Distractions helped to mask what amounted to an imperfect trial with arguably predetermined verdicts. Democratic senator Reverdy Johnson of Maryland, whom Wallace knew from his assignments in Baltimore, had volunteered to be Mary Surratt's lawyer. But the judge advocate declared that the senator was a Confederate sympathizer. The commission discouraged the counsel from appearing in court on Surratt's behalf, but they refrained from disqualifying him. Johnson attended occasionally, and he submitted a closing argument that a junior lawyer read to the court on his behalf. This early decision was one of the oddest in a series of instances in which the judge advocates and the generals overseeing the tribunal sided against the defendants and their lawyers.[45]

Wallace almost always joined the court in overruling objections by the counselors for the defendants while, at the same time, the tribunal sustained approximately four-fifths of the prosecution's objections. When one defense attorney asked for clarification of the charges against the clients, he received only a vague explanation. He merely wanted to know whether all the prisoners would be charged with conspiracy to assassinate the president, as well as his murder, or merely one of the two. Wallace tried to help the defense get some clarification on the charges but, in the end, Hunter and the other commissioners accepted the judge advocate's view that a confusingly vague charge of conspiracy sufficed. The prisoners were collectively charged with conspiracy, which also seemed to include the basic charge of murder. If the court found them guilty of taking part in the planning, then it was understood that they were essentially guilty of murder because the defendants failed to warn the government of the plot to kill Lincoln. They were part of a conspiracy that resulted in a death. According to civil code dealing with conspiracies in 1865, all eight defendants, if found guilty of a conspiracy to kidnap or kill the president, were liable for the actions of Booth, and could be punished as Booth might have been.[46]

At the same time, Federal authorities brought an additional charge against most of the defendants, separate from the blanket charge of conspiracy. Lewis Payne attempted to murder Seward and was charged for that. David Herold was alleged to be Booth's accomplice in Lincoln's assassination since he traveled with the actor before and after the killing. George Atzerodt was supposed to murder Vice President Johnson then he changed his mind, so the court charged him with planning to commit the crime. Even though there was no definitive proof, Michael O'Laughlin was alleged to have attempted to kill Grant. Samuel Arnold was not involved in the conspiracy through to the end, but the prosecution charged him with being a part of the planning before action was taken. Mary Surratt may have had no knowledge of the conspiracy, but she was separately accused of harboring and concealing the conspirators. The accused all came to her home to plot their crimes—at times the prosecution insisted that she was the mastermind of the entire operation. The court was unable to prove beyond a reasonable doubt that she knew what Booth and the others conspired to do, but that did not seem to matter in the end. Spangler claimed to have had no knowledge of the plot, but he knew the Booth family, worked at Ford's Theater, and held Booth's horse on 14 April. Spangler was prosecuted for aiding in the actor's escape. Dr. Mudd claimed to have merely set an injured man's leg, not knowing how Booth broke the limb. But, as in Spangler's case, the doctor previously knew Booth, and the judge advocates used the information as proof of his part in the conspiracy.[47]

With Hunter appointed as president of the commission, Wallace routinely deferred to him in most matters. Moreover, Joseph Holt was the lead judge advocate in charge of the prosecution's case, so the Hoosier did not make a case, prepare witnesses, or do anything else a lawyer of his caliber often carried out during a trial. On the average day, the second in command of the proceedings sat behind a long table and listened to prosecutors examine witness after witness. Having minimal patience, Wallace looked for ways to keep busy. He was a born artist, and exhibited his talent in writing, painting, sculpting, or drawing. He occupied himself by penciling excellent sketches of the people involved in the great trial. Some of the drawings portrayed striking and accurate images of the prisoners.[48] While the sketches were impressive, they most importantly demonstrated how routine the trial became; there was no challenge for the general in carrying out his legal duties.

In most cases, Wallace went along with the court's bias against the defendants. Judge Advocate Holt had a habit of introducing unreliable witnesses for the prosecution while convincing the commission to suppress evidence possibly helpful to the accused, such as Booth's diary. Mary Surratt's lawyer wanted to introduce the journal because he claimed that it proved that the woman had no knowledge of the plot against Lincoln, Seward, and Johnson. She merely coddled the friends of her beloved son, John, in her boarding house. Holt convinced the commissioners to disallow the diary. Wallace, despite this episode, continued to be rather certain of Mary Surratt's guilt as the trial reached its conclusion. Public pressure to deal out swift convictions and punishment may have encouraged the members of the court to disregard such evidence for the defense while accepting sketchy testimony for the prosecution.[49] At the same time, the diary did not appear to have totally exonerated Surratt; Booth merely failed to mention any conscious involvement on her part. In addition, a number of pages, possibly containing incriminating evidence, had been ripped out of the journal.[50]

A civil trial may have only convicted Herold, Payne, and Atzerodt since one could argue that there was reasonable doubt in the others' cases, but the nation mourned and wanted somebody to be punished soon and severely for Lincoln's death. Notably, however, later claims that a civil trial would have been significantly different have been exaggerated. The tribunal, while demonstrating some bias for the prosecution, generally adhered to the accepted practices of civil law, only differing significantly in what governmental agency controlled the proceedings. Lawyers on both sides made objections in accordance with civil code then practiced, although the prosecution was more successful in such motions. There were also logical questions about the prospects for a fair civil trial. This would likely have occurred in Washington, D.C., or Virginia, or perhaps Maryland, where southern sympathies among jurors might have prevented true justice, making the possible bias of a military commission more palatable.[51] Furthermore, no matter where the proceedings took place, intense public pressure for convictions was bound to influence the results, and the commissioners likely wanted to send a strong message to anyone who might consider taking part in a future conspiracy to kill a president.

As a result of this extraordinary military trial, Payne, Atzerodt, Herold, and Mary Surratt were sentenced to hang, and President Johnson promptly ordered the executions.[52] It seems as though Hunter and four other commissioners had second thoughts about Mrs. Surratt's guilt after the trial ended. They sent a petition for clemency to President Johnson. The chief executive never received it, maybe because Holt failed to deliver the plea. Wallace continued to believe that the tribunal did the right thing in convicting the widowed boarding house operator, refusing to sign the petition. At any rate, Americans in the following years became outraged at the manner in which Mary Surratt was convicted, especially when learning about Booth's diary.[53] This information came to light in 1867 when John Surratt was finally captured and put on trial. The problems with the conspiracy trial in 1865 created so much bad feeling among Americans that it apparently had an effect on the jurors in John Surratt's case, as those proceedings ended with his acquittal because of a hung jury.[54]

Three of the other defendants—Arnold, O'Laughlin, and Mudd—were sentenced to life in prison for their parts in the conspiracy. Based on less evidence of his involvement, the court condemned Spangler to prison for six years. All four men were sent to the military prison on one of the Dry Tortugas, islands approximately seventy miles west of Key West, Florida.[55] President Johnson pardoned these prisoners after a few years, except for O'Laughlin, who died as a prisoner.[56] Mudd saved many lives during a yellow fever epidemic, leading Johnson to free him and Arnold in 1869. Spangler was released in 1871.[57]

Support for the pardons grew because more controversial information about the case made its way to the American public. Even after no more could be done, the controversy continued. In late 1865, Holt felt compelled to defend the actions of the commission, stating that the participants in the tribunal exhibited the greatest excellence in fulfilling their duties, but many people came to believe differently.[58] Criticism existed for many years, causing Susan Wallace, finishing her dead husband's autobiography, to defend his actions in going along with Holt and the other commissioners. She echoed the defensive explanation of one of the commissioners, who stated that "the American people should be fully informed as to this most important episode in their history, in order that they may not be misled by men who were not the friends, but the enemies of our government in its struggle for its preservation and perpetuation."[59]

Lew Wallace had a great opportunity with this trial to use his expertise to the nation's benefit. He was a capable lawyer and experienced politician, and he had served on the Buell commission, making him a good choice. However, and even though all eight defendants were likely involved in the conspiracy to some degree, the general failed to object to biases exhibited during the commission's existence. At the same time, the assignment added to his résumé, making the lawyer-turned-general a prime candidate for a similar duty just a few months later.

When not sitting on the commission that met in the drab, old Penitentiary building in Washington, the Hoosier spent much of his time in Baltimore supervising the disbanding of regiments and the relieving of officers, as well as trying to secure loans for Carvajal and the Mexican liberals. The reduction in the size of the Union army and navy began in earnest in June of 1865 as all of the key Confederate commands had surrendered or disbanded by the end of May. For example, the Middle Military Division, in "accordance with instructions from the War Department," directed that "all dismounted volunteer cavalry of this command will be immediately discharged [from] the service."[60] Numerous infantry units and senior officers also received discharges. Mustering out was complicated but rushed along through the last six months of 1865.[61]

Once the assassination trial concluded, Wallace planned to allocate more of his efforts to discharging volunteers and preparing to go back to Mexico. Still inclined to pursue adventures that would prove his worth as a martial man, he even wrote letters to other veteran soldiers, encouraging them to get involved in his Mexico schemes.[62] In August, though, these designs were again cut short. Six or seven weeks after the conspiracy trial ended in Washington, Wallace found himself serving on another extraordinary military commission, one for which his past assignments made him especially qualified.

During Maj. Gen. William Tecumseh Sherman's March to the Sea, news trickled north about a prison camp holding captured Union soldiers near the town of Andersonville, Georgia. Many Civil War prison camps were horrible places for men to wait for the end of the conflict between North and South; 56,000 of 410,000 prisoners died in the Union and Confederate camps.[63] Still, Andersonville soon came to be described as the worst of the terrible. Rumors of overcrowding, diseases, starvation, and senseless death abounded, and outcries over the despicable conditions reached a fever pitch when some of the former prisoners were photographed, their pictures published in *Harper's Weekly* on 17 June.[64] Americans shuddered as they viewed pictures of living skeletons, men so emaciated that it was difficult to believe that they were still alive. Published recollections or diaries of past prisoners added to the clamor.[65] In all, some 41,000 Union soldiers inhabited the prison in 1864 and 1865, but only about 26,000 lived to go home after the war ended.[66]

Former prisoners and their families blamed some combination of "Lincoln, Jefferson Davis, [camp commander] Henry Wirz, prison guards, the government, the Union, the Confederacy, African Americans, and many other agents" for the "deprivation and cruelty."[67] The Lincoln administration certainly received blame for not doing more to bring these captured soldiers home during the war.

Arguments over the exchange of black prisoners got in the way of agreements to send Federals north and Confederates south. It was also likely that Grant and Lincoln wished to end any exchange of prisoners because it might prolong the conflict to the Confederacy's benefit. It appears that victory for the Union meant the "prioritization of some lives over others."[68] Thus, after Lee surrendered, returning soldiers and their families pressured the Johnson administration for answers. Consequently, the Union government was under pressure to prove that Confederate misconduct had caused the deaths of so many at the Georgia prison camp, not the victims' own president and war department.[69] Wallace, a political general, came to serve the administration's efforts to find one or more people directly responsible for the loss of life.

After Lincoln's death, and with the prodding of the War Department in May and June, people increasingly blamed the horrendous health of these former inmates on the commander of the Andersonville camp, Capt. Henry Wirz. A Swiss immigrant who got caught up in the Confederate cause and enlisted while living in Louisiana, Wirz insisted that he had few means to create better conditions. The commandant believed that the duties he "had to perform were arduous and unpleasant, and I am satisfied that no man can or will justly blame me for things that happened here and which were beyond my power to control." In his mind, the government could not hold him "responsible for the shortness of rations, for the overcrowded state of the prison (which was in itself a prolific source of the fearful mortality), for the inadequate supplies of clothing, want of shelters, &c." Northerners, on the other hand, believed that he should have done more, and Wirz knew that this sentiment existed, admitting that he now bore "the odium, and men who were prisoners here seem disposed to wreak their vengeance upon me for what they have suffered, who was only the medium, or, I may better say, the tool in the hands of my superiors."[70]

Understanding that his life was in danger, either through vigilante justice or more formal proceedings, the captain desperately wanted to return to Europe with his family. Thinking that U.S. authorities were not inclined to prosecute him, he asked for protection and help in leaving the country.[71] In sending such a request to Union generals, Wirz miscalculated, and U.S. officers were ordered to arrest the man before he managed to depart. Authorities also arrested a few of his subordinates.[72] On 16 May 1865, as Wallace was engrossed in the trial of conspiring assassins, cavalry general James H. Wilson reported that his men had "arrested Capt. H. Wirz, C. S. Army, notorious as commandant of the Andersonville prison." Wilson also managed to "forward herewith all the records, &c., of the prison that could be found, and also other papers relating to his cruel treatment of our men," inducing the brevet major general to echo the thoughts of many—"that this miscreant be brought before a general court-martial in Washington, D.C., where the evidence in his case can be more readily obtained."[73] Maj. Gen. George H. Thomas then ordered that the 2nd U.S. Cavalry escort Wirz to the nation's capital for interrogation and a possible trial.[74]

Having returned to Baltimore in early July, Wallace settled back into the postwar administrative duties of the Middle Department. Now that the chances for glory on the battlefield were gone, he yearned to go home in order to do business and be with his wife and boy. The situation was even more frustrating for the general since Maryland's largest city was increasingly quiet, the departmental commander having "far less to do in the office than ever before." In fact, he had gone back to working on his manual of tactics in order to pass the time.[75]

To his relief, Wallace soon received vague orders to report to the adjutant general in Washington, and the general believed that he was to be mustered out of the army. He welcomed the impending arrival of Winfield Scott Hancock, replacing him in command of the department. Wallace speculated that if he was "not to be retained in the service, I will very soon be so informed; and the sooner the better."[76] If he had achieved the glory that he relished during the war, it is likely that he would have lobbied hard for a permanent command in the U.S. Army, but he now understood that there was little prospect for such a command, especially for someone without a diploma from the Military Academy. Furthermore, his reputation still suffered due to his mediocre performance at Shiloh, and because of his problematic relationships with superiors.

The general reported to the War Department on 20 August, but instead of returning home he found himself "president of the military commission assembled for the trial of one Captain Henry Wirz," who had been "charged with starving Union prisoners at Andersonville."[77] Wallace was not thrilled with the assignment, not seeing the benefits to such duty, but he was highly qualified. He had served on the Buell commission as well as the trial of the assassination conspirators—all this in addition to his experience as a lawyer in Indiana, as well as his command of Camp Chase near Columbus, Ohio. Very few, if any, officers, West Pointers included, could have exceeded those qualifications. Still, the political general lamented that the "investigation will occupy at least two months—the hot, unwholesome, malarial months here by the Potomac."[78]

Besides Wallace, this tribunal was composed of eight officers. In his defense, Wirz chose two of his own lawyers.[79] Only one of the six generals, Adjutant

General of the Army Lorenzo Thomas, had gone to West Point. The other five had varying degrees of success in field commands, but all could have been proud of their combat service. Three of the generals under Wallace had studied law. The tribunal appeared to consist of very reputable gentlemen, but at least one historian has suggested that these officers were in a difficult position since all but two of the members had some interest in politics. If Wirz were to be found innocent, these commissioners might suffer for it later at the ballot box.[80]

Not surprisingly, Wallace learned before the commission first met that Wirz planned to defend his actions by insisting that he only followed orders from superiors.[81] The defendant had already made this argument in earlier letters to Union officials, and continued to do so before and during the trial.[82] If true, the general "expected that out of this investigation will come proof of the [Confederate] leaders' connection with that criminality."[83] This might amount to evidence that superiors explicitly hampered efforts by Wirz to help the prisoners, or that they instructed the commandant to treat the Union soldiers poorly.

Even considering the awful conditions at the Georgia prison, the defense made some sense but, as in the case of the trial of the Lincoln conspirators, the American public increasingly wanted to see someone pay for unspeakable wrongs. While there had been men above Wirz capable of doing more to help the prisoners of war, some Americans and governmental officials even wanting to indict Jefferson Davis, the Swiss immigrant was the most obvious target for the attorney general. Wirz commanded the camp, after all. Others might readily pretend an inability to make positive change in this case, but Wirz could not. At any rate, Wallace already seemed to be certain of the defendant's guilt.[84]

Still, the U.S. government seemed to be inclined to go easy on most rebels, even those at the highest levels, and it appeared that the Johnson administration decided to do the same in this case, at least at first. On 21 August, one day after Wallace received charge of the commission, he informed his wife that the secretary of war dissolved the organization, happily announcing: "So we go!" To the general's chagrin, he later learned that the commission was to reconvene on the next day. The War Department leaders changed their minds because of the public pressure, and the Indianan could only hope to soon "be released from this onerous duty."[85] This wish failed to materialize, and Wallace settled in for another lengthy stint as a military judge.

When the trial began again on 23 August, Wirz's counsel added to his earlier defense of merely following the orders of superiors. For one, the lawyer argued that his client had surrendered under the same terms as the rest of Gen. Joseph

Johnston's command at the end of the war; under those terms, "it was agreed that all officers and men should be permitted to return to their homes, not to be disturbed by the U.S. authorities so long as they observed their obligations and the laws in force where they resided." The defense also claimed that General Wilson promised that Wirz would not be harmed or imprisoned if he gave information to the government. The most compelling argument was that "the commission had no jurisdiction to try him for the offenses charged" because, on 21 August, the commandant had already been "arraigned and put on trial before the same tribunal on the same charges, and could not be tried or put to answer a second time." Moreover, this commission's "charges and specifications were too vague and indefinite, and did not make out an offense punishable by the laws of war."[86]

Wallace and his fellow commissioners rejected these motions, insisting that Wirz be brought to trial for violating the laws of war, and that the first real meeting of the commission had amounted to a decision to not bring charges; there had not been any declaration of innocence or an actual trial on that day. Relying heavily on Judge Advocates Joseph Holt and Norton P. Chipman, the court levied two charges against the prison commander. First, Wirz had "[m]aliciously, willfully, and traitorously, and in aid of the then existing armed rebellion against the United States of America" combined and conspired with at least a few others "to injure the health and destroy the lives of soldiers in the military service of the United States, then held and being prisoners of war within the lines of the so-called Confederate States, and in the military prisons thereof, to the end that the armies of the United States might be weakened and impaired, in violation of the laws and customs of war." The second charge was that of murder, again "in violation of the laws and customs of war."[87]

As the trial proceeded, Wallace seemed to be certain of Wirz's guilt. He always was suspicious of Wirz's character, commenting that in "manner he is nervous and fully alarmed, avoids your gaze, and withers and shrivels under the knit brows of the crowd." Altogether, in the general's opinion, the Swiss immigrant "was well chosen for his awful service in the warring Confederacy."[88] It was quickly obvious to Wallace that Andersonville was a thoroughly awful place, and that Wirz did little to make things easier for the inhabitants. He recounted to his wife testimony of an instance in which a parched prisoner, near death, crawled under a bar that served as the "dead line" in order to drink from a small creek. Guards were ordered to shoot anyone crossing the "dead line," and a rebel again did so in this case. The recollection so chilled the Indianan that he even planned to paint an oil-color picture of the horrible scene.[89] The commission continued to hear such distressing stories. It appeared likely that the Confederate commandant would be convicted of something.

This realization failed to bring a quick end to testimony, and Wallace complained that he had become "very dull, easily disturbed by noises, and irritable over the most pointless cross-examination of a witness that I have ever listened to, and I have suffered under many."[90] Judge Advocate Holt later explained that the victims in this case were so numerous that the amount of testimony dwarfed that of the earlier trial in May and June, so this trial lasted a few days longer. While the "number of witnesses examined was 148," fewer than in the trial of the assassins, there was much more to say and evaluate in the summer and early fall. "Besides the evidence from these sources, much important testimony obtained from the archives of the rebel Government—including the records of the prison at Andersonville—was also laid before the Commission."[91]

The investigation continued until 21 October, and it included plenty of evidence concerning the charges levied against Wirz.[92] Prisoners at Andersonville died because of diseases, starvation, and lack of shelter and clothing, and witnesses maintained that the commandant took little or no action to diminish the horrible conditions. During the investigation, Wallace and others read through the prison records, which contained "a roster of over 13,000 dead, buried naked, maimed, and putrid, in one vast sepulcher." Former prisoners further reported that three-fourths to four-fifths of these casualties "died of the treatment inflicted on them while in confinement." Judge Advocate Holt was particularly horrified. In his opinion, this human destruction was not the result of "ungovernable passion, but was accomplished slowly and deliberately, by packing upward of 30,000 men like cattle in a fetid pen—a mere cesspool—there to die for need of air to breathe, for want of ground on which to lie, for lack of shelter from sun and rain, and from the slow, agonizing processes of starvation, when air and space and shelter and food were all within the ready gift of their tormentors."[93]

In addition to the truly terrible conditions at Andersonville, former prisoners alleged that Wirz had a hand in a number of murders at the camp. The homicides allegedly committed, supporting the second charge in this case, were divided into four separate classes by Holt. The first consisted of deaths resulting "from the biting of dogs." Secondly, there were "cases of death which resulted from confinement in the stocks and chain gang." Also, the commissioners heard stories "of prisoners killed by guards pursuant to direct order of Wirz given at the time." Lastly, there were "cases of prisoners killed by Wirz's own hand."[94]

It was difficult to verify most of the testimony, especially that by Union soldiers having been imprisoned at Andersonville, but there was plenty of it. One witness recounted how he and some new prisoners received permission from a guard to retrieve water for a friend suffering from epilepsy. Wirz, upon seeing the men leave the main portion of the camp to get water from the nearby creek, shot at them, killing two of the soldiers himself. Another witness recalled how the defendant shot a man who was merely "stooping to pick up his cup which had fallen under the dead-line, and that the man died almost instantly." In many cases, the commandant allegedly ordered the guards to perform these sorts of executions.[95]

Wallace and the other commissioners heard plenty of other accusations. For example, another soldier asserted that he saw "Wirz take a prisoner who was worn out with hunger and disease by the coat collar, and because he could not walk faster, wrench him back and stamp upon him with his boots." Due to the poor treatment, "the man was borne past him bleeding from his mouth and nose, and died in a short time." They also learned about the use of dogs to capture escaping prisoners; these canines were particularly ferocious. Although Wirz was not immediately, or directly, involved in deaths caused by these mean dogs because he was not usually part of the pursuing parties, the "use of dogs was under Wirz's especial direction," and "the pursuit of prisoners was in many instances instituted under his immediate orders." The commandant also appeared to know that these canines were "dangerous to life, so as to make it probable that the men on whose track they were sent would be killed," but he still desired to use the animals in these instances. If guards caught an escapee by using dogs, and the prisoner managed to survive the ordeal, the defendant then had them shackled and chained, or possibly secured in stocks. While confined in this way, soldiers were sometimes tortured. They usually remained in this kind of captivity until they died from hunger or bleeding wounds.[96]

These stories, combined with the obviously horrific conditions at Andersonville, led the prosecution to quickly call for the ultimate punishment, hanging. The commission found Wirz guilty on both charges, citing thirteen different "specifications" in which he contributed to the murders of prisoners of war.[97] Consequently, President Andrew Johnson quickly approved the sentence, and he ordered that the execution be carried out by the Department of Washington on 3 November 1865.[98] The president made this decision, despite some pleas to overturn the commission's sentence on the accounts that nobody else could have done any better in Wirz's position, and that the rebel's health was already failing as he tried to take care of family matters.[99] Pleas for mercy could do no good. As one scholar suggests, in "looking for someone to declare culpable for the horrors of Civil War prisons [in general], the U.S. government found a perfect target in Wirz. He proved to be a malleable symbol of the Civil War prison controversy at a time when confusion abounded concerning what actually happened at Andersonville and other prison camps."[100]

A biased observer of the proceedings, one of the defendant's lawyers, Louis Schade, wrote to Johnson, arguing that wrongs committed in the trial of the assassins were also common in this case. Schade claimed that the commission had "in many instances excluded testimony in favor of the prisoner, and, on the other hand, admitted testimony against the prisoner, both in violation of all rules of law and equity." The lawyer further claimed that the "testimony for the prosecution is loose, indefinite, and in the most part contradictory." He may have been correct in stating that before "any other court but that military commission it would have been an easy matter to uncover and bring to light a tissue of perjuries."[101]

In truth, one could argue that the prosecution took advantage of military law and "good old boy" relationships to include much circumstantial evidence and managed to call forth at least a few questionable witnesses, as well as many who felt a therapeutic need to exaggerate. And, of course, "public vitriol" encouraged very "inflammatory rhetoric" on the part of the prosecution, putting a lot of pressure on the commissioners.[102] According to a historian sympathetic to Wirz, Wallace revealed a great bias in the motions he sustained—anything that might help to implicate Wirz was allowed, and evidence to the contrary was regularly disregarded "on whatever pretext General Wallace could apply."[103] Numerous former prisoners testified during the proceedings, often contradicting each other, but Wallace and the other commissioners understandably interpreted the many different stories as evidence of multiple barbaric incidents, so many that it was difficult to keep them all straight.

In the end, despite some objections, the president concluded that Wirz deserved the punishment handed down by the commissioners, and, on 10 November, the commander of the Department of Washington carried out the execution. The body of the late prison commander was then interred right next to that of George Atzerodt, executed for his part in the conspiracy to kill Lincoln, Johnson, and Seward.[104] Afterwards, the attorney general's office considered prosecuting some of Wirz's subordinates and superiors, maybe even Jefferson Davis, but Holt argued against it. The judge advocate more specifically mentioned that while Richard Bayley Winder, working under Wirz, was implicated by the court "in the conspiracy against the lives of Federal prisoners in rebel hands, no such specific overt acts of violation of the laws of war are as yet fixed upon him as to make it expedient to prefer formal charges and bring him to trial."[105] The government had punished the head of the camp, and was now content to suggest that others were merely following orders.

After these two commissions adjourned, Holt stated that both exhibited the "highest excellence," but it "was not merely in that it was unincumbered by the technicalities and inevitable embarrassments attending the administration of justice before civil tribunals, or in the fact that it could so readily avail itself of the military power of the Government for the execution of its processes and the enforcement of its orders, that its efficacy" was demonstrated. The judge advocate believed that the investigation was allowed to expand under these military tribunals, that wider conspiracies and additional evidence was uncovered because of the more efficient operation.[106] On the other hand, these trials failed to allow for the most efficient defenses. Still, in the case of the assassination conspirators, legitimate evidence suggested that all eight defendants had played a part in Booth's plans, so an imperfect trial managed to come to reasonable conclusions.

Wallace was a part of all of this, even though Holt seemed to take unofficial charge of each commission. The Indianan was second in command of the military court appointed to try the conspirators charged in Lincoln's assassination. Wallace's service on this court made sense because of his experience as a lawyer and his service on the Buell commission. This duty logically qualified him to be president of the trial of Wirz. Even though his service on these tribunals was not exemplary—unbiased proceedings may not have occurred—the political general still managed to make final contributions to the Union before resigning from the army, effective on 20 November 1865.[107]

Andrew Johnson, Stanton, and the American public wanted swift convictions and closure in these cases, and Wallace helped to make that happen. Wallace had achieved important results—though not on the battlefield—for the Union government in 1865, despite the imperfect tribunals. A trial in front of a military commission did not prohibit the officers involved from conducting a thorough investigation. Civil code and procedure could be followed in most cases. Wallace may have failed to ensure that this happened during both of these trials. In retrospect, the eight conspirators likely received acceptable punishments, and Wirz could logically be punished for at least allowing war crimes to happen—he was the officer in charge of the camp. However, if the earlier proceedings had been handled with less apparent partiality, sympathetic clamor for Surratt, Mudd, and others may have been lessened, and the rhetoric of the Wirz trial may not have negatively impacted postwar reconciliation.[108]

Now no longer a general, the Indianan was able to concentrate even more on acquiring a loan for Mexican rebels, much of this done privately as a civilian, as well as go home to support his family. Having Grant's blessing, Wallace worked all of 1866 attempting to procure supplies and weapons for the Mexican republic. He and associates successfully delivered some weapons and ammunition in late 1866, much of this financed by Wallace, but they had trouble collecting payment. The disgruntled agent settled for $2,500 in 1868, and finally received $15,000 from Mexico in 1882, far less than the $100,000 that Carvajal originally had promised.[109]

Behind all of this was Wallace's ever-present desire to prove his manliness and preserve honor by commanding troops in battle. He had been unable to secure glory on American soil, but success might come south of the Rio Grande. He managed to organize a few brigades, and Carvajal offered him a commission as major general in the republic's army; but the American was not able to lead these American troops in battle on Mexican soil. The difficulties in transporting arms and munitions, and resistance from Grant and Secretary of State Seward, delayed this part of Wallace's mission. Moreover, the French domination of Mexico ended in May of 1867. Wallace came home to Indiana that year, his wish to once again lead thousands of soldiers in a glorious battle still unfulfilled.[110]

Conclusion

Politicians became generals during the Civil War largely because President Abraham Lincoln needed them. The Union had too few West Pointers to lead brigades, divisions, corps, and armies in the field. Well-known politicians had attained commissions as a result of the United States' previous conflicts, and it quickly became evident that such men would be necessary for Lincoln's war effort. In exchange for making politically influential individuals generals, the president expected them to aid in recruiting soldiers, lead units in combat, give speeches on behalf of the Union war effort, and carry out administrative duties. Along with a number of other politicians, Lew Wallace received a volunteer general's commission to do all of those assignments, his Mexican War and militia experience making him more qualified than some new commanders. In these activities, Wallace had chances to see glorious action on the battlefield, but he often failed to perform well when he had the opportunity. Nevertheless, Wallace still fulfilled most of his duties in a satisfactory fashion.

While Wallace had contributed to the Lincoln administration's war effort in military and especially in political ways, the general had not achieved the success that he expected in 1861. He wanted more than modest credit for a satisfactory job. He wanted glory—to be a hero—and the likely political rewards that would accompany a hero's status. Unfortunately for him, few people considered him a hero after the war.

The Indianan's views on manhood led him to be quite disappointed after the war. As mentioned previously, some historians of gender differentiate between two competing masculinities in antebellum America, restrained manhood and martial manhood. Lorien Foote, on the other hand, refers to gentlemen and "roughs" in her monograph on manhood during the Civil War. Other scholars concentrate on a dominant self-made manhood that seemed to triumph over an earlier communal manhood. Wallace, who straddled the line between these dueling manhoods, often veered toward the martial and rough notions of what it meant to be a self-made man.[1]

Physical and military triumphs, bold or aggressive behavior, a distaste for restraint and discipline, and vindication for even mediocre slights to one's honor seemed to characterize Wallace's view on the traits required of a man. West Pointers, however, often embraced a more restrained, gentlemanly, and communal manhood. They professed to avoid rude and rash behavior, indiscipline, selfishness, and political fights. Political generals, including Wallace, appeared to embrace all of these negatives, leading to numerous differences between them and those who claimed a special expertise in waging war. Considering the differing views of Wallace and educated generals, his sour relationships with Halleck, Grant, and Smith make more sense.[2]

Although a natural rivalry between West Pointers and political generals may have caused tension between Wallace and professionally trained officers, this was not the primary reason for his difficulties. There were other more influential reasons for the problems that Wallace encountered during the war. For one, he was his own worst enemy at times. An ambitious and undisciplined officer, he regularly sought out mentors like Oliver Morton, Charles Smith, Henry Halleck, and Ulysses Grant, but he often proceeded to find reasons to fault them. Wallace's lack of respect for his superiors led him to occasionally criticize or disrespect them in correspondence and conversation—and this was particularly damaging to his relationships with Governor Morton, Generals Halleck and Grant, and Secretary of War Edwin Stanton.

In battle, Wallace sometimes was extremely courageous, daring, and bold at the regimental level. But later on, he demonstrated boldness in the most unfortunate situations while sometimes becoming cautious in battle as a division commander. For example, Wallace might have boldly interpreted Grant's order of 6 April 1862 to mean what suited his hope for glory, but he then cautiously moved his troops in position to engage the enemy. He showed similar tendencies at Fort Donelson. Therefore, Grant, Smith, Halleck, and Stanton decided that Wallace was unreliable—he might do well or he might not—and so they tried to compensate for that by giving him responsibilities that he could more easily execute, such as those of a garrison commander.

Wallace's inability to follow orders certainly troubled Grant, as it would anyone trained at West Point.[3] The commander of the Army of the Tennessee told

Wallace not to go on the offensive at Donelson, and the new division commander misinterpreted the order to mean that he could not come to the aid of John McClernand when that general's division gave way on the right flank in northern Tennessee. On that same evening in February of 1862, Wallace managed to take a hill that would prevent an easy escape by the Confederates at Donelson. He had done well, but then ruined the moment by rudely denouncing an order by Grant to fall back instead of apologetically explaining how the situation had changed.

At Shiloh, Wallace received an order to assist a beleaguered army near Pittsburg Landing. While Grant expected him to come to a central position behind the Union line, so that the army's commander could place the 3rd Division's regiments where needed, Wallace assumed that he should best attain glory on the far right in an attempt to turn the rebels' left flank. In that case, especially in Grant's later opinion, Wallace misinterpreted orders received in the morning of 6 April.

Embarrassment over that situation for Grant, William T. Sherman, and Wallace led Halleck and Grant to put the political general in less risky positions, performing less difficult duties—not because Wallace did not go to West Point, but because of uneven results and a lack of restraint. After Shiloh, Wallace and his 3rd Division were often held in reserve or assigned to garrison duty. Even in that capacity, Grant, in late April of 1862, lamented to the subordinate general that "often my orders and instructions are misunderstood or totally disregarded by you."[4] Wallace believed that West Pointers, strongly influenced by Halleck, had personally turned against him to ruin his career, seemingly ignoring the role his own behavior and mistakes played in his unofficial demotion.

Morton asked him to give recruiting speeches in 1862 and 1863, and the general grudgingly agreed. He refused to see Morton's requests as opportunities and declined to speak any more than was absolutely necessary. In July of 1863, when Wallace was again "on the shelf," the governor of Indiana asked him to perform the politically beneficial duty of helping to protect the people of southern and central Indiana from rebel raiders under John Hunt Morgan. If he had been the Federal general to defeat Morgan, Wallace would have gained the fame he sought, but he initially balked at the opportunity, claiming to be worried about going against orders from Halleck and Stanton to stay in Crawfordsville. Wallace may never have understood that every military opportunity, such as engaging the famous raider Morgan, also carried high risks. In this case, he sought the glory, but hesitated to take a chance.

On the other hand, Wallace energetically came to the aid of Cincinnati, Ohio, in September of 1862 in order to protect that city from Confederate troops under Edmund Kirby Smith. In that city, the general encouraged the region's citizens to come to the defense, organizing as many as 75,000 men to thwart a possible rebel advance from the south. Wallace may not have received all the credit he was due at Cincinnati.

As an administrator, Wallace realized success, politically and sometimes militarily benefiting the Lincoln administration. He also agreed to serve on a commission to investigate the actions of Maj. Gen. Don Carlos Buell in Kentucky and Tennessee during that same year. Such duties were not ones to gain anyone glory, but they were necessary for the functioning of an army. In addition, the Buell investigation was arguably politically motivated, and it received public attention, making it more than a military matter. Wallace was more inclined to perform such tasks than those that strictly involved recruitment or any other service under Governor Morton, who he failed to believe could help his chances at securing another field command at the brigade or division level.

Success at Cincinnati and on the Buell Commission may have led to his appointment in Maryland, where Wallace completed his best work of the war as primarily an administrator. Using his troops discretely to the fullest advantage as commander of the Middle Department, he was able to supervise and secure two elections in 1864 on behalf of Lincoln and the Republican Party. Confederate sympathizers were unable to get their way, and pro-Union candidates won races in most cases. The president appreciated Wallace's efforts so much that he personally invited him to the Republican Party's national convention in 1864. Wallace thus demonstrated that a political general did not have to win in a battle to contribute to winning the war.

Wallace's appointment as commander of the Middle Department and the VIII Army Corps led to another important political contribution. A Confederate corps under Jubal Early marched toward Baltimore and Washington while Lincoln, Stanton, Halleck, and Grant seemed to ignore warnings of a possibly devastating offensive move that threatened the nation's capital. Wallace did not understand these latest rebel movements at first. At the same time, to his credit, he realized the potential for danger far earlier than his superiors. If Wallace had developed better relationships with Stanton, Halleck, and Grant, he might have been able to get their attention on this matter. His superiors' lack of trust forced Wallace to confront Early's rampaging rebels near Frederick, Maryland, with only a modest force. As Grant later admitted, Wallace "moved with commendable promptitude to meet the enemy at the Monocacy. He could hardly have expected to defeat him badly, but he hoped to cripple and delay him until Washington could be put into a state of preparation for his reception."[5]

Viewed one way, Wallace's small battle with Early was a military success. Grant argued that the rebel's ultimate repulse was largely "contributed to by General Lew Wallace's leading what might well be considered almost a forlorn hope. If Early had been but one day earlier, he might have entered the capital before the arrival of reinforcements" sent from Petersburg. Politically, the lawyer from Indiana achieved through his defeat at Monocacy "a greater benefit to the cause than often falls to the lot of a commander of an equal force to render by means of victory."[6] Confederate troops marching into Washington in July of 1864 would have struck a terrible psychological blow to Union supporters, and would have damaged Lincoln's hopes to serve a second term as president.

The Battle of Monocacy allowed Wallace to demonstrate his best skill as a general in the field of battle, but it was too late in the war for him to see additional combat service. Grant eventually appreciated his gallant efforts, but he still failed to trust the political general's military decisions. When Wallace formulated a plan to assist Mexican rebels who were fighting French occupiers, Grant allowed him to negotiate with Juaristas and Confederates, but declined to let the unpredictable general take charge of troops to assist the Mexican patriots.

Grant worried less about Wallace's lust for glorious battle by April of 1865. The war was ending, and new administrative duties awaited. Less than a week after Robert E. Lee surrendered at Appomattox, Virginia, John Wilkes Booth assassinated President Lincoln. Although authorities killed Booth after a pursuit, the government captured alleged conspirators, and Andrew Johnson ordered Wallace to serve as the second in charge of the military court that tried the defendants. Experience as a lawyer and a politician, and service on the Buell Commission, made Wallace well suited for this administrative duty. Weeks after that trial concluded, the general found himself president of the trial of Capt. Henry Wirz, the commandant of the infamous Andersonville prison camp. Wallace's reluctant command of Camp Chase in Ohio made him especially qualified for the position. The political general's service on these trials brought quick decisions, if not justice. Some people later questioned aspects of these judicial proceedings, but problematic and legitimate evidence in both trials suggested that the defendants were guilty.

Wallace concluded his Civil War service having contributed politically, as well as militarily, to the war effort. The general defended Cincinnati and southern Indiana from rebels. He occasionally gave speeches to help Governor Morton recruit Indianans for the Union. His leadership of the Middle Department and his confrontation of Jubal Early with an inferior force were important to the Lincoln administration during a presidential election year. In these ways, the general managed to provide praiseworthy political contributions while often evading the usual opportunities for such service. While these duties never managed to fully win over Stanton, Halleck, and Grant, they demonstrated how a political general should be evaluated differently than most professionally trained officers; as historians David Work and Thomas J. Goss assert, their contributions to the Union could be made in multiple ways.[7]

By evaluating the performance of political generals during the Civil War, Wallace can be compared or contrasted with other generals, such as Benjamin Butler, Nathaniel Banks, Frank Blair, Franz Sigel, John Logan, and John McClernand.[8] His own efforts were not without merit, but Wallace did not have the success that Logan achieved during the war. Logan performed as well in the field as any army commander. The Democrat from Illinois also eagerly supported the war effort and Lincoln while engaging in little political intrigue. Importantly, Logan managed to tolerate West Pointers, seldom if ever appearing to resent their professional qualifications.

If Logan was the best political general, many others were no more than average in terms of overall contribution to the war effort and were modest, too often disappointing, in regard to merely battlefield performance. Similar to many of these officers, Wallace was promoted to major general and in that rank demonstrated imperfections as a commander, but he continued to be a political asset to the president. For instance, Sigel was never able to put his professional European military training to successful use, but he politically aided the president by encouraging many German immigrants to engage in the war effort. On the other hand, Wallace was a political asset in his handling of the defense of Cincinnati and Washington, and in supervising the elections of 1864 in Maryland.

But unlike Sigel, Banks, McClernand, and Butler, the political general from Indiana was more restrained in his political scheming. He contacted political connections in the hope of finding another brigade or division level command. Wallace annoyed West Pointers and arguably failed as a division commander on the battlefield, but he seldom provoked the more visible controversy and trouble that characterized the service of the other four generals. Wallace's bad relations with other generals and his announcements or general orders seldom became fodder for newspapers across the nation. His performance more closely resembled that of Frank Blair in that both caused troubles on occasion, but Lincoln could overlook their faults due to other successes. Blair achieved battlefield success while Wallace provided contributions to the war effort at Cincinnati, Baltimore, and Monocacy, as well as during his assignment to three extraordinary tribunals or investigations. Without his disagreeable temperament and flashes of impatience, Wallace might have turned such experience into a career that more closely resembled that of John Logan.[9]

The Indianan went back to his home state after he failed to secure a field command in Mexico in 1866 and 1867. He did not immediately see political benefits to his service for the Union during the late war, losing a bid for a United States congressional seat in 1870, but he had greater success in launching a career as a writer, publishing a novel based on Hernán Cortés's conquest of Mexico, *The Fair God*, in 1873. The book failed to make Wallace a household name throughout the country, but it was a good beginning.

Lawyerly duties and writing had to be put aside in 1877 when Wallace became a member of the unique committee to oversee the counting of disputed ballots in Florida, Louisiana, and South Carolina after the 1876 presidential election. This extraordinary assignment required him to spend much of his time in Florida. Just like the other committee members, he sided with his party, helping Republican Rutherford B. Hayes win the presidency.[10] The new chief executive rewarded Wallace by appointing him governor of New Mexico Territory.

Hayes hoped that the former general could put an end to New Mexico's Lincoln County Wars, which began as conflicts between ranching interests and came to include murder and mayhem on the part of William H. Bonney—popularly known as "Billy the Kid." In 1879, Wallace called for troops and arms to arrest Billy. In fact, the governor later initiated a one-on-one deal with Bonney to pardon the gunslinger in exchange for information on certain murders, but the Kid became nervous, fled the jail where he was being held, and committed more murders. Bonney escaped one more jail and a death sentence before being shot by Sheriff Pat Garrett on 15 July 1881.[11]

Wallace was governor of New Mexico Territory from 1878 to 1881, spending much of that time finishing what would become his most memorable achievement, a novel titled *Ben-Hur: A Tale of the Christ*.[12] The main character and hero of the story, Ben-Hur, seems to mirror Wallace's view of himself. Like the author, the hero "thrills at the thought of imminent battle," devotes himself to the art of war, and "like his creator, Ben-Hur is a dreamer, and the dreams are passionately defended."[13] Presenting the story of the fictional Ben-Hur alongside that of Jesus Christ, the book was published in November of 1880. The novel received some good reviews but failed to sell in great numbers during the first few years. Eventually the novel became popular among readers across the country, as 400,000 copies had been sold by 1889. By 1911, 1 million authorized copies had been purchased, along with countless pirated versions in Europe. Remarkable success continued, and the publisher conservatively estimated 2.5 million copies sold by 1944.[14]

The novel greatly pleased President James Garfield, who referred to the author as "Ben-Hur Wallace," and then named him U.S. minister to Turkey in 1881. Garfield hoped that Wallace would write another book based on his adventures in the Middle East. Wallace remained an ambassador until 1885. Once he returned to America, the famous author lectured throughout the country. He supported Benjamin Harrison, a family friend, for president, and wrote the candidate's biography. This was followed by the book President Garfield had requested, *The Prince of India*, in 1893, among numerous other short and long works written during Wallace's lifetime. In addition, he painted, sculpted, invented, played the violin, built a study, and wrote more than half of his *Autobiography*. He died in 1905 after finishing the chapter of his memoir on Monocacy; Susan Wallace, with the help of another author, completed the work.[15]

Achieving all of this political and literary success, one consistently providing opportunities for the other, the former general repeatedly thought about his inconsistent and unsatisfying career as a general. His mistakes near Shiloh haunted Wallace until his death. He spent many hours defending his actions during the Battle of Shiloh while overemphasizing his stalwart defense at Monocacy Junction in 1864. Much of this defense took place in the newspapers, and he occasionally made his case in letters and published works.[16] For example, the general recounted his actions at Fort Donelson and provided documents pertaining to Shiloh for the postwar collection of veterans' recollections that was published in a set of books with remarkable longevity, *Battles and Leaders of the Civil War*.[17]

Wallace appeared to hold a grudge against West Point and its graduates before and especially after the war, revealing this sentiment in public addresses as early as 1870. He gave at least one speech that asked why "so many of our young men are so eager to obtain West Point Cadetships? On the other hand, why is it so few of them enlist in the army proper?" He concluded that "our military system is founded on a stupendous error . . . the reasons why so few of our young men enlist in the army proper are, because the service is not regarded as honorable because the relation between officer and soldier is little better than that of master and slave, or dog and keeper." Wallace suggested that the academy offered "no education, or chance thereof, except that of the already damned," further asserting that one might find "the proof of all this in the one lamentable fact that, except in some instances, the soldiers of one enlistment are socially and morally unfitted for everything but re-enlistment."[18]

Continuing to believe that some sort of West Point conspiracy led by Henry Halleck had derailed his military career, Wallace refused to understand that his own faults and other factors played much larger parts in his demise as a commander of troops in the field. Although *Ben-Hur* and other postwar activities made Wallace famous and influential, such successes could not completely cover up the shame he felt for an unfulfilled desire to achieve military glory. Wallace contributed to the eventual victory of Lincoln and the Union, but the unfortunate truth was that rather than appreciate his own varied wartime services, he never forgave others for his own shortcomings in failing to achieve heroics, and prove his manliness, on the battlefield. Distinguished author of *Ben-Hur*, successful lawyer, notable Indiana politician, and capable military administrator—Wallace was all of those. He would have traded them all to be a general who won great battles to save the Union.

Notes

Abbreviations Used in Notes

IHS William Henry Smith Library, Indiana Historical Society, Indianapolis, Indiana
ISA Commission on Public Records, Indiana State Archives, Indianapolis, Indiana
ISL Manuscript Section, Indiana State Library, Indianapolis, Indiana
LC Manuscript Division, Library of Congress, Washington, D.C.
NARA National Archives and Records Administration, Washington, D.C.
OR *The War of the Rebellion: A Compilation of the Official Records of the Union and Confederate Armies* (1880–1901) (unless otherwise noted, all references are to series I)
RG Record Group

Introduction

1. Lew Wallace, *Lew Wallace; an Autobiography* (New York: Harper and Brothers, 1906). Wallace's *Smoke, Sound, and Fury: The Civil War Memoirs of Major-General Lew Wallace, U.S. Volunteers*, ed. Jim Leeke (Portland, Ore.: Strawberry Hill Press, 1998), is derived from the autobiography.
2. For an excellent discussion of why politically appointed officers were not unique to the Civil War, and why Lincoln resorted to offering such commissions, see David Work, *Lincoln's Political Generals* (Urbana: University of Illinois Press, 2009), 1–5 and 227–34.
3. Ibid., 228.
4. Carol Reardon, *With a Sword in One Hand and Jomini in the Other: The Problem of Military Thought in the Civil War North* (Chapel Hill: University of North Carolina Press, 2012), 10 and 55–58.
5. Work, *Lincoln's Political Generals*, 228–34 and 25.
6. Brooks D. Simpson, "Lincoln and His Political Generals," *Journal of the Abraham Lincoln Association* 21, no. 1 (2000), 63–77.

7. Thomas J. Goss, *The War within the Union High Command: Politics and Generalship during the Civil War* (Lawrence: University Press of Kansas, 2003), xv–xvi, xx, and 105.

8. Irving McKee, *"Ben-Hur" Wallace* (Berkeley: University of California Press, 1947) and Robert E. Morsberger and Katharine M. Morsberger, *Lew Wallace: Militant Romantic* (New York: McGraw-Hill, 1980) provide popular histories of Wallace's life and times. Lee Scott Thiesen's "The Public Career of General Lew Wallace, 1854–1905" (PhD diss., University of Arizona, 1973) offers a more academic approach to the subject, suggesting that Wallace "showed more ability than most political generals in the field" (427). See also the older brief study, Jesse Roy Smith, "The Military Career of Lew Wallace" (MA thesis, Indiana University, Bloomington, 1935). Gail Stephens, *Shadow of Shiloh: Major General Lew Wallace in the Civil War* (Indianapolis: Indiana Historical Society Press, 2010) is the best of the lot; see more in reference to her work below. Understandably, Stephens's account fails to mention this author's dissertation on Wallace, which was released a little over two years prior to the publication of *Shadow of Shiloh*. That graduate work is titled "Lew Wallace and the Civil War: Politics and Generalship" (PhD diss., Texas A&M University, 2007).

9. McKee, *"Ben-Hur" Wallace*, 42–46.

10. Thiesen, "The Public Career of General Lew Wallace, 1854–1905," 104.

11. Morsberger and Morsberger, *Lew Wallace*, 79–102 and 503–4.

12. The best of the other works is Gail Stephens's *Shadow of Shiloh*. But I do believe there are key differences between her book and this one. For one, there is more focus on rehabilitating Wallace's image, as it pertains to Shiloh, in the former volume. And, while the author dredges up a lot of interesting evidence, thinking that it somehow exonerates Wallace, the fact that nobody has the written order given to the general at Shiloh still means that there will always be very reasonable doubt. Stephens also believes that because the Indianan had to march sixteen or seventeen miles, he could not be expected to do better than he did on the first day of the battle. But, again, I would argue that he should not have marched where he marched, causing the march to be longer—thus not exonerating him. There was plenty of blame to go around for Ulysses S. Grant and Wallace. This issue will be covered, in more detail, in chapter 4.

While both books focus on political generalship, this treatment of Wallace is more of a case study for such. Stephens focuses maybe a little more on a perceived (by the author and Wallace) feud between Wallace and West Pointers. While I agree with her to a point, I think the greater truth is that the political general happened to continually upset his superiors, who were almost always West Pointers—but also included the likes of Oliver Morton and Edwin Stanton. While Stephens's volume has different foci, including the "Shiloh" theme, it is also an oversized book. This author's Civil War biography of Wallace is meant to provide a shorter and even more accessible accounting of the officer's career.

In addition, Kevin Getchell's *Scapegoat of Shiloh: The Distortion of Lew Wallace's Record by U. S. Grant* (Jefferson, N.C.: McFarland, 2013) focuses even more on that controversy, but comes off as a lawyer's brief that is trying too hard. It is not a biography, like the volumes mentioned above. Charles G. Beemer's *"My Greatest Quarrel with Fortune": Major General Lew Wallace in the West, 1861–1862* (Kent, Ohio: Kent State University Press, 2015) seems to mirror Getchell's book, at least in its lawyerly defense of actions at Shiloh, as well as an indictment of a possible "conspiracy" to criticize his actions at the battle. Furthermore, it merely covers the first two years of the war; it does not discuss the great administrative contributions that Wallace makes later in the war.

13. For more on this subject, see Goss, *The War within the Union High Command.*

14. One historian has attributed most of Wallace's later difficulties in attaining a field command to his high rank of major general. His seniority, measured by the date of his commission, may have discouraged army commanders from giving the Indianan command of a division or corps in the field; he outranked many West Pointers. This notion, however, tends to discount Wallace's tendency to irritate superiors, causing them to mistrust or disregard him for reasons other than his high rank. See Stacy D. Allen, "If He Had Less Rank," in *Grant's Lieutenants: From Cairo to Vicksburg,* ed. Stephen E. Woodworth (Lawrence: University Press of Kansas, 2001), 63–89.

15. Amy S. Greenberg, *Manifest Manhood and the Antebellum American Empire* (New York: Cambridge University Press, 2005), 11–13.

16. Lorien Foote, *The Gentlemen and the Roughs: Violence, Honor, and Manhood in the Union Army* (New York: New York University Press, 2010), 3–5, 15–16, and 121.

17. Michael Kimmel, *Manhood in America: A Cultural History* (New York: The Free Press, 1996), x, 6–7, and 69.

18. See Gail Bederman, *Manliness and Civilization* (Chicago: University of Chicago Press, 1995), 11 and 17; and E. Anthony Rotundo, *American Manhood: Transformations in Masculinity from the Revolution to the Modern Era* (New York: Basic Books, 1993), 1 and 3–4.

19. For discussions on the views of West Pointers, see Samuel J. Watson, "Flexible Gender Roles during the Market Revolution: Family, Friendship, Marriage, and Masculinity among U.S. Army Officers, 1815–1846," *Journal of Social History* 29, no. 1 (Autumn 1995): 82–83 and 96; as well as Ethan S. Rafuse, "'To Check . . . the Very Worst and Meanest of Our Passions': Common Sense, 'Cobbon Sense,' and the Socialization of Cadets at Antebellum West Point," *War in History* 16, no. 4 (2009): 408–10, 413, 418–19, and 421. For an analysis of a West Pointer who had problems somewhat related to those of Wallace, and certainly related to dueling masculinities, see Christopher S. Stowe, "George Gordon Meade and the Boundaries of Nineteenth-Century Military Masculinity," *Civil War History* 61, no. 4 (December 2015): 365 and 387. For more on the lack of discipline among many volunteer soldiers, and some officers, see Steven J. Ramold, *Baring the Iron Hand: Discipline in the Union Army* (DeKalb: Northern Illinois University Press, 2010), 3, 214, and 217; as well as Steven J. Ramold, "Discipline and the Union Army," *North and South* 13, no. 4 (November 2011): 45. For more on the teachings at West Point and the development of a common set of values among regular officers, see two articles by Samuel Watson, "How the Army Became Accepted: West Point Socialization, Military Accountability, and the

Nation-State during the Jacksonian Era," *American Nineteenth Century History* 7, no. 2 (June 2006): 233; and "Continuity in Civil-Military Relations and Expertise: The U.S. Army during the Decade before the Civil War," *Journal of Military History* 75 (January 2011): 233, 238–39, and 244. Also see three works by William B. Skelton, "Officers and Politicians: The Origins of Army Politics in the United States Before the Civil War," *Armed Forces and Society* 6, no. 1 (Fall 1979): 27, 29, 38, and 41; "The Commanding Generals and the Question of Civil Control in the Antebellum U.S. Army," *American Nineteenth Century History* 7, no. 2 (June 2006): 167–168; and *An American Profession of Arms: The Army Officer Corps, 1784–1861* (Lawrence: University Press of Kansas, 1992), xiii, 167, and 362.

20. Thomas B. Buell, *The Warrior Generals: Combat Leadership in the Civil War* (New York: Three Rivers Press, 1997), xxvii–xxxiii.

21. Bruce Catton, *America Goes to War: The Civil War and Its Meaning Today* (Middletown, Conn.: Wesleyan University Press, 1958), 40. Also see James M. McPherson, *Abraham Lincoln and the Second American Revolution* (New York: Oxford University Press, 1991), 71. For more on the relationships between regulars and volunteers, as well as the "martial" spirit that encouraged men like Wallace to become volunteer officers, see also Marcus Cunliffe's *Soldiers and Civilians: The Martial Spirit in America, 1775–1865* (Boston: Little, Brown and Company, 1968).

22. Halleck to W. T. Sherman, 29 April 1864, in U.S. War Department, *The War of the Rebellion: A Compilation of the Official Records of the Union and Confederate Armies*, (Washington, D.C.: Government Printing Office, 1880–1901) [hereafter, *OR*], 34(3):333. Again, for more on the nineteenth-century debate over the proper qualifications for generals, see Reardon, *With a Sword in One Hand and Jomini in the Other*, 10 and 55–58.

Chapter 1. Militia, Mexico, and Politics

1. Morsberger and Morsberger, *Lew Wallace: Militant Romantic*, 3.
2. Martha E. Schaaf, *Lew Wallace, Boy Writer* (Indianapolis: Bobbs-Merrill, 1961), 18.
3. McKee, *"Ben-Hur" Wallace*, 1.
4. Wallace, *Lew Wallace; an Autobiography*, 5.
5. Lew Wallace was born on 10 April 1827 in Brookville, Indiana; see ibid., 8.
6. McKee, *"Ben-Hur" Wallace*, 2.
7. Ibid., 3.
8. See Kimmel, *Manhood in America*, 58–59; as well as Rotundo, who mentions Wallace's account of the "dares" in *American Manhood*, 21, 25, 42–43, and 50–51. Rotundo also mentions that father Wallace eventually had to resort to kicking Lew out of the house, sometime in his middle teens, effecting a very abrupt end of his boyhood; see *American Manhood*, 53.
9. Wallace, *Lew Wallace; an Autobiography*, 7.
10. Ibid., 5–7. Lew Wallace discussed his father's career in some detail in his memoir. David Wallace's gubernatorial administration provided some positive achievements while establishing an overall mixed record, including allegations of embezzlement

of funds meant for internal improvements. Though no one could prove the charges made, the state's Whig Party convention, in 1840, declined to renominate Wallace to run in the general election for governor. Despite such an embarrassment, the lame-duck governor successfully campaigned for his father's old friend, William Harrison, who won the presidential election of 1840. After serving one term in the U.S. Congress, David Wallace had passed the height of his political career. Still, in 1850, Marion County chose him to be their delegate to a convention intent on revising the state's constitution. Afterwards, he served until his death as the elected judge of the Court of Common Pleas.

11. Morsberger and Morsberger, *Lew Wallace*, 16.
12. Amy S. Greenberg discusses young men's desire to prove a more martial manhood through such excursions in *Manifest Manhood and the Antebellum American Empire*, 79 and 138. Also see Kimmel, *Manhood in America*, 62–63.
13. McKee, *"Ben-Hur" Wallace*, 11. Wallace's discovery of Winfield Scott's combat training manual, *Infantry Tactics*, further stimulated an interest in officership and tactics. He believed that intense study of this work might make him a "drill-master," and he spent plenty of time discussing the book and various tactical drills with the company captain; see ibid., 94–95.
14. Ibid., 93–94. See Lorien Foote's description of roughs in *The Gentlemen and the Roughs*, 1–18.
15. McKee, *"Ben-Hur" Wallace*, 93–94.
16. Wallace to Isaac Blackford, in Wallace, *Lew Wallace; an Autobiography*, 112.
17. Isaac Blackford to Wallace, ibid., 113.
18. Wallace, *Lew Wallace; an Autobiography*, 114.
19. "The Quota Filled," *Indiana Democrat*, 12 June 1846, reprinted in *Indiana in the Mexican War*, compiled by Oran Perry (Indianapolis: Wm. B. Burford, 1908), 45.
20. Watson, "How the Army Became Accepted," 233.
21. "Drake's Company Leaves for New Albany," *Indiana Sentinel*, 20 June 1846, reprinted in Perry, *Indiana in the Mexican War*, 56.
22. Morsberger and Morsberger, *Lew Wallace*, 25. The Morsbergers suggest that Wallace was promoted to first lieutenant while the Indianans were camped near New Albany, Indiana. No other source confirms that assertion. Muster rolls that indicate the promotions of James Drake and John McDougal list Wallace as a second lieutenant. Wallace's *Lew Wallace; an Autobiography* states that "Sergeant Charles C. Smith, a school-mate, fine looking and clever, was by my nomination promoted to the vacant first lieutenancy, McDougal becoming captain," oddly adding that as "a rule, jealousies among men come with years and competition." Such jealousies with regard to the election of regimental officers might have led to increased tension between Wallace and McDougal. A copy of the muster rolls is in Perry, *Indiana in the Mexican War*, 359; also see Wallace, *Lew Wallace; an Autobiography*, 116. Note that primary documents in Perry's *Indiana in the Mexican War* spell the above captain's name as "McDougal" or "McDougall." Since Wallace insisted on the former, this author has used that spelling; see 45, 58–59, 67, 85, 91, 95, 111, 137, 196, 228, 243, 247, 256–57, 291, 322, 359.

23. The Indianans left New Albany, Indiana, for New Orleans, and eventually Brazos Santiago, on 5 July 1846; see "Off for Mexico," *Indiana Sentinel*, 11 July 1846, reprinted in Perry, *Indiana in the Mexican War*, 74. Also see McKee, *"Ben-Hur" Wallace*, 14–15.

24. "Letter from Colonel Drake," *Indiana Democrat*, 21 August 1846, reprinted in Perry, *Indiana in the Mexican War*, 84.

25. Wallace to William "Bill" Wallace, from Brazos Santiago, 26 July 1846, Lew Wallace Collection, Box 1, Folder 1, William Henry Smith Library, Indiana Historical Society, Indianapolis, Indiana (hereafter, IHS).

26. Ibid. Recounting how squads of Georgians, Louisianans, and Kentuckians made for interesting acquaintances, he also observed that they had their share of disputes and scuffles. He discovered something "which might open the eyes of those of our citizens whom long and unbroken peace has made blind, and that is the jealousy—and I might say the hatred—observable in the conduct and actually existing in the hearts of our soldier citizens." Lamentably, those southerners were "armed to [the] teeth day and night; being uneducated and ill-enlightened they've no better sense than a fight to the death." These comments reflected, or demonstrated, the growing animosities between Northerners and Southerners.

27. Wallace claimed that McDougal became so domineering that the "cusses of the boys are deep if not loud, and when the expiration of the year shall have removed the barrier of the army superiority they will have a vengeance which . . . he will feel to his sorrow." In "a word we are *slaves* and the army is a *military despotism* as absolute as a Turkish government!" Wallace, however, was not interested in making real, lasting peace; he intended to cut "off every connection with him by forming another mess and ceasing all conversation save such as is absolutely necessary in the discharge of my duty." See ibid. Wallace occasionally underlined words in his letters, italicized here to show his emphasis.

28. For the first time in his life, on the other hand, Wallace suggested a desire to come home and practice law, at least as an alternative to his current dilemmas; see ibid.

29. Foote, *The Gentlemen and the Roughs*, 15–16 and 168.

30. Wallace to William "Bill" Wallace, from Camp Rio Grande, 22 October 1846, Lew Wallace Collection, OMB23, Box 1, Folder 8, IHS.

31. Ibid.

32. Wallace to William "Bill" Wallace, from Camp Rio Grande, 29 October 1846, Lew Wallace Collection, Box 1, Folder 1, IHS. Emphasis in original; Wallace occasionally underlined words in his letters. Wallace asserted to his brother, William, that "I might have written that he *was* sick, and with truth; as he himself informed me that he was so; but that I wrote that I *would be Capt*, to any one else than Bill Ricketts, is false; and that you will remember was written a month or so ago—long before McDougal became sick, or was so reported to me."

33. McDougal claimed that Wallace "*was indebted to company $100; that I went to Matamoras, drew my pay, and refused to refund it.*" It appeared that the second lieutenant owed some money to the captain, by his own admission, but claimed that it was a small amount that would be properly paid at the end of the month. No matter the entire truth, the two men hated each other, and the confrontation would not

end soon. The tension and anger between the two men led McDougal to assert that Wallace would be court-martialed if he did not amend his ways, causing William to ask if Lew had any friends. The lieutenant replied that such a trial would never occur, and that Colonel Drake, as well as Maj. Henry S. Lane, would come to his rescue in any case. The controversy depressed Wallace, and he further agonized that another late incident would make matters worse. He and some of his men guarded some supplies that had washed ashore as a result of a shipwreck. The lieutenant wore one of the overcoats from a broken box, and one of the shipmates claimed that the officer was stealing. See ibid. Later, Wallace was again accused of rifling through the hogsheads, but he was acquitted by a court of inquiry; see Wallace to William "Bill" Wallace, from Camp Rio Grande, 11 November 1846, Lew Wallace Collection, Box 1, Folder 1, IHS.

34. Wallace to William "Bill" Wallace, from Matamoras, 4 March 1847, Lew Wallace Collection, Box 1, Folder 2, IHS.

35. Wallace, *Lew Wallace; an Autobiography*, 177–92.

36. Wallace to William "Bill" Wallace, from Matamoras, 4 March 1847, Lew Wallace Collection, Box 1, Folder 2, IHS. Wallace felt that news of Taylor's woes confirmed his notion that the Indianans would be fighting soon, especially since they had "received marching orders for Monterey; orders this time coming direct from the head quarters and about which accordingly there are no doubts or uncertainties." They would have left already, but they had to wait to be "relieved by some of the new regiments which have been lately ordered to the Rio Grande." Many in the 1st Indiana likely wanted to leave for Monterrey, considering the growing number of "volunteers who have been roaming about the streets for the last week or two, apparently disordered in their intellects and giving evidence of having been brought to this state of wretchedness by sickness and suffering." American troops, as in most conflicts before World War II, never evaded disease until they returned to their home states. See "Wretched Condition of Volunteers," *Madison Banner*, 25 November 1846, reprinted in Perry, *Indiana in the Mexican War*, 105.

37. Wallace noted that on the way to Monterrey, "Rancheros" followed the Americans and "made several demonstrations of attack; but finding us always prepared [they] . . . refrained and drew . . . off to our great disappointment." After camping near Monterrey, the men's experiences resembled those in Matamoras. They were never called forth to fight with Taylor, and the Indianans spent their time securing and occupying the city. As is often the case in war, Wallace saw more death due to disease than battle, and more administrative and guard duty than attacking. This array of duties and experiences continued to be the norm until the end of the regiment's service. Considering that the true offensive actions were now in the hands of Ge. Winfield Scott, farther south near Mexico City, the lack of "more honorable" action should not have been a surprise to Wallace. See Wallace to William "Bill" Wallace, from Monterrey, 26 March 1847, Lew Wallace Collection, Box 1, Folder 2, IHS.

38. Wallace, *Lew Wallace; an Autobiography*, 193–200, 212–13. E. Anthony Rotundo mentions what might have been Wallace's only great draw to his new profession. The gender scholar quotes the Indianan's recollection of the spirited competition,

or "bouts," between himself and Daniel Vorhees in the courtroom. Wallace enjoyed these bouts, and eventually became a great friend of Vorhees; see Rotundo, *American Manhood*, 198.

39. At the conclusion of Wallace's service, the general had made a point to compliment Colonel Drake on the performance of the 1st Indiana during the war, and he even emphasized his "regret that it was not your good fortune as well as your excellent regiment, to have participated in one, at least, of the hard fought battles which have taken place since our arrival in Mexico." Drake read the letter to the men before they left Mexico, but Wallace still continued to hold an intense, almost irrational, grudge against the general for not allowing the 1st Indiana to join in real battle, and for his accusations of cowardice against the 2nd Indiana. See Zachary Taylor to James P. Drake, 22 May 1847, reprinted in Perry, *Indiana in the Mexican War*, 164.

40. Wallace, *Lew Wallace; an Autobiography*, 205.

41. Wallace and his wife, Susan, had one of their few fights over the number of children they would have. Eventually, with the help of an arbitrator, the father-to-be "consented to *one*, in consideration of a solemn promise on her part that that one should be a *boy*." See Wallace to William "Bill" Wallace, 17 February 1853, Lew Wallace Collection, Box 1, IHS.

42. Wallace, *Lew Wallace; an Autobiography*, 224. Wallace also comments on the benefits of the position in a letter to William "Bill" Wallace, 11 September 1851, Lew Wallace Collection, Box 1, IHS.

43. Wallace to William "Bill" Wallace, from Covington, 23 August 1850, Lew Wallace Collection, Box 1, Folder 2, IHS. Wallace also mentions this episode in his "Autobiographical Sketch" to Benson J. Lossing, 16 August 1863, Lew Wallace Collection, Series 10, Box 23, IHS; however, while his previous, more contemporary, letters suggest that he attained office earlier as a result of such actions, the sketch mentions a later year.

44. Michael Thomas Smith mentions a similar display of aggression in "Abraham Lincoln, Manhood, and Nineteenth-Century American Political Culture," in *This Distracted and Anarchical People: New Answers for Old Questions about the Civil War–Era North*, ed. Andrew L. Slap and Michael Thomas Smith (New York: Fordham University Press, 2013), 37. That incident, a wrestling match between a young Abraham Lincoln and another Illinoisan, paved the way for a career in western politics. However, later in life, Lincoln was embarrassed by the incident.

45. Stephens, *Shadow of Shiloh*, 12–13.

46. Wallace won the election by a vote of 2,112 to 2,020. See "Official Vote of Montgomery County," *Montgomery Weekly Journal*, 23 October 1856. At least one author suggests that Wallace won his senatorial seat in 1858, but it appears that the wording of his autobiography may have led to the confusion, especially since the actual service in office would have run from 1857 into 1859. See Wallace, *Lew Wallace; an Autobiography*, 251; and Stephens, *Shadow of Shiloh*, 13.

47. *Montgomery Weekly Journal*, 4 December 1856.

48. Wallace, *Lew Wallace; an Autobiography*, 245. One such challenge appeared in the *Crawfordsville Journal*, 26 July 1860. The resulting performance, in Indianapolis, was lauded by the same paper; see "The Montgomery Guards," *Crawfordsville Journal*, 20 September 1860.

49. Wallace's militia unit was so popular that he was elected commander of an Indiana encampment of militia in September of 1860; see Stephens, *Shadow of Shiloh*, 14–15. Around this time, he also attained some West Point textbooks to shore up his skills, but he had some trouble acquiring them. In fact, he had to write to a congressman to succeed in the undertaking. This trouble seems to have further convinced him that military professionals were a terrible "club" of elites; see ibid., 15. Also see Beemer, *"My Greatest Quarrel with Fortune,"* 19.

50. "Lew Wallace—Negro Equality," *Crawfordsville Journal*, 26 July 1860.

51. On the Thursday after the election in Montgomery County, a local paper reported that Lincoln's majority over all opposition was fifty votes; see "Montgomery County," *Crawfordsville Journal*, 8 November 1860.

52. Morton was originally elected lieutenant governor in 1860 while Henry S. Lane won the governorship. But, Morton became governor when Lane took office as a U.S. senator, thus resigning the governorship in early 1861; see "Resignation of the Governor," *Crawfordsville Journal*, 31 January 1861.

53. According to Wallace, the secession crisis led Democratic leaders to hold a party meeting in Indianapolis shortly after the election. He arrived late to the meeting and discovered that the delegates were discussing the possibility of siding with the South should a civil war erupt. Many believed that the Union could not be saved should Abraham Lincoln be inaugurated. This treasonous talk was too much for Wallace, so he quickly left the meeting after rebuking an older party veteran who tried to convince him to stay. He had reached a crossroads, personally and politically. See Wallace, *Lew Wallace; an Autobiography*, 257–61.

54. Emma Lou Thornbrough, *Indiana in the Civil War Era, 1850–1880* (Indianapolis: Indiana Historical Society, 1965), 114–15; and Stephens, *Shadow of Shiloh*, 17–18.

55. Wallace to Henry S. Lane, from Crawfordsville, with an endorsement by Lane to Simon Cameron, 6 April 1861, Lew Wallace Collection, Box 1, IHS. Americans in the first half of the 1800s debated whether born genius or learned expertise made for great generals, and Wallace would side with the former argument throughout the century; for more on the debate, see Reardon, *With a Sword in One Hand and Jomini in the Other*, 10–11 and 55–56.

Chapter 2. "The Fruits of Victory"

1. Wallace, *Lew Wallace; an Autobiography*, 261.

2. Wallace's commission as the "Adjutant General of the Indiana Militia," 15 April 1861, Lew Wallace Collection, Box 1, IHS. For evidence of Wallace's continuing dislike for Taylor, see Wallace, *Lew Wallace; an Autobiography*, 121–28, 143–57, 177–92, and 201–5.

3. Wallace, *Lew Wallace; an Autobiography*, 265. Wallace later appointed Archibald Harrison as an assistant adjutant general, with duties exclusively concerning Camp Morton, where new companies first reported in Indianapolis. See General Orders No. 7, Adjutant General's Office, Indianapolis, 18 April 1861, Governor Oliver P. Morton Papers, Microfilm Reel 1, Commission on Public Records, Indiana State Archives, Indianapolis, Indiana (hereafter, ISA).

4. Wallace, *Lew Wallace; an Autobiography*, 266.

5. For more on the nineteenth-century belief that genius or born ability counted for more than expertise, see Reardon, *With a Sword in One Hand and Jomini in the Other*, 10–12 and 55–58.

6. *Crawfordsville Weekly Review*, 20 April 1861. Zouave battle tactics were not significantly different from those used by other U.S. regiments, but much more emphasis was placed on complicated drill (resembling a kind of rapid gymnastics) and parades. Compared to the average Civil War soldier, those in Zouave regiments were no more likely to be elite fighters. One historian suggests that these units were anti-Regular Army by nature, possibly appealing to Wallace for that reason. See Cunliffe, *Soldiers and Civilians*, 5, 244–46, 358, and 404. For a detailed explanation of Zouave tactics and drill, see E. E. Ellsworth, *Manual of Arms for Light Infantry, Adapted to the Rifled Musket, with, or without, the Priming Attachment, Arranged for the U.S. Zouave Cadets, Governor's Guard of Illinois* (Chicago: P. T. Sherlock, 1861).

7. Thomas Wise Durham, *Three Years with Wallace's Zouaves: The Civil War Memoirs of Thomas Wise Durham*, ed. Jeffrey L. Patrick (Macon, Ga.: Mercer University Press, 2003), 32.

8. Wallace, *Lew Wallace; an Autobiography*, 266–67. Wallace later recollected that 130 companies had reported to Camp Morton. But a letter of the following Sunday reported 109 companies and his resignation as adjutant general of Indiana. See Wallace to Morton, 21 April 1861, Governor Oliver P. Morton Papers, Microfilm Reel 1, ISA.

9. Wallace, *Lew Wallace; an Autobiography*, 267–68. Contrary to Wallace's recollection, he and Morton likely made this decision during a meeting on the day Wallace accepted the position of adjutant general, or the day after when he was officially commissioned. The unique numbering of regiments is mentioned in the adjutant's first general order of 15 April 1861, reprinted in the *Crawfordsville Weekly Review*, 20 April 1861.

10. Indiana, under Morton, eventually enlisted approximately 200,000 soldiers; See William F. Fox, *Regimental Losses in the American Civil War, 1861–1865* (Albany, N.Y.: Albany Publishing, 1889), 501–5.

11. Foote, *The Gentlemen and the Roughs*, 6.

12. Commission as "Colonel in and for the . . . 11th Regiment of the Volunteers," 26 April 1861, Lew Wallace Collection, Box 1, IHS. Also see Morton to Simon Cameron, 28 April 1861, followed by an "inclosure," dated 27 April 1861, in *OR*, series III, 1:125–27.

13. Morton to Wallace, 26 April 1861, Correspondence of the 11th Indiana Volunteer Infantry Regiment, Microfilm Reel 6, Records of the Adjutant General of Indiana, ISA.

14. Dumont, Wallace, Benton, Milroy, Crittenden, and Manson to Abraham Lincoln, 21 May 1861, with an "indorsement" of 24 May 1861, *OR*, series III, 1:220.
15. Durham, *Wallace's Zouaves*, 8.
16. Wallace, *Lew Wallace; an Autobiography*, 270. The Indianan stated, in regard to the uniforms, that there "was nothing of the flashy, Algerian colors . . . no red fez, a head-gear exclusively Mohammedan, and therefore to be religiously avoided by Christians; no red breeches, no red or yellow sash with tassels big as early cabbages."
17. Schaaf, *Lew Wallace, Boy Writer*, 154.
18. *Crawfordsville Weekly Review*, 11 May 1861.
19. Durham, *Wallace's Zouaves*, 34–6.
20. Wallace, *Lew Wallace; an Autobiography*, 274.
21. Ibid., 274–75. Also see Durham, *Wallace's Zouaves*, 8–10.
22. Wallace to an unknown recipient, 6 May 1861, Lew Wallace Collection, Box 1, IHS. Various companies of the 11th Indiana provided similar protection for other nearby Indiana towns while the regiment was based in Evansville, possibly breaking up the monotony for some soldiers; see Morton to Thomas A. Morris, 27 May 1861, Governor Oliver P. Morton Papers, Microfilm Reel 1, ISA.
23. Wallace to Susan Wallace, 11 May 1861, Lew Wallace Collection, Box 1, IHS.
24. Stephens, *Shadow of Shiloh*, 23.
25. Durham, *Wallace's Zouaves*, 10. Wallace admitted later that the order had quite an effect on him; after all, it was exciting to "be known to Winfield Scott, to be addressed by him—what an appeal to my vanity!" See Wallace, *Lew Wallace; an Autobiography*, 277.
26. Durham, *Wallace's Zouaves*, 38.
27. According to a telegraph, the troops "made a splendid appearance and were enthusiastically received" in Cincinnati, Ohio; see the *Crawfordsville Weekly Review*, 8 June 1861. The counties that included the towns of Grafton, Romney, and New Creek soon became part of the new state of West Virginia in 1863.
28. Patterson, in General Orders No. 27, moved his headquarters from Chambersburg to Hagerstown on 15 June 1861, XII Army Corps—General and Special Orders Issued, part II, number 127, entry 2205, vol. 22 (1 of 3), Record Group (hereafter, RG) 393, National Archives and Records Administration, Washington, D.C. (hereafter, NARA).
29. Wallace, *Lew Wallace; an Autobiography*, 279–80.
30. Fitz John Porter to Wallace, from Chambersburg, 6 June 1861, XII Army Corps—Letters Sent, part II, number 127, entry 2192, vol. 4 of 6, RG 393, NARA.
31. Wallace, *Lew Wallace; an Autobiography*, 282.
32. Durham, *Wallace's Zouaves*, 11.
33. Porter to Wallace, 11 June 1861, General's Papers, Lewis Wallace (1827–1905), being "Miscellaneous official Letters Received, Orders, and Telegrams" (hereafter, Lewis Wallace Papers), entry 159, RG 94, NARA.
34. Watson, "Flexible Gender Roles during the Market Revolution," 83.
35. Rafuse, "'To Check . . . the Very Worst and Meanest of Our Passions'," 413.
36. Report of Wallace, 14 June 1861, *OR*, 2:123–24. There is good evidence that the dates in this report are incorrect at times; see Stephens, *Shadow of Shiloh*, 24. Furthermore,

along the way, the men came to a small "hamlet," and one of the residents, according to Wallace, got on his horse and rode to Romney to warn the rebels; see Wallace, *Lew Wallace; an Autobiography*, 285–86.

37. Report of Wallace, 14 June 1861, *OR*, 2:123–24.

38. Ibid. Once Romney had been taken, and the spoils collected, the regiment headed down the hill toward the river. At the bottom, Wallace discovered that the brick house had not been burned; an old farmer convinced the company not to burn his house. Rebels had taken the house from the man, using it to fire on the Union men. The owner professed loyalty to the Union, so Wallace acquiesced in the subordinate's decision to let the house stand; see Wallace, *Lew Wallace; an Autobiography*, 289–90.

39. Report of Wallace, 14 June 1861, *OR*, 2:123–24.

40. Wallace, *Lew Wallace; an Autobiography*, 288.

41. Report of Wallace, 14 June 1861, *OR*, 2:123–24.

42. One "High Private" later suggested that the rebels, when "about a mile distant," could be seen already "running for the woods" well before the regiment came to the bridge; see the *Crawfordsville Weekly Review*, 22 June 1861.

43. Report of Wallace, 14 June 1861, *OR*, 2:123–24.

44. Wallace, *Lew Wallace; an Autobiography*, 289.

45. Report of Wallace, 14 June 1861, *OR*, 2:123–24.

46. Robert Patterson to Wallace, 13 June 1861, XII Army Corps—Letters Sent, part II, number 127, entry 2192, vol. 4 of 6, RG 393, NARA.

47. Report of Wallace, 14 June 1861, *OR*, 2:123–24.

48. "Wanted—A Fair Field," *New York Times*, 15 June 1861.

49. *Indianapolis Journal*, 17 June 1861; reprinted in the *Chicago Tribune*, 18 June 1861.

50. For example, see the *Crawfordsville Weekly Review*, 22 June 1861; and the *New York Times* of 14, 15, 20, 21, and 28 June 1861; as well as the *Chicago Tribune* of 14, 25, and 27 June 1861.

51. Wallace, *Lew Wallace; an Autobiography*, 292. Also see McKee, *"Ben-Hur" Wallace*, 38.

52. Durham, *Wallace's Zouaves*, 42.

53. Two letters from Fitz John Porter to Wallace, and one from Patterson to McClellan, 15 June 1861, XII Army Corps—Letters Sent, part II, number 127, entry 2192, vol. 4 of 6, RG 393, NARA. Another note on the same day worried Wallace. While not yet being able to send reinforcements, Porter suggested that Johnston's army might retreat toward Romney, endangering Cumberland; see second communication from Porter to Wallace, 15 June 1861, ibid. Wallace, in a reply, complained to Fitz John Porter about not receiving enough support from Generals Morris, McClellan, and, in some sense, Porter. It was an early sign of his inability to keep quiet; the communication is quoted in Beemer, *"My Greatest Quarrel with Fortune,"* 36.

54. Wallace's division commander, Brig. Gen. George Cadwalader, planned to send aid in the form of cavalry, artillery, and infantry under Col. Ambrose Burnside; see George Cadwalader to Wallace, 16 June 1861, Lewis Wallace Papers, entry 159, RG 94, NARA. But an earlier note from Wallace suggesting the absence of the enemy, and

orders from Scott asking that extra units be held for a major action soon to come, convinced Patterson's assistant adjutant general to overturn Cadwalader's order; see Porter to Wallace, 17 June 1861, ibid. Letter also found in XII Army Corps—Letters Sent, part II, number 127, entry 2192, vol. 4 of 6, RG 393, NARA.

55. Wallace to Porter, 18 June 1861, *OR*, 2:704.
56. Wallace, *Lew Wallace; an Autobiography*, 295–96.
57. Ibid., 293–95.
58. Porter to Wallace, 24 June 1862, XII Army Corps—Letters Sent, part II, number 127, entry 2192, vol. 4 of 6, RG 393, NARA.
59. Porter to Wallace, 26 June 1861, ibid.
60. Wallace to Patterson, 27 June 1861, *OR*, 2:134–35.
61. Wallace, *Lew Wallace; an Autobiography*, 301.
62. Wallace to Patterson, 27 June 1861, *OR*, 2:134–35
63. Ibid. Wallace also mentions this episode in his "Autobiographical Sketch" to Benson J. Lossing, 16 August 1863, Lew Wallace Collection, Series 10, Box 23, IHS.
64. Wallace to McClellan, 27 June 1861, forwarded to Scott on 28 June 1861, *OR*, 2:134.
65. Ibid. Also see Wallace to Patterson, 27 June 1861, *OR*, 2:134–35.
66. General Orders No. 29, by order of Patterson, 30 June 1861, reprinted in Wallace, *Lew Wallace; an Autobiography*, 305–6. The successes of the 11th Indiana made such an impression that Patterson again made particular note of events at and near Romney in a letter to the Indianan in January of 1865, Wallace then being a major general in charge of the Middle Department; see Patterson to Wallace, 14 January 1865, Lew Wallace Collection, Box 3, IHS.
67. McClellan to Wallace, 28 June 1861, reprinted in Wallace, *Lew Wallace; an Autobiography*, 306. Wallace later stated that the Pennsylvania governor sent that state's units to Cumberland only when the Indianans received orders to leave the town on 7 July; see Wallace, *Lew Wallace; an Autobiography*, 309.
68. Schuyler Colfax to Wallace, 28 June 1861, Lew Wallace Collection, Box 1, IHS.
69. In the meantime, the regiment and Cumberland prepared for an Independence Day celebration. The townspeople provided a wonderful feast, and the officers, including Wallace, even performed guard duty for a few hours so all troops could participate in the festivities; they enjoyed their time with the citizens. But, unbeknown to the revelers, the protection of the regiment would soon be ordered away. Durham, *Wallace's Zouaves*, 42–3. Also see the *Crawfordsville Weekly Review*, 13 July 1861.
70. Wallace's report to McClellan, for example, was reprinted in the *New York Times*, 29 June 1861. Also see McKee, *"Ben-Hur" Wallace*, 38.
71. Patterson, in General Orders No. 30, moved his headquarters to Martinsburg, Virginia, on 3 July 1861, XII Army Corps—General and Special Orders Issued, part II, number 127, entry 2205, vol. 22 (1 of 3), RG 393, NARA. Porter sent the order to Wallace on 5 July 1861, XII Army Corps—Letters Sent, part II, number 127, entry 2192, vol. 4 of 6, RG 393, NARA. The 11th Indiana arrived in Martinsburg on 11 July 1861; see Durham, *Wallace's Zouaves*, 46.

72. Wallace, *Lew Wallace; an Autobiography*, 310–11.

73. Wallace to Susan Wallace, 10 July 1861, Lew Wallace Collection, Box 1, IHS.

74. Wallace, *Lew Wallace; an Autobiography*, 313–14. He also mentions the incident in a letter to Susan Wallace, 14 July 1861, Lew Wallace Collection, Box 1, IHS.

75. Wallace to Susan Wallace, 14 July 1861, Lew Wallace Collection, Box 1, IHS. Wallace describes Scott's order in Wallace, *Lew Wallace; an Autobiography*, 317.

76. Wallace, *Lew Wallace; an Autobiography*, 320. Also see Durham, *Wallace's Zouaves*, 13.

77. Porter to Wallace, 19 July 1861, XII Army Corps—Letters Sent, part II, number 127, entry 2192, vol. 4 of 6, RG 393, NARA.

78. Wallace, *Lew Wallace; an Autobiography*, 322–23. Wallace later recounted that Patterson complimented the Wisconsin and Indiana units in an appreciative speech when the regiments marched to his house.

79. Durham, *Wallace's Zouaves*, 50.

80. Patterson relinquished his command of the XII Corps in General Orders No. 88, 25 July 1861, XII Army Corps—General and Special Orders Issued, part II, number 127, entry 2205, vol. 22 (1 of 3), RG 393, NARA.

81. Wallace may have realized that the situation resembled one of his own in 1862. See Wallace, *Lew Wallace; an Autobiography*, 322.

82. Durham, *Wallace's Zouaves*, 51–2. Patterson ordered the 11th Indiana to depart for Indianapolis, via Hagerstown, in Special Orders No. 124, 23 July 1861, XII Army Corps—General and Special Orders Issued, part II, number 127, entry 2205, vol. 22 (1 of 3), RG 393, NARA.

83. Durham, *Wallace's Zouaves*, 60.

84. *Crawfordsville Weekly Review*, 3 August 1861. Also see Wallace's "Autobiographical Sketch" to Benson J. Lossing, 16 August 1863, Lew Wallace Collection, Series 10, Box 23, IHS.

85. Learning of the regiment's continued service, George McClellan supposedly offered Wallace and his men the opportunity to serve in the Army of the Potomac; surprisingly, the colonel turned it down, believing that the Indiana regiment would be out of place in an army of easterners; see Wallace, *Lew Wallace; an Autobiography*, 323–27. Fremont, through Simon Cameron, asked Morton for any available regiments on 5 September 1861, Governor Oliver P. Morton Papers, Microfilm Reel 1, ISA.

86. Durham, *Wallace's Zouaves*, 59.

87. Wallace, *Lew Wallace; an Autobiography*, 327.

88. Wallace's reluctance to complete more political tasks will contrast with the willingness of other political appointees. See Work, *Lincoln's Political Generals*, 1–5, 25, 156, and 202–14; as well as Goss, *The War within the Union High Command*, 39, 44, 105, 138, and 205.

89. Wallace, *Lew Wallace; an Autobiography*, 332. In 1863, Wallace spoke more fondly of Fremont's abilities; see Wallace's "Autobiographical Sketch" to Benson J. Lossing, 16 August 1863, Lew Wallace Collection, Series 10, Box 23, IHS.

Chapter 3. Forts Henry and Donelson

1. Wallace, *Lew Wallace; an Autobiography*, 338.
2. Wallace to Susan Wallace, 22 September 1861, Lew Wallace Collection, Box 1, IHS.
3. Wallace, *Lew Wallace; an Autobiography*, 339–41.
4. Wallace to Susan Wallace, 9 November 1861, Lew Wallace Collection, Box 1, IHS.
5. McKee, *"Ben-Hur" Wallace*, 41. The commission is dated 3 September 1861, and Wallace read about his rumored promotion as early as 13 September, but he likely received notice much later. See Wallace, *Lew Wallace; an Autobiography*, 345; also see Wallace to Morton, 13 September 1862, Governor Oliver P. Morton Papers, Microfilm Reel 2, ISA.
6. Wallace, *Lew Wallace; an Autobiography*, 342–45. Smith's advice mirrored that taught to all West Point students; again, see works such as William B. Skelton, *An American Profession of Arms: The Army Officer Corps, 1784–1861* (Lawrence: University Press of Kansas, 1992), 167; Watson, "How the Army Became Accepted," 233; and Rafuse, "'To Check . . . the Very Worst and Meanest of Our Passions'," 413.
7. Wallace, *Lew Wallace; an Autobiography*, 347. Wallace actually wrote to the secretary of war to request two of the regiments, which must not have made General Smith happy. To Wallace's credit, he also wrote letters home in support of the war effort and of Morton, in exchange for Morton's help in securing new uniforms for some of Indiana's troops; see Stephens, *Shadow of Shiloh*, 38–39. He would not be so willing to help recruit support for the war effort as the months passed.
8. Wallace to Morton, 24 September 1861, Governor Oliver P. Morton Papers, Microfilm Reel 2, ISA.
9. Wallace to Morton, 1 November 1861, ibid.
10. Wallace, *Lew Wallace; an Autobiography*, 350.
11. Morsberger and Morsberger, *Lew Wallace*, 64.
12. Ramold, "Discipline and the Union Army," 45. Also see Ramold, *Baring the Iron Hand*, 214 and 217.
13. Morsberger and Morsberger, *Lew Wallace*, 64.
14. Wallace claimed to have written the order, which was signed by Smith, but there is no corroborating evidence; see Wallace, *Lew Wallace; an Autobiography*, 350–51.
15. Ibid., 351. For example, see "The Late Affair at Paducah," *Chicago Tribune*, 3 December 1861. That article mentions correspondents from the *Missouri Democrat* and the *Evansville* (Indiana) *Journal*. Also see "Gen. Smith, of Paducah—His Loyalty," *Chicago Tribune*, 5 December 1861; information for that article came from the *Cincinnati Commercial*, 3 December 1861.
16. Wallace, *Lew Wallace; an Autobiography*, 351.
17. See ibid., 351–53, as well as Morsberger and Morsberger, *Lew Wallace*, 64. No documents existed to verify these rumors, but they still lingered; see Brooks D. Simpson, *Ulysses S. Grant: Triumph over Adversity, 1822–1865* (Boston: Houghton Mifflin, 2000), 58–62.
18. McKee, *"Ben-Hur" Wallace*, 41. Wallace later remembered that a raid to destroy a rebel camp was a feint in conjunction with Grant's attack, but he was mistaken. That

raid occurred in late December, not early November; see Wallace, *Lew Wallace; an Autobiography*, 354–55. Also see a report of Wallace on the expedition to Camp Beauregard and Viola, Kentucky, 1 January 1862, in *OR*, 7:66–68.

19. Wallace to Susan Wallace, 9 November 1861, Lew Wallace Collection, Box 1, IHS. For a more objective, yet similar, explanation of events near Belmont, see Simpson, *Ulysses S. Grant*, 99–101; also see John Y. Simon, "Grant at Belmont," *Military Affairs* 45 (December 1981): 164. Another historian acknowledges the confusion at the end of the battle but points out that the Confederates lost more troops and materials than the Union during the full length of the engagement; see Nathaniel Cheairs Hughes Jr., *The Battle of Belmont: Grant Strikes South* (Chapel Hill: University of North Carolina Press, 1991), 147–63, 184–85.

20. Report of Wallace, 1 January 1862, *OR*, 7:66–68.

21. Wallace, *Lew Wallace; an Autobiography*, 356–64; it was the first such incident mentioned in his postwar memoir. Susan Wallace, while momentarily with her husband in Kentucky, also managed to be moved by her first observations of the peculiar institution; see Benjamin Franklin Cooling, *Forts Henry and Donelson: The Key to the Confederate Heartland* (Knoxville: University of Tennessee Press), 64–65.

22. Wallace to Susan Wallace, 22 December 1861, Lew Wallace Collection, Box 1, IHS.

23. Wallace to Susan Wallace, 5 February 1862, ibid.

24. Draft of a report of U. S. Grant, 30 August 1861 through 6 April 1862, Papers of Ulysses S. Grant, Series 10, Container 17 (Military File—Reports), Manuscript Division, Library of Congress, Washington, D.C. (hereafter, LC).

25. Spencer C. Tucker, *Unconditional Surrender: The Capture of Forts Henry and Donelson* (Abilene, TX: McWhiney Foundation Press, 2001), 55–56. Also see General Field Orders No. 1, District of Cairo, 5 February 1862, Department of the Tennessee— General and General Field Orders Received, part II, number 171, entry 2733, vol. 3 (4 of 4), RG 393, NARA.

26. Wallace to Susan Wallace, 7 February 1862, Lew Wallace Collection, Box 1, IHS.

27. Cooling, *Forts Henry and Donelson*, 101–10.

28. Wallace, *Lew Wallace; an Autobiography*, 375–77. Also see Richard L. Kiper, *Major General John Alexander McClernand: Politician in Uniform* (Kent, Ohio: Kent State University Press, 1999), 73–74. John A. McClernand served as a Democratic congressman from Illinois before receiving a commission as a brigadier general. President Lincoln offered the appointment to "the most powerful politician in Illinois," counting on McClernand to keep "Egypt," more formally known as southern Illinois, "in the Union fold." He did not disappoint the president; Kiper, *McClernand*, 24–25.

29. General Field Orders No. 7, District of Cairo, 10 February 1862, Papers of Ulysses S. Grant, Series 10, Container 17 (Military File—Reports), LC.

30. Draft of a report of U.S. Grant, 30 August 1861 through 6 April 1862, Papers of Ulysses S. Grant, Series 10, Container 17 (Military File—Reports), LC.

31. Grant to Wallace, 12 February 1862, Department of the Tennessee—Letters Sent, part II, number 171, entry 2730, vol. G1, RG 393, NARA. Also see Special Field Orders No. 6, District of Cairo, 11 February 1862, *OR*, 7:606.

32. Wallace to Susan Wallace, 11 February 1862, Lew Wallace Collection, Box 1, IHS.

33. Grant to Wallace, 12 February 1862, Department of the Tennessee—Letters Sent, part II, number 171, entry 2730, vol. G1, RG 393, NARA. Also see Special Field Orders No. 6, District of Cairo, 11 February 1862, OR, 7:606.

34. Grant to Wallace, 15 February 1862, Department of the Tennessee—Letters Sent, part II, number 171, entry 2730, vol. G1, RG 393, NARA. Also found in the OR, 7:618–19.

35. Wallace to Susan Wallace, 13 February 1862, Lew Wallace Collection, Box 1, IHS.

36. Cooling, *Forts Henry and Donelson*, 282. Also see General Field Orders No. 12, District of Cairo, 14 February 1862, Department of the Tennessee—General and General Field Orders Received, part II, number 171, entry 2733, vol. 3 (4 of 4), RG 393, NARA. In addition, see General Field Orders No. 14, U. S. Grant, 14 February 1862, Lew Wallace Collection, Box 1, IHS.

37. Draft of a report of U. S. Grant, 30 August 1861 through 6 April 1862, Papers of Ulysses S. Grant, Series 10, Container 17 (Military File—Reports), LC.

38. Wallace, *Lew Wallace; an Autobiography*, 387–88. In his report on the battle, however, Wallace stated that his "orders, received from General Grant, were to hold my position and prevent the enemy from escaping in that direction; in other words, to remain there and repel any sally from the fort. Under the orders I had no authority to take the offensive." This wording does not suggest that Grant specifically ordered him to "not assume the aggressive," and it did not, in any way, prevent him from coming to McClernand's defense. See Report of Wallace, 20 February 1862, OR, 7:236–40. May also find the same report in the Lew Wallace Collection, Box 1, IHS.

39. During the gunfight, a rebel "128-pounder was spiked by the incompetence of its own gunner, [but] the remaining ten 32-pounders and a 10-inch columbiad kept up a barrage that bounced iron balls off the sides of the ironclads with the noise of an amplified smithy." See Morsberger and Morsberger, *Lew Wallace*, 73. Also see Cooling, *Forts Henry and Donelson*, 153–61; and Simpson, *Ulysses S. Grant*, 114–15.

40. Morsberger and Morsberger, *Lew Wallace*, 73–74.

41. Wallace, *Lew Wallace; an Autobiography*, 387–88. And again, see different wording in his report on the battle; see Report of Wallace, 20 February 1862, OR, 7:236–40. May also find the same report in the Lew Wallace Collection, Box 1, IHS. At least one historian agrees with Wallace on the subject of Grant's initial order to the division commander; see Beemer, *"My Greatest Quarrel with Fortune,"* 84.

42. Draft of a report of U. S. Grant, 30 August 1861 through 6 April 1862, Papers of Ulysses S. Grant, Series 10, Container 17 (Military File—Reports), LC. On the other hand, Grant merely suggested, in his *Memoirs*, that "Wallace was nearer the scene of conflict [than Smith] and had taken part in it" by the time Grant arrived on the scene, and he "had, at an opportune time, sent Thayer's brigade to the support of McClernand and thereby contributed to hold the enemy within his lines." He failed to mention that Wallace delayed in helping McClernand until finally ordered to do so. See Ulysses S. Grant, *Personal Memoirs of U. S. Grant*, 2 vols. (New York: Charles L. Webster and Company, 1886), 1:306.

43. Wallace, *Lew Wallace; an Autobiography*, 399–400. In his post-battle report, however, Wallace admitted that when he began preparations to support McClernand, "Captain

Rawlins was conversing with me at the time;" see the Report of Wallace, 20 February 1862, *OR*, 7:236–40.

44. Draft of a report of U. S. Grant, 30 August 1861 through 6 April 1862, Papers of Ulysses S. Grant, Series 10, Container 17 (Military File—Reports), LC.

45. Wallace, *Lew Wallace; an Autobiography*, 405–7.

46. Draft of a report of U. S. Grant, 30 August 1861 through 6 April 1862, Papers of Ulysses S. Grant, Series 10, Container 17 (Military File—Reports), LC.

47. Ibid.

48. Wallace, *Lew Wallace; an Autobiography*, 411–12.

49. Draft of a report of U. S. Grant, 30 August 1861 through 6 April 1862, Papers of Ulysses S. Grant, Series 10, Container 17 (Military File—Reports), LC. Also see Grant, *Personal Memoirs*, 1:305–8.

50. Report of Wallace, 20 February 1862, *OR*, 7:236–40.

51. Ibid.

52. Ibid.

53. Tucker, *Unconditional Surrender*, 55–56.

54. Report of Wallace, 20 February 1862, *OR*, 7:236–40.

55. Ibid.

56. Wallace, *Lew Wallace; an Autobiography*, 411–12. Wallace added the italics.

57. Draft of a report of U. S. Grant, 30 August 1861 through 6 April 1862, Papers of Ulysses S. Grant, Series 10, Container 17 (Military File—Reports), LC.

58. Cooling, *Forts Henry and Donelson*, 200–9; also see Tucker, *Unconditional Surrender*, 55–56.

59. Grant to Simon B. Buckner, 16 February 1862, Papers of Ulysses S. Grant, Series 10, Container 2, LC. Also see Grant, *Personal Memoirs*, 1:312–13. On that same day, Abraham Lincoln sent a telegraph to Halleck, suggesting that Fort Donelson was "safe unless Grant shall be overwhelmed from outside, to prevent which latter will I think require all the vigilance energy and skill of yourself and Gen [Don Carlos] Buell acting in full cooperation." He further stressed that the Union's "success or failure at Fort Donelson is vastly important and I beg you to put your soul in the effort." See Abraham Lincoln to Henry Halleck, 16 February 1862, Henry W. Halleck Papers, LC. The note was a little late in coming as Grant's reply to Buckner induced the Confederate to surrender the fort and its garrison; see Buckner to Grant, 16 February 1862, Department of the Tennessee—General and General Field Orders Received, part II, number 171, entry 2733, vol. 3 (3 of 4), RG 393, NARA. Lincoln's thoughts, on the other hand, foreshadowed a lack of cooperation on the parts of Halleck, Buell, and Grant.

60. Report of Wallace, 20 February 1862, *OR*, 7:236–40.

61. Grant, *Personal Memoirs*, 1:312.

62. Wallace, *Lew Wallace; an Autobiography*, 426–33. Also see Beemer, *"My Greatest Quarrel with Fortune,"* 106–8.

63. Rafuse, "'To Check . . . the Very Worst and Meanest of Our Passions,'" 413.

64. Draft of a report of U. S. Grant, 30 August 1861 through 6 April 1862, Papers of Ulysses S. Grant, Series 10, Container 17 (Military File—Reports), LC.

65. Wallace, *Lew Wallace; an Autobiography*, 434–35.
66. John Rawlins to Wallace, 16 February 1862, Lew Wallace Collection, Box 1, IHS. Slightly different wording in records of the Department of the Tennessee—Letters Sent, part II, number 171, entry 2730, vol. G1, RG 393, NARA.
67. Wallace, *Lew Wallace; an Autobiography*, 434–35.
68. Wallace to Rawlins, 17 February 1862, Lew Wallace Collection, Box 1, IHS.
69. W. S. Hillyer to Wallace, 16 February 1862, ibid.
70. Wallace to Susan Wallace, 19 February 1862, ibid.
71. Wallace, *Lew Wallace; an Autobiography*, 401, 435–36. There appears to be some evidence that the incident at least turned Hillyer against Wallace, considering that the former circulated a lampoon of the latter's actions at Forts Henry and Donelson to other officers; see Stephens, *Shadow of Shiloh*, 61–62.
72. The 1st Brigade of the 3rd Division included the 8th Missouri and the 11th, 24th, and 52nd Indiana, as well as a battery of artillery. The 2nd Brigade included the 1st Nebraska and the 58th, 68th, and 78th Ohio, as well as four companies of cavalry. The 3rd Brigade included the 20th, 56th, and 76th Ohio and the 23rd Indiana, as well as the remainder of the aforementioned cavalry regiment. See General Orders No. 6, District of West Tennessee, 21 February 1862, Department of the Tennessee—General and General Field Orders Received, part II, number 171, entry 2733, vol. 3 (4 of 4), RG 393, NARA. Also see Wallace, *Lew Wallace; an Autobiography*, 437.
73. Report of Grant to General G. W. Cullum, Chief of Staff, Department of the Missouri, 16 February 1862, *OR*, 7:160.
74. Wallace, *Lew Wallace; an Autobiography*, 439.
75. Grant to Wallace, 19 February 1862, Department of the Tennessee—Letters Sent, part II, number 171, entry 2730, vol. G1, RG 393, NARA.
76. Wallace to Susan Wallace, 24 February 1862, Lew Wallace Collection, Box 1, IHS.
77. Again, see works such as Skelton, *An American Profession of Arms*, 167; Watson, "How the Army Became Accepted," 233; and Rafuse, "'To Check . . . the Very Worst and Meanest of Our Passions'," 413.

Chapter 4. Shiloh

1. Wallace to Susan Wallace, 27 February 1862, Lew Wallace Collection, Box 1, IHS.
2. Draft of a report of U. S. Grant, 30 August 1861 through 6 April 1862, Papers of Ulysses S. Grant, Series 10, Container 17 (Military File—Reports), LC.
3. Ibid.
4. Larry J. Daniel, *Shiloh: The Battle That Changed the Civil War* (New York: Simon and Schuster, 1997), 77.
5. Halleck to McClellan, 4 March 1862, in *OR*, 7:682.
6. Wallace, *Lew Wallace; an Autobiography*, 443–45.
7. Wallace to Susan Wallace, 12 March 1862, Lew Wallace Collection, Box 1, IHS.
8. Wallace, *Lew Wallace; an Autobiography*, 445. Gail Stephens found little evidence to support Wallace's story; see *Shadow of Shiloh*, 65–66. However, Wallace also mentions the injury in his "Autobiographical Sketch" to Benson J. Lossing, 16 August 1863, Lew Wallace Collection, Series 10, Box 23, IHS.

9. Report of Wallace to Captain McMichael from Linton's Farm, 13 March 1861, *OR*, 10(1):9. Also see a draft of a report of U. S. Grant, 30 August 1861 through 6 April 1862, Papers of Ulysses S. Grant, Series 10, Container 17 (Military File—Reports), LC.

10. Report of Wallace to Captain McMichael from Linton's Farm, 13 March 1861, *OR*, 10(1):9.

11. Ibid., 9–10. Also see a draft of a report of U. S. Grant, 30 August 1861 through 6 April 1862, Papers of Ulysses S. Grant, Series 10, Container 17 (Military File—Reports), LC.

12. Grant to Halleck, 19 March 1862, copy in a draft of a report of U. S. Grant, 30 August 1861 through 6 April 1862, Papers of Ulysses S. Grant, Series 10, Container 17 (Military File—Reports), LC.

13. Grant to Wallace, 20 March 1862, ibid. Grant later determined, on the 21st, that the wet weather would cause problems with moving artillery; thus, he suggested that he would wait a few days for further orders from Halleck. He also noted that they could not take Corinth without meeting a force of about 30,000 rebels.

14. See a map, which is a bit different from Wallace's map, in James Lee McDonough's *Shiloh—in Hell Before Night* (Knoxville: University of Tennessee Press, 1977), 51. Wallace describes the roads, and his inspection of them, in his *Lew Wallace; an Autobiography*, 451–52.

15. Wallace, *Lew Wallace; an Autobiography*, 451–52.

16. Report of Wallace to John Rawlins, and a report of Charles H. Murray of the 5th Ohio Cavalry to C. R. Woods, 1 April 1862, *OR*, 10(1):78–79. Whatever the reason for Wallace's concentration on the Shunpike, he failed to understand alternate routes, possibly planning to rely on his cavalry in such cases. Furthermore, while he assumed that the Shunpike would be his route to aid the rest of the army, Grant may have mistakenly believed that Wallace's Bridge had been named after Lew Wallace, not William H. L. Wallace; see Stephens, *Shadow of Shiloh*, 75. Such assumptions could have easily led to miscommunications later on 6 April.

17. Wallace, *Lew Wallace; an Autobiography*, 453–54.

18. John J. Hardin to Maj. J. A. Cravens in Washington, D.C., 25 March 1862, J. A. Cravens Mss., Manuscripts Department, Lilly Library, Indiana University, Bloomington, Indiana.

19. Ibid.

20. For more on the teachings at West Point and the development of a common set of values among regular officers, see two articles by Samuel Watson, "How the Army Became Accepted," 233; and "Continuity in Civil-Military Relations and Expertise," 233, 238–39, and 244. Also see three works by Skelton, "Officers and Politicians," 27, 29, 38, and 41; "The Commanding Generals and the Question of Civil Control in the Antebellum U.S. Army," 167–168; and *An American Profession of Arms*, xiii, 167, and 362.

21. Draft of a report of U. S. Grant, 30 August 1861 through 6 April 1862, Papers of Ulysses S. Grant, Series 10, Container 17 (Military File—Reports), LC.

22. Daniel, *Shiloh*, 300.

23. Ibid., 319–20. Also see McDonough, *Shiloh*, 226–34.

24. Extract from a return of the Department of the Mississippi, March 1862, *OR*, 10(2):84.

25. Draft of a report of U. S. Grant, 30 August 1861 through 6 April 1862, Papers of Ulysses S. Grant, Series 10, Container 17 (Military File—Reports), LC. Grant's description of Wallace's note is correct; see *OR*, 10(2):90–91.

26. Simpson, *Ulysses S. Grant*, 129–30.

27. McDonough, *Shiloh*, 9–11.

28. Daniel, *Shiloh*, 320–21.

29. Leonidas Polk, an Episcopal bishop from Louisiana and formerly in charge at Columbus, Kentucky, commanded the I Corps, Braxton Bragg, a strict disciplinarian, headed the II Corps, and the reliable William J. Hardee commanded the III Corps. John C. Breckinridge, a presidential candidate in 1860 and former vice president of the United States, led a reserve corps, including three brigades and some unattached regiments; see McDonough, *Shiloh*, 7, 16–17, 70, 96, 240–47. Another scholar suggests that the effective strength of the Union Army of the Tennessee on 6 April may have been greater; see Daniel, *Shiloh*, 106, 322.

30. Wallace to Aaron Blair in Crawfordsville, Indiana, 3 April 1862, Lew Wallace Collection, Box 2, IHS.

31. Wallace, *Lew Wallace; an Autobiography*, 454–57.

32. In retrospect, Wallace even admitted that sometimes "I think the report should have been forwarded by an officer of my staff specially." See ibid., 458.

33. Ibid., 457–58.

34. McDonough, *Shiloh*, 86.

35. Grant to Don Carlos Buell, 6 April 1862, copy in a draft of a report of U. S. Grant, 30 August 1861 through 6 April 1862, Papers of Ulysses S. Grant, Series 10, Container 17 (Military File—Reports), LC.

36. Wallace, *Lew Wallace; an Autobiography*, 459–60.

37. Draft of a report of U. S. Grant, 30 August 1861 through 6 April 1862, Papers of Ulysses S. Grant, Series 10, Container 17 (Military File—Reports), LC. Emphasis added.

38. McDonough, *Shiloh*, 122.

39. Ibid., 122–24. Also see Daniel, *Shiloh*, 175.

40. Draft of a report of U. S. Grant, 30 August 1861 through 6 April 1862, Papers of Ulysses S. Grant, Series 10, Container 17 (Military File—Reports), LC. See a similar explanation in Grant, *Personal Memoirs*, 1:336.

41. Morsberger and Morsberger, *Lew Wallace*, 89. It could have been earlier, considering that Grant seemed to have expected Wallace as early as 12:00 P.M. See McDonough, *Shiloh*, 128.

42. Wallace, *Lew Wallace; an Autobiography*, 463–64.

43. Report of Wallace to John Rawlins, 12 April 1862, *OR*, 10(1):170.

44. Wallace to Colonel Nicholson, 11 April 1896, Miscellaneous Manuscripts—Lew Wallace, LC.

45. Grant, *Personal Memoirs*, 1:337.

46. Ibid., 1:337–38.
47. At the same time, Wallace did not likely understand that he might end up well in the rear of the Confederate left flank; see Daniel, *Shiloh*, 256–59.
48. Again, see aforementioned works on the development of a common set of values among regular officers, one being Watson, "How the Army Became Accepted," 233.
49. Wallace to Grant, 28 February 1868, in *The Papers of Ulysses S. Grant,* 28 vols, ed. John Y. Simon (Carbondale: Southern Illinois University Press, 1967–2005), 18:191–95. Wallace, in 1863, echoed such a sentiment in his "Autobiographical Sketch" to friend Benson J. Lossing, 16 August 1863, Lew Wallace Collection, Series 10, Box 23, IHS. In fact, in that sketch, he seems to suggest that Grant's staff accidentally created the miscommunications of the day. At the time he was particularly concerned because, and due to his supposed tardiness on 6 April 1862, his "enemies have manufactured all manner of falsehoods against me."
50. Grant to Wallace, 10 March 1868, *The Papers of Ulysses S. Grant*, 18:191. One author argues that Grant "exonerated" Wallace in a published letter of 1885, just before he died. However, Grant only went so far as to say that he was no longer certain of the contents of the controversial order of 6 April 1862, at least in terms of the paper received by Wallace; see Stephens, *Shadow of Shiloh*, 232. While not truly exonerating anyone, such postwar correspondence leaves plenty of doubt. On the other hand, Stephens's chapter on Shiloh offers an interesting interpretation of the events on 6 April. She seems to be a little too caught up in proving that Wallace was less at fault than Grant—something that cannot be proven without reasonable doubt—but the chapter still makes a good case that the senior officer, Grant, deserves some serious blame for the miscommunications of the day. See Stephens, *Shadow of Shiloh*, 79–92.
51. Morsberger and Morsberger, *Lew Wallace*, 90.
52. Wallace, *Lew Wallace; an Autobiography*, 465–66.
53. Ibid., 467–68.
54. Ibid., 468. Emphasis in original.
55. Ibid., 467–69.
56. McDonough, *Shiloh*, 158.
57. Wallace, *Lew Wallace; an Autobiography*, 469.
58. McDonough, *Shiloh*, 159.
59. Wallace, *Lew Wallace; an Autobiography*, 469–72.
60. McDonough, *Shiloh*, 159.
61. Report of Wallace to John Rawlins, 12 April 1862, *OR*, 10(1):170. Author Gail Stephens recounts an attempt to duplicate the march of Wallace's division on 6 April 1862. It appears that Wallace made good time, considering the marching and countermarching. See Stephens, *Shadow of Shiloh*, 91–92. Still, one could argue that the march should not have been that long in the first place.
62. Report of Wallace to John Rawlins, 12 April 1862, *OR*, 10(1):170.
63. Wallace, *Lew Wallace; an Autobiography*, 544–45.
64. McDonough, *Shiloh*, 206.
65. Report of Wallace to John Rawlins, 12 April 1862, *OR*, 10(1):170.

66. Ibid.

67. Ibid., 10(1):172–73.

68. Ibid., 10(1):173.

69. A table representing a "Return of casualties in the Third (Wallace's) Division, at the battle of Pittsburg Landing, April 7, 1862," which follows the report of Wallace to John Rawlins, 12 April 1862, *OR*, 10(1):190.

70. Wallace to Susan Wallace, 9 April 1862, Lew Wallace Collection, Box 2, IHS.

71. Buell, *The Warrior Generals*, xxvii–xxxiii. Buell asserts in total that "fighting spirit, courage, intelligence, stamina, and good fortune" allowed the most able volunteers to deal with assuming the obligations of the Civil War general, being "the intelligent employment of the army's combat power; the discipline, morale, and well being of the troops; transportation and supply; rapid and secure communications; the gathering of intelligence; the need for accurate maps; interactions with irregular forces and hostile civilians; relations with politicians, the public, and the media."

Chapter 5. "On the Shelf" and Off to Cincinnati

1. Wallace to Susan Wallace, 9 April 1862, Lew Wallace Collection, Box 2, IHS.

2. Wallace, *Lew Wallace; an Autobiography*, 570.

3. John F. Marszalek, *Commander of All Lincoln's Armies: A Life of General Henry W. Halleck* (Cambridge: Belknap Press of Harvard University Press, 2004), 123–25. A recently embarrassed Grant also discouraged anything risky, especially since Halleck argued for caution; see Grant to Wallace, 12 April 1862, *OR*, 10(2):135.

4. Wallace, *Lew Wallace; an Autobiography*, 571–72.

5. Wallace claimed to have a copy of his *Light Infantry Tactics* when writing his memoir, but it has not been found; see ibid.

6. Perry D. Jamieson, *Crossing the Deadly Ground: United States Army Tactics, 1865–1899* (Tuscaloosa: University of Alabama Press, 1994), 4, 94, 99, and 112. Also see Skelton, *An American Profession of Arms*, 255.

7. Wallace, *Lew Wallace; an Autobiography*, 579–80.

8. T. Harry Williams, *Lincoln and His Generals* (New York: Alfred A. Knopf, 1952), 137.

9. Herman Hattaway and Archer Jones, *How the North Won: A Military History of the Civil War* (Urbana: University of Illinois Press, 1983), 54.

10. Ibid., 64–65, 77, and 209.

11. Wallace to Susan Wallace, 26 April 1862, Lew Wallace Collection, Box 2, IHS.

12. Special Field Orders No. 35, by command of Henry Halleck, 30 April 1862, Papers of Ulysses S. Grant, Series 10, Container 16, LC.

13. Grant, *Personal Memoirs*, 1:372.

14. Wallace to Susan Wallace, 10 May 1862, Lew Wallace Collection, Box 2, IHS.

15. Report of Wallace to John A. Rawlins, 12 April 1862, *OR*, 10(1):169–70.

16. An "indorsement" by Grant, attached to Wallace's report, which he "Respectfully forwarded to headquarters of the department," 25 April 1862, *OR*, 10(1):173.

17. For examples, see *Chicago Tribune*, 15–17 April 1862.

18. John A. Rawlins to Wallace, 23 April 1862, Lew Wallace Collection, Box 2, IHS.

19. Grant to Wallace, 28 April 1862, *OR*, 10(2):135.

20. These words were copied in an endorsement book which usually acknowledges only the receipt of letters by the headquarters; see Grant's "endorsement" acknowledging a message from Wallace, 28 April 1862, Department of the Tennessee—Letters Received and General Orders, part II, number 171, entry 2733, vol. G3 (including old vols. 3 and 4), RG 393, NARA.

21. Again, for more on the teachings at West Point and the development of a common set of values among regular officers, see Watson, "How the Army Became Accepted," 233, and "Continuity in Civil-Military Relations and Expertise," 233, 238–39, and 244. Also see Skelton, "Officers and Politicians," 27, 29, 38, and 41; "The Commanding Generals and the Question of Civil Control in the Antebellum U.S. Army," 167–168; and *An American Profession of Arms*, xiii, 167, and 362.

22. Grant to Wallace, 29 April 1862, *OR*, 10(2):140.

23. Wallace to Susan Wallace, 23 May 1862, Lew Wallace Collection, Box 2, IHS.

24. McDonough, *Shiloh*, 220–21.

25. Morsberger and Morsberger, *Lew Wallace*, 108; also see Grant, *Personal Memoirs*, 1:392–93. Halleck personally "assumed command of the Army as General-in-Chief on the 23d of July, 1862;" see General Orders No. 101, War Department, 11 August 1862, Papers of Ulysses S. Grant, Series 10, Container 16, LC.

26. Wallace to Susan Wallace, 14 June 1862, Lew Wallace Collection, Box 2, IHS.

27. Morsberger and Morsberger, *Lew Wallace*, 108–9. Also see C. T. Hotchkiss, by command of John A. McClernand, to Wallace, 22 June 1862, *OR*, 17(2):25. Gail Stephens addresses the destruction of a train and the capture of some Union troops in *Shadow of Shiloh*, 114.

28. Morsberger and Morsberger, *Lew Wallace*, 108–9.

29. Grant, *Personal Memoirs*, 1:385.

30. Ibid., 1:385–93.

31. Morsberger and Morsberger, *Lew Wallace*, 109.

32. Wallace, *Lew Wallace; an Autobiography*, 589.

33. Ibid., 589–90.

34. Ibid., 590. It is not entirely clear as to whether Wallace had a choice in the matter, and it is also possible that Morton deceived Wallace, not explaining that there was a choice; see Stephens, *Shadow of Shiloh*, 122–23. Even if there was technically a choice, Wallace must have felt a lot of pressure to make his governor happy, and to stay away from Halleck.

35. Wallace, *Lew Wallace; an Autobiography*, 590.

36. President Lincoln expected these contributions from political generals, and tried to reward them; see Goss, *The War within the Union High Command*, xv–xvi, xx, and 105; and Work, *Lincoln's Political Generals*, 1–5, 25, and 227–34.

37. Wallace, *Lew Wallace; an Autobiography*, 590–91.

38. For an example of criticism of Grant, see *Chicago Tribune*, 3 May 1862. Also see Morsberger and Morsberger, *Lew Wallace*, 109–14.

39. Halleck to Wallace by telegraph, 31 July 1862, Lew Wallace Collection, Box 2, IHS.

40. Bruce Tap, "Inevitability, Masculinity, and the American Military Tradition: The Committee on the Conduct of the War Investigates the American Civil War," *American Nineteenth Century History* 5, no. 2 (Summer 2004): 20–21, 26, and 42; as well as Bruce Tap, *Over Lincoln's Shoulder: The Committee on the Conduct of the War* (Lawrence: University Press of Kansas, 1998), x, 2, 8, 21, 24, 27, 35, 47, 54, 60, 78, 137, 165–66, and 256–57.

41. Ibid., 8 and 256.

42. Stephens, *Shadow of Shiloh*, 119–21. Also see Beemer, *"My Greatest Quarrel with Fortune,"* 93 and 143–49.

43. Ibid., 157–58.

44. Morsberger and Morsberger, *Lew Wallace*, 115; also see Wallace, *Lew Wallace; an Autobiography*, 591.

45. James Lee McDonough, *War in Kentucky: From Shiloh to Perryville* (Knoxville: University of Tennessee Press, 1994), 1–116.

46. Wallace, *Lew Wallace; an Autobiography*, 591–92.

47. Ibid., 593–94.

48. J. T. Boyle to Wallace, 18 August 1862, *OR*, 52(1):271.

49. J. T. Boyle to Wallace, 20 August 1862, *OR*, 52(1):272–73.

50. Morsberger and Morsberger, *Lew Wallace*, 115–17. Buell's order is explained in a message from Horatio G. Wright to Wallace, 23 August 1862, *OR*, 16(2):405.

51. McDonough, *War in Kentucky*, 126–46.

52. Wright to Wallace, 1 September 1862, Lewis Wallace Papers, entry 159, RG 94, NARA.

53. Wright from Lexington to Wallace, 1 September 1862, *OR*, 16(2):470. Also see McKee, *"Ben-Hur" Wallace*, 59.

54. "Proclamation" by Wallace, 2 September 1865, Lew Wallace Collection, Box 2, IHS; also in *Cincinnati Enquirer*, 2 September 1862.

55. *Cincinnati Enquirer*, 2 September 1862. Wallace received letters from owners hoping to reopen businesses for a variety of reasons, but he seldom granted the requests unless the business might help in the defense; see one such request by George Wood, of a theatre company, to Wallace, 6 September 1862, and another to Wallace from the Gibson House, 4 September 1862, Lew Wallace Papers, Collection #L173, Manuscript Section, Indiana State Library, Indianapolis, Indiana (hereafter, ISL).

56. "Proclamation" by Wallace, 2 September 1865, Lew Wallace Collection, Box 2, IHS; also in *Cincinnati Enquirer*, 2 September 1862.

57. "Mayor's Proclamation" by George Hatch of Cincinnati, 2 September 1865, *OR*, 52(1):278. Wallace also authorized Maj. Malcom McDowell "to raise and organize all the volunteer companies and parts of companies in this city," taking "such steps as are necessary to arm and equip" the soldiers; see Special Orders No. 1, U.S. Forces at Cincinnati, 2 September 1862, Lew Wallace Papers, Collection #L173, ISL. McDowell would soon be authorized to group the companies into regiments; see Special Orders No. 7, by order of Wallace, 3 September 1862, Lew Wallace Papers, Collection #L173, ISL.

58. Another "Mayor's Proclamation" by George Hatch of Cincinnati, 2 September 1865, *OR*, 52(1):278–79; also in *Cincinnati Enquirer*, 2 September 1862. A proclamation,

dated 2 September, by Mayor John A. Goodson of Covington, echoed Tod's wishes; see *Cincinnati Enquirer*, 3 September 1862.

59. Ibid.

60. "The Cincinnati Times Again Issued," *Cincinnati Enquirer*, 6 September 1862.

61. General Orders No. 1, by order of Wallace, signed by I. C. Elston, 2 September 1865, *OR*, 52(1):278; also in *Cincinnati Enquirer*, 2 September 1862.

62. Vernon L. Volpe, "Squirrel Hunting for the Union: The Defense of Cincinnati in 1862," *Civil War History* 33 (September 1987): 243–47.

63. Ibid.

64. Ibid., 247.

65. McKee, *"Ben-Hur" Wallace*, 60. For a list of the gunboats, see a memorandum by John A. Darble, 19 September 1862, Lew Wallace Papers, Collection #L173, ISL.

66. "Enrollment of Members of Teacher's [*sic*] Rifle Company," 3 September 1862, Lew Wallace Papers, Collection #L173, ISL; also see letter from a company of "Frenchmen" to Wallace, 4 September 1862, Lew Wallace Papers, Collection #L173, ISL.

67. McKee, *"Ben-Hur" Wallace*, 60. A provost from Warsaw, Kentucky, estimated that five thousand rebels approached Covington; see Robinson to Wallace, 8 September 1862, Lew Wallace Papers, Collection #L173, ISL.

68. A. C. Kemper to Wright, 10 September 1862, Lew Wallace Papers, Collection #L173, ISL.

69. Sent from the Gibson House in Cincinnati to Wallace, 4 September 1862, ibid.

70. David Tod to Wright, 10 September 1862, *OR*, 16(2):504.

71. Tod to E. M. Stanton, 11:00 A.M. on 10 September 1862, *OR*, 16(2):504.

72. See a "List of [some] Companies from the Country," 11 September 1862, Lew Wallace Papers, Collection #L173, ISL.

73. Volpe, "Squirrel Hunting for the Union," 243.

74. N. H. McLean to "His Honor Mayor Hatch," 10 September 1862, *OR*, 16(2):504–5. One officer crafted a long letter dispelling one of the few complaints raised against blacks working on or near the trenches; see W. M. Dicheron to Col. A. F. Perry, 18 September 1862, Lew Wallace Papers, Collection #L173, ISL.

75. For example, see a complaint from someone near Covington to Wallace, 5 September 1862, Lew Wallace Papers, Collection #L173, ISL. It helped that Provost Marshal A. E. Jones issued detailed instructions to commanders, telling them, among other things, that citizens were "not to be molested" as the troops passed from town to town; see Jones to "Captain Provost Guard," 15 September 1862, ibid.

76. McKee, *"Ben-Hur" Wallace*, 61.

77. Wallace to Wright, 12 September 1862, Lewis Wallace Papers, entry 159, RG 94, NARA. Also in *OR*, 16(2):511.

78. A. J. Smith to Wallace, 17 September 1862, *OR*, 52(1):282.

79. Capt. Sam D. Carey to Wallace, 14 September 1862, Lew Wallace Collection, Box 2, IHS.

80. "General Lew. Wallace," *Cincinnati Enquirer*, 14 September 1862.

81. "To the People of Cincinnati, Newport and Covington," ibid.

82. Wallace to Wright, 17 September 1862, *OR*, 16(2):525.

83. Halleck to Wallace, 17 September 1862, *OR*, series II, 4:522.

84. Wallace, *Lew Wallace; an Autobiography*, 632.

85. Wright to Wallace, 18 September 1862, *OR*, 52(2):283.

86. "Joint resolutions relative to a vote of thanks to Maj. Gen. Lew. Wallace for service rendered at Cincinnati," signed by James R. Hubbell, P. Hitchcock, and W. W. Armstrong, 4 March 1863, *OR*, 52(1):337.

87. Volpe, "Squirrel Hunting for the Union," 253.

88. Goss, *The War within the Union High Command*, xv–xvi, xx, and 105; and Work, *Lincoln's Political Generals*, 1–5, 25, and 227–34.

Chapter 6. Columbus, Buell, and Morgan

1. Henry W. Halleck to Wallace, 17 September 1862, *OR*, series II, 4:522.

2. William S. Rosecrans to Halleck, 26 September 1862, *OR*, 17(2):239. Earlier in the same note, Rosecrans stated that he had been "promoted junior to men who have not rendered a tithe of the services nor had a tithe of the success" that he had earlier in the war in western Virginia.

3. Wallace to Horatio G. Wright, 17 September 1862, Lewis Wallace Papers, entry 159, RG 94, NARA.

4. G. W. Berry, from Falmouth, Kentucky, to Wallace, 18 September 1862, *OR*, 16(1):989–90.

5. Wallace, *Lew Wallace; an Autobiography*, 632.

6. Ibid., 632–33.

7. Paul J. Springer, *America's Captives: Treatment of POWs from the Revolutionary War to the War on Terror* (Lawrence: University Press of Kansas, 2010), 81.

8. Benjamin G. Cloyd, *Haunted by Atrocity: Civil War Prisons in American Memory* (Baton Rouge: Louisiana State University Press, 2010), 7.

9. Wallace, *Lew Wallace; an Autobiography*, 629–30.

10. Ibid., 634.

11. Ibid., 634–35.

12. Wallace to Lorenzo Thomas, 22 September 1862, *OR*, series II, 4:546. Ohio's governor sent a telegram to Edwin Stanton, reaffirming that it would "be impossible for General Wallace to bring them [prisoners] to any kind of order or discipline" until the soldiers received back pay; see David Tod to Stanton, 22 September 1862, *OR*, series II, 4:545–46. See Wallace's embellished description of events in his *Lew Wallace; an Autobiography*, 636–37.

13. Cary H. Fry to Lorenzo Thomas, 23 September 1862, *OR*, series II, 4:546.

14. Edwin M. Stanton to Wallace, 23 September 1862, ibid., series II, 4:548.

15. Wallace to Lorenzo Thomas, 28 September 1862, ibid., series II, 4:569–71. Wallace referred to the same camp as "Camp Tod" in his postwar memoir, but admitted that the name was "from recollection," not from wartime correspondence; see Wallace, *Lew Wallace; an Autobiography*, 637.

16. Stanton to Wallace, 23 September 1862, *OR*, series II, 4:548.

17. Wallace to Stanton, 26 September 1862, *OR*, series II, 4:563. Also see Wallace's description of events in his *Lew Wallace; an Autobiography*, 639.

18. Ramold, *Baring the Iron Hand*, 230; as well as Ramold, "Discipline and the Union Army," 47.

19. Michael Thomas Smith, "The Most Desperate Scoundrels Unhung: Bounty Jumpers and Recruitment Fraud in the Civil War North," *American Nineteenth Century History* 6, no. 2 (June 2005): 159.

20. Wallace to Lorenzo Thomas, 28 September 1862, *OR*, series II, 4:569.

21. Ibid., 4:569–71. The unfortunate and bizarre situation also led the general to recommend that the army "give a dishonorable discharge to every man who refuses to be attached to an organization or who deserts after being paid." And since whoever "gets into Camp Chase or comes in contact with its inmates is instantly seized with the mutinous spirit," the Indianan begged the secretary of war "not to send more troops to this place."

22. Wright to Wallace by telegraph from Cincinnati, 8 October 1862, Lewis Wallace Papers, entry 159, RG 94, NARA.

23. Lane, later in December, even managed to get forty-eight signatures on a petition to Lincoln requesting that Wallace receive a command; Halleck appears to have "filed the petition away." See Beemer, *"My Greatest Quarrel with Fortune,"* 163.

24. Telegram from Grant, 10 November 1862, Lew Wallace Collection, Box 2, IHS. Also see Wallace, *Lew Wallace; an Autobiography*, 641, and Stephens, *Shadow of Shiloh*, 141.

25. Wallace to Susan Wallace, 13 November 1862, Lew Wallace Collection, Box 2, IHS.

26. E. D. Townsend, by order of Halleck, to Wallace, 20 November 1862, reprinted in Wallace, *Lew Wallace; an Autobiography*, 641–42.

27. James M. McPherson, *Battle Cry of Freedom: The Civil War Era* (New York: Oxford University Press, 1988), 511–17.

28. Ibid., 516–22.

29. Wallace, *Lew Wallace; an Autobiography*, 642.

30. Stephen D. Engle, *Don Carlos Buell: Most Promising of All* (Chapel Hill: University of North Carolina Press, 1999), 328–34.

31. Rafuse, "'To Check . . . the Very Worst and Meanest of Our Passions'," 422.

32. Wallace, *Lew Wallace; an Autobiography*, 643.

33. Wallace to Susan Wallace from Nashville, 14 December 1862, Lew Wallace Collection, Box 2, IHS.

34. Wallace, *Lew Wallace; an Autobiography*, 642–44.

35. Wallace to Susan Wallace from Nashville, 22 December 1862, Lew Wallace Collection, Box 2, IHS.

36. Engle, *Don Carlos Buell*, 333–34.

37. Nothing substantial or official came from the five-month-long inquiry until the entire record was published in the *Official Records* well after the war; see ibid. Also see *OR*, 16(1):6–726.

38. "Indorsement" by Grant, "forwarded [and attached to Wallace's report on Shiloh] to headquarters of the department," 25 April 1862, *OR*, 10(1):174.

39. Grant to Halleck, December 1862, quoted in *How the North Won*, by Hattaway and Jones, 309. Also see *OR*, 17(1):475 and 52(2):313–14.
40. Wallace's first draft of a letter to Halleck, 3 March 1863, Lewis Wallace Papers, entry 159, RG 94, NARA. Also see the final draft of the same letter, 14 March 1863, *OR*, 10(1):174–76.
41. Wallace's first draft of a letter to Halleck, 3 March 1863, Lewis Wallace Papers, entry 159, RG 94, NARA. Emphasis in original. Also see the final draft of the same letter, 14 March 1863, *OR*, 10(1):174–76. For other explanations of early events on 6 April, see the draft of a report of U. S. Grant, 30 August 1861 through 6 April 1862, Papers of Ulysses S. Grant, Series 10, Container 17 (Military File—Reports), LC; and Grant, *Personal Memoirs*, 1:336; as well as Wallace, *Lew Wallace; an Autobiography*, 461.
42. Wallace's first draft of a letter to Halleck, 3 March 1863, Lewis Wallace Papers, entry 159, RG 94, NARA. Also see the final draft of the same letter, 14 March 1863, *OR*, 10(1):174–76.
43. Grant to Col. J. C. Kelton from before Vicksburg, 13 April 1863, *OR*, 10(1):178. Grant's note is followed by three "inclosures" by W. R. Rowley, James B. McPherson, and John A. Rawlins, respectively dated 4 April, 26 March, and 1 April 1863, *OR*, 10(1):178–88.
44. Three "inclosures" by W. R. Rowley, James B. McPherson, and John A. Rawlins, respectively dated 4 April, 26 March, and 1 April 1863, *OR*, 10(1):178–88.
45. "Inclosure No. 3" by John A. Rawlins, addressed to Grant, 1 April 1863, *OR*, 10(1):185.
46. Grant to Col. J. C. Kelton from before Vicksburg, 13 April 1863, *OR*, 10(1):178.
47. Stanton to Wallace via telegraph, 25 May 1863, Lewis Wallace Papers, entry 159, RG 94, NARA.
48. Wallace to Halleck, date unknown, ibid. The telegram also appears in Wallace, *Lew Wallace; an Autobiography*, 655.
49. Wallace to Halleck, 24 June 1863, Lewis Wallace Papers, entry 159, RG 94, NARA.
50. Halleck to Wallace, 24 June 1863, ibid.
51. Wallace, *Lew Wallace; an Autobiography*, 654.
52. Wallace to Halleck, 26 June 1863, Lewis Wallace Papers, entry 159, RG 94, NARA.
53. Halleck to Wallace, 27 June 1863, ibid.
54. Halleck to Wallace, 2 and 4 July 1863, ibid.
55. Wallace to Grant, 27 June 1863, Lew Wallace Collection, Box 2, IHS.
56. Oliver P. Morton to Halleck, 10 July 1863, *OR*, 52(1):398.
57. W. R. Holloway to Wallace, 10 July 1863, Lewis Wallace Papers, entry 159, RG 94, NARA.
58. Halleck to Wallace, sent at 12:20 P.M., 11 July 1863, ibid.
59. Report of Wallace on Morgan's Raid, 27 July 1863, *OR*, 52(1):68.
60. Ibid., 68–69.
61. Orlando B. Willcox to Wallace, 11 July 1863, Lewis Wallace Papers, entry 159, RG 94, NARA.
62. Report of Wallace on Morgan's Raid, 27 July 1863, *OR*, 52(1):68–69.
63. Wallace also ordered that nobody leave the cars, for he feared an attack against the train. Most heeded the command to stay in the cars, accounting "for the airy condition of the box-cars in my trains, which was doubtless observed by the railroad

agents" on the following morning; see ibid., 69. While Wallace and his troops were on their way, in the middle afternoon of 11 July, Morgan and his cavalry approached the town of Vernon, quickly finding out the town was ready to fight. Barricades "had been thrown up in the streets, and several hundred militiamen were waiting with rifles at ready." Morgan sent in some men, who demanded the surrender of the town, but the Union colonel in charge refused. The cavalry raider decided that an attack on Vernon would result in too many losses, so he and his subordinates directed their brigades to another road that led southeast toward the small town of Dupont. See Dee Alexander Brown, *Morgan's Raiders* (New York: Konecky and Konecky, 1959), 199. Morgan made a second demand for surrender in order to gain time to re-form his columns. At about this time, Love and his troops arrived on board a train from the north, and the Union general soon demanded that the Confederates surrender. The cavalry commander had no intention of giving up, so he informed Love that the Union soldiers had "thirty minutes to remove women and children, after which time the raiders would begin shelling Vernon with artillery." Love and his men excitedly moved noncombatants to a safe place north of town. As Union troops worked to protect Vernon's citizens, "Morgan's rear guard slipped away, and concealed by darkness hurried on after the forward columns," traveling all night to Dupont, Indiana. See Brown, *Morgan's Raiders*; also see James A. Ramage, *The Life of General John Hunt Morgan* (Lexington: University of Kentucky Press, 1986), 171.

64. Report of Wallace on Morgan's Raid, 27 July 1863, *OR*, 52(1):69.

65. Wallace to Willcox, 12 July 1863, ibid., 52(1):400.

66. Wallace, by telegraph from Vernon, to William Nelson, 12 July 1863, Lewis Wallace Papers, entry 159, RG 94, NARA.

67. Report on troop strength from Wallace to Willcox, 13 July 1863, ibid.

68. Wallace to Willcox, 14 July 1863, *OR*, 52(1):410.

69. Wallace to Willcox, 14 July 1863, Lewis Wallace Papers, entry 159, RG 94, NARA.

70. See letters from Willcox to Wallace, 12 July 1863, *OR*, 52(1):404.

71. Telegram from Ambrose Burnside copied into a telegram from Willcox to Wallace, 14 July 1863, ibid., 411.

72. Morton to Wallace, 15 July 1863, Lewis Wallace Papers, entry 159, RG 94, NARA.

73. Wilcox to Wallace, 15 July 1863, ibid.

74. General Orders No. 1, by Wallace from Sunman, Indiana, 15 July 1863, ibid.

75. Report of Wallace on Morgan's Raid, 27 July 1863, *OR*, 52(1):69–70.

76. Ibid., 52(1):70.

77. Wallace to Stanton, 17 July 1863, Lewis Wallace Papers, entry 159, RG 94, NARA. Same letter, but dated 18 July, appears in *OR*, 10(1):189.

78. Ibid.

79. Ibid., 10(1):189–90.

80. "Indorsement" by James A. Hardie, by order of Stanton, ibid., 10(1):190.

81. Wallace, *Lew Wallace; an Autobiography*, 662. Wallace sent the letter on 16 August 1863.

82. Sherman to Rawlins, confidential, 27 August 1863, *OR*, 30(3):183–84.

83. Sherman to Wallace, 27 August 1863, Lew Wallace Collection, Box 2, IHS; also reprinted in Wallace, *Lew Wallace; an Autobiography*, 662–64.

84. Ibid. Emphasis added.

85. See Watson, "Flexible Gender Roles during the Market Revolution," 83; as well as Rafuse, "'To Check . . . the Very Worst and Meanest of Our Passions'," 408–9. For more on the influence West Point had on it graduates, see Watson, "How the Army Became Accepted," 233; as well as Skelton, *An American Profession of Arms*, 362.

86. Sherman to Wallace, 27 August 1863, Lew Wallace Collection, Box 2, IHS; also reprinted in Wallace, *Lew Wallace; an Autobiography*, 662–64.

87. Wallace to Stanton, 16 September 1863, Lew Wallace Collection, Box 2, IHS; also in *OR*, 10(1):189–90.

88. *OR*, 10(1):189–90.

89. W. R. Holloway to Wallace, 18 September 1863, Lewis Wallace Papers, entry 159, RG 94, NARA.

90. Stanton to Morton, 19 September 1863, *OR*, 30(3):738.

91. W. R. Holloway to Wallace, 20 and 21 September 1863, Lewis Wallace Papers, entry 159, RG 94, NARA.

92. For examples, including thoughts on Wallace's earlier stint as adjutant general in Indiana, see Goss, *The War within the Union High Command*, 39–44.

93. Wallace to Stanton, 21 September 1863, *OR*, 30(3):760. See the same telegram, misdated 20 July 1863, Lewis Wallace Papers, entry 159, RG 94, NARA.

94. Wallace, *Lew Wallace; an Autobiography*, 667.

95. Morton to Stanton, 2 October 1863, *OR*, 30(4):31.

96. Stanton to Morton, 2 October 1863, *OR*, 30(4):32.

97. Wallace to Stanton, 3 October 1863, *OR*, 30(4):57.

98. Sherman further softened the bad news by divulging some of his own. He explained to Wallace that he was having a hard time because his little boy had recently died; see Sherman to Wallace, 9 October 1863, Lew Wallace Collection, Box 2, IHS. Also see Wallace, *Lew Wallace; an Autobiography*, 665–66.

Chapter 7. "A Command Worthy of His Rank"

1. *Crawfordsville Journal*, 10 March 1864.

2. The Middle Department was created on 22 March 1862. Its boundaries varied during the war, at times including portions of New Jersey, Pennsylvania, Delaware, Maryland, and Virginia. Wallace took over command two years after the department had been created. By that time, the department included most of Maryland and all of Delaware. His command also included the VIII Army Corps. See Frederick H. Dyer, *A Compendium of the War of the Rebellion*, 3 parts (Des Moines, Iowa: Dyer Publishing, 1908), 1:256.

3. G. R. Tredway, *Democratic Opposition to the Lincoln Administration in Indiana* (Indianapolis: Indiana Historical Bureau, 1973), xiii.

4. Wallace, *Lew Wallace; an Autobiography*, 668–69.

5. It is possible that Halleck did object, but there is no direct evidence, except for Wallace's own words, that the chief of staff actively tried to persuade the president to cancel the appointment. Some authors have taken the Indianan's word on this particular issue, but Wallace, in his autobiography, does not reveal a source, or suggest when he heard this news. For example, see Morsberger and Morsberger, *Lew Wallace*, 132.

6. Wallace to Susan Wallace, from the National Hotel, 13 March 1864, Lew Wallace Collection, Box 3, IHS.

7. Wallace, *Lew Wallace; an Autobiography*, 669–70.

8. Wallace to E. M. Stanton, 21 September 1863, *OR*, 30(3):760.

9. Wallace, *Lew Wallace; an Autobiography*, 670–73. For more on the participation of soldiers in the electoral process, see Jonathan W. White, *Emancipation, the Union Army, and the Reelection of Abraham Lincoln* (Baton Rouge: Louisiana State University Press, 2014), 1–4.

10. In the order, Wallace was certain to acknowledge the "zeal and rare ability" of his predecessor, Brig. Gen. Henry H. Lockwood; see Wallace, Headquarters at Baltimore, General Orders No. 16, 22 March 1864, Lew Wallace Collection, Box 3, IHS. Also in the *OR*, 33:717. The new department chief delivered a wise compliment. It turned out that Lockwood would be a brigade commander under Wallace from 20 July to the end of the war; see Dyer, *Compendium of the War of the Rebellion*, 1:343. The new commander of the department understood what it was like to lose a command, and he acted accordingly.

11. Wallace, Headquarters at Baltimore, General Orders No. 16, 22 March 1864, Lew Wallace Collection, Box 3, IHS. Also in the *OR*, 33:717.

12. Susan Wallace to Helen Lossing, 20 July 1864, Collection LS1995, Box 10, The Huntington Library, San Marino, CA. Henry Winter Davis was a Republican, and Reverdy Johnson was a Democrat, but both claimed to be members of Maryland's Unionist party during the war. See Richard Walsh and William Lloyd Fox, eds., *Maryland: A History, 1632–1974* (Baltimore: Maryland Historical Society, 1974), 380–82.

13. Wallace to William Wallace, from Crawfordsville, 8 February 1864, Lew Wallace Collection, Box 3, IHS. Wallace underlined "Conservatism is a necessity" in the original letter.

14. Goss, *The War within the Union High Command*, 94 and 105.

15. For example, see letters of 25, 26, 28, and 29 March 1864, signed by judges of election, in Middle Department and VIII Army Corps—Letters Received, part I, entry 2343, box 4 (1864 A-G), RG 393, NARA.

16. Augustus Bradford was a supporter of the Union, and he had visited Lincoln on occasion, but Wallace's staff was not aware of this. See Charles B. Clark, "Politics in Maryland During the Civil War: Slavery and Emancipation in Maryland, 1861–1865," *Maryland Historical Magazine* 41 (June 1946): 139–43.

17. Wallace, *Lew Wallace; an Autobiography*, 681–82.

18. Wallace italicized this question in his memoir; see ibid., 682.

19. Work, *Lincoln's Political Generals*, 168–77.
20. Bradford had been a Whig before the war. When the Whig Party collapsed in the 1850s, Bradford declined to join the Democrats or Republicans. In 1861, he became one of the more conservative members of Maryland's Union Party. Bradford ran for the governorship as a Union Party candidate and won, taking office in January of 1862. The Union party later split into different groups, with Bradford allying himself with one of the more conservative wings that criticized those who unconditionally supported the Union. See J. Thomas Scharf, *History of Maryland from the Earliest Period to the Present Day*, 3 vols. (1879; reprint, Hatboro, Pa.: Tradition Press, 1967), 3:202, 378–79, and 568–69. And see Walsh and Fox, *Maryland*, 353–56 and 371–77.
21. Again, see White, *Emancipation, the Union Army, and the Reelection of Abraham Lincoln*, 1–4.
22. Wallace to Governor Bradford, 24 March 1864, Middle Department and VIII Army Corps—Letters Sent, part I, entry 2327, vol. 31 (5 of 5), RG 393, NARA.
23. "Disloyal Candidates—Declination of E. G. Kilbourn [*sic*]," *Baltimore Daily Gazette*, 2 April 1864. For more on Kilbourne's involvement in the secession crisis, see Scharf, *History of Maryland*, 3:443.
24. Shelby Clark to Stanton, 14 March 1864, Middle Department and VIII Army Corps—Letters Received, part I, entry 2343, box 4 (1864 A-G), RG 393, NARA.
25. Edward W. Belt to Wallace, 29 March 1864, ibid. The incident, one in which the army freed blacks who had been arrested for a number of crimes, occurred at a most unfortunate time, possibly hindering the general's efforts at guarding an election without bad publicity. It is unclear whether authorities found Perkins guilty; evidence painted a clear picture of someone who did something possibly humane, but certainly illegal. See Col. S. W. Bowman to Samuel B. Lawrence, 5 April 1864, ibid.
26. Organization of the Army of the Potomac, *OR*, 36(1):114. Also see *OR*, 46(1):579. Joseph G. Perkins eventually rose to the rank of colonel during the war; see Francis B. Heitman, ed., *Historical Register and Dictionary of the United States Army*, 2 vols. (Washington, D.C.: Government Printing Office, 1903), 2:136.
27. Samuel B. Lawrence to Lockwood, E. B. Tyler, D. Tyler, and Porter, 25 March 1864, Middle Department and VIII Army Corps—Letters Sent, part I, entry 2327, vol. 31 (5 of 5), RG 393, NARA.
28. White, *Emancipation, the Union Army, and the Reelection of Abraham Lincoln*, 120.
29. Lawrence to Generals Lockwood, E. B. Tyler, Daniel Tyler, and Colonel Waite (?), 29 March 1864, Middle Department and VIII Army Corps—Letters Sent, part I, entry 2327, vol. 31 (5 of 5), RG 393, NARA.
30. White, *Emancipation, the Union Army, and the Reelection of Abraham Lincoln*, 9.
31. Wallace, *Lew Wallace; an Autobiography*, 684.
32. Abraham Lincoln to Stanton, 31 March 1864, Lew Wallace Collection, Box 3, IHS.
33. "Negro Equality," *Baltimore Daily Gazette*, 25 March 1864.
34. Lawrence to Editor, *Baltimore Daily Gazette*, 29 March 1864, Middle Department and VIII Army Corps—Letters Sent, part I, entry 2327, vol. 31 (5 of 5), RG 393, NARA.

35. Another letter from Lawrence to Editor, *Baltimore Daily Gazette*, ibid.
36. Wallace to Augustus W. Bradford, 30 March 1864, ibid.
37. For example, see Wallace to Brig. Gen. H. H. Lockwood, 3 April 1864, ibid. Also Samuel B. Lawrence to General Lockwood and Colonel Porter, 5 April 1864, ibid.
38. Wallace to Susan Wallace, 3 April 1864, Lew Wallace Collection, Box 3, IHS.
39. Wallace, *Lew Wallace; an Autobiography*, 682–83.
40. White, *Emancipation, the Union Army, and the Reelection of Abraham Lincoln*, 153.
41. For examples, see Lawrence to Col. P. A. Porter, and Lawrence to Brig. Gen. H. H. Lockwood, 6 April 1864, Middle Department and VIII Army Corps—Letters Sent, part I, entry 2327, vol. 31 (5 of 5), RG 393, NARA.
42. George W. Krebs to Wallace, with a reply on the back, 6 April 1864, Middle Department and VIII Army Corps—Letters Received, part I, entry 2343, box 4 (1864 A-G), RG 393, NARA.
43. Clark, "Politics in Maryland During the Civil War," 148.
44. H. Winter Davis to Wallace, 7 April 1864, Lew Wallace Collection, Box 3, IHS.
45. Wallace to Susan Wallace, 8 April 1864, ibid.
46. According to Morsberger, "Wallace required voters to answer a questionnaire that allowed election judges to disqualify those of dubious loyalty." This list of questions was occasionally abused by judges of election; however, this was not Wallace's intention, and abuses did not regularly occur. See Robert E. Morsberger, "Latter-Day Lord of Baltimore," *Maryland Magazine* 9 (Summer 1977): 4.
47. *Baltimore Daily Gazette*, 7 through 12 April 1864.
48. For example, on 28 March, Wallace received notice of the arrival of C. J. Simpson, from Montgomery, Alabama, a man he viewed as a "dangerous and disloyal citizen of the U.S." His adjutant asked the provost marshal to investigate the matter and have the man arrested. See Assistant Adjutant General Max Woodhull to Lt. Col. John Woolley, 28 March 1864, Middle Department and VIII Army Corps—Letters Sent, part I, entry 2327, vol. 31 (5 of 5), RG 393, NARA. Such actions took up much of Wallace's time in Maryland.
49. Lawrence to John Woolley, 30 March 1864, ibid.
50. Unsigned letter to Col. P. A. Porter, 26 April 1864, ibid.
51. A second letter from Lawrence to John Woolley, 30 March 1864, ibid.
52. Mark Grimsley, *The Hard Hand of War: Union Military Policy toward Southern Civilians, 1861–1865* (Cambridge, UK, and New York: Cambridge University Press, 1995), 53–54; as well as i, 2, 204.
53. William H. Gooding to Provost Marshal Goldsborrough, 21 April 1864, Middle Department and VIII Army Corps—Letters Received, part I, entry 2343, box 4 (1864 A-G), RG 393, NARA. Gooding underlined "Seceshism" and "Lincoln Catechism" in the original letter.
54. Wallace to Susan Wallace, 24 April 1864, Lew Wallace Collection, Box 3, IHS.
55. Wallace to E. D. Townsend, 28 April 1864, *OR*, 33:1008.
56. Wallace to Townsend, 3 May 1864, *OR*, 37(1):375.
57. Townsend to Wallace, 12 May 1864, Middle Department and VIII Army Corps—Letters Received, part I, entry 2343, box 4 (1864 A-G), RG 393, NARA.

58. Stephen V. Ash, *When the Yankees Came* (Chapel Hill: University of North Carolina Press, 1995), 124. Ash mentions, for example, that while "secessionists were a majority in nearly every section of no-man's-land," occupied areas between garrisoned towns and the Confederate frontier, "and in most cases a very large majority, the absence of Confederate authority and the proximity of the Federal posts diminished their power and strengthened the Unionists. The result was a degree of desperation on the part of the secessionists and a degree of defiance on the part of the Unionists that fueled one another and ultimately exploded into savage fratricide." Though such violence could occur in Maryland, a Union state, it was not as problematic in 1864 as in parts of the Confederate South.

59. Wallace to the Commissioners of Police, City of Baltimore, 5 May 1864, *OR*, 37(1):391–92.

60. Morsberger, "Latter-Day Lord of Baltimore," 5.

61. General Orders No. 30 and 33, 26 April and 1 May 1864, Middle Department and VIII Army Corps—General Orders (Printed), part I, entry 2352, vol. 61 (2 of 3), RG 393, NARA.

62. Stanton to Wallace, 14 June 1864, *OR*, series III, 4:431. Also see Wallace to Edward Bates, 30 May 1864, ibid., 413–15.

63. Wallace to Stanton, 14 June 1864, ibid., 432.

64. Samuel B. Lawrence to Lockwood, E. B. Tyler, D. Tyler, and Porter, 25 March 1864, Middle Department and VIII Army Corps—Letters Sent, part I, entry 2327, vol. 31 (5 of 5), RG 393, NARA.

65. Wallace to Susan Wallace, 10 April 1864, Lew Wallace Collection, Box 3, IHS.

66. Wallace to Brig. Gen. Lorenzo Thomas, 14 April 1864, Middle Department and VIII Army Corps—Letters Sent, part I, entry 2327, vol. 31 (5 of 5), RG 393, NARA.

67. Wallace to E. D. Townsend, 22 April 1864, ibid.

68. Halleck to U. S. Grant, 29 April 1864, *OR*, 34(3):332.

69. Halleck to W. T. Sherman, 29 April 1864, *OR*, 34(3):333.

70. Robert Whott to Wallace, 6 May 1864, Middle Department and VIII Army Corps—Letters Received, part I, entry 2343, box 4 (1864 A-G), RG 393, NARA.

71. Morsberger, "Latter-Day Lord of Baltimore," 5. Also see White, *Emancipation, the Union Army, and the Reelection of Abraham Lincoln*, 99.

72. In May, and then June, the general found himself regularly sending men to the Army of the Potomac, which was maneuvering to capture Richmond. Wallace also spent a lot of time providing transportation and guards for recently captured and paroled prisoners; for example, see Lawrence to Col. Alexander Bliss, 23 April 1864, Middle Department and VIII Army Corps—Letters Sent, part I, entry 2327, vol. 31 (5 of 5), RG 393, NARA. These duties became even more troublesome to the departmental commander once the death tolls of Grant's Wilderness Campaign multiplied the extent of these duties; for example, see Halleck to Wallace, 15 May 1864, *OR*, 36(2):802. In the midst of all this confusion, the general assisted Governor Bradford with efforts to recruit young Marylanders, at least for one hundred days' service; see Wallace to Stanton, and a reply, 14 May 1864, *OR*, 37(1):458–59.

Chapter 8. "A Forlorn Hope"

1. Furthermore, in May and June, Wallace regularly sent men to the Army of the Potomac, as it endeavored to capture Richmond. He spent much of his time providing transportation and guards for recently captured or paroled prisoners. Grant's Wilderness Campaign added to these duties. As a consequence, the meager forces of the Middle Department could not defend the approaches to Baltimore and Washington, D.C., in an emergency. For examples, see Samuel B. Lawrence to Col. Alexander Bliss, 23 April 1864, Middle Department and VIII Army Corps—Letters Sent, part I, entry 2327, vol. 31 (5 of 5), RG 393, NARA; and see Henry W. Halleck to Wallace, 15 May 1864, *OR*, series I (all references to series I unless indicated), 36(2):802.

2. Wallace to Halleck, 9 June 1864, *OR*, 37(1):617–18.

3. Benjamin Franklin Cooling, *Monocacy: The Battle That Saved Washington* (Shippensburg, Pa.: White Mane Publishing, 1997), 9.

4. Robert E. Lee to Gen. Jubal A. Early, at Lynchburg, 18 June 1864, in *The Wartime Papers of R. E. Lee*, ed. Clifford Dowdy (Boston: Little, Brown, 1961), 791.

5. Cooling, *Monocacy*, 12.

6. "Excursion to the Capes," *Baltimore Sun*, 28 June 1864.

7. Franz Sigel to the Adjutant General of the Army, from Martinsburg in Virginia, received at 12:00 P.M. on 2 July 1864, Lew Wallace Collection, Box 3, IHS.

8. Cooling, *Monocacy*, 20.

9. Wallace to Darius N. Couch, 3 July 1864, *OR*, 37(2):32.

10. Couch to Wallace, sent at 4:30 P.M. by telegraph, 3 July 1864, ibid.

11. Ulysses S. Grant to Halleck, 5:00 P.M. on 3 July 1864, Lew Wallace Collection, Box 3, IHS.

12. Charles Dana to Edwin Stanton, from City Point in Virginia, 3:30 P.M. on 3 July 1864, ibid.

13. T. Harry Williams, *Americans at War: The Development of the American Military System* (Baton Rouge: Louisiana State University Press, 1960), 81; as well as Williams's *Lincoln and His Generals*, 291.

14. For more on this breakdown in the command structure, see four books by Benjamin Franklin Cooling, including *Symbol, Sword, and Shield: Defending Washington during the Civil War* (Hamden, Conn.: Archon Books, 1975), 189; *Monocacy*, 42; *Jubal Early: Robert E. Lee's "Bad Old Man"* (Lanham, Mass.: Rowman and Littlefield, 2014), 101; and *Jubal Early's Raid on Washington, 1864* (Baltimore: Nautical and Aviation Publishing Company of America, 1989), 221. Also see Albert Castel, with Brooks D. Simpson, *Victors in Blue: How Union Generals Fought the Confederates, Battled Each Other, and Won the Civil War* (Lawrence: University Press of Kansas, 2011), 282; Simpson, *Ulysses S. Grant*, 367; Brooks D. Simpson, *The Civil War in the East: Struggle, Stalemate, and Victory* (New York: Praeger, 2011; reprint, Lincoln, Nebr.: Potomac Books, 2013), 113; and Marszalek, *Commander of All Lincoln's Armies*, 210. For more on how a state's reaction to a crisis greatly depends on organizational behavior and governmental politics, see Graham Allison and Philip Zelikow, *Essence of Decision:*

Explaining the Cuban Missile Crisis, 2nd ed. (New York: Longman, 1999), vii, 2–8, 11, 15–18, 143–44, 152, 157, 164–66, 172–73, 255–58, 297–98, 379, 390, and 401–4.

15. *Baltimore Daily Gazette*, 4 July 1864, as well as "Highly Important War News," *Baltimore Sun*, 4 July 1864.

16. "Local Matters," *Baltimore Sun*, 6 July 1864.

17. Wallace to Stanton, 6 July 1864, *OR*, 37(2):91.

18. Papers of Jubal Anderson Early, container 5 (1868, Feb. 7—1871, Apr. 24), LC.

19. For more on Early's number of troops, see Cooling, *Monocacy*, 2–3, and Frank E. Vandiver, *Jubal's Raid: General Early's Famous Attack on Washington in 1864* (Westport, Conn.: Greenwood Press, 1974; originally published, New York: McGraw Hill, 1960), 26, 60.

20. Wallace, *Lew Wallace; an Autobiography*, 613–14.

21. Samuel B. Lawrence to Wallace, 6 July 1864, Lewis Wallace Papers, entry 159, RG 94, NARA. Also in the *OR*, 37(2):92.

22. Max Woodhull to Samuel B. Lawrence, 6 July 1864, *OR*, 37(2):93.

23. Special Order, Middle Department and the VIII Army Corps, 6 July 1864, Lewis Wallace Papers, entry 159, RG 94, NARA.

24. Stanton to Wallace, 6 July 1864, ibid. Stanton wrote to Wallace: "Please report to this Dept. the cause for imprisoning Mr. Reed of Balto and in the mean time discharge him immediately from prison and withdraw the guard from his dwelling house."

25. Stanton to Couch, 3:10 P.M. on 6 July 1864, *OR*, 37(2):95.

26. Wallace to Samuel B. Lawrence, 6 July 1864, p. 17 of a compilation of letters on Monocacy, Lew Wallace Collection, Box 3, IHS.

27. Headquarters Monocacy to Colonel Gilpin, 7 July 1864, Lewis Wallace Papers, entry 159, RG 94, NARA.

28. Samuel B. Lawrence to Wallace, 7 July 1864, ibid.

29. For example, see two letters from John W. Garrett to Samuel B. Lawrence, 7 July 1864, Middle Department and VIII Army Corps—Letters Received, part I, entry 2343, box 4 (1864 A-G), RG 393, NARA.

30. J. W. Garrett to Stanton, from Camden Station in Maryland, received at 7:40 P.M. on 7 July 1864, *OR*, 37(2):100.

31. Morsberger and Morsberger, *Lew Wallace*, 144.

32. Wallace to Samuel B. Lawrence, 7 July 1864, *OR*, 37(2):110; and J. W. Garrett to Stanton, from Camden Station in Maryland, received at 8:20 P.M. on 7 July 1864, *OR*, 37(2):100–101.

33. Ulysses S. Grant to George G. Meade, from City Point in Virginia, 5 July 1864, #54 in a list of dispatches pertaining to Monocacy, Lew Wallace Collection, Box 3, IHS.

34. J. W. Garrett to Stanton, from Camden Station in Maryland, received at 8:20 P.M. on 7 July 1864, *OR*, 37(2):100–101.

35. Stanton to Wallace, sent at 10:00 P.M., 7 July 1864, Lewis Wallace Papers, entry 159, RG 94, NARA. Also in *OR*, 37(2):108.

36. Halleck to Wallace, sent at 9:40 P.M., 7 July 1864, Lewis Wallace Papers, entry 159, RG 94, NARA. Also in *OR*, 37(2):108.

37. Halleck to Commanding Officer and Chief Quartermaster in Baltimore, sent at 9:42 P.M., 7 July 1864, *OR*, 37(2):111. Also see Halleck to James B. Ricketts (at Baltimore), 7 July 1864, #101 in a list of dispatches pertaining to Monocacy, Lew Wallace Collection, Box 3, IHS.

38. Samuel B. Lawrence to Halleck, received at 10:20 P.M., 7 July 1864, *OR*, 37(2):111.

39. Samuel B. Lawrence to Ricketts, 7 July 1864, ibid.

40. "The Rebel Raid," *Crawfordsville Journal*, 12 May 1864.

41. Wallace to Halleck, 8:00 P.M. on 8 July 1864, p. 25 of a compilation of letters on Monocacy, Lew Wallace Collection, Box 3, IHS.

42. Wallace to Sigel or Brigadier General Howe, from Frederick, 12:00 P.M. on 8 July 1864, *OR*, 37(2):124–25.

43. Gloria Baker Swift and Gail Stephens, "Honor Redeemed: Lew Wallace's Military Career and the Battle of Monocacy," *North and South* 4 (January 2001): 42.

44. Max Woodhull to Ricketts, 9 July 1864, *OR*, 51(1):1175.

45. Gary W. Gallagher, *Stephen Dodson Ramseur: Lee's Gallant General* (Chapel Hill: University of North Carolina Press, 1985), 126.

46. Morsberger and Morsberger, *Lew Wallace*, 149.

47. Swift and Stephens, "Honor Redeemed," 44.

48. Wallace to Commanding Officer Detachment VI Army Corps, 2:30 P.M. on 9 July 1864, *OR*, 51(1):1177.

49. Morsberger and Morsberger, *Lew Wallace*, 150–51.

50. Ricketts to Wallace, afternoon of 9 July 1864, Lewis Wallace Papers, entry 159, RG 94, NARA.

51. Morsberger and Morsberger, *Lew Wallace*, 151.

52. Swift and Stephens, "Honor Redeemed," 44.

53. Wallace to Halleck, received at 11:40 P.M. on 9 July 1864, *OR*, 37(2):145.

54. Lincoln to J. W. Garrett, 5:15 P.M. on 9 July 1864, #119 in a list of dispatches pertaining to Monocacy, Lew Wallace Collection, Box 3, IHS.

55. J. W. Garrett to Lincoln, received at 7:15 P.M. on 9 July 1864, *OR*, 37(2):138–39.

56. Halleck to Grant, sent at 9:00 P.M. on 9 July 1864, received at 11:20 A.M. on 10 July 1864, p. 29 of a compilation of letters on Monocacy, Lew Wallace Collection, Box 3, IHS. Also in *OR*, 40(3):93.

57. Graham Allison's discussion of the effect governmental politics can have on decision making during a crisis could certainly pertain to the "battles" between regular and political generals, Halleck and Wallace in this case. See Allison and Zelikow, *Essence of Decision*, 255–314.

58. Thomas Swann, Evan T. Ellicott, William E. Hooper, Thomas S. Alexander, and Michael Warner to the President of the United States, received at 11:50 P.M. on 9 July 1864, *OR*, 37(2):140. The men stated that they had "been appointed by the mayor a committee to confer with you upon this subject and to impress upon you the absolute necessity of sending large re-enforcements." The proximity of Early's raiders led them to believe that it was "too late to organize the citizens to any extent before the enemy will be upon us." They desperately hoped for prompt help from the president.

59. Halleck to Wallace, 11:55 P.M. on 9 July 1864, Lewis Wallace Papers, entry 159, RG 94, NARA. Also on p. 31 of a compilation of letters on Monocacy, Lew Wallace Collection, Box 3, IHS.

60. Grant now ordered that the "balance of the 6th Corps . . . be forwarded to Washington," along with as much of the XIX Corps as Halleck deemed necessary; see Grant to Meade, from City Point in Virginia, 5:40 P.M. on 9 July 1864, #125 in a list of dispatches pertaining to Monocacy, ibid. Halleck only accepted the VI Corps because he believed that the timely "arrival of the 19th corps is very uncertain"; see Halleck to Grant, 11:00 P.M. on 9 July 1864, p. 30 of a compilation of letters on Monocacy, ibid.

61. Wallace to Ricketts from Ellicott's Mills, 10 July 1864 at 2:30 P.M., Lewis Wallace Papers, entry 159, RG 94, NARA.

62. Samuel B. Lawrence to Colonel Bowman, as well as a separate letter from Lawrence to Colonel Comegys, 10 July 1864, *OR*, 37(2):177–78.

63. Stephens, *Shadow of Shiloh*, 202–3.

64. Susan Wallace to Helen Lossing, 20 July 1864, Collection LS1995, Box 10, The Huntington Library, San Marino, CA. Also see "Local Matters" in the *Baltimore Daily Gazette*, 11 July 1864, for confirmation of this panic in the city.

65. "Proclamation," *Baltimore Sun*, 11 July 1864, as well as the *Baltimore Daily Gazette*, 11 July 1864.

66. See the *Baltimore Sun*, 12 July 1864, and 13 July 1864, and the *Baltimore Daily Gazette*, 13 July 1864.

67. Wallace to Halleck, received at 1:00 P.M. on 11 July 1864, *OR*, 37(2):214.

68. Halleck to Wallace, 1:20 P.M. on 11 July 1864, ibid.

69. General Orders No. 228, 11 July 1864, ibid.

70. Grant to Halleck, 12:50 P.M. on 10 July 1864, p. 40 of a compilation of letters on Monocacy, Lew Wallace Collection, Box 3, IHS.

71. Grant's order confused Wallace because it said nothing about his status. Would he be relieved, or placed in another command? Maybe Ord was supposed to report to Wallace? He sent a note to Stanton relaying these concerns; see Wallace to Stanton, 11 July 1864, p. 42 of a compilation of letters on Monocacy, ibid. Later that evening, Stanton responded, stating that "General Ord is assigned to the command of the Eighth Army Corps and all the troops in the [Middle] department." Wallace was to report to Ord, "your relations to him being precisely similar to those of General [George H.] Thomas and [James B.] McPherson to [William T.] Sherman and [Nathaniel P.] Banks." See Stanton to Wallace, 9:30 P.M. on 11 July 1864, *OR*, 37(2):215. The administration lost any faith it had in Wallace's ability to command troops in the field. It needed to ensure the safety of Baltimore.

72. For example, see letters dated 12 July 1864, *OR*, 37(2):253–55.

73. Charles A. Dana to Brig. Gen. John A. Rawlins, sent on 13 July, received on 14 July 1864, Papers of Ulysses S. Grant, series 10, container 3, LC.

74. Charles A. Dana to Rawlins (Chief of Staff), sent in cipher at 9:00 P.M. on 12 July, received on 13 July 1864, ibid. Also see Simon, *The Papers of Ulysses S. Grant*, 11:230–32.

75. Ibid.
76. "The War News," *Baltimore Sun*, 15 July 1864.
77. Edward O. C. Ord to Wallace, 14 July 1864, *OR*, 37(2):324.
78. "The Great Rebel Raid Terminated—Washington Safe," *Crawfordsville Weekly Review*, 16 June 1864.
79. "General Wallace," *Crawfordsville Weekly Review*, 23 June 1864.
80. However, Wallace was not officially reinstated as commander of the VIII Army Corps until July 28, 1864. See General Orders No. 237, Lew Wallace Collection, Box 3, IHS.
81. "Insignificant Force of the Enemy," by a special correspondent of the *New York Tribune*, published in the *Baltimore Daily Gazette*, 18 July 1864.
82. Charles A. Dana to John A. Rawlins, sent in cipher on 11 July, received on 14 July 1864, Papers of Ulysses S. Grant, series 10, container 3, LC.
83. Wallace to Halleck, received at 2:50 P.M. on 18 July 1864, *OR*, 37(2):381.
84. Wallace to John W. Garrett, 18 July 1864, ibid.
85. A "circular" by Lew Wallace to the Loyal Citizens of Baltimore, dated 18 July 1864, *Baltimore Daily Gazette*, 19 July 1864. The commander also declared that orders had "been given to the brigade commanders to procure lists of all citizens who rendered service, and copies of the lists will be furnished to the city government, as 'rolls of honor' for future reference."
86. Ibid.
87. Grant to Capt. C. N. Turnbull, 15 July 1864, *OR*, 37(2):346.
88. Grant to Halleck, 1:00 P.M. on 17 July 1864, *OR*, 37(2):361.
89. Grant to Lincoln, 25 July 1864, Papers of Ulysses S. Grant, series 10, container 3, LC. Also see Simon, *The Papers of Ulysses S. Grant*, 11:308–10. Grant wished that the four departments "be merged into one," while suggesting "Gen [William B.] Franklin as a suitable person to command the whole." Generals Hunter, Sigel, Weber, Couch, and Wallace never had managed to coordinate their efforts. The VIII Corps' commander tried more than the rest, but to little avail, and the administration was increasingly under the impression that Wallace had not met the threat with utmost vigilance. The details of the arrangement were not as important as the goal. No matter the technical arrangements, Grant begged that "one General Officer in whom I, and yourself [Lincoln], have confidence in, should command the whole." Of course, Grant also suggested that the four departments could be placed under a "Military Division" with General George G. Meade as the division commander.
90. See Simpson, *The Civil War in the East*, 114; Cooling, *Jubal Early's Raid on Washington*, 221–23; Marszalek, *Commander of All Lincoln's Armies*, 211; and Williams, *Lincoln and His Generals*, 333.
91. Simon, *Papers of Ulysses S. Grant*, 11:308–10.
92. "Gen. Lew. Wallace," *Crawfordsville Journal*, 28 July 1864. Wallace's hometown newspaper may have been referring to articles in the *New York Times*, 22 and 28 July 1864, as well as "Siege of Washington," *Chicago Tribune*, 17 July 1864. Also see the *Philadelphia Inquirer*, 18 July 1864.

93. "Major General Wallace," *Crawfordsville Journal*, 4 August 1864.

94. Adjutant General E. D. Townsend to Wallace, 13 September 1864, Middle Department and VIII Army Corps—Letters Received, part I, entry 2343, box 4 (1864 A-G), RG 393, NARA.

95. Wallace to Delia (Mrs. William) Wallace, 30 July 1864, Lew Wallace Collection, Box 3, IHS. Wallace underlined the words "vice versa" in the original letter.

96. Morsberger and Morsberger, *Lew Wallace*, 154.

97. Grant, *Personal Memoirs*, 2:304–6.

98. Ibid.

Chapter 9. Victory and Mexico

1. See Greenberg, *Manifest Manhood and the Antebellum American Empire*, i–17.

2. Thomas Hicks to Wallace, 13 August 1864, Lew Wallace Collection, Box 3, IHS. Emphasis in original.

3. Ibid.

4. See Work, *Lincoln's Political Generals*, 1–5, 25, and 227–34; as well as Goss, *The War within the Union High Command*, xv–xvi, xx, and 105.

5. Wallace to Henry W. Halleck, 18 July 1864, *OR*, series I (all references to series I unless indicated), 37(2):381.

6. Susan Wallace to Helen Lossing, 20 July 1864, Collection LS1995, Box 10, The Huntington Library, San Marino, California.

7. Wallace to John W. Garrett, 25 July 1864, *OR*, 37(2):442.

8. Wallace to Edward D. Townsend, 26 July 1864, ibid., 37(2):459.

9. Commo. Thomas A. Dornin to Wallace, 26 July 1864, ibid., 37(2):459–60.

10. Daniel Link to Wallace, 26 July 1864, ibid., 37(2):461.

11. Wallace to E. D. Townsend, 26 July 1864, ibid., 37(2):459.

12. Edwin M. Stanton to Halleck, 27 July 1864, Lew Wallace Collection, Box 3, IHS.

13. General Orders No. 237, 28 July 1864, War Department, ibid.

14. Wallace to Halleck, 27 July 1864, *OR*, 37(2):475.

15. Halleck to Wallace, 27 July 1864, ibid.

16. Special Orders No. 186, Middle Department and VIII Army Corps, 27 July 1864, ibid.

17. E. D. Townsend to Wallace, 9 August 1864, *OR*, 43(1):750. Wallace replied to Townsend that same day, 9 August 1864, *OR*, 43(1):750.

18. Special Orders No. 187, Middle Department and VIII Army Corps, 28 July 1864, *OR*, 37(2):489–90.

19. Jubal A. Early, *Autobiographical Sketch and Narrative of the War between the States* (Philadelphia: J. B. Lippincott, 1912), 396–400.

20. Ulysses S. Grant to Halleck, 1 August 1864, in *Personal Memoirs*, 2:317–18.

21. Everard H. Smith, "Chambersburg: Anatomy of a Confederate Reprisal," *American Historical Review* 96 (April 1991): 432–55.

22. Wallace to Susan Wallace, 3 August 1864, Lew Wallace Collection, Box 3, IHS.

23. Wallace to J. H. Lemmon, Postmaster of Dublin, 2 August 1864, *OR*, 37(2):581–82.

24. Wallace's frustration with the Dublin postmaster did not cause him to ignore, or hold contempt for, anyone asking for the protection or aid of the army. The ability to successfully fly a flag over a post office seemed unimportant at such a troublesome time. But another complaint, received a day later, did receive a respectful and positive answer. A Reverend L. Van Bokkelen was "under the pressure of the secessionists of" his congregation "to retire from the pastorship of Saint Timothy's Church, over which," according to Wallace, "you have so long and so creditably presided." The situation was more important than a flag pole; disloyal persons were forcing a patriotic gentleman to resign his post. In response to the news, the commander asserted "that in the event of your retirement services will not be allowed in that church, except by a successor of undoubted loyalty." The reverend was to announce this order to the entire congregation. As added encouragement, Wallace assured "that if you choose to remain in charge, as heretofore, you shall have all the protection that lies in my power." The Indianan concluded by emphasizing that after "this presentation it is hoped you will regard it as your duty to remain at your post." Again, the commander demonstrated his ability to motivate others to action, a quality that might have earned him a field command if the blue-coated officer had more enthusiastically done his penance as a recruiter for the Union army. See Wallace to Reverend L. Van Bokkelen, 3 August 1864, ibid., 590.
25. For more on recruiting, and receiving commands in exchange, see Work, *Lincoln's Political Generals*, 208–26; as well as Goss, *The War within the Union High Command*, 43–44.
26. Williams, *Lincoln and His Generals*, 333.
27. According to the Indianan, "the First Separate Brigade, commanded by Brig. Gen. E. B. Tyler . . . is composed of four regiments of infantry, for duty about 1,800 men; First Delaware Cavalry, for duty about 190 men; one battery of artillery, for duty about 120 men. . . . The Second Separate Brigade, commanded by Bvt. Brig. Gen. W. W. Morris, U.S. Army," included Forts "McHenry, Marshall, Federal Hill, Carroll. The entire garrison of the four forts is, one regiment of infantry, about 800 men; two companies Second U.S. Artillery (dismounted), about 75 men." In addition, the "Third Separate Brigade, commanded by Brig. Gen. H. H. Lockwood," was composed of 2,600 men scattered across the department. Wallace believed that Tyler's brigade was best suited to supporting Sheridan's movements in the Valley if necessary, the issue then troubling the chief of staff. But if Sheridan did need the First Brigade, "concentrated in the vicinity of the Monocacy Junction," the most the commander could do "to strengthen General E. B. Tyler . . . will be but little." See Wallace to Lt. Col. James W. Forsyth, 19 August 1864, *OR*, 43(1):854.
28. Wallace to Charles A. Dana, 30 August 1864, ibid., 43(1):969–70.
29. Ibid.
30. Ibid.
31. Wallace to Susan Wallace, 12 September 1864, Lew Wallace Collection, Box 3, IHS.
32. Robert E. Lee to Jubal A. Early in Winchester, VA, 17 September 1864, *OR*, 43(1):873.
33. Lee to Early, 18 September 1864, ibid., 43(1):876.

34. Wallace to Benjamin J. Lossing, 27 September 1864, Miscellaneous Manuscript Collections—Lew Wallace, LC.

35. Wallace to Samuel B. Lawrence, 4 October 1864, Lew Wallace Collection, Box 3, IHS.

36. Ibid.

37. Ibid.

38. A "true American" to Wallace, 4 October 1864, ibid.

39. William Cannon to Wallace, 28 October 1864, *OR*, 43(1):485. Also see White, *Emancipation, the Union Army, and the Reelection of Abraham Lincoln*, 120.

40. Philip H. Sheridan to Wallace, 1 November 1864, *OR*, 43(1):522.

41. Samuel B. Lawrence to Wallace in Crawfordsville, 13 October 1864, ibid., 43(1):362.

42. Grant to Stanton, 10 November 1864, Papers of Ulysses S. Grant, series 10, container 3, LC.

43. White, *Emancipation, the Union Army, and the Reelection of Abraham Lincoln*, 6 and 112.

44. John C. Waugh, *Reelecting Lincoln: The Battle for the 1864 Presidency* (New York: Crown Publishers, 1997), 354–55. Also see White, *Emancipation, the Union Army, and the Reelection of Abraham Lincoln*, 115–16 and 153.

45. Stephens, *Shadow of Shiloh*, 168–70.

46. Wallace to E. D. Townsend, 21 November 1864, *OR*, 43(2):657.

47. E. D. Townsend to Wallace, 21 November 1864, ibid.

48. T. S. Bowers to Wallace, 11 January 1865, *OR*, 46(2):104.

49. An "inclosure" from S. S. Brown to Wallace, 13 January 1865, *OR*, 48(1):512–13. For another description of problems near the Rio Grande, see James Fisk to Winfield Scott Hancock, 9 January 1865, Lew Wallace Collection, Box 3, IHS.

50. Ibid.

51. Wallace to Grant, 14 January 1865, *OR*, 48(1):512. Also see Greenberg, *Manifest Manhood and the Antebellum American Empire*, i–17, for more on the "aggressive vision of expansionism and an equally martial vision of manhood" embraced by many American men after the Mexican-American War.

52. Wallace to Grant, 14 January 1865, *OR*, 48(1):512.

53. Ibid.

54. Special Orders No. 16, by command of U. S. Grant, 22 January 1865, Lew Wallace Collection, Box 3, IHS.

55. Wallace to Grant, 27 January 1865, *OR*, 46(2):279. Grant did not agree, asking that Ambrose E. Burnside be placed in command; see E. S. Parker to Burnside, 2 February 1865, ibid., 46(2):353.

56. General Orders No. 20, 1 February 1865, Middle Department and VIII Army Corps—General Orders (Printed), part I, entry 2352, vol. 62 (3 of 3), RG 393, NARA.

57. J. W. Forsyth to Wallace, 30 January 1865, *OR*, 46(2):310.

58. Wallace to Oliver P. Morton, addressed merely to "Governor," 10 February 1865, Lew Wallace Collection, Box 3, IHS.

59. Wallace to Susan Wallace, 17 February 1865, ibid.

60. Lt. Col. C. G. Sawtelle to Wallace, 20 February 1865, ibid.
61. "Form No. 22," headed "The United States, to Major General Lew Wallace," 21 February 1865, ibid.
62. Wallace to Grant, 22 February 1865, ibid.
63. Ibid.
64. Ibid.
65. Wallace arranged for the meeting through Special Agent Charles Worthington, officially with the Treasury Department. See Charles Worthington to James E. Slaughter and Slaughter to Worthington, 6 March 1865, ibid. Also see Worthington to Wallace, 7 March 1865, ibid.
66. Robert Ryal Miller, "Lew Wallace and the French Intervention in Mexico," *Indiana Magazine of History* 59 (March 1963): 34.
67. Wallace to J. E. Slaughter and John S. Ford, 12 March 1865, Lew Wallace Collection, Box 3, IHS.
68. Wallace to Susan Wallace, 14 March 1865, ibid.
69. Wallace to Grant, 14 March 1865, *OR*, 48(1):1166–67.
70. John G. Walker to Wallace, 25 March 1865, Lew Wallace Collection, Box 3, IHS. Walker also politely chastised Slaughter for negotiating with Wallace; see J. G. Walker to J. E. Slaughter, 27 March 1865, ibid.
71. Wallace to J. G. Walker, 2 April 1865, ibid.
72. Greenberg, *Manifest Manhood and the Antebellum American Empire*, 30–31.
73. Miller, "Lew Wallace and the French Intervention in Mexico," 35.

Chapter 10. Assassination and Andersonville

1. Wallace to S. A. Hurlbut from New Orleans, 6 April 1865, *OR*, 48(2):37.
2. General Orders No. 85, Middle Department and the VIII Army Corps, by Wallace, 19 April 1865, *OR*, 46(3):843.
3. E. D. Townsend to W. W. Morris, 19 April 1865, ibid., 46(3):842.
4. Stanton to Major General Dix and "Same to Governor Fenton, Albany; John W. Garrett, esq., Baltimore; Governor Curtin, Harrisburg; General Cadwalader, Philadelphia," 19 April 1865, ibid., 46(3):843.
5. Wallace to Augustus W. Bradford, 19 April 1865, ibid.
6. E. D. Townsend to Stanton, 3 May 1865, ibid., 46(3):1081.
7. Wallace to Townsend, 19 April 1865, ibid., 46(3):842–43.
8. Wallace to E. D. Townsend, 23 April 1865, *OR*, series II, 8:505.
9. Wallace to Brig. Gen. W. A. Nichols, 26 April 1865, ibid., series II, 8:515.
10. Ibid.
11. Wallace to Nichols, 3 May 1865, *OR*, 46(3):1080. In late April and early May, Wallace also dealt with issues that he likely expected to confront at the war's conclusion. For example, some "disloyal manifestations on the part of some of the people" in Delaware led Washington to send a brigade of infantry, now under Wallace's command, to that state to keep order. See Bvt. Brig. Gen. C. H. Morgan to Wallace, 3 May 1865, ibid., 46(3):1080–81.

12. Lew Wallace to U. S. Grant, 19 April 1865, *OR*, 48(2):122. Also in the Lew Wallace Collection, Box 3, IHS.

13. Two early drafts of this "continuation" of Wallace's 14 March report to Grant, both dated 18 April 1865, are in the Lew Wallace Collection, Box 3, IHS.

14. Wallace to Grant, 19 April 1865, *OR*, 48(2):122. Also in the Lew Wallace Collection, Box 3, IHS.

15. Ibid.

16. Report by Wallace to Grant, 16 May 1865, including inclosures of various dates, *OR*, 48(2):457–63. The same report, but minus the inclosures, is also in the Lew Wallace Collection, Box 3, IHS.

17. The Indianan had been communicating with Stanton and Halleck concerning wartime laws on the navigation of his department's waterways. Transportation of people and materials had been heavily regulated on the Potomac River and in the Chesapeake Bay during the war, especially when boats intended to cross the state line between Maryland and Virginia. Not fully understanding that such activity might still be necessary, Wallace sent a telegram to Stanton, 23 April 1865, *OR*, 46(3):915.

18. Stanton to Wallace, 23 April 1865, ibid.

19. When Halleck, temporarily taking care of matters in Richmond, asked about proper orders regarding trade in and with Virginia, the secretary of war sent him an equally grumpy reply. This note contained no threat as in the response to Wallace, but Stanton declared that any order from Halleck "in respect to trade as you deem proper will be approved. Please prepare and telegraph it immediately, so that the public may know and this department be relieved from the incessant annoyance of questions that I am unable to answer." See Stanton to Halleck, 24 April 1865, ibid. Halleck and Stanton quickly ironed out new regulations on domestic commerce and trade in Virginia; see another message from Halleck to Stanton, as well as Stanton's reply, 24 April 1865, ibid., 46(3):916.

20. For example, see J. H. Taylor, Chief of Staff of the Department of Washington, to Colonel Thompson, commanding at Darnestown, 14 April 1865, ibid., 46(3):752. Also see Stanton to Major General Dix, sent at 4:44 A.M. on 15 April 1865, ibid., 46(3):781. There was also speculation that the fugitives would head into western Maryland; see Col. W. G. Mitchell to General Emory in Cumberland, 19 April 1865, ibid., 46(3):840.

21. For example, see Gideon Welles to Cdr. F. A. Parker of the Potomac Flotilla, 17 April 1865, ibid., 46(3):816.

22. Wallace to Stanton, 24 April 1865, ibid., 46(3):936–37.

23. Assistant Adjutant General Samuel B. Lawrence to Colonel Sewell commanding in Annapolis, 24 April 1865, ibid., 46(3):937.

24. Wallace, *Lew Wallace; an Autobiography*, 848. The postwar portion of Wallace's memoir was actually written by his wife, Susan, since the elderly general died in 1905, not able to finish the work.

25. Ibid., 847–48.

26. Ramold, *Baring the Iron Hand*, 342.

27. Wallace, *Lew Wallace; an Autobiography*, 847.

28. George H. Thomas to Stanton, 15 April 1865, *OR*, 49(2):359.

29. Bvt. Maj. Gen. John W. Geary to Lt. Col. H. W. Perkins, 31 May 1865, *OR*, 47(1):699–702.

30. For example, Wallace's hometown paper, like most others throughout the country, lamented the loss of the "Late Abraham Lincoln" regardless of political affiliation; see the Democratic *Crawfordsville Weekly Review*, 22 April 1865.

31. Proclamation titled "SURRATT. BOOTH. HEROLD." by Stanton, 20 April 1865, *OR*, 46(3):847–48. Baltimore advertised a $10,000 reward across the country for the capture of Booth; the announcement even appeared in the *Crawfordsville Journal*, 20 April 1865.

32. "A Proclamation" by Andrew Johnson, 2 May 1865, *OR*, 49(2):566–67. Also see a note from Stanton to Holt, on behalf of the president, asking for the names of possible accomplices in the assassination attempts, 2 May 1865, *Investigation and Trial Papers Relating to the Assassination of President Lincoln* (hereafter, *Investigation and Trial Papers*), Microcopy No. 599, Microfilm Reel 16, NARA.

33. Jefferson Davis was captured on 10 May 1865—the same day that the trial of the conspirators in Lincoln's assassination began; see Stanton's report to Andrew Johnson on officers arrested and imprisoned in 1865, 4 January 1866, *OR*, series II, 8:843–44.

34. Edward Steers Jr., *Blood on the Moon: The Assassination of Abraham Lincoln* (Lexington: University Press of Kentucky, 2001), 223–25; and William A. Tidwell, *April '65: Confederate Covert Action in the American Civil War* (Kent, Ohio: Kent State University Press, 1995), 1–13 and 160–96.

35. Report by Wallace to Grant, 16 May 1865, including inclosures of various dates, *OR*, 48(2):457–63.

36. Wallace, *Lew Wallace; an Autobiography*, 849. As the defense lawyers and judge advocates prepared for trial, Wallace handed over most departmental duties during the commission's existence, but he still supervised and seemed to be involved in most of the more important or interesting business. For example, he received an order from the War Department that attempted to protect the constitutional rights of the press and of individual Americans. Stanton's office stated that if any of three departmental commanders had "prohibited the sale of photograph likenesses of J. Wilkes Booth the Secretary of War directs that the prohibition be removed." The Indianan certainly honored such instructions. See E. D. Townsend to Maj. Gen. J. A. Dix, Maj. Gen. George Cadwalader, and Wallace, 27 May 1865, *OR*, 46(3):1227.

37. Joseph Holt, Judge Advocate General of the Army, to Stanton, 13 November 1865, *OR*, series III, 5:490–91. Wallace actually drew a diagram of the hearing's room and tables, including seat placement and the names of the main participants; see drawing dated 10 May 1865, Lew Wallace Collection, Box 3, IHS.

38. Ezra J. Warner, *Generals in Blue: Lives of the Union Commanders* (Baton Rouge: Louisiana State University Press, 1964), 239.

39. Ibid., 158–59, 209–10, 239–40, 243–44, and 257–58.

40. Wallace tallied these statistics as the proceedings continued. He also counted 4,300 pages of testimony, making a manuscript that was twenty-six inches thick; see a page

later dated 10 May 1865 and following the drawing of the same date, 10 May 1865, Lew Wallace Collection, Box 3, IHS.

41. Holt to Stanton, 13 November 1865, *OR*, series III, 5:491. "A prominent lawyer in his early career, [Joseph] Holt was also a respected political figure. He had served as Postmaster General and, after the resignation of John Floyd, Secretary of War in the final months of James Buchanan's administration. Despite his association with Buchanan's Democratic administration, Holt threw his support behind the Lincoln administration and used his influence to ensure that his native Kentucky remained loyal to the Union. Holt remained in his post for the rest of the war, overseeing several major legal debates and major cases," in addition to those discussed in this chapter; see Ramold, *Baring the Iron Hand*, 312.

42. Morsberger and Morsberger, *Lew Wallace*, 169–71.

43. Issues of the *Daily National Intelligencer*, Washington, D.C., were photocopied for the *Investigation and Trial Papers*, Microcopy 599, Reel 16, NARA.

44. *Daily National Intelligencer*, Washington, D.C., 16 May 1865, *Investigation and Trial Papers*, Microcopy 599, Reel 16, NARA.

45. Bernard C. Steiner, *Life of Reverdy Johnson* (1914; reprint, New York: Russell & Russell, 1970), 115–16.

46. Morsberger and Morsberger, *Lew Wallace*, 171. A few historians have contended that all of the eight defendants, most notably Dr. Mudd and Mary Surratt, were likely guilty of the charges of conspiracy, and that their refusal to stop the assassination of Lincoln was still a serious felony, possibly punishable by death or many years in prison. See, for example, William Hanchett, *The Lincoln Murder Conspiracies* (Urbana: University of Illinois Press, 1983), 47–50 and 57; and William A. Tidwell, with James O. Hall and David Winfred Gaddy, *Come Retribution: The Confederate Secret Service and the Assassination of Lincoln* (Jackson: University Press of Mississippi, 1988), 3–29; and Steers, *Blood on the Moon*, 135–54 and 209–11.

47. Holt to Johnson, including the "Charge and Specification" against the defendants, 5 July 1865, *Investigation and Trial Papers*, Microcopy 599, Reel 16, NARA.

48. Morsberger and Morsberger, *Lew Wallace*, 172–73. Also see Wallace, *Lew Wallace; an Autobiography*, 850–51.

49. Steers, *Blood on the Moon*, 214. Also see Morsberger and Morsberger, *Lew Wallace*, 173–74.

50. Hanchett, *The Lincoln Murder Conspiracies*, 83–85, 227–30, and 246.

51. Steers, *Blood on the Moon*, 211–13.

52. Holt to Stanton, 13 November 1865, *OR*, series III, 5:491.

53. Even before the existence of the diary was made public, many Americans were sympathetic with Mary Surratt; for example, see "A Change in Mrs. Surratt" in the *Crawfordsville Journal*, 8 June 1865. After the executions, the *Crawfordsville Weekly Review*, 22 July 1865, insisted that justice had not been done in this trial, further claiming that General Hunter was "a fanatic of the most violent description" who would "hesitate at no crime to achieve success for his principles." The same issue

of the *Weekly Review* also borrowed a "Heart-rending and Affecting" description of Surratt's execution from a Cincinnati newspaper. The *Crawfordsville Journal*, 20 July 1865, described that a "desperate effort is being made to prove that Mrs. Surratt was innocent," but it also surmised that this effort was largely designed to discredit a trial that might lead to a similar indictment of Jefferson Davis.

54. Hanchett, *The Lincoln Murder Conspiracies*, 86–88. Also see Morsberger and Morsberger, *Lew Wallace*, 175.

55. Holt to Stanton, 13 November 1865, *OR*, series III, 5:491.

56. Wallace, *Lew Wallace; an Autobiography*, 849.

57. Morsberger and Morsberger, *Lew Wallace*, 175. Johnson was at odds with Holt before, during, and after the trial, over the pardoning of ex-rebels and the surviving assassination conspirators. See Elizabeth D. Leonard, *Lincoln's Avengers: Justice, Revenge, and Reunion after the Civil War* (New York: W. W. Norton, 2004), xi–xiv and 199–200.

58. Holt to Stanton, 13 November 1865, *OR*, series III, 5:493.

59. Brig. Gen. T. M. Harris, quoted in Wallace, *Lew Wallace; an Autobiography*, 850.

60. General Orders No. 55, Middle Military Division, 6 June 1865, *OR*, 46(3):1261.

61. For example, see Wallace to Lt. Col. T. S. Bowers, 6 June 1865, ibid., 46(3):1261–62.

62. The *Crawfordsville Weekly Review*, 29 July 1865, learned that the town's favorite son again designed "going to Mexico." Newspapers also described a letter from Wallace to "a military friend" in which the Indianan argued for veteran soldiers to come to Mexico's aid in expelling the French invaders; see the *Cincinnati Gazette*, 8 July 1865, as well as the *Crawfordsville Journal*, 13 July 1865.

63. Cloyd, *Haunted by Atrocity*, 1.

64. *Harper's Weekly*, 17 June 1865, 379–80.

65. Charles W. Sanders Jr., *While in the Hands of the Enemy: Military Prisons of the Civil War* (Baton Rouge: Louisiana State University Press, 2005), 295. Also see William Marvel, *Andersonville: The Last Depot* (Chapel Hill: University of North Carolina Press, 1994), 243.

66. Marvel, *Andersonville: The Last Depot*, ix.

67. Cloyd, *Haunted by Atrocity*, 19.

68. Ibid., 11.

69. Marvel, *Andersonville*, x–xi.

70. Capt. Henry Wirz to Maj. Gen. J. H. Wilson, 7 May 1865, *OR*, series II, 8:537–38. See an example of former prisoners blaming Wirz for the evils of Andersonville in the *Crawfordsville Journal*, 8 June 1865.

71. Wirz to Wilson, 7 May 1865, *OR*, series II, 8:538.

72. Almost one month after Bvt. Maj. Gen. J. H. Wilson arrested Wirz, other unaware Union officers were still ordering subordinates to find the prison commander; for example, see Assistant Adjutant General W. L. M. Burger of the Department of the South to Provost Marshal B. W. Thompson, 4 June 1865, ibid., 8:639. Also see Assistant Adjutant General S. L. McHenry of the District of Florida in the Department of the South to Provost Marshal E. C. Woodruff, 12 June 1865, *OR*, 47(3):645–46.

73. Wilson to the Adjutant General of the U.S. Army, 16 May 1865, *OR*, 49(2):800.

74. "Second indorsement" by George H. Thomas, 26 May 1865, *OR*, series II, 8:538.

75. Wallace to Susan Wallace, 10 July 1865, reprinted in Wallace, *Lew Wallace; an Autobiography*, 853. For more on infantry manuals in the nineteenth century, again see Jamieson, *Crossing the Deadly Ground*, 4, 94, 99, and 112; as well as Skelton, *An American Profession of Arms*, 255.

76. Wallace to Susan Wallace, 10 July 1865, reprinted in Wallace, *Lew Wallace; an Autobiography*, 853.

77. Wallace to Susan Wallace, 20 August 1865, reprinted in ibid.

78. Ibid.

79. Holt to Stanton, 13 November 1865, *OR*, series III, 5:491.

80. R. Fred Ruhlman, *Captain Henry Wirz and Andersonville Prison: A Reappraisal* (Knoxville: University of Tennessee Press, 2006), 181. Also see Warner, *Generals in Blue*, 41–42, 152–53, 169–70, 337–38, and 502–3.

81. Wallace to Susan Wallace, 20 August 1865, reprinted in Wallace, *Lew Wallace; an Autobiography*, 853.

82. Wirz to Wilson, 7 May 1865, *OR*, series II, 8:537–38. The *Crawfordsville Journal*, 17 August 1865, noted that Wirz promised "to show that he acted under direct and positive orders from Jeff. Davis."

83. Wallace to Susan Wallace, 20 August 1865, reprinted in Wallace, *Lew Wallace; an Autobiography*, 853.

84. Marvel, *Andersonville*, 243.

85. Wallace to Susan Wallace, 21 August 1865, reprinted in Wallace, *Lew Wallace; an Autobiography*, 853–54.

86. Holt to Andrew Johnson, 31 October 1865, *OR*, series II, 8:775–76.

87. "GENERAL COURT MARTIAL ORDERS NO. 607," War Department, Adjutant-General's Office, Washington, signed by E. D. Townsend, November 6, 1865, ibid., series II, 8:785–86. Also see *Trial of Henry Wirz: Letter from the Secretary of War Ad Interim, in answer to a resolution of the House of April 16, 1866, transmitting a summary of the trial of Henry Wirz,* House of Representatives, 40th Congress, 2nd Session, Executive Document No. 23 (Washington, D.C.: Government Printing Office, 1868), 3–8.

88. Wallace to Susan Wallace, 21 August 1865, reprinted in Wallace, *Lew Wallace; an Autobiography*, 853–54.

89. Wallace to Susan Wallace, 4 September 1865, reprinted in ibid., 854–55.

90. Ibid.

91. Holt to Stanton, 13 November 1865, *OR*, series III, 5:491.

92. Holt to Andrew Johnson, 31 October 1865, *OR*, series II, 8:776.

93. Ibid., 8:781.

94. Ibid., 8:777.

95. Ibid.

96. Ibid., 8:778–79.

97. "GENERAL COURT MARTIAL ORDERS NO. 607," War Department, Adjutant-General's Office, Washington, signed by E. D. Townsend, November 6, 1865, ibid., 8:784–92. Also see *Trial of Henry Wirz*, 805–8.

98. Order by Andrew Johnson, 3 November 1865, reprinted as part of "GENERAL COURT MARTIAL ORDERS NO. 607," War Department, Adjutant-General's Office, Washington, signed by E. D. Townsend, November 6, 1865, *OR*, series II, 8:791.

99. For example, see Estwick Evans to Andrew Johnson, 8 and 9 November 1865, ibid., 8:792. Also see John Hitz, Consul General of Switzerland, to Johnson, 9 November 1865, 8:792.

100. Cloyd, *Haunted by Atrocity*, 34.

101. Louis Schade to Andrew Johnson, 26 October 1865, *OR*, series II, 8:773–74. Paul J. Springer and Glenn Robins echo these concerns in *Transforming Civil War Prisons: Lincoln, Lieber, and the Politics of Captivity* (New York: Routledge, 2015), 75–80.

102. Cloyd, *Haunted by Atrocity*, 32–33 and 35.

103. Marvel, *Andersonville*, 244–46. Springer and Robins support this concern in *Transforming Civil War Prisons*, 75–80.

104. Maj. Gen. C. C. Augur to the Adjutant General of the Army, 11 November 1865, *OR*, series II, 8:794. See same letter in *Trial of Henry Wirz*, 815.

105. Holt to the Secretary of War, 16 November 1865, *OR*, series II, 8:799. The Johnson administration likely would have prosecuted Richard Winder's second cousin, John H. Winder, the commissary general of prisoners east of the Mississippi River, but he died of natural causes in February of 1865; see Arch Fredric Blakey, *General John H. Winder, C.S.A.* (Gainesville: University of Florida Press, 1990), xi–xvi and 175–215.

106. Holt to Stanton, 13 November 1865, *OR*, series III, 5:493.

107. Wallace, *Lew Wallace; an Autobiography*, 865.

108. For more on how the prison controversies played a part in encouraging postwar bitterness between North and South, see Cloyd, *Haunted by Atrocity*, 36–37.

109. Miller, "Lew Wallace and the French Intervention in Mexico," 37–50.

110. It appears that Grant was wary of Wallace leading U.S. soldiers into Mexico, preferring a trusty subordinate, John M. Schofield. In addition, Secretary of State Seward disliked the idea of any Americans getting involved in the Mexican conflict, fearing war with France; see ibid.

Conclusion

1. See Greenberg, *Manifest Manhood and the Antebellum American Empire*, 11–13, 139–40, 168–69, and 269; Foote, *The Gentlemen and the Roughs*, 3–5, 15–16, and 121; Bederman, *Manliness and Civilization*, 11 and 17; Rotundo, *American Manhood*, 1 and 3–4; and Kimmel, *Manhood in America*, x, 6–7, and 69.

2. For discussions on the views of West Pointers, see Watson, "Flexible Gender Roles during the Market Revolution," 82–83 and 96; as well as Rafuse, "'To Check . . . the Very Worst and Meanest of Our Passions,'" 408–10, 413, 418–19, and 421. For an analysis of a West Pointer who had problems somewhat related to those of Wallace, and certainly related to dueling masculinities, see Stowe, "George Gordon Meade and the Boundaries of Nineteenth-Century Military Masculinity," 365 and 387. For more on the lack of discipline among many volunteer soldiers, and some officers, see Ramold, *Baring the Iron Hand*, 3, 214, and 217; as well as Ramold, "Discipline

and the Union Army," 45. Carol Reardon discusses the nineteenth-century debate over the primacy of "genius" or "expertise" as a better indicator of military success in *With a Sword in One Hand and Jomini in the Other*, 10 and 55–58.

3. For more on the teachings at West Point and the development of a common set of values among regular officers, including the expectation of good discipline and quiet respect for superiors, see two articles by Watson, "How the Army Became Accepted," 233; and "Continuity in Civil-Military Relations and Expertise," 233, 238–39, and 244. Also see three works by Skelton, "Officers and Politicians," 27, 29, 38, and 41; "The Commanding Generals and the Question of Civil Control in the Antebellum U.S. Army," 167–168; and *An American Profession of Arms*, xiii, 167, and 362.

4. These words were copied in an endorsement book, which usually acknowledges only the receipt of letters by the headquarters; see Grant's "endorsement" acknowledging a message from Wallace, 28 April 1862, Department of the Tennessee—Letters Received and General Orders, part II, number 171, entry 2733, vol. G3 (including old vols. 3 and 4), RG 393, NARA.

5. Grant, *Personal Memoirs*, 2:304–6.

6. Ibid.

7. Work, *Lincoln's Political Generals*, 1–5, 25, and 227–34; and Goss, *The War within the Union High Command*, xv–xvi, xx, and 105.

8. See biographies of these generals: James P. Jones, *"Black Jack:" John A. Logan and Southern Illinois in the Civil War Era* (Tallahassee: Florida State University, 1967); William E. Parrish, *Frank Blair: Lincoln's Conservative* (Columbia: University of Missouri Press, 1998); Richard L. Kiper, *Major John Alexander McClernand: Politician in Uniform* (Kent, OH: Kent State University Press, 1999); Stephen D. Engle, *Yankee Dutchman: The Life of Franz Sigel* (Baton Rouge: Louisiana State University Press, 1993); Dick Nolan, *Benjamin Franklin Butler: The Damnedest Yankee* (Novato, CA: Presidio Press, 1991); and James G. Hollandsworth Jr., *Pretense of Glory: The Life of General Nathaniel P. Banks* (Baton Rouge: Louisiana State University Press, 1998).

9. Again, for more on politics and generalship, see David Work, "Lincoln's Political Generals" (PhD diss., Texas A&M University, 2004), 355–63; Goss, *The War within the Union High Command*, 192–211; and Stephen R. Taaffe, *Commanding the Army of the Potomac* (Lawrence: University Press of Kansas, 2006), 208–18.

10. For more on Wallace's role on the committee of "visiting statesmen" after the election of November 1876, see William H. Rehnquist, *Centennial Crisis: The Disputed Election of 1876* (New York: Alfred A. Knopf, 2004), 101–2; and Hans L. Trefousse, *Rutherford B. Hayes* (New York: Henry Holt, 2002), 76–78. Also see Ari Hoogenboom, *The Presidency of Rutherford B. Hayes* (Lawrence: University Press of Kansas, 1988), 26–31.

11. Robert M. Utley, *Billy the Kid: A Short and Violent Life* (Lincoln: University of Nebraska Press, 1989), 115–88.

12. Lew Wallace, *Ben-Hur: A Tale of the Christ* (New York: Harper and Brothers, 1880).

13. McKee, *"Ben-Hur" Wallace*, 169–70.

14. Ibid., 173–74.

15. Ibid., 189–269. Also see Stephens, *Shadow of Shiloh*, 203–4 and 236.

16. For example, see letters and drafts in the Lew Wallace Collection, Box 12, especially Folder 6, IHS. Also see a map, dated 3 August 1873, on which Wallace defended his marching route of 6 April 1862, Container 20, Benjamin Holt Ticknor Papers, Manuscript Division, Library of Congress, Washington, D.C. He evidently inserted this map into a letter sent to the publisher, Benjamin Ticknor, demonstrating that he still had Shiloh on his mind eleven years later.

17. Robert Underwood Johnson and Clarence Clough Buel, eds., *Battles and Leaders of the Civil War*, 4 vols. (1884–88; reprint, New York: Thomas Yoseloff, 1956), 1:398–428 and 607–10.

18. Undated speech that was likely given after the war, Lew Wallace Collection, Box 12, Folder 1, IHS. Also see a newspaper clipping that recounts a visit to West Point in July of 1870, Lew Wallace Collection, Box 17, Folder 3, IHS. In addition, President Benjamin Harrison appointed Wallace to West Point's Annual Board of Visitors in 1889, and he tried to exert some influence over personnel decisions while also making numerous other recommendations. The superintendent and secretary of war ignored his efforts. See Morsberger and Morsberger, *Lew Wallace*, 375–76.

Bibliography

Primary Sources

Manuscripts and Archives

Huntington Library, San Marino, California
    Collection LS1995
Indiana Historical Society, William Henry Smith Library, Indianapolis, Indiana
    Lew Wallace Collection
Indiana State Archives, Indianapolis, Indiana
    Oliver P. Morton Papers
    Records of the Adjutant General of Indiana
Indiana State Library, Indianapolis, Indiana
    Lew Wallace Papers
Library of Congress, Washington, D.C.
    Miscellaneous Manuscript Collections—Lew Wallace
    Papers of Jubal Anderson Early
    Papers of Ulysses S. Grant
    Papers of Benjamin Holt Ticknor
Lilly Library, Indiana University, Bloomington, Indiana
    J. A. Cravens Manuscripts
National Archives and Records Administration, Washington, D.C.
    Record Group 94: Special Civil War Collections, "Generals' Papers"
    Record Group 153: Records of the Office of the Judge Advocate General (Army);
        Investigation and Trial Papers Relating to the Assassination of President Lincoln,
        Microcopy 599, 16 rolls
    Record Group 393: Records of U.S. Army Continental Commands, 1821–1920

Newspapers

Baltimore Daily Gazette
Baltimore Sun

Chicago Tribune
Cincinnati Commercial
Cincinnati Enquirer
Cincinnati Gazette
Crawfordsville (Indiana) *Journal*
Crawfordsville (Indiana) *Weekly Review*
Daily National Intelligencer (D.C.)
Evansville (Indiana) *Journal*
Harper's Weekly (New York)
Indianapolis Journal
Missouri Democrat
Montgomery (County of Indiana) *Weekly Journal*
New York Times
New York Tribune
Philadelphia Inquirer

United States Government Publications

Davis, George B., et al. *Atlas to Accompany the Official Records of the Union and Confederate Armies*. Washington, D.C.: Government Printing Office, 1891–95.

Trial of Henry Wirz: Letter from the Secretary of War Ad Interim, in answer to a resolution of the House of April 16, 1866, transmitting a summary of the trial of Henry Wirz. House of Representatives, 40th Congress, 2nd Session, Executive Document No. 23. Washington, D.C.: Government Printing Office, 1868.

U.S. War Department. *The War of the Rebellion: A Compilation of the Official Records of the Union and Confederate Armies*. 4 series, 128 vols. Washington, D.C.: Government Printing Office, 1880–1901.

Autobiographies, Memoirs, Diaries, and Accounts by Contemporaries

Durham, Thomas Wise. *Three Years with Wallace's Zouaves: The Civil War Memoirs of Thomas Wise Durham*. Edited by Jeffrey L. Patrick. Macon, Ga.: Mercer University Press, 2003.

Early, Jubal A. *Autobiographical Sketch and Narrative of the War between the States*. Philadelphia: J. B. Lippincott, 1912.

Ellsworth, E. E. *Manual of Arms for Light Infantry, Adapted to the Rifled Musket, with, or without, the Priming Attachment, Arranged for the U.S. Zouave Cadets, Governor's Guard of Illinois*. Chicago: P. T. Sherlock, 1861.

Grant, Ulysses S. *The Papers of Ulysses S. Grant*. Edited by John Y. Simon. 28 vols. Carbondale: Southern Illinois University Press, 1967–2005.

———. *Personal Memoirs of U. S. Grant*. 2 vols. New York: Charles L. Webster, 1886.

Johnson, Robert Underwood, and Buel, Clarence Clough, eds. *Battles and Leaders of the Civil War*. 4 vols. New York: Thomas Yoseloff, 1956.

Lee, Robert E. *The Wartime Papers of Robert E. Lee*. Edited by Clifford Dowdy. New York: Bramhall House, 1961.

Perry, Oran, compiler. *Indiana in the Mexican War.* Indianapolis: Wm. B. Burford, 1908.

Wallace, Lew. *Lew Wallace; an Autobiography.* New York: Harper and Brothers, 1906.

———. *Smoke, Sound, and Fury: The Civil War Memoirs of Major-General Lew Wallace, U.S. Volunteers.* Edited by Jim Leeke. Portland, Oreg.: Strawberry Hill Press, 1998.

Secondary Sources

Books and Articles

Allison, Graham, and Philip Zelikow. *Essence of Decision: Explaining the Cuban Missile Crisis.* 2nd ed. New York: Longman, 1999.

Ash, Stephen V. *When the Yankees Came.* Chapel Hill: University of North Carolina Press, 1995.

Bederman, Gail. *Manliness and Civilization.* Chicago: University of Chicago Press, 1995.

Beemer, Charles G. *"My Greatest Quarrel with Fortune": Major General Lew Wallace in the West, 1861–1862.* Kent, Ohio: Kent State University Press, 2015.

Blakey, Arch Fredric. *General John H. Winder, C.S.A.* Gainesville: University of Florida Press, 1990.

Brown, Dee Alexander. *Morgan's Raiders.* New York: Konecky & Konecky, 1959.

Buell, Thomas B. *The Warrior Generals: Combat Leadership in the Civil War.* New York: Three Rivers Press, 1997.

Castel, Albert, with Brooks D. Simpson. *Victors in Blue: How Union Generals Fought the Confederates, Battled Each Other, and Won the Civil War.* Lawrence: University Press of Kansas, 2011.

Catton, Bruce. *America Goes to War.* Middletown, Conn.: Wesleyan University Press, 1958.

Clark, Charles B. "Politics in Maryland during the Civil War: Slavery and Emancipation in Maryland, 1861–1865." *Maryland Historical Magazine* 41 (June 1946): 132–58.

Cloyd, Benjamin G. *Haunted by Atrocity: Civil War Prisons in American Memory.* Baton Rouge: Louisiana State University Press, 2010.

Cooling, Benjamin Franklin. *Forts Henry and Donelson: The Key to the Confederate Heartland.* Knoxville: University of Tennessee Press, 1987.

———. *Jubal Early: Robert E. Lee's "Bad Old Man."* Lanham, Mass.: Rowman and Littlefield, 2014.

———. *Jubal Early's Raid on Washington, 1864.* Baltimore: Nautical and Aviation Publishing Company of America, 1989.

———. *Monocacy: The Battle That Saved Washington.* Shippensburg, Pa.: White Mane Publishing, 1997.

———. *Symbol, Sword, and Shield: Defending Washington during the Civil War.* Hamden, Conn.: Archon Books, 1975.

Cunliffe, Marcus. *Soldiers and Civilians: The Martial Spirit in America, 1775–1865.* Boston: Little, Brown, 1968.

Daniel, Larry J. *Shiloh: The Battle That Changed the Civil War.* New York: Simon and Schuster, 1997.

Dyer, Frederick H. *A Compendium of the War of the Rebellion.* 3 parts. Des Moines, Iowa: Dyer, 1908.

Engle, Stephen D. *Don Carlos Buell: Most Promising of All.* Chapel Hill: University of North Carolina Press, 1999.

———. *Yankee Dutchman: The Life of Franz Sigel.* Baton Rouge: Louisiana State University Press, 1993.

Foote, Lorien. *The Gentlemen and the Roughs: Violence, Honor, and Manhood in the Union Army.* New York: New York University Press, 2010.

Fox, William F. *Regimental Losses in the American Civil War, 1861–1865.* Albany, N.Y.: Albany Publishing, 1889.

Gallagher, Gary W. *Stephen Dodson Ramseur: Lee's Gallant General.* Chapel Hill: University of North Carolina Press, 1985.

Getchell, Kevin. *Scapegoat of Shiloh: The Distortion of Lew Wallace's Record by U. S. Grant.* Jefferson, N.C.: McFarland, 2013.

Goss, Thomas J. *The War within the Union High Command: Politics and Generalship during the Civil War.* Lawrence: University Press of Kansas, 2003.

Greenberg, Amy S. *Manifest Manhood and the Antebellum American Empire.* New York: Cambridge University Press, 2005.

Grimsley, Mark. *The Hard Hand of War: Union Military Policy toward Southern Civilians, 1861–1865.* Cambridge, UK, and New York: Cambridge University Press, 1995.

Hanchett, William. *The Lincoln Murder Conspiracies.* Urbana: University of Illinois Press, 1983.

Hattaway, Herman, and Archer Jones. *How the North Won: A Military History of the Civil War.* Urbana: University of Illinois Press, 1983.

Heitman, Francis B., ed. *Historical Register and Dictionary of the United States Army.* 2 vols. Washington, D.C.: Government Printing Office, 1903.

Hollandsworth, James G., Jr. *Pretense of Glory: The Life of General Nathaniel P. Banks.* Baton Rouge: Louisiana State University Press, 1998.

Hoogenboom, Ari. *The Presidency of Rutherford B. Hayes.* Lawrence: University Press of Kansas, 1988.

Hughes, Nathaniel Cheairs, Jr. *The Battle of Belmont: Grant Strikes South.* Chapel Hill: University of North Carolina Press, 1991.

Jamieson, Perry D. *Crossing the Deadly Ground: United States Army Tactics, 1865–1899.* Tuscaloosa: University of Alabama Press, 1994.

Jones, James P. *"Black Jack:" John A. Logan and Southern Illinois in the Civil War Era.* Tallahassee: Florida State University Press, 1967.

Kimmel, Michael. *Manhood in America: A Cultural History.* New York: The Free Press, 1996.

Kiper, Richard L. *Major General John Alexander McClernand: Politician in Uniform.* Kent, Ohio: Kent State University Press, 1999.

Leonard, Elizabeth D. *Lincoln's Avengers: Justice, Revenge, and Reunion after the Civil War.* New York: W. W. Norton, 2004.

Marszalek, John F. *Commander of All Lincoln's Armies: A Life of General Henry W. Halleck.* Cambridge, Mass.: Belknap Press of Harvard University Press, 2004.

Marvel, William. *Andersonville: The Last Depot*. Chapel Hill: University of North Carolina Press, 1994.

McDonough, James Lee. *Shiloh—In Hell before Night*. Knoxville: University of Tennessee Press, 1977.

———. *War in Kentucky: From Shiloh to Perryville*. Knoxville: University of Tennessee Press, 1994.

McKee, Irving. *"Ben-Hur" Wallace*. Berkeley: University of California Press, 1947.

McPherson, James M. *Abraham Lincoln and the Second American Revolution*. New York: Oxford University Press, 1991.

———. *Battle Cry of Freedom: The Civil War Era*. New York: Oxford University Press, 1988.

Miller, Robert Ryal. "Lew Wallace and the French Intervention in Mexico." *Indiana Magazine of History* 59 (March 1963): 31–50.

Morsberger, Robert E. "Latter-Day Lord of Baltimore." *Maryland Magazine* 9 (Summer 1977): 2–6.

Morsberger, Robert E., and Katharine M. Morsberger. *Lew Wallace: Militant Romantic*. New York: McGraw-Hill, 1980.

Nolan, Dick. *Benjamin Franklin Butler: The Damnedest Yankee*. Novato, Calif.: Presidio Press, 1991.

Parrish, William E. *Frank Blair: Lincoln's Conservative*. Columbia: University of Missouri Press, 1998.

Rafuse, Ethan S. "'To Check . . . the Very Worst and Meanest of Our Passions': Common Sense, 'Cobbon Sense,' and the Socialization of Cadets at Antebellum West Point." *War in History* 16, no. 4 (2009): 406–24.

Ramage, James A. *The Life of General John Hunt Morgan*. Lexington: University of Kentucky Press, 1986.

Ramold, Steven J. *Baring the Iron Hand: Discipline in the Union Army*. DeKalb: Northern Illinois University Press, 2010.

———. "Discipline and the Union Army." *North and South* 13, no. 4 (November 2011): 44–51.

Reardon, Carol. *With a Sword in One Hand and Jomini in the Other: The Problem of Military Thought in the Civil War North*. Chapel Hill: University of North Carolina Press, 2012.

Rehnquist, William H. *Centennial Crisis: The Disputed Election of 1876*. New York: Alfred A. Knopf, 2004.

Rotundo, E. Anthony. *American Manhood: Transformations in Masculinity from the Revolution to the Modern Era*. New York: Basic Books, 1993.

Ruhlman, R. Fred. *Captain Henry Wirz and Andersonville Prison: A Reappraisal*. Knoxville: University of Tennessee Press, 2006.

Sanders, Charles W., Jr. *While in the Hands of the Enemy: Military Prisons of the Civil War*. Baton Rouge: Louisiana State University Press, 2005.

Schaaf, Martha E. *Lew Wallace, Boy Writer*. Indianapolis: Bobbs-Merrill, 1961. Originally published in Baltimore: John B. Piet, 1879.

Scharf, J. Thomas. *History of Maryland from the Earliest Period to the Present Day.* 3 vols. 1879. Reprint, Hatboro, Pa.: Tradition Press, 1967.

Simon, John Y. "Grant at Belmont," *Military Affairs* 45 (December 1981): 161–66.

Simpson, Brooks D. *The Civil War in the East: Struggle, Stalemate, and Victory.* New York: Praeger, 2011. Reprint, Lincoln, Nebr.: Potomac Books, 2013.

———. "Lincoln and His Political Generals." *Journal of the Abraham Lincoln Association* 21, no. 1 (2000): 63–77.

———. *Ulysses S. Grant: Triumph over Adversity, 1822–1865.* Boston: Houghton Mifflin, 2000.

Skelton, William B. *An American Profession of Arms: The Army Officer Corps, 1784–1861.* Lawrence: University Press of Kansas, 1992.

———. "The Commanding Generals and the Question of Civil Control in the Antebellum U.S. Army." *American Nineteenth Century History* 7, no. 2 (June 2006): 153–72.

———. "Officers and Politicians: The Origins of Army Politics in the United States before the Civil War." *Armed Forces and Society* 6, no. 1 (Fall 1979): 22–48.

Slap, Andrew L., and Michael Thomas Smith, eds. *This Distracted and Anarchical People: New Answers for Old Questions about the Civil War-Era North.* New York: Fordham University Press, 2013.

Smith, Everard H. "Chambersburg: Anatomy of a Confederate Reprisal." *American Historical Review* 96 (April 1991): 432–55.

Smith, Michael Thomas. "The Most Desperate Scoundrels Unhung: Bounty Jumpers and Recruitment Fraud in the Civil War North." *American Nineteenth Century History* 6, no. 2 (June 2005): 149–72.

Springer, Paul J. *America's Captives: Treatment of POWs from the Revolutionary War to the War on Terror.* Lawrence: University Press of Kansas, 2010.

Springer, Paul J., and Glenn Robins. *Transforming Civil War Prisons: Lincoln, Lieber, and the Politics of Captivity,* New York: Routledge, 2015.

Steers, Edward, Jr. *Blood on the Moon: The Assassination of Abraham Lincoln.* Lexington: University Press of Kentucky, 2001.

Steiner, Bernard C. *Life of Reverdy Johnson.* Baltimore: The Norman, Remington Co., 1914. Reprint, New York: Russell & Russell, 1970.

Stephens, Gail. *Shadow of Shiloh: Major General Lew Wallace in the Civil War.* Indianapolis: Indiana Historical Society Press, 2010.

Stowe, Christopher S. "George Gordon Meade and the Boundaries of Nineteenth-Century Military Masculinity." *Civil War History* 61, no. 4 (December 2015): 362–99.

Swift, Gloria Baker, and Gail Stephens. "Honor Redeemed: Lew Wallace's Military Career and the Battle of Monocacy." *North and South* 4 (January 2001): 34–46.

Taaffe, Stephen R. *Commanding the Army of the Potomac.* Lawrence: University Press of Kansas, 2006.

Tap, Bruce. "Inevitability, Masculinity, and the American Military Tradition: The Committee on the Conduct of the War Investigates the American Civil War." *American Nineteenth Century History* 5, no. 2 (Summer 2004): 19–46.

———. *Over Lincoln's Shoulder: The Committee on the Conduct of the War.* Lawrence: University Press of Kansas, 1998.

Thornbrough, Emma Lou. *Indiana in the Civil War Era, 1850–1880.* Indianapolis: Indiana Historical Society, 1965.

Tidwell, William A. *April '65: Confederate Covert Action in the American Civil War.* Kent, Ohio: Kent State University Press, 1995.

Tidwell, William A., with James O. Hall and David Winfred Gaddy. *Come Retribution: The Confederate Secret Service and the Assassination of Lincoln.* Jackson: University Press of Mississippi, 1988.

Tredway, G. R. *Democratic Opposition to the Lincoln Administration in Indiana.* Indianapolis: Indiana Historical Bureau, 1973.

Trefousse, Hans L. *Rutherford B. Hayes.* New York: Henry Holt, 2002.

Tucker, Spencer C. *Unconditional Surrender: The Capture of Forts Henry and Donelson.* Abilene, Tex.: McWhiney Foundation Press, 2001.

Utley, Robert M. *Billy the Kid: A Short and Violent Life.* Lincoln: University of Nebraska Press, 1989.

Vandiver, Frank E. *Jubal's Raid: General Early's Famous Attack on Washington in 1864.* Westport, Conn.: Greenwood Press, 1974. First published 1960 by McGraw Hill (New York).

Volpe, Vernon L. "Squirrel Hunting for the Union: The Defense of Cincinnati in 1862." *Civil War History* 33 (September 1987): 242–55.

Wallace, Lew. *Ben-Hur: A Tale of the Christ.* New York: Harper and Brothers, 1880.

Walsh, Richard, and William Lloyd Fox, eds. *Maryland: A History, 1632–1974.* Baltimore: Maryland Historical Society, 1974.

Warner, Ezra J. *Generals in Blue: Lives of the Union Commanders.* Baton Rouge: Louisiana State University Press, 1964.

Watson, Samuel. "Continuity in Civil-Military Relations and Expertise: The U.S. Army during the Decade before the Civil War." *Journal of Military History* 75 (January 2011): 221–50.

———. "Flexible Gender Roles during the Market Revolution: Family, Friendship, Marriage, and Masculinity among U.S. Army Officers, 1815–1846." *Journal of Social History* 29, no. 1 (Autumn 1995): 81–106.

———. "How the Army Became Accepted: West Point Socialization, Military Accountability, and the Nation-State during the Jacksonian Era." *American Nineteenth Century History* 7, no. 2 (June 2006): 219–51.

Waugh, John C. *Reelecting Lincoln: The Battle for the 1864 Presidency.* New York: Crown Publishers, 1997.

White, Jonathan W. *Emancipation, the Union Army, and the Reelection of Abraham Lincoln.* Baton Rouge: Louisiana State University Press, 2014.

Williams, T. Harry. *Americans at War: The Development of the American Military System.* Baton Rouge: Louisiana State University Press, 1960.

———. *Lincoln and His Generals.* New York: Alfred A. Knopf, 1952.

Woodworth, Stephen E., ed. *Grant's Lieutenants: From Cairo to Vicksburg.* Lawrence: University Press of Kansas, 2001.

Work, David. *Lincoln's Political Generals.* Urbana: University of Illinois Press, 2009.

Theses and Dissertations

Mortenson, Christopher R. "Lew Wallace and the Civil War: Politics and Generalship." PhD diss., Texas A&M University, College Station, 2007.

Smith, Jesse Roy. "The Military Career of Lew Wallace." MA thesis, Indiana University, Bloomington, 1935.

Theisen, Lee Scott. "The Public Career of General Lew Wallace, 1854–1905." PhD diss., University of Arizona, Tucson, 1973.

Work, David. "Lincoln's Political Generals." PhD diss., Texas A&M University, College Station, 2004.

Index

Page numbers in *italics* indicate pages with photos and maps

Abercrombie, John J., 32, 33
Adamsville, Tenn., *56*, 58
Andersonville prison camp: bias during Wirz trial, 187, 188; blame for conditions and deaths at, 180–81, 194; conditions at and condition and treatment of men at, 97, 180, 183, 184–86; criticisms of trial and outcome, 187; death of prisoners at, 180, 185–86; length of and number of witnesses to testify during Wirz trial, 185; military commission for trial of Wirz, 182–88, 194; number of Union soldiers at, 180; officers, prosecutors, and defense counselors involved in, 182–83; punishment for Wirz, 186–89; testimony of former prisoners during Wirz trial, 185–86, 187; trial of Wirz subordinates and superiors at, 187–88, 248n105; Wirz arrest for conditions at, 181–82, 246n72; Wirz defense for actions at, 183–84, 188, 247n82
Annapolis, Md., 118–19, 135, 143, 173
Appomattox Courthouse, Va., 169, 194
armies: concern about standing armies, 117; speech about army service enlistment, 198, 250n18

Army Corps, VIII: command of, 115, 193, 229n2; command reinstatement of Wallace, 145, 148, 150, 238n80; command relief of Wallace, 143, 145, 237n71; department lines, order to ignore, 136–37; experience of troops assigned to, 154; Lee uncertainty about location of, 158; Ord command of, 143, 237n71; troop reassignment from to Army of the Potomac, 117, 127–28, 129–30, 153–55, 156, 158, 233n72, 234n1
Army of Northern Virginia, 106, 132, 169. *See also* Lee, Robert E.
Army of the Mississippi: organization and force strength, 60, 219n29; Shiloh battle retreat and defeat, 68–70; Shiloh battle role of, 60–63, 65–66, 67
Army of the Ohio, 68–69, 72, 101–3. *See also* Buell, Don Carlos
Army of the Potomac: chief of staff offer from Grant, 157; defeat of by Lee forces, 106; Lee surrender to, 169; McClellan offer to Wallace and 11th Indiana for service in, 212n85; Perkins and regiment transfer to, 119–20, 231n26; resources for, 158; Richmond

Army of the Potomac (*continued*)
operations of, 233n72, 234n1;
troop reassignment from Middle
Department to, 117, 127–28, 129–30,
153–55, 156, 158, 233n72, 234n1
Army of the Tennessee: commanders of
divisions in, 44, 59; Corinth assault
plans, 71–72; departure from, 115;
force strength of, 59, 60, 219n29;
Fort Donelson battle, 44–51, *45*, 52,
191–92; regiments in 3rd Division, 52,
217n72; reorganization of, 52; Wallace
command of 3rd Division, 44, 52, 54
Arnold, Samuel, 173, 177, 179
assassination of Lincoln: bias against
defendants on trial for role in,
176–79, 188; conspiracy charges and
conviction of the conspirators, 176–79,
188, 245n46, 245–46n53; cornering and
shooting of Booth, 173; criticisms of
trial and outcome, 179, 194; diary of
Booth as evidence during trial, 178,
179, 245–46n53; events of, 169–70, 194;
length of and number of witnesses
to testify during trial for, 175–76,
244–45n40; military trial of suspects
and accessories in the assassination
plot and escape, *94*, 173–80, 182,
194, 244n33; names of suspects and
accessories in the plot or escape, 173;
officers, prosecutors, and defense
counselors involved in, *94*, 175,
244n37; pardoning of defendants after
a few years in prison, 179, 246n57;
peaceful reuniting of nation after, 174,
244n30; public observation of and
printed transcripts from trial for, 176;
public pressure for convictions related
to, 178; punishment of conspirators,
176–77, 178–79, 188–89, 245n46, 245–
46n53; rebel officers regrets for, 174–75;
rewards for capture of conspirators or
information about, 174, 244nn31–32;

search and capture of assassin and
accomplices, 172–73, 243n17, 243n20;
Wallace sketches of people during the
trial, 177, 244n37
Atzerodt, George A., 173, 177, 178, 187
Augur, Christopher, 133–34, 144

Baltimore, Md.: black recruits and
units, organization in, 156–57, 158;
defense from rebel raids, 127–28,
129–30, 141, 152–58, 233n72; disloyal
activity, rebel sympathizers, and spies
in, 117, 124–27, 151, 161–62, 232n48;
Early threat to, failure to appreciate
seriousness of, 141, 193; forces for
defense of and reinforcement
requests, 134–35, 141–43, 146, 152–55,
156–58, 234n1; Lincoln funeral train
in, 170; martial law in, 126–27; Middle
Department headquarters in, xi, 115;
Negro Equality article in newspaper
in, 121–22; organization for defense
of, 131; paroled rebel prisoners in,
transportation arrangements for,
170–71; rebel attack threats to, 133–34,
137, 141–44, 152–53, 154–56, 236n58;
rebel prisoners, supplies for, 161–62;
reorganization of departments for
defense of, 146–47, 153, 156, 238n89;
retreat from Monocacy Junction to,
140–41; saloons in, complaints about,
125; success of Wallace and praise for
success in, 144–46, 147–49, 155, 193–94;
thank you to its citizens by Wallace,
146, 238n85; vessel search to find
Booth and accomplice, 173
Baltimore & Ohio (B&O) Railroad, 24,
29, 134, 135–36, *136*, *139*
Banks, Nathaniel, 8, 128–29, 195
Battles and Leaders of the Civil War, 197
Baxter, A. S., 63–66
Beauregard, P. G. T., 25, 29, 32, 33, 60,
69, 77

Belmont, Battle of, 39–40, 65,
    213–14nn18–19
Ben-Hur (Wallace), 3, 197, 198
Biddle, Charles, 29, 32
Bingham, John A., *94*
black recruits and units organization,
    156–57, 158
Blair, Frank, 195, 196
Bonney, William H. "Billy the Kid," 3,
    196
Booth, John Wilkes, 170, 172–73, 178, 179,
    194, 244n36, 245–46n53
Boyle, J. T., 81–82
Bradford, Augustus W., 170; authority
    of, Wallace acknowledgement of,
    118; black men in militias, opinion
    about, 156–57; crime investigation
    request from, 119–20; disloyal people
    as candidates in elections, 122;
    Kilbourne arrest, request for help
    with, 119; meeting with about election
    guards, 118–19; oath of allegiance
    given by, 122; photo of, *93*; political
    affiliations of and Union support by,
    118–19, 230n16, 231n20; recruitment of
    soldiers for, 233n72; relationship with
    Wallace, 118–19, 121
Bragg, Braxton, 60, 81, 101, 103, 219n29
brigade: bridge destruction order from
    Grant to, 44; brigadier general
    commission, 19, 36–37, 213n5; cavalry
    scouts, proposal to raise regiment of,
    37; disciplining troops in, 38; force
    strength of and units assigned to, 36,
    37, 213n7; Fort Donelson attack and
    counterattack, 44–51; Fort Donelson
    departure with regiments not
    assigned to Wallace, 51–52, 53; Fort
    Heiman attack and capture, 41–42, 43,
    44; Fort Henry guarding by, 43–44;
    lie prone and fire from position
    tactic, 49; plea to Morton to be sent
    into battle, 37; rebel flag incident in

Paducah, 37–39, 213nn14–15; Viola
    reconnaissance operation, 40,
    213–14n18
Brookville, Ind., 9
Buckner, Simon B., 46, 50
Buell, Don Carlos: Chattanooga
    operations of, 101–3; commission
    to investigate operations of units
    under, 101–3, 114, 179, 182, 188, 193, 194,
    226n37; contributions to war effort,
    8; cooperation between Halleck,
    Grant, and, 216n59; dislike for, 102,
    103; force strength of units under,
    57; Fort Donelson importance and
    cooperation in holding, 216n59; order
    of Wallace to Cincinnati, 82, 223n50;
    photo of, *92*; rebel threat to forces
    under in Kentucky and Tennessee,
    81–82; reinforcements for Shiloh, 62;
    Shiloh battle role of, 57, 68–69
bugle for commands on battlefield, 72
Bull Run, Battle of, 33
Bunker Hill, 33
Burnside, Ambrose, 109, 210–11n54
Butler, Benjamin "Beast," 8, 125, 128–29,
    195

Cadwalader, George, 210–11n54
Cameron, Simon, 19, 212n85
Camp Beauregard, 40, 213–14n18
Camp Chase: command of, 96, 114, 182,
    194; conditions at and condition of
    men at, 97–98, 99, 100; desertions
    from, 99–100, 226n21; dishonorable
    discharge recommendation for men
    at, 226n21; guards for, 100; paroled
    Union prisoners organization for
    service in Minnesota to police
    Indians, 96–100, 114; payments to
    paroled troops, 98–99, 100, 225n12,
    226n21; regiment organization at, 100,
    226n21; Wallace speech to prisoners
    at, 97–98

Camp Morton, 21–22, 208n3, 208n8

Camp Thomas, 99, 100, 225n15

Camp Tod, 225n15

Cannon, William, 160

Carvajal, José Maríe Jesús, 167–68, 169, 170, 172, 180, 189

Cavalry, U.S., 4th, 37

Chambersburg, Pennsylvania, 24, 155, 209n28

Charlestown, Va., 33

Chase, Salmon P., 97

Chattanooga, Tenn.: Buell operations in, 101–3; railroad lines to move troops to, 60; visit to lobby for field command, 113, 114

Cheatham, Benjamin F., 55, 57

Chipman, Norton P., 184

Cincinnati, Ohio: awaiting orders in, 101, 106; blacks as wartime laborers in, 84–86, 87–88; Buell investigation commission meeting in, 101, 103; command of Covington, Newport, and, 82–83; cooperation of citizens in, 85–86, 193, 224nn74–75; cultural and political divisions in, 84–86, 224nn74–75; daily life conditions in, 83–86, 223n55; force strength for defense of, 85, 134–35; martial law declaration in, 83–84; Morgan raid on and threat of another attack, 84, 85; rebel attack threats to and defense of, xi, 5, 82–86, 96, 193, 195, 223–24nn57–58; rebel force strength for attack on area, 85, 224n67; rebel retreat from, 86, 87; reinforcements for defense of, request for, 85; success of Wallace and praise for success in, 86, 87–88, 96, 193; travel through on way to Cumberland, 24, 209n27; Wallace order to, 82, 223n50

City Greys militia, 11–12

Civil War: avoidance of risky and intense battles by officers, 11; Committee on the Conduct of the War (CCW), 80, 101, 103; desertions during, 99–100; deviation from rules and orders during, 12; end of in the East, 168; Fort Sumter attack and start of, 20; hard-war policy during, 125; Lee retreat and Union victory, 158; military career of Wallace during, writings about, 3; military justice during, 173–74; morale erosion and damaged war effort by political generals, 5; occupation of border states duty, 125; peaceful reuniting of nation after, 174, 244n30; Reconstruction after, 130; report from committee on conduct of war, 80; support for and political general appointments, 3, 118, 190; testimony before committee on conduct of war, 80; transport of soldiers back to home states at end of war, 170–71; Union success, maintaining impression of, 118; war for the Union and emancipation of slaves, 40–41

Colfax, Schuyler, 31–32

Columbus, Ky., 36, 37, 39–40, 55

Columbus, Ohio: paroled Union prisoners organization for service in Minnesota to police Indians, 87, 96–100, 114; paymaster in capitol building to pay paroled prisoners, 98–99, 100, 225n12. See also Camp Chase

Committee on the Conduct of the War (CCW), 80, 101, 103

Conestoga, 40, 214n21

Confederacy/The South: animosity between Northerners and, 204n26; Democratic Party support for in event of civil war, 207n53; loss of heart after Romney raid, 28; occupation of cities in, 125; secession crisis, 18, 207n53;

sympathizers and spies for, 117, 124–27, 232n48; women spying for, 124–25
Confederate army: assassination of Lincoln, accusations about role in, 174–75; Camp Beauregard, 40, 213–14n18; Chattanooga operations of, 101–3; Corinth importance to in defense of the South, 60; deaths during fighting near Romney, 30–31; force strength at Corinth, 57, 60, 218n13, 219n29; force strength at Purdy, 60; meetings with Wallace about getting back into the Union, 166–67, 168, 169, 171–72, 242n65, 242n67; opinions about Southern soldiers, 28, 204n26; organization of for Shiloh, 60, 219n29; resources for, 158; Shiloh defeat of, 68–70; supplies and resources coming from Mexico, 163–64, 165, 167, 168; surrender and disbanding of, 180; transport of soldiers back to home states at end of war, 170–71; Viola reconnaissance operation, 40; Winchester camp, Patterson order to hold, 32–33
Corinth, Miss.: assault on, 71–72; destruction of railroad lines to, 76–77, 222n20; rebel evacuation from, 77; rebel force strength at, 57, 60, 77, 218n13, 219n29; rivers to transport troops to, 41; siege and seizure of by Union, 72, 73, 74, 77, 101–3; strategic importance of, 53, 60; Union force strength at, 77; Union move against Confederate army near, 59; Wallace complaint about not being part of battle at, 77
Couch, Darius N., 133, 134, 135, 137, 145
courage: dare activity to prove, 10, 202n8; of successful volunteer generals, 70, 221n71; of Wallace, 5, 8, 70, 191
Covington, Ind., 9–10, 16

Covington, Ky., 82–86, 223–24n58, 224n67
Crawfordsville, Ind.: awaiting orders in, 107, 110, 192; Elston home in, 16; leave of absence to return to, 78–79; move to after marrying Susan, 17; reactions to Wallace performance by newspapers in, 145, 147–48, 238n92; request to return to, 107; state senate election and service of Wallace, 17, 206n46; sword and scabbard for gallantry at Donelson from citizens of, 53; Wallace education in, 10; Wallace law practice in, 17
Cruft, Charles, 44, 47–49
Crump's Landing: artillery reinforcement at, 60; Confederate camp near, 55; Division camp at, 54, 55, 57; force strength at, 60; horse left at for messenger, 63; location of, 56; order to leave force to guard, 63, 64, 105; rebel attack threat on, 58, 61, 63
Cumberland, Md.: additional troops to defend, requests for, 29, 31, 210–11nn53–54, 211n67; appreciation of regiment by townspeople, 211n69; campsite at, looking for and pretending not to find an appropriate, 25, 26; cavalry scouts to warn of rebel advance on, 29–30; guarding of, 26; Independence Day celebration in, 211n69; order to secure and gather information in, 24–25; Pennsylvania units for defense of, 32; rebel column advance on and retreat, 30; Scott order to Wallace to go to, 24, 209n25; threat of attack from Confederate troops in Romney, 29–30, 210n53; threat of attack on, 25; trip to, 24, 209n27
Cumberland River, 36, 41
Curtin, Andrew, 29, 31, 32, 106–7, 211n67
Curtis, Samuel, 128–29

Dana, Charles, 133, 143–44, 145, 156

Davis, Henry Winter, 117, 121, 123–24, 151, 230n12

Davis, Jefferson, 15, 23, 174–75, 180, 187, 244n33, 247n82

Delaware: defense of from rebel raids, 127–28; election security in, 160; furlough of soldiers to vote in, 160; Middle Department authority over, 115, 229n2; postwar tension in, 242n11

Democratic Party: Republican Party emergence and losses for elected Democrats, 17; slavery support by, 18; state senate election and service of Wallace, 17, 206n46; support for South in event of civil war, 207n53; Wallace joining of, 15–16; Wallace split with, 18, 207n53; Wallace support of, 18

Department of the Tennessee, 100

District of West Tennessee, 59

Division, 3rd: break up of, 79–80; camp of and visitors to camp, 73; casualties at Shiloh, 70, 221n69; command relief of Wallace, 78–79, 222n34; countermarch and approach to Pittsburg Landing in correct order, 67, 70, 75, 220n61; Crump's Landing camp of, 54, 55, 57; delays and lack of urgency in movement toward Pittsburg Landing, 66–68, 70, 75, 220n61; duty assignments after Shiloh, 192; force strength of, 59; movement of, failure to notify Grant of, 66; order to destroy railroad connection between Purdy and Columbus, 55, 57; railroad lines destruction by, 76–77, 222n20; readiness to move to Pittsburg Landing, 57, 218n13; rebel attack threat on Crump's Landing camp of, 58, 61, 63; regiments in, 52, 217n72; reorganization of, request for, 80; Shiloh battle role of, 65–70, 192,

220n47; Wallace command of, 44, 52, 54

Douglas, Stephen, 17, 18

Drake, James P., 12, 13, 203n22, 204–5n33, 206n39

Dublin, Md., 155–56, 240n24

Early, Jubal A.: advance into Maryland by, 132–34, 144, 193–94; attack threat from, 146, 154–55; force strength of units assigned to, 134, 145; photo of, 94; seriousness of threat from, failure to appreciate, 141, 193; Wallace contributions against raids by, 148–49, 193–94; Washington raid by, 131, 132, 144, 193–94

Ekin, James A., 94, 175

elections: army interference in and validity of, 119, 158–59; arrest of anti-Union candidate, 119; commission to oversee disputed ballots, 196; constitutional convention representatives, election for, 115, 117, 119, 120, 123; disloyal people as candidates in, 122; furlough of soldiers to vote, 120–21, 122, 123, 124, 150–51, 160, 161; judges of election and oath administration to voters, 124, 232n46; presidential election, 158–61; presidential election and winning Maryland, 116; security of and guarding polling places, 118–19, 120–21, 122, 123, 124, 150–51, 158–60, 193; soldier participation in, concern about, 117; successful management of, 123–24, 127, 129, 130, 193; supervision of Reconstruction elections based on Wallace management of presidential election, 130

Elston, Susan, 16. See also Wallace, Susan (wife)

Emancipation Proclamation, 41, 88, 120

Evansville, Ind., 23–24

Fair God, The (Wallace), 196
fame. *See* glory, fame, and honor
flag incident in Paducah, 37–39,
    213nn14–15
Floyd, John B., 46, 50, 245n41
Foote, Andrew, 42, 44–46, 47, 50
Forrest, Nathan B., 46, 77, 101
Fort Donelson: attack on and
    capture of, 41; attack on and rebel
    counterattack, 44–50, *45*, 65, 215n38;
    bridge destruction to impede rebel
    reinforcements, 44; brigade departure
    with regiments not assigned to
    Wallace, 51–52, 53; casualties of
    attack on, 46; courage displayed at,
    5; credit for victory at, 6, 52, 111, 192;
    garrison for defense of, 54; Grant
    frustration with, criticism of, and lack
    of initiative by Wallace at, 6, 46, 47,
    48, 49, 50–52, 53, 54, 65; importance
    of, 216n59; ironclads and gunboats
    role in attack on, 44–46, 50, 215n39; lie
    prone and fire from position tactic,
    49; McClernand request for assistance
    from Wallace, xi, 46–47, 49, 50, 52,
    53, 191–92, 215–16nn41–43; order to
    by Grant, 43, 65; plan for attack on,
    42–43; promotions after battle at, 53,
    59; rebel escape, blocking of, 48–49,
    192; report about battle, correction
    of, 52; surrender of and surrender
    acceptance by Wallace, 50–51, 216n59;
    Wallace order to hold center, 44–45,
    215n38, 215–16nn41–43; Wynn's Ferry
    Road defense, 47–48
Fort Heiman, 41–42, 43–44
Fort Henry: attack on and capture of,
    41–42; *Conestoga* trip to investigate
    status of, 40; distrust of Wallace by
    Grant after, 53, 54, 141; Grant order to
    return to, 51; guarding of, 43–44, 54
Foster, Robert, 175
Franklin, William B., 238n89

Frederick, Md., 135, 136–37, 140–41,
    193–94
Fremont, John C., 33–34, 35, 74, 212n85,
    212n89

Garfield, James, 197
Garrett, John W., 135–37, 140–41, 146
Getchell, Kevin, 200–201n12
glory, fame, and honor: Baltimore and
    Washington defense success and
    praise for success, 144–46, 147–49,
    193–94; Columbus order and injury
    of Wallace pride, 87; command relief
    and honor as a man, 78–79, 230n10;
    concern about honor and friction
    with superiors, 39; fear of being
    dishonored, 32; hero status, desire
    for, 190; major general promotion
    and status as honorable man, 58;
    manhood concept and honor, 7,
    65, 70; Mexican War service and
    no chance to gain, 14, 15, 205n37;
    praise for successes of Wallace
    and 11th Indiana, 27–29, 31–32, 34,
    65, 211n66; praise for success in
    Cincinnati, 87–88, 96; pursuit and
    attainment of by Wallace, xi, 11, 53,
    65, 182, 190; regimental command
    and pursuit of, 22, 65; regret and
    shame about unfulfilled glory, 198;
    risky actions and need for glory, 28,
    53, 192; Romney raid as pursuit of
    honor, 25–26, 65; self-worth of a man
    and honor, 22; Shiloh decisions and
    performance for, 64–70
Grafton, Va., 24, 28, 30, 209n27
Grant, Ulysses S.: assassination attempt
    on, 177; Baltimore and Washington
    defense success, opinion about,
    143, 193–94; Baltimore defense
    improvements order, 152; Belmont
    battle, 39–40, 213–14nn18–19; blame
    for errors during Shiloh battle, 70,

Grant, Ulysses S. (*continued*)
75, 80, 104, 200–201n12; breakfast in
Savannah at start of Shiloh battle, 62;
bridge destruction orders from, 44,
53; command position after Halleck
promotion, 77; command relief of
Wallace, 143, 237n71; command
retention of, 55; command system
flaws and defense of Washington,
133–34, 145; communication skills of,
66; cooperation between Halleck,
Buell, and, 216n59; cordial meeting
with and chief of staff offer, 157; credit
for Fort Donelson victory, 6, 53;
demotion and relief of command by
Halleck, 54–55, 74; distrust of Wallace
by, 39, 51–52, 53, 54, 65, 80, 164, 191,
192, 194; drinking and smoking
evening in Paducah, 39, 213n17;
drinking of, 55, 144; Early threat,
failure to appreciate seriousness of,
135, 141, 193; Fort Donelson attack and
counterattack, 44–50, 215n38; Fort
Donelson attack plan, 42–43; Fort
Donelson departure with regiments
not assigned to Wallace, 51–52, 53;
Fort Donelson order from, 43, 65;
Fort Donelson surrender, 50–51,
216n59; frustration with, criticism
of, and lack of initiative by Wallace
at Donelson, 6, 46, 47, 48, 49, 50–52,
65; Lee surrender to, 169; letter to
about Shiloh, 107; major general
commission, 53, 59; Memphis transfer
of, 78; Mexico covert operations
approval, 163–64, 165–66; Mexico
mission, meeting with and letter and
report to about, 171–72, 175; Mexico
mission of Wallace, resistance to,
189, 194, 248n110; military costs of
political generals to, 4; mistakes
about Early troops, 133; note from
Wallace about attack on Pittsburg
Landing, 61–62, 70, 219n32; orders
about direction of attack, 68; orders to
subordinates, expectations to follow,
49–50, 53, 65–66, 76; photo of, 92; plea
to not be left out of the action, 51–52;
political connections and alliances,
65; political connections and alliances
of, 66; portrayal of Wallace actions
at Shiloh, 64–65, 66, 75–76, 103–6,
110–11, 220n50, 221n16; presidential
campaign of, 66; prisoner parole
and exchange system during war,
181; railroad lines destruction order
from, 76–77, 222n20; relationship
with Halleck, 54–55, 78; relationship
with Wallace, 6, 7, 8, 35, 37, 39, 51, 53,
54, 64–65, 66, 70, 74, 75–76, 96, 115,
130, 191; relief of duty under Halleck,
requests of, 78; reorganization of
departments around Washington
and Baltimore, 146–47, 238n89;
rising star status of, 80; risky actions
discouragement by, 221n3; Shiloh
battle, 62–70; Shiloh reports, review
of and response to, 75–76, 77, 103–4,
110–11, 221n16; telegram sending
Wallace to Cincinnati, 100–101; visit
to in Vicksburg, 106, 107; Wallace
contributions against Early raids,
148–49; Wallace disregard for orders
from, 192, 249n4; Wallace Division
movement, failure to notify, 66;
Wallace move to Pittsburg Landing,
delay in, 57, 218n13; Wallace opinion
of, 40; Wallace order to Pittsburg
Landing and the written order given
to Wallace, 63–67, 75, 104–6, 192,
200–201n12, 219n41, 220nn49–50;
Wallace plea to not be left out of the
action, 51–52; Wilderness Campaign,
127–28, 129, 233n72, 234n1
guerrilla activity, 126, 233n58

Hagerstown, Md., 24, 30, 209n28, 212n82
Halleck, Henry: abilities and competence of, 73–74; Baltimore and Washington defense success, opinion about, 143; blame for confusion about Baltimore and Washington defenses, 144, 147; blame for errors during Shiloh battle, 80; blame for failure of Chattanooga operations, 103; Buell commission, Wallace assignment to, 101, 102; caution of and Corinth siege, 71–72, 73, 77, 221n3; character and behavior of, 73; Cincinnati defense, failure to acknowledge, 96; Columbus order and injury of Wallace pride, 87; command of military operations by, 153; command relief of Wallace, 143; cooperation between Buell, Grant, and, 216n59; Corinth seizure by, 77; criticism of by Wallace, 73, 76; dislike of Buell by, 103; distrust of Wallace by, 39, 79, 80, 141, 153, 191, 192; Early threat, failure to appreciate seriousness of, 135, 141, 193; encouraging meeting with, 71; forces for defense of Baltimore and Washington, request to, 131, 141, 142–44; Fort Donelson importance and cooperation in holding, 216n59; Fremont removal and cleaning up of mess left in Missouri, 74; general in chief promotion, 74, 77, 222n25; letters between Wallace and, 153; letter to about Shiloh, 104, 110; meeting with Wallace, 71; Memphis actions, irritation with Wallace about, 77–78; Middle Department, removal of Wallace from command of, 129; Middle Department command by Wallace, objection to, 116, 230n5; military career of, 73–74; Monocacy Junction operations orders, 137; nickname of, 55, 74; opinion about political generals, 8, 73, 128–29, 141, 202n22; Pennsylvania service request, denial of, 106–7; performance and responsibilities during the war, 74; petition for command for Wallace, 226n23; photo of, 92; regulations on commerce and trade in and with Virginia, 243n19; relationship with Grant, 54–55, 78; relationship with Wallace, 6, 7, 8, 39, 74, 76, 79, 96, 103, 115, 116, 128–29, 130, 153, 191; request to go to Vicksburg to, 106; transportation on waterways, regulation of during war, 243n17; Wallace dislike for and blame for troubles and mistakes, 73, 192, 198
Hancock, Winfield Scott, 182
Hardee, William J., 60, 219n29
Hardin, John, 58–59
Harpers Ferry, 24, 28, 33, 128, 134, 141, 152
Harris, Thomas, 94, 175
Harrison, Archibald, 208n3
Harrison, Benjamin, 197
Harrison, William Henry, 9, 34, 202–3n10, 250n18
Hatch, George, 83–84, 223–24nn57–58
Hay, David, 30–31
Hayes, Rutherford B., 196
Herold, David E., 173, 177, 178
Hicks, Thomas, 151
Hillyer, W. S., 46–47, 51–52, 217n71
Holt, Joseph: Lincoln assassination trial role, 176, 177, 178, 179; pardoning of Lincoln assassination defendants, opinion about, 246n57; photo of, 94; political career of, 245n41; trial of Wirz subordinates and superiors, opinion about, 187–88; Wirz trial role of, 184, 185
honor. See glory, fame, and honor
Hood, John Bell, 158
Hooker, Joseph, 106, 145
Howe, Albion, 175

Hunter, David: area of responsibility of, 134; combat record of, 175; command relief of, 155; coordination of operations of, 238n89; criticism of, 133; defeat and retreat of, 132, 134; military trial of Lincoln assassination suspects, role of, 173, 175, 176, 177, 178–79, 245–46n53; photo of, 94; troop support from Wallace for, 154

Hurlbut, Stephen A., 59, 169, 172

Illinois, funeral train to transport Lincoln to, 170, 171
Illinois Infantry regiments, 44, 47
Illinois Light Artillery, Battery A, 44, 47
Indiana: adjutant general appointment, 19, 20–22, 65, 208n3; Buena Vista battle as embarrassment to, 14, 15, 23, 28, 206n39; desire to attain honor for, 14; governorship of David Wallace, 10, 21, 202–3n10; Lincoln support in, 18, 115, 137, 207n51; Morgan raid on and defense of, xi, 107–10, 114, 117, 192, 227–28n63; secessionists in towns along Ohio River, 23–24, 209n22
Indiana Brigade, 13
Indiana Infantry, 1st: active service in Mexico, hope for and blame for lack of action, 14, 20, 206n39; court-martial threat from McDougal, 204–5n33; election of officers in, 12, 203n22; farewell celebration for, 12; first lieutenant promotion of Wallace, 203n22; formation of, 12, 19; illnesses and deaths of soldiers, 13–14, 205nn36–37; Matamoras occupation by, 14–15; military experience gained in, 19, 20, 21; money owed by Wallace to the company, dispute about, 14, 204–5n33; Monterrey marching orders and occupation duty, 15, 205nn36–37; return to Indianapolis, 15; second

lieutenant election of Wallace, 12, 203n22; shipwrecked supplies and stealing claims, 204–5n33; Taylor compliment of performance of during war, 206n39; trip to and arrival at Brazos de Santiago, 12–13, 204n23
Indiana Infantry, 2nd, 15, 23, 206n39
Indiana Infantry Regiment, 11th: aggression and fighting capabilities of, 30–31; appreciation of by Cumberland townspeople, 211n69; Army of the Potomac service offer to, 212n85; Army of the Tennessee assignment, 217n72; assignment to VIII Army Corps, 162; challenge to Massachusetts regiment, 32; colonel commission in, 19, 22; command of, 22; Cumberland defense role of, 24–32, 210–11nn53–54, 211n69; death during fighting near Romney, 30–31; departure ceremony for, 23; drilling of, 36; Evansville and Ohio River boat search duty, 23–24, 209n22; favoritism of Wallace toward, 58–59; Fort Donelson attack and counterattack, 44; Fort Donelson departure while assigned to Smith, 51, 53; horses and equipment from rebels near Romney, 30–31, 32; Martinsburg order and arrival of, 32, 211n71; McGinnis command of, 37; Missouri order and arrival of, 33, 65, 212n85; Montgomery Guards as part of, 22; offering services to Morton to form, 18, 19; Paducah order and arrival of, 34, 35, 65; praise for success of, 27–29, 31–32, 34, 211n66; reenlistment of, 33, 212n78; reinforcements for, questions about need for, 31; return to Indianapolis, 33, 212n82; ridicule of Zouaves by Massachusetts regiment, 32; rifles for, 19, 22; Romney raid by,

24–29, 209–10n36, 210n38, 210n42; scouts fight with rebel troops near Romney, 30–31, 211n66; support for, 19; uniforms for, 23, 209n16; Zouave uniforms, drills, and tactics, 22–23, 162

Indiana Infantry Regiment, 23rd, 37, 58–59, 217n72

Indiana Infantry Regiment, 24th, 217n72

Indiana Infantry Regiment, 31st, 44, 48

Indiana Infantry Regiment, 44th, 44

Indiana Infantry Regiment, 52nd, 217n72

Indiana Infantry Regiment, 66th, 81

Indianapolis, Ind.: investment in Free-Soil publication in, 15–16; militias in, 11–12; return of 11th Indiana to, 33, 212n82; state library in, 10–11; Wallace family move to, 10

Indiana regiments for Civil War: Camp Morton to house recruits, 21–22, 208n3, 208n8; command of regiment in exchange for adjutant general duties, 20, 22, 65, 208n8; enlistment term length, 22, 33; numbering of regiments, 22, 208n9; number of companies and regiments, 22, 208n8, 208n10; quota for and recruitment of volunteer soldiers, 21–22, 208n10; recruitment of soldiers for, 32, 213n7; recruitment speeches of Wallace, 78–79, 112–14, 116–17, 156, 192, 195; reenlistment of, 33; rifles for, 22. *See also specific regiments*

Infantry Tactics (Scott), 11, 203n13

intelligence: Baltimore and Washington attacks, information about, 144; Confederate march toward Pittsburg Landing, Wallace information about, 61–62, 70, 219n32; use by Wallace, 8; use of by successful volunteer generals, 70, 221n71

John J. Roe (Wallace headquarters), 55, 62–63

Johnson, Andrew, 186–87; Andersonville prison camp, pressure to investigate, 181; assassination attempt on, 170, 173, 177; execution orders for assassination conspirators, 178–79; pardoning of defendants after a few years in prison, 179, 246n57; Wallace appointment to Lincoln assassination commission, 173, 194

Johnson, Reverdy, 117, 124, 151, 176, 230n12

Johnston, Albert Sidney: Corinth operations of, 59; mortal wound received at Shiloh, 69; Nashville operations of, 46, 50; Pittsburg Landing attack plan of, 60; Shiloh battle role of, 65, 69

Johnston, Joseph: action against, Wallace hope to participate in, 25, 29; Harper's Ferry evacuation by, 28; Harper's Ferry operations of and Romney operations, 24, 210n53; surrender of, 183–84; Winchester operations of, 32–33

Jones, John Paul, 9

Kautz, August V., 94, 175

Kentucky: Buell operations in, 81–82; commission to investigate operations of units under Buell, 101–3, 114, 179, 182, 188, 193, 194, 226n37; loyalty to Union of, 245n41; rebel retaking of Cumberland Gap and central Kentucky, 81–82; secessionists in towns along Ohio River, 23–24; success of Wallace in defense of Covington and Newport, 86. *See also specific cities*

Kentucky Infantry regiments, 44, 48

Kilbourne, Elbridge G., 119, 120

Kneffler, Fred, 21

Lane, Henry S.: assistance from, refusal to ask, 130; assistance from to find a command, 100–101, 226n23; better assignment for 11th Indiana, role in, 24; contributions of Wallace, forcing administration acknowledgement of, 147; court-martial threat and rescue of Wallace by, 204–5n33; infantry regiment formation, support for, 19; marriage of and relationship to Wallace, 16; Middle Department command by Wallace, support for, 116; political connections of and Wallace appointment during Civil War, 16, 116; praise for success of 11th Indiana by, 34; Republican Party role of, 16; Senate service of, 16, 207n52; service in Mexico with Wallace, 16; support for Wallace by, 71, 124

Lane, Joseph, 13

law career: bar exam before leaving for Mexico, 12; bar exam passing, 15; courtroom experiences with Vorhees, 205–6n38; Covington practice, 16; Crawfordsville practice, 17; experience from and qualification for military commissions, 182; fight with Mallory at debate, 16–17; prosecuting attorney election, 16–17, 206n42; study of law with father, 11, 12, 15

Lawrence, Samuel B.: adjutant role of, 120; Baltimore defense, organization of companies for, 135; Baltimore defense responsibility of, 142; election security responsibility of, 160; Negro Equality article investigation by, 121–22; Ricketts order to Monocacy, 137; troops for election security, decisions about, 159

Lee, Robert E.: assassination of Lincoln, accusations about role in, 175; intelligence about Wallace corps location, 158; northern advance of and attack threat from, 106, 132, 137; retreat to Petersburg, 158, 169; Shenandoah Valley operations, 131; strength of forces with, 133; surrender of, 169, 170, 174, 181, 194

Lexington, Ky., 81–82

Light Infantry Tactics (Wallace), 72, 76, 182, 221n5

Lincoln, Abraham: assistance from, refusal to ask, 130; Baltimore and Washington defense success, opinion about, 143; benefits of and need for political general appointments, 3–4, 8, 118, 190, 199n2; blame for conditions and deaths at Andersonville, 180–81; confiscation of funds of citizens, opinion about, 127; Early threat, failure to appreciate seriousness of, 193; election of, 18, 207n51; Emancipation Proclamation of, 41, 88, 120; Fort Donelson importance to, 216n59; funeral train to transport body to Illinois, 170, 171; McClernand commission by, 214n28; meeting with Wallace, 116, 121; opposition to in Ohio, 84; political and military benefits of appointment of Wallace, 115–17, 121, 123–24, 129, 130, 190, 193, 195; political rights for blacks, 41; praise for success of 11th Indiana by, 32, 34; reelection of, 160–61; Republican Party convention invitation for Wallace, 129, 193; rewards for political generals from, 222n36; social and political equality, charges of support of, 18; support for in Indiana, 18, 115, 137, 207n51; Union success, maintaining impression of, 118; wrestling match and political career of, 206n44. See also assassination of Lincoln

Lincoln County Wars, 196

Lockwood, Henry H., 120, 230n10, 240n27
Logan, John, 195, 196
Louisville, Ky., 81, 86, 96, 103
Love, John, 108, 227–28n63

manhood: boyhood-to-manhood role of mothers, 10; communal concept of, 7, 26, 191; gentlemen concept of, 6–7, 13, 99, 190; honor and, 7, 70; martial concept and Marion Rifles experience, 11–12; martial concept of, xi, 6, 7, 10, 11, 19, 21, 65, 81, 180, 190–91, 203n12; nineteenth-century concepts of, 6–7; Northern understanding of, 7; respect for, 7; restrained concept of, 6, 7, 190; roughs concept of, xi, 6–7, 10, 13, 81, 190–91; self-made concept of, 7, 10, 191; self-worth of a man and honor, 22; Southern understanding of, 7; Wallace traits and character, 7, 10, 11, 13, 19, 21, 65, 99, 180, 190–91; West Pointers traits, 7, 26, 191, 201–2n19, 248–49n2
maps, use and value of, 8
Marion (County) Rifles militia, 11–12
martial law, 126–27
Martinsburg, Va., 32, 211n71
Maryland: command system for defense of, 133–34; Confederate army invasion of, 130, 144; confiscation of funds of citizens in, 127; constitutional amendment on slavery in, 115–16, 123, 159, 161; constitutional convention representatives election in, 115, 117, 119, 120, 123; defense of from rebel raids, 127–28, 129–30, 233n72; disloyal activity, rebel sympathizers, and spies in, 117, 124–27, 232n48; disloyal people as candidates in elections, 122; Dublin request for aid and Wallace response, 155–56, 240n24; Early advance into, 132–34, 144, 193–94; election guards in, 118–19; election of 1864 role of Wallace, 5; expulsion of disloyal citizens, 124–25; forces for defense of, 134–35, 141–43; furlough of soldiers to vote in, 120–21, 122, 123, 124; guerrilla activity in, 126, 233n58; martial law declaration in, 126–27; Middle Department authority over, 115, 229n2; oath of allegiance taken by legislative body, 122; oath of allegiance to the United States to regain residence in, 171; occupation and guarding of, 15, 125–27; paroled rebel prisoners in, transportation arrangements for, 170–71; political distractions in and military preparedness, 130; postwar tension in, 171; rebel attack threats to, 152–53, 154–56; release of ex-slaves and free black men from jail, 119–20, 231n25; reorganization of departments for defense of, 146–47, 238n89; Republican Party divisions in, 117, 121, 230n12, 231n20; search for Booth and accomplice in, 172–73, 243n17, 243n20; slavery future in, 120, 121–22; transportation on waterways, regulation of during war, 243n17; vessel search order to find Booth and accomplice, 172–73. *See also specific cities*
McArthur, John, 41
McClellan, George: Army of the Potomac service offer to Wallace, 212n85; contributions to war effort, 8; Peninsula Campaign of, 175; plan to support march to Richmond, 35–36; praise for success of 11th Indiana by, 34; presidential candidacy of, 158, 160; reinforcements for 11th Indiana, questions about need for, 31; reinforcements for Cumberland, request to, 29, 210n53; Romney rebel skirmish report to, 31, 211n70

McClernand, John A.: assistance request to Wallace, 46–47, 49, 50, 52, 53, 191–92, 215–16nn41–43; brigadier general commission of, 214n28; credit for Fort Donelson victory, 53; division command by, 44, 59; evaluation of contributions of, 195; Fort Donelson attack and counterattack, 44–45, 46–48, 49, 50; Fort Donelson attack plan, 42–43; Fort Donelson duty before being sent forward, 51; Fort Henry attack and capture, 41–42; Halleck opinion about, 8; major general commission, 53, 59; opinions about, 129; political career of, 42–43, 214n28; Wallace "on the shelf" complaint about, 74–75

McCook, Alexander M., 145, 164

McDougal, John, 13; confrontations and tension between Wallace and, 12, 13, 14, 203n22, 204n27, 204–5nn32–33; court-martial threat to Wallace, 204–5n33; election of as officer, 12, 203n22; money owed by Wallace, dispute about, 14, 204–5n33; promotion of, 13; spelling of last name of, 203n22; tyrannical nature of, 13, 204n27

McDowell, Irvin, 33

McGinnis, George, 22, 37

McKee, Irving, 5

McPherson, James B., 67–68, 75, 105, 227n43, 237n71

Memphis, Tenn., 35, 60, 77–78

Mexican-American War: Buena Vista battle, 14, 15, 23, 28, 206n39; declaration of, 12; excitement of and experiences with southern soldiers during, 13, 204n26; logistics and supply experience during, 14; Marion Rifles experience and preparation for, 11; Matamoras occupation during, 14–15; Mexico City actions of Scott, 205n37; military experience gained during, 19, 20, 21. *See also* Indiana Infantry, 1st

Mexico: attacks on and French annexation of territory in, 166; Confederacy supplies and resources coming from, 163–64, 165, 167, 168; covert operations to provide supplies to liberals in and stop provisions of supplies to Confederacy, 150, 162–68, 169, 171–72, 189, 194; delay in mission to, 175; expulsion of French from, 162–63, 172, 194, 246n62; French domination of, end of, 189; loans for rebels in, 168–69, 180, 189; love of books about, 11, 12; rebel officers meetings about getting back into the Union, 166–67, 168, 242n65, 242n67; resistance to Wallace mission in, 189, 194, 248n110; return to with soldiers, plans for, 180, 189, 194, 196, 246n62, 248n110

Middle Department: aid requests from loyal citizens, 155–56, 240n24; appointment to and command of, xi, 115, 150, 193, 211n66; appropriation of too much authority by Wallace, 127; assistance related to, refusal to ask, 130; Baltimore headquarters of, 115; best work of war while in command of, 130; black recruits and units organization in, 156–57, 158; blame and criticism about condition of department, 129; challenges and problems faced by Wallace, 117–18, 151–52; command relief of Wallace, 143, 145, 237n71; creation and boundaries of, 229n2; disbanding of regiments and discharge of officers and men, 180; duties of Wallace during Lincoln assassination trial, 175, 244n36; end of duty and replacement for, 182; espionage and rebel sympathizers, management

by, 117, 124–27, 232n48; experience
of troops assigned to, 154; forces
assigned to, 115, 156, 229n2, 240n27;
forces for defense of Baltimore
and Washington and requests for
reinforcements, 134–35; Halleck
command over military operations of,
153; Halleck removal of Wallace from,
concern about, 129; Lane support
for Wallace command of, 116; leave
from to go to Mexico, 164, 241n55;
Lincoln funeral train security duty
of, 170, 171; Middle Military Division
jurisdiction over, 147, 156; objections
to Wallace command of, 116, 129,
230n5; occupation duty of, 15, 125–27;
opportunity to redeem negative
impression, 115; Ord command of,
143, 237n71; order taking command
of, 117, 230n10; political benefits
of appointment of Wallace, 115–17,
121, 123–24, 129, 130, 193; political
cooperation and challenges, 117,
230n12; postwar duties in, 182;
successful management of, 130, 151–52,
157, 193–94, 195; troop reassignment
from to Army of the Potomac, 117,
127–28, 129–30, 153–55, 156, 158, 233n72,
234n1
Middle Military Division, 147, 156, 180
Military Academy, U.S.: Abercrombie
as classmate of David Wallace
at, 32; Annual Board of Visitors
appointment, 250n18; David Wallace
education and teaching experience
at, 9; textbooks from, acquisition of,
207n49; Wallace grudge against, 197–
98, 250n18. *See also* West Pointers/
Military Academy–trained officers
militias: basic military training
through, 17–18; black men in militias,
Bradford opinion about, 156–57; City
Greys, 11–12; commander of militia

encampment election, 207n49;
horses for, need for and shortage of,
109–10; Marion Rifles, 11–12; military
experience gained in, 19, 20, 21;
Montgomery County Guards, 17–18,
207nn48–49
Minnesota, policing Indians in, 96, 97,
98, 99, 100
Missouri: Belmont battle, 39–40, 65,
213–14nn18–19; Fremont removal and
cleaning up of mess left in, 74; St.
Louis order of 11th Indiana, 33, 65,
212n85; Wallace opinion of Fremont
and headquarters at St. Louis, 33–34,
35, 212n89
Missouri Infantry Regiment, 8th, 37, 44,
51, 59, 217n72
Monocacy Junction: Battle of Monocacy
and confrontation with Early, 137–41,
139, 195; casualties of battle at, 140;
defeat at and retreat from, 140–41,
142, 144, 145, 194; defense of, xi,
135–36, 137–41, 197; delay of Early raid
on Washington because of battle at,
141, 144, 148–49, 194; skill of Wallace
at, 194; success of Wallace and praise
for success at, 5, 147, 148–49, 193–94
Montgomery County Guards: challenges
to other militia companies, 18,
207n48; drills and training of, 18;
infantry regiment assignment of, 22;
organization of, 17–18; popularity of,
18, 207nn48–49; Zouave outfits for, 18
Morgan, John Hunt: Cincinnati raid
on and threat of another attack, 84,
85; Indiana raid by and defense of
Indiana from, 107–10, 114, 117, 192,
227–28n63; supply lines destruction
by, 101
Morris, Thomas, 24, 210n53
Morris, William W., 164, 170, 240n27
Morsberger, Katherine, 5–6
Morsberger, Robert, 5–6

Morton, Oliver P.: apology to, 18; assistance from, failure to give, 80; assistance from, refusal to ask, 130; assistance from in finding a command, 100–101, 113, 193; command relief of Wallace, 78–79, 222n34; dislike of Buell by, 103; governorship of, 18, 207n52; ill feelings between Wallace and, 79, 101, 112–14, 116–17; infantry regiment formation, support for, 19; Mexico covert operations role of, 164–65; Missouri order to Wallace and 11th Indiana by, 33, 65, 212n85; offer of service in event of war, 18, 20; Paducah order to Wallace and 11th Indiana, 34, 65; photo of, 91; plea to be sent into battle, 37, 65; praise for experience working under, 21; praise for success of 11th Indiana by, 34; quota for and recruitment of volunteer soldiers, 21–22, 208n10; recruitment request to Wallace, 78–79, 80, 112–14, 116–17, 156, 192, 195; relationship with Wallace, 103, 115, 191; resentment toward for leaving Democratic Party, 18; Stanton communication with about Wallace, 113–14; support for Wallace by, 71; temporary command position for Wallace, 81; uniforms for troops, help in securing, 213n7
Mudd, Samuel A., 173, 177, 179, 189, 245n46

Nashville, Tenn., 41, 46, 50, 103
Nebraska Infantry Regiment, 1st, 44, 47, 217n72
Nelson, William, 62, 63, 82
New Creek, Va., 25, 26, 30, 209n27
New Jersey, 161, 229n2
New Mexico Territory: governorship of, 196–97; Lincoln County Wars, 3, 196
New Orleans, La., 15, 125, 165, 169, 172, 204n23
Newport, Ky., 82–86, 223–24n58, 224n67

New York artillery units, 128
Northerners/The North: animosity between Southerners and, 204n26; self-worth of a man and honor, 22; Virginian support for Union after Romney raid, 28

Ohio: assistance from friend in finding a command, 100–101; Lincoln opposition in, 84; praise for and thanks to Wallace for success in Cincinnati, 87–88; rebel attack threats to, 146; recruitment of soldiers in, 87. *See also specific cities*
Ohio Infantry regiments, 44, 47, 217n72
O'Laughlin, Michael, 173, 177, 179
Ord, Edward O. C., 101, 143, 144–45, 237n71

Paducah, Ky.: boredom of duty in, 36, 37, 39; drinking and smoking evening in, 39, 213n17; order of 11th Indiana to, 34, 65; picket operations against attack on, 36, 37, 39, 65; rebel flag incident in, 37–39, 213nn14–15; Wallace opinion about, 36; welcome for 11th Indiana arrival at, 35
Patterson, Robert: Bull Run campaign failure blame of, 33, 212n80; Chambersburg camp of, 24, 209n28; Cumberland order to Wallace by, 24–25; Hagerstown camp of, 209n28; Hagerstown order for Wallace, 30; Martinsburg headquarters of, 211n71; Martinsburg order to Wallace, 32, 211n71; order to Cumberland and report to, 24; praise for success of 11th Indiana by, 31, 34, 211n66; reenlistment request to regiments, 33, 212n78; reinforcements for Cumberland, request to, 29; Romney raid, caution about from, 25; Romney raid report to, 28; Romney rebel skirmish report to, 31; Wallace

meeting of, 32; Wallace plea to not be left out of the action, 25, 29; Winchester camp, order from Scott to hold, 32–33

Payne, Lewis, 173, 177, 178

Pennsylvania, 32; Chambersburg burning by rebels, 155; Middle Department authority over, 229n2; plea for volunteers and officers for defense of, Wallace response to, 106–7; rebel attack threats to, 154; State Reserve units on state line to defend against rebel advance, 29, 31; State Reserve units orders to Cumberland, 31, 211n67

Perkins, Joseph G., 119–20, 231nn25–26

Petersburg, Va., 132, 134, 152, 158, 171, 175, 194

Piatt, Donn, 101, 102

picket and patrol duties: experience gained in Mexico for, 15, 205n37; frustration of Wallace with, 36, 65; Paducah operations, 36, 37, 39, 65; Sherman pickets against rebel attacks, 60, 62

Pillow, Gideon, 46, 50

Pittsburg Landing: army camp at, 57; arrest of Wallace because of lack of urgency, suggestion of, 68; delays and lack of urgency in 3rd Division movement toward, 66–68, 70, 75, 104–6, 110, 220n61; force strength at, 60, 219n29; intelligence about Confederate march toward, 61–62, 70, 219n32; location of, 56; rebel attack on Union army at, 60–63; River Road as direct route to, 58, 64, 65, 105–6; River Road to, 56, 57–58, 218n14; Shunpike to, 56, 57–58, 63, 64–67, 105–6, 218n14, 218n16; Union camps and division lines near, 61, 63; Union repulsing rebels at, 64; Wallace order to Pittsburg Landing and the written

order given to Wallace, 63–67, 75, 104–6, 110, 192, 200–201n12, 219n41, 220nn49–50; Wallace readiness to move to Pittsburg Landing, 57, 218n13

political generals, 74–75; abilities and competence of Wallace, 7–8, 19, 21, 36–37, 77, 115, 190, 191–96; administrative capabilities of, 4; avoidance of risky and intense battles by, 11; behaviors compared to West Pointers, 7, 42–43, 191; benefits and support gained through, 3–4, 8, 118, 190; capabilities and qualifications of, 21; character and traits of successful volunteer generals, 70, 221n71; commissioning of through political connections, 3, 190; contribution of and rewards for, 222n36; disciplining of troops by, 38; evaluation of contributions of volunteer generals, xi, 5, 8, 195–96; expectations for and opinions about, 8, 33–34, 35, 42–43, 73, 96–97, 128–29, 141, 202n22; focus of partisan political struggle in war, 4–5; Fremont performance as, 33–34, 35, 212n89; manhood concept embraced by, 7; military experience of, 3; political and military benefits and costs of appointment of, 4, 5, 8, 195–96; political connections to secure positions and commands, 34; recruitment of soldiers by, xi, 4, 21, 78–79, 190, 222n36, 233n72; relationships with regular officers, 5, 6, 74–75, 96–97, 191, 195–96, 225n2, 236n57; reluctance to complete political tasks, 34, 212n88; rivalry and tension between West Pointers and, xi, 4–5, 191, 195–96, 200–201n12; speeches by to support Union army, xi, 4; stereotypes of, 4; tradition of turning politicians and civilians into military officers, 3–4

Polk, Leonidas, 36, 37, 60, 219n29

Porter, Fitz John, 24–25, 29, 32, 175, 210–11nn53–54

Porter, P. A., 120

Prentiss, Benjamin A., 59, 62

Prince of India, The (Wallace), 197

prisoners: conditions in prisoner camps, 180; death of during Civil War, 180; Middle Department troops to guard and transport, 233n72; parole and exchange system during war, 97, 180–81; paroled rebel prisoners, transportation arrangements for, 170–71; paroled Union prisoners organization for service in Minnesota to police Indians, 87, 96–100, 114; rebel prisoners in Baltimore, supplies for, 161–62. *See also* Andersonville prison camp

Purdy, Tenn., 55, 60

Rawlins, John A.: Fort Donelson departure with regiments not assigned to Wallace, 51; McClernand assistance request to Wallace, role in, 52; Paducah visit with Grant, 39; relay of Grant's command to Baxter by, 63, 105; Sherman letter to about field command for Wallace, 111; Shiloh report, note about, 75–76; shortcut to River Road and frustration with pace, 67–68

Reconstruction, 130

Republican Party: convention invitation for Wallace, 129, 193; divisions in, 117, 118, 121, 230n12, 231n20; emergence of and losses for elected Democrats, 17; Grant and Wallace roles in, 65, 66; Lane role in, 16; slavery views of, 40–41; Union Party name for, 18; Wallace support for and switch to, 18, 40–41

Richmond, Ky., 81

Richmond, Va.: Army of the Potomac operations for capture of, 233n72, 234n1; capture of, 174; defeated rebels sent to Maryland from, 171; Grant operations near, 132, 134; plan to support march to, 35–36; troops for capture of, 233n72, 234n1

Ricketts, James B., 136, 137, 138–40, 141, 142, 143

Ristine, Joseph, 16–17

River Road: as direct route to Pittsburg Landing, 58, 64, 65, 105–6; inspection and decision to not repair, 57–58, 218n14; location of, 56

Romney, Va., 27; Confederate troops in and threat of attack on Cumberland from, 29–30, 210n53; courage displayed at, 5; decision to raid, 24–25; feeding of troops after raid, 27; Patterson caution about raid of, 25; raid on, 26–27, 210n38; raid plan, 25–26; rebel force strength at, 25; rebels retreat from, 27, 210n42; rebel troops occupation of, 24; report and press coverage about rebel skirmish at, 31, 32, 65, 211n70; successful rout of rebel forces and praise for Wallace, 27–29, 65; trip to and arrival at for raid, 26, 209–10n36; Union scouts fight with rebel troops near Frankfort, 30–31; warning to rebels about attack, 26, 209–10n36; West Virginia location of, 209n27

Rosecrans, William, 96–97, 128–29, 145, 225n2

Sanders, Zerelda Gray, 10

Sanderson, W. C., 37

Savannah, Tenn., 53, 54–55, 59, 62, 63

Scapegoat of Shiloh (Getchell), 200–201n12

Schofield, John M., 248n110

Scott, John S., 82

Scott, Winfield: *Infantry Tactics*, 11, 203n13; Mexico City actions of, 205n37; note from after Romney raid, 28; order to Cumberland by, 24, 209n25; praise for success of 11th Indiana by, 34; units for upcoming action, order to hold back, 29, 210–11n54; Wallace admiration of, 34; Winchester camp, order to Patterson to hold, 32–33

secession crisis, 18, 207n53

Seward, William H., 165, 170, 172, 173, 177, 189, 248n110

Shadow of Shiloh (Stephens), 200n8, 200–201n12

Shenandoah Valley operations, 131, 133, 134, 135, 136, 146, 154–55, 175, 240n27

Sheridan, Philip: Middle Military Division command of, 147, 156; Shenandoah Valley operations of, 146, 154–55, 175, 240n27; troops for election security, request to, 160

Sherman, William T.: death of son of, 229n98; division command by, 59; field command correspondence with Wallace, 111–12, 114, 228n81, 229n98; force strength at Corinth, report on, 57; Grant remaining in department, role in, 78; Halleck complaint about Banks to, 129; pickets against rebel attack on rearguard divisions, 60, 62; professional advice to Wallace, 112, 114; Shiloh battle role of, 68, 69, 70; Wallace movement to assist, 64

Shiloh, Battle of: advantage of rear attack on rebels, 67; blame and criticism for errors related to, 66, 70, 75, 80, 103–6, 110–11, 200–201n12, 220nn49–50; casualties of, 70, 221n69; character faults and performance at, 8; Confederate army defeat at, 68–70; courage displayed at, 70; delays and lack of urgency in 3rd Division

movement toward Pittsburg Landing, 66–68, 70, 75, 104–6, 110, 220n61; distrust between Wallace and Grant, 53; division movement and ending up behind enemy line, 65–67, 220n47; exhaustion after, 71; failure of Wallace and lingering negative impressions after, 80, 115; Grant review of and response to reports about, 75–76, 77, 103–4, 110–11, 221n16; Grant's order and the written order given to Wallace, 63–67, 75, 104–6, 110, 192, 200–201n12, 219n41, 220nn49–50; intelligence about Confederate march toward Pittsburg Landing, 61–62, 70, 219n32; investigation of performance at, request for and Sherman advice about, 110–11, 112; map of area, 56; miscommunications during, 63–67, 70, 218n16, 220nn49–50; mistakes near, haunting of Wallace by, 197, 250n16; official reports about, 75–76, 77, 103–6, 110–11, 221n16; orders about direction of attack, 68; performance on first day of battle, 63–68, 70, 75, 103–6, 110–11, 182, 200–201n12, 219n41, 220n61; performance on second day of battle, xi, 68–70; portrayal of Wallace actions by Grant, 64–65, 66, 75–76, 103–6, 110–11, 220n50, 221n16; rebel arms left on battlefield, 70; rebel attack on Union army at Pittsburgh Landing, 60–63; rebel force strength for, 57, 60, 218n13, 219n29; Sherman pickets report of rebel activity near Shiloh Church, 62; Union camps and division lines, 61, 63; Union force strength for, 60, 219n29; Union repulsing rebels at, 64; victory of Union at, 68–70; Wallace Division role at, 65–70, 220n47; Wallace letter to Halleck in response to Grant note about, 104, 110; writings about battle, 5–6, 200n8, 200–201n12

Shunpike: inspection and repair of, 57–58, 218n14, 218n16; location of, 56; route to Pittsburg Landing, 63, 64–67, 105–6, 218n16

Sigel, Franz: coordination of operations of, 238n89; Harpers Ferry and operations against Early, 132–34; Maryland Heights operations of, 132–33, 136; opinions about capabilities and performance of, 8, 128–29, 145, 195; rebel attack threats to Maryland, reports on, 135

Slaughter, James E., 166–67, 172, 242n65, 242n67

slaves and slavery: black recruits and units organization, 156–57, 158; blacks as wartime laborers in, 84–86, 87–88; *Conestoga* trip and rescue of runaway slave, 40, 214n21; equality between races, opinion about, 18, 118; Free-Soil publication support of antislavery cause, 15–16; future of in Maryland, 120, 121–22; Maryland constitutional amendment on, 115–16, 123, 159, 161; "Negro Equality" article, 121–22; political rights for blacks, 41; release of ex-slaves and free black men from jail, 119–20, 231n25; support of right to secure and expand slavery, 18; Union victory and end of slavery, 158; Wallace views on, 18, 40–41, 117–18, 158, 214n21

Smith, Charles F., 36; advice to Wallace after promotion, 36–37, 213n6; command given to W. H. L. Wallace, 59; credit for Fort Donelson victory, 6, 53; death of, 59, 74; distrust of Wallace by, 51, 52, 65, 191; drinking and smoking evening in Paducah, 39, 213n17; Fort Donelson attack and counterattack, 44–45, 48–49, 50; Fort Donelson attack plan, 42–43; Fort Donelson departure of regiments

assigned to, 51, 53; Fort Donelson duty before being sent forward, 51; Fort Henry attack and capture, 41–42; Fort Henry guarding by Wallace, 43; injury while leaving boat, 55, 59, 74, 217n8; major general commission, 53, 59; military career of, 36; opinions about and admiration of, 74; photo of, 91; rebel flag incident, response to, 37–39, 213nn14–15; relationship with Wallace, 7, 35, 37–39, 52, 54, 55, 65, 74, 191; transfer to 11th Indiana to serve under, 34, 65

Smith, Edmund Kirby: Chattanooga operations of, 101; Cincinnati, Covington, and Newport attack threat by, 82–83, 85, 193, 195; Cumberland Gap retaking by, 81; force strength under, 82; Lexington operations of, 82; meetings with about getting back into the Union, 166, 167, 168, 169, 172; retreat from Cincinnati, 86, 87

Smith, Morgan, 37, 48–49, 51, 106

Southerners/The South. *See* Confederacy/The South

Spangler, Edward, 173, 177, 179

Stanton, Edwin: arrest of men, concern about, 135, 235n24; assistance request to find field command, 106; Baltimore and Washington defense success, opinion about, 143; Camp Chase conditions and supplies, communications about, 98–99, 100; command relief of Wallace, 78–79, 116–17, 222n34; confiscation of funds of citizens, opinion about, 127; department lines, order to ignore, 136–37; dislike of Buell by, 103; distrust of Wallace by, 191; duty request from Wallace for any duty, 112–14; martial law declaration, opinion about, 126; meeting with

Wallace, 116–17; Middle Department command by Wallace, objection to, 116; Middle Department troop reassignments , exchanges about, 128; Morton communication with about Wallace, 113–14; political savvy of Wallace, opinion about, 121; rebel threat, lack of concern about, 135, 193; regulations on commerce and trade in and with Virginia, 243n19; reinforcements for defense of Cincinnati, 85; relationship with Wallace, 6, 8, 76, 103, 112–14, 115, 130, 153, 191; tactics book submission to, 72; transportation on waterways, regulation of during war, 243n17; vessel search order from to find Booth and accomplice, 172–73

Stantonville, Tenn., 76–77

Stephens, Gail, 200n8, 200–201n12

Stoney Lonesome, 56, 57, 58, 62, 63

Surratt, John, 173, 178, 179

Surratt, Mary E., 173, 176, 177, 178–79, 189, 245n46, 245–46n53

tactics book, 72, 76, 182, 221n5

Taylor, Zachary, 14, 15–16, 20, 23, 205nn36–37, 206n39

Tennessee: Buell operations in, 81–82; commission to investigate operations of units under Buell, 101–3, 114, 179, 182, 188, 193, 194, 226n37; rebel retaking of Cumberland Gap and central Tennessee, 81–82. See also specific cities

Tennessee River: *Conestoga* trip to investigate status of Fort Henry, 40; destruction of railroad bridge across, 53; importance of, 36; operations against forts on, 41; troop transport of, 41

Test, Esther French. *See* Wallace, Esther French Test (mother)

Test, John (grandfather), 9

Texas: meetings with rebel officers in about getting back into the Union, 166–67, 169, 171–72, 242n65, 242n70; surrender of rebel forces in, 169; travel to and joining Texas Navy, failed attempt at, 11, 65

Thayer, John M., 44, 47, 50, 51, 57, 58, 215n42

Thiesen, Lee Scott, 5

Thomas, George H., 74, 174, 182, 237n71

Thomas, Lorenzo, 98, 128, 183

Tigress, 62–63

Townsend, E. D.: Baltimore defense communications with, 152–53; paroled rebel prisoners in, transportation arrangements for, 170–71; rebel prisoners in Baltimore, supplies for, 162; troop reassignment from Middle Department requests from, 128, 154, 239n17; troop request to enforce martial law, 126; Wallace performance as less trouble than other dpeartment commanders, 157

Turkey, minister to, 197

Tyler, Daniel, 101, 120

Tyler, Erastus B., 120, 134, 137, 138, 140, 240n27

Union army: Bull Run campaign failure and unwillingness of regiments to reenlist, 33; command system flaws and defense of Washington, 133–34, 145, 234–35n14; desertions from, 99–100; disbanding of regiments and discharge of officers and men, 180; force strength and organization of, 4; Halleck as general in chief, 74, 77, 222n25; horses for defending militias, need for and shortage of, 109–10; Lee retreat and victory of, 158; number of West Pointers serving in, 4; recruitment of black troops to, 88;

Union army (*continued*)
recruitment of soldiers for, xi, 4,
23, 190; reenlistment of regiments,
33, 212n78; reorganization of
departments in, 146–47, 153, 156,
238n89; reputation concerns related
to Early raid threat, 133–34; shortage
of professional officers for, 4, 190;
speeches to support, xi, 4. *See also*
Indiana regiments for Civil War;
specific units

Union Party, 18. *See also* Republican
Party

United States (U.S.): citizen and regular
soldiers in military service to, 6;
tradition of turning politicians and
civilians into military officers, 3–4

Vernon, Ind., 108–9, 227–28n63
Vicksburg, Miss., 60, 104, 106, 107, 111
Viola, Ky., 40, 213–14n18
Virginia: citizen support for Union after
Romney raid, 28; Middle Department
authority over, 229n2; regulations
on commerce and trade in and with,
243n19. *See also specific cities*
Vorhees, Daniel, 205–6n38

Walker, John G., 166, 167, 168, 169, 172,
242n67
Wallace, Andrew (grandfather), 9
Wallace, David (father): Brookville law
practice of, 9; Covington move of,
9–10; death of, 10; Indianapolis move
of, 10; kicking Lew out of house by,
202n8; law, interest in returning
home to practice, 204n28; marriage
and family of, 9; political career of,
10, 21, 202–3n10; political connections
of, 10; study of law by Lew, support
for, 11, 12, 15; travel of, 10; West Point
education and teaching experience of,
9, 32; Whig politics of, 9

Wallace, Esther French Test (mother),
9–10
Wallace, Henry (son), 16, 206n41
Wallace, John (brother), 9–10
Wallace, Lewis "Lew": aggressive, bold
behavior as successful strategy,
16–17, 206n43; ambition, arrogance,
and pride of, 17, 19, 21, 36–37, 115,
191; *Ben-Hur*, 3, 197, 198; Ben-Hur
Wallace nickname, 197; birth and
family of, 9–10; challenge to integrity
of, 16–17; early life and education of,
10; equality between races, opinion
about, 18, 118; *The Fair God*, 196;
friends, difficulty in making, 17;
grudge against West Point and
graduates of, 197–98, 250n18; happy
marriage of, 16; kicking out of house
by father, 202n8; *Light Infantry
Tactics*, 72, 76, 182, 221n5; manhood
concept embraced by, 7, 10, 11, 13, 19,
21, 65, 99, 180, 190–91; marriage and
family of, 16, 206n41; memoir of, 179,
197, 243n24; photos of, *89, 90*; postwar
career of, 196–98; pride in writings
and presentations by, 17; *The Prince
of India*, 197; reading and writing
interests of, 10–11; rebellious ways
of, 10, 12; relationship with Lane, 16;
scarlet fever illness of, 10; slavery
views of, 18, 40–41, 117–18, 158, 214n21;
writing career of, 196, 197. *See also*
law career; military career; political
career and interests
Wallace, Lewis "Lew," military career:
abilities and competence to be an
officer, 7–8, 19, 21, 36–37, 77, 115, 190,
191–96; active service, hope for and
blame for lack of action, 14, 20, 39,
206n39; adjutant general appointment
and resignation, 19, 20–22, 65, 208n3,
208n8; aggressive and bold behavior,
19, 21, 31, 32, 34, 35, 39, 40, 43, 127,

191–96; ambition, arrogance, and pride as limitations on career, 19, 36–37, 115, 191; Andersonville prison camp trial role, 180–89; Army of the Potomac service offer from McClellan, 212n85; arrogance after promotion, 59; art of war, learning about, 103; assistance in finding a command, 100–101, 226n23; audacity in writing tactics book, 72; basic military training, 17–18; blaming others for own faults, 70, 75, 198; bold acts, with or without permission, 28; brigadier general commission, 19, 36–37, 116, 213n5; Buell investigation commission role, 101–3, 114, 179, 188, 193, 194, 226n37; Civil War career, writings about, 3; colonel commission, 19, 22, 65; command in field worthy of rank, 115; command relief, 78–79, 222n34, 230n10; communication skills and inability to keep quiet, 19, 39, 66, 76, 141, 210n53; contributions to war effort, xi, 8, 71, 88, 148–49, 190, 191–96; cordial relations with and respect from regular officers, 157; courage during, 5, 8, 70, 191; courage of Wallace, 5, 8, 70; departmental administrator potential, 24; departmental experience, failure to use during Reconstruction, 130; deviation from rules and orders, 12; distrust and troublemaker status, 39, 51–52, 53, 54, 65, 80, 141, 153, 164, 191, 192, 194, 217n71; drills, officership, and tactics interests, 11, 203n13; duty assignments after Shiloh, 192; end of, feelings about, 150; evaluation of and writings about Civil War career, 5–6, 200n8, 200–201n12; evaluation of contributions and success, 8, 195–96; excitement of battle, love for,

54; failures and damaged image, xi, 6, 51–52, 70, 80, 96–97, 115; fear and humility after promotion, 36–37; fear war was over and "on the shelf" complaints, 53, 65, 74–75, 80, 97, 100, 192; field command, desire for and unlikelihood of, 80, 96, 100, 106, 111–14, 115, 182, 193; field command assistance from Morton and ill feelings about recruitment, 79, 112–14; field command correspondence with Sherman, 111–12, 114, 228n81, 229n98; flag incident in Paducah, 37–39, 213nn14–15; genius or learned expertise in military matters, 19, 207n55; Halleck as superior until end of war, 74; Halleck to blame for troubles and ruining career, 73, 192, 198; hatred for officers, 15, 52, 55, 206n39; leave of absence, 78–79; Lincoln assassination trial role, 173–80, 188, 194, 244n37, 244–45n40; major general commission, 19, 53, 58–59; Marion Rifles experience and preparation for, 11; mentors during, 191; military accomplishments during, 5, 88, 191–96; military experiences in pre–Civil War career, 19, 20, 21; military professionals as club of elites, 207n49; motivational letters and speeches, 155–56, 240n24; mustering out of the army, 182; negative attitude of Wallace, 14; obedience to superiors, Smith advice about, 37, 213n6; objective analysis of, 6; orders from superiors, neglect to follow, 25–26, 49–50, 53, 65–66, 106–7, 191–92, 249n4; overconfidence issues, 35–36, 43; patience and modesty traits, 43; Patterson Bull Run campaign decisions, opinion about, 33, 212n81; pleas to be sent into battle and not be left out of the action, 25, 29, 37, 51–52,

Wallace, Lewis "Lew," military career
(*continued*)
65; political amends for military
blunders, reluctance to make,
34, 212n88; political benefits of
appointment of Wallace, 5, 6, 8,
88, 115–17, 121, 123–24, 129, 130, 190,
193–96; political connections to
secure positions and commands,
34; procedural experience from
Buell commission role, 103, 188, 194;
professional advice from Sherman,
112, 114; promotions, 5, 36–37, 53,
58–59, 213n5; rank, seniority, and
field command duty, 201n14; reaction
to major general promotion, 58–59;
rebellious ways of Wallace, 13;
recruitment speeches, 78–79, 80,
112–14, 116–17, 156, 192, 195, 233n72;
regrets about by Wallace, 197, 198,
250n16; relationship with and lack
of respect for superiors, xi, 6, 8, 13,
19, 43, 53, 65–66, 73–74, 107, 113–14,
141, 191, 201n14; relationship with
regular officers, 5, 6, 37–39, 128–29,
195–96; Shiloh report and operation
assignments, 76; successes of, xi, 53,
190; support for by Lane and Morton,
19; sympathetic analyses of, 5–6;
unreliability during, 191; volunteer
general commission of, 190; West
Point textbooks, acquisition of,
207n49. *See also specific wars and
duty assignments*
Wallace, Lewis "Lew," political career
and interests of: arrogance and
erosion of political support, 17;
congressional campaign after war,
196; political affiliation, 15–16;
political aspirations, 16, 21; political
connections and alliances, 10, 16, 65,
66; prosecuting attorney election,
16–17, 206n42; state senate election

and service, 17, 206n46
Wallace, Susan (wife): Baltimore
raid threat, concern about,
142; frustrations about Middle
Department duties, 151–52; happy
marriage of, 16; marriage and family
of, 16, 206n41; memoir of husband,
writing postwar portion of, 179, 197,
243n24; slavery views of, 214n21
Wallace, William (brother), 9–10
Wallace, William H. L., 47, 59, 60, 63,
218n16
Wallace, Zerelda (stepmother), 10
Wallace's Bridge, 55, 56, 57, 58, 68, 218n16
Washington, D.C.: Carvajal trip to
with Wallace, 168, 169; command
system flaws and defense of, 133–34,
145, 234–35n14; credit for stopping
rebel advance on, 131; Early raid
on, 131, 132, 193–94; Early threat to,
failure to appreciate seriousness of,
141, 193; forces for defense of and
reinforcement requests, 131, 134–35,
141–43, 234n1, 237n60; force strength
of Early for raid on, 134; guarding
approaches to, 137–38; Middle
Department troops and defense of,
128, 129–30, 233n72; organization
for defense of, 131; questions about
threat to, 131; rebel attack threats to,
132–34, 141–44, 153; reorganization of
departments for defense of, 146–47,
153, 156, 238n89; success of Wallace
and praise for success in, 143, 144–46,
147–49, 193–94
Weber, Max, 132–34, 238n89
West Pointers/Military Academy-
trained officers: behavior and ethics
of, 7, 26, 59, 112, 191; behaviors
compared to political generals, 7, 191;
focus of military problems in war,
4–5; manhood concept embraced
by, 7, 26, 191, 201–2n19, 248–49n2;

military actions by mediocre officers, 8; number of officers serving in Union army, 4; orders to subordinates, expectations to follow, 25–26, 43, 49–50, 53, 76, 222n21; Reconstruction departmental commands for, 130; regulations, procedures, and discipline traditions of, 26, 51, 249n3; relationships with political generals, 5, 6, 74–75, 96–97, 191, 195–96, 225n2, 236n57; respect for authority and orders of, 7, 26; rivalry and tension between political generals and, xi, 4–5, 191, 195–96, 200–201n12; volunteer general investigation of, 102; Wallace grudge against, 197–98, 250n18

Whig party, 9, 10, 15–16, 202–3n10, 231n20

Wilderness Campaign, 127–28, 129, 233n72, 234n1

Wilson, James H., 181–82, 184, 246n72

Winchester, Va., 32–33, 134

Winder, John H., 248n105

Winder, Richard Bayley, 188, 248n105

Wirz, Henry, 95, 180, 181–89, 194, 246n72, 247n82

Wisconsin regiment, 2nd, 33, 212n78

Woolley, John, 164

Wright, Horatio G., 82; appreciation of Wallace for defense of Cincinnati, 87, 96; Cincinnati defense role of, 85–86; request for troops from to guard Camps Chase and Thomas, 100; Wallace order to Cincinnati, 223n50; Wallace order to Columbus, 87, 97

Wynn's Ferry Road defense, 47–48

Zouave regiments: Algerian Zouaves, 18; drills and battle tactics of, 21, 208n6; Montgomery County Guards uniforms, 18; recruitment for, 21; ridicule of by Massachusetts regiment, 32; uniforms, drills, and tactics of 11th Indiana, 22–23, 162

CPSIA information can be obtained
at www.ICGtesting.com
Printed in the USA
LVHW092241230119
605049LV00004B/14/P

9 780806 161952